THE FOUNDING OF
NEW ENGLAND

THE FOUNDING OF
NEW ENGLAND

BY

JAMES TRUSLOW ADAMS

An Atlantic Monthly Press Book

LITTLE, BROWN AND COMPANY · BOSTON · TORONTO

ATLANTIC–LITTLE, BROWN BOOKS
ARE PUBLISHED BY
LITTLE, BROWN AND COMPANY
IN ASSOCIATION WITH
THE ATLANTIC MONTHLY PRESS

To
A. L. A.

One duty that was always incumbent on the historian has now become a duty of deeper significance and stronger obligation. Truth, and Truth only, is our aim. We are bound as historians to examine and record facts without favor or affection to our own nation or to any other.

LORD BRYCE,
Presidential Address, at the
International Congress of Historical Studies, 1913

PREFACE

THE following account of the founding of New England is intended to serve as an introduction to the later history of that section, and to the study of its relations with other portions of the Empire and with the mother-country, as well as of the section's influence upon the nation formed from such of the colonies as subsequently revolted. The book thus necessarily deals mainly with origins, discussing the discovery and first settlement of the region; the genesis of the religious and political ideas which there took root and flourished; the geographic and other factors which shaped its economic development; the beginnings of that English overseas empire, of which it formed a part; and the early formulation of thought—on both sides of the Atlantic—regarding imperial problems.

There is no lack of detailed narratives, both of the entire period covered by the present volume and, on an even larger scale, of certain of its more important or dramatic episodes. New material brought to light within the past decade or two, however, has necessitated a revaluation of many former judgments, as well as changes in selection and emphasis. Moreover, our general accounts do not, for the most part, adequately treat of those economic and imperial relations which are of fundamental importance; for the one outstanding fact concerning any American colony in the colonial period is that it was a dependency, and formed merely a part of a larger and more comprehensive imperial and economic organization. Consequently, the evolution of such a colony can be viewed correctly only when it is seen against the background of the economic and imperial conditions and theories of the time.

While the author, accordingly, has endeavored to place the local story in its proper imperial setting, he has endeavored also to distinguish between its various elements, and to display the conflicting forces at work in the colonies themselves. The old conception of New England history, according to which that section was considered to have been settled by persecuted religious refugees, devoted to liberty of conscience, who, in the disputes with the mother-country, formed a united mass of liberty-loving patriots unanimously opposed to an unmitigated tyranny, has, happily, for many years, been passing. In his own narrative of the facts, based upon a fresh study of the sources, the author has tried to indicate that economic as well as religious factors played a very considerable part in the great migration during the early settlement period, in the course of which over sixty-five thousand Englishmen left their homes for various parts of the New World, of which number approximately only four thousand were to join the New England churches. He has also endeavored to exhibit the workings of the theocracy, and to show how, in the period treated, the domestic struggle against the tyranny exercised by the more bigoted members of the theocratic party was of greater importance in the history of liberty than the more dramatic contest with the mother-country.

While the local narrative is based wholly upon original records, much use has been made also of the rapidly increasing number of scholarly monographs upon particular topics, the indebtedness to which will be found more particularly set forth in the footnotes. It is true that many points — such as land-tenure, in spite of all that has been written upon it — yet remain to be cleared up before we can be quite sure that we understand a number of matters connected with colonial institutions. Nevertheless, so much work of this character has already been done, which has only in part found its way into popular accounts, that it seems as if the time had come for a serious attempt to recast the story of early New England, and to combine these results of recent research with the more modern spirit, in a new presentation of the period.

To those who first encouraged him to undertake the work,— interrupted by the war,— and who, in one way and another, have assisted him in his enterprise, the author takes this opportunity to offer his most sincere and grateful thanks.

J. T. A.

BRIDGEHAMPTON, NEW YORK,
November 9, 1920.

CONTENTS

CONTENTS

THE FOUNDING OF
NEW ENGLAND

THE FOUNDING OF
NEW ENGLAND

CHAPTER I

THE AMERICAN BACKGROUND

In the name of the country which to-day occupies the major part of the inhabitable portion of North America is indicated the twofold nature of its history; for the story of the United States may evidently be approached, either from the standpoint of a federal nation, or from that of its component political units. These units, although in themselves separate states, are geographically divided from one another, for the most part, by boundaries which are purely artificial. Natural frontiers consist of the sea, deserts, mountains, rivers, and the now almost obsolete ones of forests and swamps. A glance at the map shows that such natural barriers are only a negligible part of the boundaries between our various states and territories. Rivers alone form an exception, and these, for several reasons, are the least satisfactory for the purpose.[1] Were the federal tie dissolved, and these now united commonwealths to become completely independent, and possibly hostile, the artificial character of their limits would at once become obvious.

From this it has followed, as settlement has gradually spread over the continent, bringing innumerable communities into existence, that these have tended to group themselves into sections, united by common modes of thought, ways of life, and economic needs. Histories of the individual states are almost as arbitrarily localized as the histories of the counties within

[1] *Cf.* C. B. Fawcett, *Frontiers* (Oxford, 1918), pp. 50 *ff.* Also, Lord Curzon, *Frontiers* (Oxford, 1908), pp. 13 *ff.*

them; but the story of any of the sections into which the country has divided from time to time possesses an organic unity created by the forces of life itself.

Some of these divisions have tended to remain permanent, while others have passed with the development of the country. During the colonial period, when the English inhabited only the comparatively narrow strip of land between the sea and the mountain-barrier of the Appalachian system, the colonists fell into three natural groups,— the New England, the Middle, and the Southern,— determined by climatic, economic, and cultural conditions. These factors, operating with others somewhat more fortuitous, made the distinctions both lasting and marked, the extreme northern and southern groups exhibiting their differences more clearly than the intermediate one lying between them.

When the frontier was extended west of the mountain-barrier, — and, indeed, on a smaller scale, even earlier,— another grouping came into existence, that of East and West, or old settlement and frontier. This division was also to persist, with an ever-enlarging East and an ever-retreating West. If the economic and political ideas of these new sections were to remain somewhat sharply contrasted, the distinctions between the original extreme eastern groups were also continued, like lengthening shadows across the mountain ridges, and the whole country was to find itself aligned in two hostile groupings in the most tragic division that it has yet had to face — that between the North and the South.

In the New England group we have one which, in spite of minor differences, is unusually homogeneous. Not only are the boundaries between the six states which now form it negligible, but the section, as a whole, is a geographical unit, within which a common life, based upon generally similar economic, political, and religious foundations, has constituted a distinct cultural strain in the life of the nation. The "New England idea" and the "New England type" have been as sharply defined as they have been persistent; and, if, in our own day, they seem, to some extent, to be passing, their influence may be no less living because spread broadcast throughout the whole land, and absorbed into the common national life.

Effective natural boundaries, defining a limited area, are of determining influence in fostering the life of primitive peoples or of civilized colonies. Diffusion over an unlimited space, in the one case, tends to weaken the hold on the land and the growth of the state, while, in the other, it greatly retards the development of those elements that make for civilized life. Aside from other factors, the possession by the English, in the settlement period, of a limited and protected area, naturally restricted by the sea and the mountains, resulted, speaking broadly, in the building up of thickly settled, compact colonies as contrasted with the boundless empire of the French, opened to them by their control of the Mississippi and the St. Lawrence rivers. It is noteworthy that, of the great river-highways leading to the interior of the continent,— the St. Lawrence, the Hudson–Mohawk, and the Mississippi,— none was at first possessed by the English, who had everywhere, unwittingly but fortunately, selected portions of the coast where their natural tendency to expand was temporarily held in check.

The Appalachian barrier, which thus served to protect and to concentrate the efforts of the English, may be said to extend from the Gulf of St. Lawrence to Alabama, coming nearest to the coast in passing across New York. In the northern part of Maine, where the mountains descend to a low water-shed, enormous forests, with no easy river-route facilitating peaceful or warlike travel, formed almost as effective a barrier; while passage southward, along the coast, was impeded during the early period by the presence of a foreign nation, the Dutch. There were, indeed, certain narrow entrances to this enclosed territory from the north, as the larger streams, flowing southward from the water-shed along the Canadian boundary, could be utilized, in connection with those flowing northward from its other slope to the St. Lawrence. The many falls along their courses, entailing laborious carries in the dense forest, together with the necessary longer ones across the height of land, made these routes more suitable, however, for the military needs of savages than for the movement of troops in large bodies, or for the purposes of trade.[1] The main passage for travel and transport from Canada to the south lay wholly to the west of New England, by way of the Richelieu River and Lake Champlain, which latter well deserved its Indian name of "key to the country."

Within the boundaries thus roughly defined and the sea, lies a land said to contain a greater diversity of natural features than any other of equal area in the United States. To the west and north are the Berkshire Hills of Massachusetts, the Green Mountains of Vermont, the White Mountains of New Hampshire, and the scattered peaks of Maine. From a height of fifteen hundred to two thousand feet at the base of the mountains, a gently sloping upland descends gradually to Long Island Sound and the Atlantic. Although, at first glance, its surface seems to present only a confused mass of low-lying hills, their tops are seen to show a marked uniformity of level as they gradually slope downward toward the south and east; and geological evidence makes it almost certain that, at one time, this region was a plain, resulting from the wearing down, by denudation, of an earlier mountain range. Subsequent alterations in its surface, due to erosion and other factors, gave rise to the present uplands and lowlands, which have been of determining influence in the peopling of the section, the rugged uplands offering so hard a subsistence that they were nowhere willingly chosen for settlement so long as land might still be had in the lowlands.

Although, largely in the eighteenth century, economic pressure in the happier valleys forced many farmers to move to the hills, the opening of the West drew many of them to the prairies during the following century, and the population, like

[1] The three most important of these routes were: 1, from the headwaters of the St. John to a branch of the Chaudière; 2, from the head of the Kennebec to the Chaudière proper (the route of Col. Arnold in 1775); and 3, from a branch of the Connecticut to a stream entering Lake Memphremagog, and so down the St. Francis. *Cf.* A. B Hulbert, *Portage Paths;* Cleveland, 1903. Many of the early maps also show the more important portages and carrying-places.

water which had been forced above its level, slowly drained off the uplands again, through the sluiceway of the Mohawk Valley. To-day, dying hill-towns, abandoned farms, and the yet unpeopled wilderness of northern Maine, tell the story of this struggle against geographical conditions.[1]

This formation of upland and valley extends to the shore-line of Sound and ocean, the broad coastal plain, which is so marked a feature from New Jersey southward, being almost wholly absent in New England. This is probably due to a subsidence of the shore, which allowed the ocean to flow back over part of the land, and which also explains the many hundred islands off the coast of Maine, and the drowned river valleys along the Sound. So numerous are the islands, bays, and headlands of the rugged coast north of the Isles of Shoals, that they expand the two hundred and thirty miles of shore to nearly three thousand, if all are included in the measurement. In this section, also, there are many good harbors, particularly that of Portland, but the coast is so greatly dissected as to make land communication along it very difficult; while the small boats, which partially served the needs of commerce and travel in early days, were seriously interfered with by the great rise and fall of the tides. Both these conditions tended to isolate the colonial settlements and hinder their development. The upland country, with its poorer soil and more difficult conditions of life, also approaches nearer to the sea in Maine and New Hampshire than farther south, so that, although Portsmouth, too, has a fine harbor, those states have always been more thinly settled than the others.

The coast of Massachusetts is less rugged, but more varied. South of the granite headland of Cape Ann, the shores of Boston Bay are still rocky and irregular; but both shores of the great sandy curve of the Cape Cod peninsula, which, with Cape Ann, encloses the waters of Massachusetts Bay, are smooth and moulded by wind and wave. The coast again becomes rough around Buzzard's Bay, while the almost land-

[1] W. M. Davis, *The Physical Geography of Southern New England* (New York, 1896), pp. 26 *ff.*

locked waters of Rhode Island have drowned the old river-system of that state. Opposite Connecticut lies Long Island, the only island of any considerable size along the entire Atlantic coast; so that the Sound, or inland sea, thus formed between it and the mainland, gives to Connecticut the advantage of a quiet, protected waterway for all its ports.

The value of a coast-line, however, depends not alone upon its own features, but upon its relations with the interior, both as to means of communication, and as to the soil and products of the back-country. During the colonial period, the lines of communication were naturally along waterways. With the small tonnage of the vessels then employed, even the sea-going ones, by utilizing rivers, could pass far inland; and we find Henry Hudson penetrating to Albany in the same ship in which he had crossed the ocean. The almost interminable length of the St. Lawrence and the Mississippi lured the French ever deeper into the wilderness in quest of the retreating fur-trade, so that their empire became hardly more than a series of far-flung forts and trading-posts. The rivers of New England, on the other hand, having their rise in the Appalachian barrier, and inter-rupted by many falls in their short courses, led to no vast domain beyond, and offered little temptation to the settler to leave their fertile valleys and tide-swept mouths. This lack of inland navigation not only tended to concentrate settlement near the coast, or on the lower navigable reaches of such streams as the Connecticut, but, also, in a later period, hastened the progress of turnpikes and railroads more quickly in New Eng-land than anywhere else in the country.[1]

At first, however, rivers were the only means of communi-cation with the interior, and settlements along the coast of Massachusetts, and on Buzzard's and Narragansett bays, tended to remain maritime in character, extending inland but slowly; whereas those located on such streams as the Kennebec and the Connecticut absorbed the rich fur-trade for which they formed the main routes. This trade, it may be noted, was exhausted earlier in New England than elsewhere, on account

---

[1] E. C. Semple, *Influences of Geographic Environment* (New York, 1911), p. 354.

of the comparatively limited drainage basins of the river-system, so that the people were sooner forced to depend upon agriculture, fishing, commerce, and manufactures.

Land travel continued both difficult and costly in all the colonies throughout the whole of the earlier industrial period, and roads were so poor, even a century after New England was settled, that not until 1722 was a team driven for the first time from Connecticut to Rhode Island. To emphasize the effect of rivers, we may note that in New York, where the Hudson was the highway, the average cost of carrying a bushel of wheat one hundred miles was but two pence, compared with a shilling in Pennsylvania, where forty wagons, one hundred and sixty horses, and eighty men were required to transport the same amount of freight handled by two or three men on a scow in New York. This high cost of land carriage, which, added to the ocean freights, had the effect of fostering home manufactures as against importations from England, also restricted the areas of distribution, and tended to localize industry.[1]

It was not, however, merely the lack of an adequate system of river transport that served to stimulate manufacturing in New England in competition with the mother-country. The character of such rivers as she possessed peculiarly adapted them for the purpose of supplying power, for not only are falls and rapids numerous in all of them, but the "fall-line" in New England is nearer tidewater than it is anywhere else along the coast. In addition, the regularity of the rainfall, and the great number of lakes, which form natural reservoirs, cause the flow of the rivers to be more constant than in other parts of the country. From all these causes, the little Merrimac, for example, which is otherwise insignificant as an American river, is the most noted water-power stream in the world.[2]

The soil of New England is of glacial origin, about three quarters of it being of boulder-clay, stubborn in character and

---

[1] V. S. Clark, *History of Manufactures in the U. S., 1607–1860* (Carnegie Institution, Washington, 1916), pp. 88 *ff.*

[2] *Report on the Water-Power of the U. S.;* Census Report, 1885.

difficult to cultivate, but of fair and lasting fertility, due to the steady decomposition of the smaller pebbles. The remainder, largely in the southeast, is sandy and of little or no use for agriculture, owing to the rapid draining away of all moisture.[1] That on the uplands is thinner and poorer than in the valleys, and the uplands predominate.

A hard living may be forced from such a soil; but the lazy or unskilled fail to subsist, much less leave a surplus. Tests of white and colored farmers in the north indicate that, if the efficiency of the former be taken as 100, that of the latter is but 49,[2] from which fact the economic impossibility of slavery would seem to be established for New England, as that institution requires the production of a considerable surplus over individual needs, even by inefficient labor. In Barbadoes, on the other hand, a hundred acres planted in sugar were tended by fifty slaves and seven white servants; a similar amount of land, if cotton were raised, required forty-five blacks and five whites; while the cultivation of ginger necessitated the labor of seven and a half persons per acre.[3] The economic, social, and political results of such utilization of the soil, as compared with the subsistence farming of New England, are too obvious to need elaboration. As we shall see, the Puritans were not wholly averse to owning slaves, and were often wont, in ethical cases, to weigh both religious scruples and economic considerations. In this case, the latter prevailed, without detriment to the former, and the abolition sentiment of the nineteenth century was rooted in the glacial soil of the seventeenth.

The soil was one which did not foster large plantations, as in the South, but small farms tilled by their owners, with little help from slave or indented servant. There was, therefore, no economic factor at work in New England tending to wide dispersal, as against the obvious need of compact settlement for purposes of protection, mutual help, and social intercourse.

[1] N. S. Shaler, *United States*, vol. 1, p. 54.

[2] E. Huntington, *Civilization and Climate* (Yale University Press, 1915), p. 22.

[3] Dalby Thomas, *An historical account of the rise and growth of the W. I. Collonies and of the great advantages they are to England in respect to Trade* (London, 1690), pp. 14, 21 f.

The early New Englander was a somewhat hesitating believer in the injustice of slavery. He was a strong believer in a town grouped about a church. The soil confirmed and strengthened him in both convictions.

This compact form of settlement, in turn, however, caused the village lands of New England to become exceedingly high-priced as compared with the plantation lands of the southern colonies. In the seventeenth century, New England farms very rarely contained over five hundred acres, in contrast to the average Virginian plantation of five thousand; but New England land was worth about fourteen times as much per acre as that in Virginia, and a hundred-acre homestead in the north was equal in value to a fair-sized plantation in the south.[1] All these factors, operating with others, emphasized the character-istic nature of New England expansion, which was almost in-variably a migration, not of individuals, but of churches and towns, or, at least, of small neighborhood groups.

When the land was first settled, it was everywhere covered by a dense forest, except for meadows here and there, along the shore or in the larger river-bottoms. Even to-day, of the thirty thousand square miles of land-surface in Maine, the forest is said to extend over twenty-one thousand, a district as large as New Hampshire, Massachusetts, and Connecticut combined.[2] These forests, mainly of hard-wood, deciduous trees, with an admixture of conifers in Maine, had been prac-tically untouched by the natives, except by burning the under-brush. In fact, Whitney claims that more trees had been destroyed by the beavers than by the Indians.[3] Although building stone is plentiful in New England, this abundance of timber along the Atlantic coast determined the form of the colonial architecture, and developed a type of wooden building little used in England. It also provided the materials for ship-building, the forests growing to the very edge of a shore in-

[1] J. C. Ballagh, "The Land System in the South," in *American Historical Association Report*, 1897, p. 109.
[2] H. A. Pressey, *Water-Powers of the State of Maine*; U. S. Geological Survey, 1902, p. 15.
[3] J. D. Whitney, *The United States* (Boston, 1889), p. 176.

dented almost everywhere by suitable harbors; and, in the early period, this industry is found scattered along the entire shore. But it tended to concentrate at fewer points, as the lumber-supply near at hand became exhausted, and the tonnage of vessels increased. "In reading the early commercial history of New England," however, as Miss Semple well says, "one seems never to get away from the sound of the shipbuilder's hammer, and the rush of the launching vessel." [1]

The climate, though varying in intensity from northern Maine and New Hampshire to southern Connecticut, and also from inland to the sea, is, on the whole, a severe one. Snow falls to a considerable depth everywhere, remaining in the mountains till late in the spring, the lower mean temperature of the year, as compared with the coast farther south, being due to the greater cold of winter rather than to a cooler summer. The seasonal changes, indeed, are very marked, and the cultural influence of "the harshness of contrasts and extremes of sensibility," of a "winter which was always the effort to live," and a summer which was "tropical license," must formerly have been even greater than to-day.[2] A noteworthy feature of our Atlantic coast, climatically, is the crowding together of the isothermal lines, so that the frigid and tropical zones are brought within twenty degrees of latitude, as compared with forty in Europe. This bringing the products of so many climatic regions comparatively near to one another greatly stimulated intercolonial trade, which New England early claimed the largest share in carrying.[3]

We thus see how the mountain-barrier kept the New Englander within bounds; how the lack of long navigable rivers prevented him from advancing far inland, even within his

---

[1] E. C. Semple, *American History and its Geographic Conditions* (Boston, 1903), p. 122.

[2] *The Education of Henry Adams* (Boston, 1918), pp. 7 *ff.*

[3] Semple, *Influences of Geographic Environment*, p. 618. Both Miss Semple and A. P. Brigham (*Geographic Influences in American History*, New York, 1903) lay their main stress on land-forms. For climatic influences, *vide* W. N. Lacy, "Some Climatic Influences in American History," in *Monthly Weather Review*, vol. xxxvi, pp. 169 *ff*; Huntington, *Civilization and Climate, ubi supra*; and *The Red Man's Continent* (Yale University Press, 1919).

narrow limits; how the bleak and stony uplands held him along the coast and lower river valleys; how the soil discouraged him from agriculture; and, on the other hand, how his numerous harbors, the quantity of timber for ship-building, and his central position for the carrying trade, all drew him out to sea.

There was another, and most important factor, however, luring him to quit the land, for the banks and shoals, extending from Cape Cod to Newfoundland, were the feeding grounds of enormous masses of cod, herring, and other fish, which swarmed in the cold waters of the Labrador current. If no precious metals rewarded search, if the beaver retreated farther and farther into the wilderness, if the soil gave but grudging yield, here, at least, was limitless wealth. The industry, thanks to the combination of shoals and icy waters, became the corner-stone of the prosperity of New England; and in the colonial history of that section, commerce smells as strongly of fish as theology does of brimstone. Together with lumber, fish became the staple of exchange with old England and the rich West Indian settlements, and the industry bred a hardy race of seamen, who manned New England's merchant fleet, and, later, the American navy.[1]

In two other aspects the sea exerted marked influence upon both the discovery and the settlement of the new lands, as well as upon their later history. The fact that America and Europe are separated by three thousand miles of water must be considered in relation to culture at various periods; for geographic factors are relative, and not absolute, in their historic connotations. Countries may be said to be habitable or uninhabitable, distances to lengthen or shorten, heights to rise or fall, according to the measure of man's control over nature at any given time. As a distinguished French geographer has said: "Tout se transforme autour de nous; tout diminue ou s'accroît. Rien n'est vraiment immobile et invariable."[2] Increase in

---

[1] For the influence of the sea on subsidiary industries, *vide* M. Keir, "Some Influences of the Sea upon the Industries of New England," *American Geographical Review*, vol. v, pp. 399 ff.

[2] Jean Brunhes, *La géographie humaine* (Paris, 1912), p. 6.

speed of vessels, with increased storage capacity for food and water, is equivalent to an actual reduction of the distance in miles; and, measured by the standards of modern ships in speed alone, without considering other factors, we may say that twenty to thirty thousand miles of uncharted seas had kept America hidden from European eyes.

Across this wide expanse, in the latitude of Europe, the currents of both air and water set from America toward the Old World, and almost precluded the possibility, under primitive conditions, of European voyaging and discovery. North of this eastward track, however, lie not only the stepping-stones of the Faroe Islands, Iceland, and Greenland, but, once at Iceland, the prevailing wind carries the European mariner to Greenland, whence the Labrador current leads him close inshore and along the coasts of Canada and New England.[1] To the south of the central eastward track, is the zone of the trade-winds and the great westward flowing equatorial current; and there, again, we find island stepping-stones. Thus nature clearly indicated the two ways by which America might be found; and, for long, the routes followed were the northerly one to the Newfoundland fisheries and New England, and the southerly one to the Canaries, the West Indies, and, thence, to Virginia. The earliest English efforts at colonization in North America were at the two points lying nearest to England by wind and ocean current.

One other feature in the geographic control over the life of New England may here be noted. The main imports of England were naturally those commodities which she did not produce herself, and these were found in the southern and West Indian colonies rather than in New England, whose fish and cereals competed with similar products in the home market. Destined, from her position and other geographic factors, to occupy the leading place among the colonies in trade and commerce, New England was thus forced to find outlets for her

---

[1] In the Middle Ages there was apparently an additional volcanic island, known as Gunnbiörn's Skerries, between Iceland and Greenland, destroyed by eruption in 1456. R. H. Major, *Voyages of the Zeni* (Hakluyt Society, 1873), pp. lxxiv ff.

products in intercolonial and foreign trade, rather than in that with England. In order to pay for the manufactured and other articles imported from the old country, she exported, in turn, not to that country, as, in the main, did the other colonies, but to her sister colonies and to foreign ports. According to the accepted economic theories of the colonizing period, this not only made her less valuable to the mother-country, but would evidently give her a considerable interest in breaking those laws for regulating commerce that were the logical expression of the current imperial theory. If we consider, therefore, the nature of the commodities she produced, the competing character of her trade, the democratic ideas of the groups of self-governing land-holders, such as the soil and climate combined to develop, and the economic beliefs of the day, it becomes evident that, when a heavy strain should be put upon the imperial structure, the tendency to break would be likely to appear first in New England.

In the foregoing sketch, an attempt has been made to trace, very briefly, some of the influences of geography upon Puritan development in New England. The early history of all peoples is largely to be found in their struggle against their environment, and its effect upon them. These effects are subtle and far-reaching, and, in connection with them, it may not be wholly idle to speculate upon what might have been had events followed a slightly different course. Had the Jamestown settlers planted themselves upon the coast of Massachusetts, they would probably have failed. On the other hand, had the Pilgrims and Puritans, as both seriously thought of doing, settled in the tropics, where the nature of the climate and the soil would have turned the scale for slavery, where the conditions of life would have strongly combatted their notions of town and church, and where luxury and easy living would have been quickly attained by their inherent energy, what would then have become of what we call the New England element in our national life? To carry the speculation far would be futile, but it serves to bring out into somewhat clearer relief the influences of the geographic environment upon those colonists whose history it is our task to trace.

The distant land to which they came was not an uninhabited wilderness. They found there, as occupants of the soil, an unknown race, in the lower stage of barbarism, with whom they had to contend for its possession. With a few notable exceptions, the relations of the whites with the Indians were the same in all the colonies. The natives were traded with, fought with, occasionally preached to, and then, as far as possible, exterminated. "The precepts Christianity delivers," wrote Lord Bryce, of the relations between advanced and backward races, "might have been expected to soften the feelings and tame the pride of the stronger race. It must, however, be admitted that in all or nearly all the countries . . . Christianity . . . has failed to impress the lessons of human equality and brotherhood upon the whites. . . . Their sense of scornful superiority resists its precepts." [1]

This comment, which is only too true in the present day, was still more true in the seventeenth century. Even in history, the Indian has usually been treated as, at best, a picturesque element, to give color to the somewhat drab homespun of the colonial story; while the Indian policy of the several colonies, the history of the Indian trade, and the influence of the Indian upon the settler, yet await adequate treatment.

The Indian's character and mental traits, which were frequently misinterpreted, were those to be expected in a savage at his stage of culture. If, on the one hand, he was not the noble being painted by Cooper, on the other, he was not the demon often conceived. Indeed, in scanning the list of epithets hurled at him by some of New England's ministers of Christ, one is reminded of Professor Murray's comment on the Greek story of Œdipus. "Unnatural affection, child-murder, father-murder, incest, a great deal of hereditary cursing, a double fratricide and a violation of the sanctity of dead bodies—when

[1] Lord Bryce, *The Relations of the Advanced and Backward Races of Mankind* (Romanes Lecture; Oxford, 1902), p. 40. He contrasts the failure of Christianity with the success of Islam in that regard.

one reads," writes this scholar, "such a list of charges brought against any tribe or people, either in ancient or in modern times, one can hardly help concluding that somebody wanted to annex their land." [1]

The nature of the life the Indian led inclined to render him improvident and lazy, although capable at need of great exertion and endurance. He was dirty in his person, and yet possessed of a childish vanity as to his appearance. The popular idea of him as reserved, silent, and dignified probably came from the fact that his etiquette demanded that he thus appear on ceremonial occasions, social or religious, and it was at such times, at first, that the whites usually saw him. In reality, in his ordinary life, he was a sociable body, cheerful and chatty, with a considerable sense of humor, fond of punning and joking.[2] Hysterical in his nervous make-up, he was peculiarly liable to suggestion and religious excitement. As he was passionate and quick to take offense, like other savages and children, public opinion demanded that he seek revenge; and when a crime was committed against any member of a clan, the punishment of the guilty party became the duty of every other member. Under the compelling influence of such a code, the individual may often have had to appear more revengeful than he really was; and, as a matter of fact, the old law of an eye for an eye had already become softened by possibilities of compensation, through adoption or otherwise, even in the case of murder. Although prisoners of war were frequently tortured with fiendish ingenuity before being killed, in this case, also, adoption offered a milder alternative, often exercised. Scalping, as a sign of victory, was supposed to be performed only on the dead, and, although this theory did not always hold good,[3] it must be remembered that the whites, as well as the Indians, engaged in the practice, with the difference that,

[1] Gilbert Murray, *The Rise of the Greek Epic* (Oxford, 1911), p. 54.

[2] F. W. Hodge, *Handbook of American Indians north of Mexico* (Bureau of American Ethnology, 1911), vol. I, pp. 578, 88, 286; L. Farrand, *Basis of American History* (New York, 1904), p. 265.

[3] G. Friederici, *Skalpieren u. ähnliche Kriegsgebräuche in Amerika* (Braunschweig, 1906), p. 106.

while the natives did it for honor, the settlers did it for money. New England men, and even New England women, sold scalps to the authorities at so much a head; and, among the Pennsylvanians, prices went as high as fifty dollars for a female scalp, and one hundred and thirty for that of a boy under ten.[1] With the Indian, it was merely a custom to which he had become inured; and it should be noted that he wore his own hair accordingly, and carefully refrained from shaving the scalplock, which it might be his enemy's glory, some day, to remove.

The influence of a formal code is seen also in his bearing of pain. In public, he would suffer torture of the most excruciating sort with complete stoicism, as required by the opinion of his fellows; whereas, in private, when not thus sustained, he would be childish in his self-abandon over the tooth-ache or other discomfort.[2] Hospitality was a cardinal virtue, to such an extent that "in some languages there was but one word both for generosity and bravery, and either was a sure avenue to distinction."[3] Fierce and bloodthirsty in war, in domestic life he was affectionate to an extreme, especially toward children. His code, though different from the white man's, was apparently adhered to quite as strictly; but, when the two were brought into contact, the vices inherent in each tended to develop, and it is natural that the weaker came to be considered hopelessly lazy, cruel, drunken, and untrustworthy.

At the time of discovery, the natives encountered along the Atlantic coast had advanced from savagery to the lower status of barbarism, and were still in the Stone Age. Although agriculture was practised to a considerable extent, the Indians, having no domestic animals, were still dependent upon the chase for a material part of their diet, and so must be considered as in the hunting stage, their advancement in culture being limited by that condition.[4]

---

[1] G. E. Ellis, *The Red Man and the White Man in America* (Boston, 1882), p. 123.

[2] Farrand, *Basis*, p. 265; Roger Williams, *A Key into the Languages of America* (*Narragansett Club Publications*, vol. I), p. 138.

[3] Hodge, *Handbook*, vol. I, p. 572.

[4] L. Carr, "The Food of certain American Indians and their Method of preparing it"; *Proceedings American Antiquarian Society*, New Series, vol. IV, p. 156.

Their political organization was much misunderstood by the whites, with disastrous results. The settlers, utterly ignorant of savage life, tried to interpret such things as they saw in terms of their own institutions; whence came the kings, princes, and nobles, who parade the pages of our early writers. It is needless to say that nothing in Indian society in any way corresponded to these terms; and the failure of the whites to apprehend that Indian institutions had almost nothing in common with their own was the source of endless trouble and much needless bloodshed.

Among such Indians as had attained to some degree of social organization, which included the majority on the continent and all of those with whom the settlers came in contact, the primary unit was the clan, or gens. Within a clan, or gens, everyone was, or was supposed to be, descended from a common ancestor, and thus related to all the others — in the former the line of descent being traced through the female, and in the latter, through the male. Otherwise, the two organizations were identical, and we shall, therefore, speak in terms of the clan only. Clan members were absolutely forbidden to intermarry; they had the right to elect and depose the sachem and chiefs, to bestow names upon individuals, and to adopt strangers. They possessed common religious observances, were buried in one place, had mutual rights of inheritance in the property of deceased members, were under obligation to defend one another, and participated in the council.[1] The latter was essentially democratic, every man and woman in the clan having a voice, the sachem and chiefs being elected and deposed at will. The sachem was a civil officer having nothing to do with war, and the office was hereditary within the clan, though the succeeding relative, usually a brother or nephew, was elected. Chief was a very vague term, merely indicating one who had been elected for some special fitness, the number of chiefs being roughly proportioned to the size of the clan. Both sachem and chiefs attended the larger council of the tribe.

[1] L. H. Morgan, *Ancient Society* (London, 1877), pp. 71 *ff.*

While articles of personal property, such as clothes or weapons, were owned by the individual, the title to all land was in the clan, and the individual had the right of use only.   Ownership in fee by the individual, as practised by the whites, was not known at all to the natives, nor was the native institution understood by the whites during the first years, so that the so-called land sales by the Indians were the cause of constant misunderstandings and ill-feeling.[1]

Generally, each clan possessed a totem, or animal, from which it derived its name.   These names, however, were not, as a rule, the common ones for the animal or object, but denoted a characteristic feature or haunt, and were less childish than they have been made to seem.   Thus the Turtle Clan did not use the common word, *ha'nowa*, but *hadiniaden*, "they have upright necks." [2]   A curious importance was attached by the Indian to the names of individuals, and that first given in infancy was usually changed at puberty, and even at other times. Certain names were given only in certain clans, and the individual had property rights in his own name, which he could lend, sell, or even pawn.

The clan was thus the Indian's little world.   To its organization, and his own position in it, he owed almost all that made life worth living from the social standpoint — his name, to which a potent influence attached, his ceremonial rights, his rights of inheritance, his property rights in land, his obligation to defend and succor his fellow clansmen, his right to be protected in return, and, finally, his political right to elect and depose his sachem and chiefs.   Notwithstanding the extremely democratic and individualistic nature of Indian society, and the looseness of its political organization, the influence of the clan sentiment upon the individual must have had enormous weight.[3]

---

[1] *Cf.* Ellis, *The Red Man*, pp. 207 *ff*.   [2] Hodge, *Handbook*, vol. 1, p. 304.

[3] The phratry was a combination of two or more clans, forming a larger exogamous group, and originating, perhaps, in the division of overgrown clans.   Although it frequently had the power of veto over the election of clan sachems and chiefs, its functions were social rather than political.   In ball games, phratry played against phratry, while at funerals and other ceremonies the organization appears clearly. There was no chief or head.

Above the clan was the tribe, which is difficult to define, but clearly marked, and which was the highest form of organization ordinarily attained by the natives — confederacies, such as the Iroquois, being exceptional. Tribal organization is more obvious to the untrained observer than that of clans, and whenever the settlers found a body of natives possessing an apparent degree of independence or territorial isolation, they gave them a tribal designation, derived from the dialect, locality, or name of the leader, though such designations are of almost no value for scientific classification.[1] The tribe, which was composed of several clans, may be said to have had a common religious worship, a name, a definite territory, and the exclusive use of a dialect, together with the right to invest and depose the sachems and chiefs of the several clans.[2] These chiefs and sachems formed the tribal council, which controlled the tribe's "foreign policy," sent and received ambassadors, made alliances, and declared war and peace, although it was a weak organization for military purposes. The assumed natural condition was war, not peace, and every tribe was theoretically at war with every other, unless a specific treaty of peace had been made. On the other hand, there was no forced military service, and public opinion or personal inclination alone sent the warrior along the war-path. Any person could organize an expedition at any time, and service was voluntary, operations, as a rule, being conducted suddenly, secretly, and on a small scale.

As among all primitive peoples, the food-quest was one of the dominating factors in the Indian's mode of life. This included hunting, both with weapons and with traps, fishing, by net and line, and agriculture, with primitive implements and manuring. Game was fairly abundant for a sparse population, and the bays, rivers, and lakes swarmed with many sorts of fish. Maize, the fundamental food-crop of all eastern North America, was raised as far north as northern Maine; pumpkins, beans, and other native vegetables were cultivated also, and tobacco

---

[1] Clark Wissler, *The American Indian* (New York, 1917), p. 152.
[2] Morgan, *Ancient Society*, pp. 112 *ff*.

was grown even beyond the northern limits of maize. Not only these crops, but the whole complex of cultivation which the Indians had developed, was of profound importance to the settlers, who, it may be noted, also adopted in its entirety the native method of making maple-sugar.

In many cases, the quest of these various foods gave rise to seasonal migrations, from which was derived the false idea that the Indians were nomadic. Although this was not true, they nearly always did have two, and even three, places of residence — one in the summer, conveniently located for their fields of corn; one in the winter, in some sheltered valley; and, perhaps, one for the fall months, for the hunting.[1] Moreover, as Williams tells us, "the abundance of fleas" in their homes would occasionally make them "remove on a sudden" to a more exclusive spot. Most communities had one or more fortified enclosures, consisting of from one to a score of houses inside a stockade, which were resorted to in time of danger, and frequently formed their winter dwellings.[2]

In traveling, birch-bark or dugout canoes were used along the coasts and water-courses, and, on the land, well-established trails extended, with few breaks, across the length and breadth of the continent.[3] The most noted of these in New England, and among the earliest used by the settlers, were the Bay Path and Old Connecticut Path, the latter of which ran from what are now Boston and Cambridge, through Marlborough, Grafton, Oxford, and Springfield, to Albany, where it joined the great Iroquois trail along the Mohawk Valley to Niagara.[4]

In their travel, as in their domestic life, labor was more or

[1] Williams, *Key*, p. 74.

[2] C. C. Willoughby, "Houses and Gardens of the New England Indians," *American Anthropologist*, New Series, vol. VIII, p. 126.

[3] Rolle, for example, in 1697, followed one from Quebec to Illinois, 2400 miles. *Maine Historical Society Collections*, vol. V, p. 325.

[4] The Bay Path went from Boston to Springfield along the same line, except that it passed through South Framingham instead of Marlborough and Worcester, joining the Connecticut Path at Oxford. See map, in L. B. Chase, "Interpretation of Woodward's and Saffery's Map of 1642," in *New England Historical and Genealogical Register*, vol. IV. pp. 155 *ff*. For other early trails, see the same author's "Early Indian Trails," in *Worcester Society of Antiquity Collections*, vol. XIV. pp. 105 *ff*., and A. B. Hulbert, *Indian Thoroughfares*; Cleveland, 1902.

less equally divided between the sexes; and, although woman's position was subordinate, it is a mistake to paint her as drudge, toiling for a lazy master. In building the house, for example, the man cut and set the poles, on which the woman arranged the covering of mats or bark. The tillage of the soil in comparative safety was her share, while the man undertook the more dangerous work of hunting. While she had the care of the household, and the nurture of the children, he laboriously chipped the stone implements used in war and the chase, built the boats, and, in some cases, made the women's clothes as well as his own. The boys and old men helped her about the crops; to the other males were intrusted the duties of a warrior, and the conducting of public business and ceremonials, including the memorizing of the tribal records, treaties, and rituals.[1] In the production of household goods, the women made baskets and mats; the men, dishes and pots and spoons.[2]

Such a division of labor was calculated to provide the community, under the conditions of its savage and war-like life, with the largest possible measure of food and protection, and did not indicate a degraded position for woman. On the contrary, descent was usually traced through her, and the titles of the chiefs of the clans belonged to her, as did the family lodge and all its furnishings. She had ownership rights in the tribal lands; possessed the children exclusively; had the right of selecting from her sons candidates for the chieftaincy, of preventing them from going on the war-path, and of adopting strangers into the clan. She also had other powers, including that of life and death over alien prisoners, and was not seldom elected a chief or sachem herself. Among the Iroquois, the penalty for killing a woman was twice that exacted for a man; and it is noteworthy that no attempt against the chastity of a white woman prisoner has been charged against the savage— a record distinctly better than that of the white settlers. Although polygamy was not forbidden, it was rare except in the

[1] Hodge, *Handbook*, vol. ii, p. 284.
[2] D. Gookin, "Historical Collections of the Indians in New England, 1674"; *Massachusetts Historical Society Collections*, Series I, vol. i, p. 151.

case of chiefs, priests, and shamans (or medicine-men), and monogamic unions were the rule. The tie, however, was loose, and could readily be dissolved by either party, the children, in any case, remaining with the mother. Constancy was expected, and its breach, particularly in the case of the woman, was severely punished. Chastity was not expected before marriage, but, as Wissler points out, it was essential in certain religious ceremonies, and so may have been an ideal.[1]

In their relations with their children, we find some of the highest traits in the character of the natives. Both parents were, as a rule, excessively fond of their offspring, and boys and girls were carefully instructed. In general, moral suasion alone was used; force but rarely. The girls, from an early age, were taught sewing, weaving, cooking, and the other household arts; the boys were initiated into the methods of hunting, fishing, war, and government. Etiquette was carefully observed by all, in such matters as sitting, standing, precedence in walking, interrupting a speaker, respect to elders, passing between a person and the fire, and the other niceties of life according to native standards.

The New England Indians had made but slight progress in the arts. The character of the native music is even yet not well understood, and much preliminary work remains to be done before any generalizations can be made.[2] We know, however, that in the same song the instrumental and vocal rhythms were different, and that there was a characteristic one for every ceremony. Music, indeed, was an important element in life, all ceremonies, public and private, being accompanied by songs, which were the property of clans, societies, or individuals, and were bought and sold. In design, both in pottery and weaving, the patterns used were geometrical only, and simple; but the later New England native pottery showed the influence of the superior art of the Iroquois, in form as well as decoration.[3]

[1] Wissler, *The American Indian*, p. 176.   [2] *Ibid.*, p. 146.
[3] C. C. Willoughby, "Pottery of the New England Indians," in *Putnam Anniversary Volume of Anthropological Essays* (New York, 1909), pp. 83 *ff.*

In their economic life, the most interesting feature was the use of wampum, or shell-beads, as a primitive medium of exchange. These little black or white cylinders, of which the former were worth twice as much as the latter, were made with great care from certain shells found along the coast. Besides their use as currency, they were prized by the Indians as ornament, and were strung into belts, to perform their well-known symbolic and historical functions.[1]

One of the most popular misconceptions of the Indian is that of his belief in a "Great Spirit." Nowhere in American aboriginal life do we find anything approaching such a conception. The Indian was in the animistic stage of religious belief. The *manitou* of the Algonquins, like the *orenda* of the Iroquois, was merely the magic power which might exist in objects, forces, animals, and even men, superior to man's natural qualities; and the Indian's religious beliefs centred about his relations to some embodied form of this power. He believed in good spirits and bad, which could be controlled or invoked by prayer, offerings, charms, or incantations, and had developed a large body of myths to explain the universe and his relation to it. No moral concept attached to any of his deities, nor had he developed any idea of future rewards and punishments, although there was a belief in some vague form of life after bodily death. The rites of their primitive religion were in the hands of priests, whose power and influence increase as we proceed southward toward the highly developed ritualism of the Incas and their neighboring civilizations. The priest, acting for the tribe, must not be confused with the "medicine-man," who depended solely upon his personal ability to establish relations with the magic powers, which he won by extraordinary experiences derived from fasting, prayer, and nervous excitement.

The exact classification of the Indians by cultural, archæological, linguistic, and other tests, is a matter of considerable

[1] W. B. Weeden, *Indian Money as a Factor in New England Civilization*, Johns Hopkins University Studies, 1884; A. C. Parker, *The Constitution of the Five Nations*, N. Y. State Museum Bulletin, 1916.

difficulty, but the linguistic, on the whole, is the best.   Judged
by all of them, however, the aborigines of New England possessed a high degree of unity.[1]   At the time of settlement, the
entire country along the coast, from Maryland to Hudson
Strait, was occupied by natives of the widely distributed Algonquin stock, except for a small number of Beothuks in Newfoundland, and the Esquimaux along the Labrador shore.[2]
The Algonquins also extended westward to the Mississippi, and
two-thirds of the way across Canada.   Imbedded in this otherwise homogeneous mass, the great body of the Iroquois dwelt
on both sides of the St. Lawrence, surrounded Lake Erie, and
covered all central Pennsylvania and the state of New York,
except the lower Hudson.   Although not included in the confines
of New England, the influence of this highly organized and war-
like confederacy was felt far beyond their bounds in every
direction.[3]   It is impossible to state the numbers which composed the New England tribes at the coming of the whites.
Perhaps the original settlers faced in all, throughout New England, five thousand warriors, although this may be too high a
figure, and all estimates can be only guesses.[4]

Such, in outline, was the Indian when he met the astonished
and anxious gaze of the first settlers.   Enough has been said to
show that in the contact of the races an irrepressible conflict
was bound to develop.   Even had the savage never received
any but kind and just treatment from his white neighbor, it is
improbable that he could have readjusted his entire life so as

[1] See maps, in Wissler, *The American Indian*, pp. 205, 246, 282.

[2] In recent years, evidences of a pre-historic culture in the Penobscot valley, wholly
different from that of the Algonquin or Beothuks, have been found.   *Vide* W. K.
Moorehead, "Prehistoric Cultures in the State of Maine," *Proceedings of the 19th
International Congress of Americanists* (Washington, 1917), pp. 48 *ff*.   Also his "Red-
Paint People," in *American Anthropologist*, New Series, vol. xv.

[3] L. H. Morgan, *The League of the Iroquois;* New York, 1901, *passim*.   Though
considered a different stock from the Algonquin, they seem to have been identical
physically.   A. Hrdlička, *Physical Anthropology of the Lenape;* Bureau of American
Ethnology, Bulletin 62, 1916, p. 127.

[4] Gookin, *Historical Collection*, pp. 145 *ff*.   Another writer, in 1629, says: "The
greatest Saggamores about us cannot make above three hundred men, and other
lesser Saggamores have not above fifteen subjects, and others neere about us but
two." [Higginson] "New England's Plantation, 1630," in *Mass. Hist. Soc. Coll.*
Series I, vol. I, p. 122.

to compete with, or to accept, civilization. That test, however, was never made. To say that his lands were bought, and that, therefore, he was justly treated, is a mockery. To have expected sympathy, understanding, and justice in the situation as it developed in the seventeenth century is asking too much, both of human nature and of the period. Indeed, it is questionable whether, in the competition between races of higher and lower civilizations, when the former intrude upon the lands of the latter, justice, in its strictest sense, is ever possible. One cannot believe that the world would have been either better or happier had the land which to-day supports a hundred million self-governing people been left to the half-million barbarians who barely gained a subsistence from it four centuries ago. Man, in the individual treatment of his fellow, is, indeed, bound by the laws of justice and of right; but in the larger processes of history we are confronted by problems that the ethics of the individual fail to solve. The Indian in the American forest, and the Polynesian in his sunny isle, share, in the moral enigma of their passing, the mystery of the vanished races of man and brute, which have gone down in the struggle for existence in geological or historic ages, in what, one would fain believe, is a universe governed by moral law.

CHAPTER II

STAKING OUT CLAIMS

As we saw in the first chapter, nature had clearly defined the paths by which America might be found. The time when the discovery would be made was almost as definitely determined by events in the Old World. For countless centuries, Europe, by many routes and through many intermediaries, had traded with the vaguely localized countries of the Orient. Throughout the Middle Ages, not only had she been dependent on the East for most of her luxuries, but many of these, from long usage, had become necessities.[1] About the beginning of the fourteenth century, this commerce, "the oldest, the most extensive, and the most lucrative trade known to Europe," began to be interfered with by the internal changes in the East, mainly due to conquests by the Ottoman Turks. Beginning about 1300, marked by the fall of Constantinople in 1453, and continuing until all the seaports of the eastern Mediterranean, including those of Egypt, were in their possession by 1522, the process was a gradual one. At first uneasy, then alarmed, finally facing commercial ruin by the almost complete strangulation of her Oriental trade, Europe struggled frantically against geographical conditions, in her efforts to find a new and unimpeded route to the East.

During the latter part of the same period, geographical science had been making many strides; while the theory of the earth's sphericity had been held, by some at least, since the days of Plato. After nearly two thousand years, motives developed which led men to turn that idea into action by use of the new discoveries, and in one generation Columbus sailed

[1] *Cf.* E. P. Cheyney, *European Background of American History* (New York, 1904), pp. 3–41.

west to America, and Da Gama east to India, and Magellan circumnavigated the globe. The thought advanced by philosophy, denied by common sense, and fought by the Church, finally wrought the greatest change yet known in the world's history through the commonplace necessities of trade.

Voyaging toward the northwest, in the hope of finding the treasures of the East, had possibly been undertaken annually from 1491, by certain citizens of Bristol, England, when the Italian, John Cabot, domiciled in their city, applied to King Henry VII for letters patent "for the discovery of new and unknown lands." The Cabots themselves left no account of their voyages, and the story must be made up from a few contemporary documents, some hearsay evidence, and a large amount of inference. Apparently, John Cabot sailed, some time in 1497, under the patent granted to himself and his sons, and by the end of August was back in England, after a voyage of several months. The location of the landfall, made June 24, is wholly uncertain.[1] A second voyage was made the following year, and a considerable part of the northeast coast appears to have been explored, although it is impossible to place the limits of the discovery. Whether he was accompanied on either or both of the voyages by his son Sebastian is uncertain, but it is probable that he was.[2] As for the rest, one is tempted to echo Dawson's remark, that "as for John Cabot, Sebastian says he died, which is one of the few undisputed facts in the discussion."[3] To us, the importance of the voyage lies in the fact that upon it England based her claims, in later times, to a portion of the New World, though she made no

[1] Prowse favors Newfoundland; d'Avezac, Deane, Réclus, Winsor, Brevoort, Eggleston, Winship, Biggar, and Dawson believe in Cape Breton; Biddle, Humboldt, Kohl, Stevens, Kretschmer, and Harrisse point to Labrador. The question is not important, and the alignment is given merely to show the uncertainties of this and other early voyages. The original sources are most accessible to the general reader in C. R. Beazley, *John and Sebastian Cabot*; London, 1898.

[2] In regard to the 1497 voyage, opinion ranges from R. Biddle, *Memoir of Sebastian Cabot* (Philadelphia, 1831), p. 50, who doubts if the father went, to H. Harrisse, *John Cabot* (London, 1896), p. 48, who doubts if the son did!

[3] S. E. Dawson, "Voyages of the Cabots," *Transactions of the Royal Society of Canada*, Series II, 1894, p. 53.

effort to colonize for another eighty years, and the immediate
effect of the discovery was not great.   The times were not yet
ripe.   Exploration and land-grabbing were games for kings,
and not for private endeavor, as the merchants of Bristol had
doubtless found; and Henry, as the Milanese ambassador observed, was "not lavish."

Owing to the great demand for fish in a Catholic Europe,
however, the shores of Newfoundland soon became the accustomed resort of English, French, and Portuguese.[1]   The coast
between Canada and Florida, nevertheless, remained practically
unexplored, and the maps of the period either break the continent into islands, or connect the two known portions by a
fanciful delineation, considered by some students to represent
the eastern coast of Asia.[2]   Where nothing is certain, all is
possible, and it was thought that the passage to the East, so
vainly sought elsewhere, might yet be found in this unknown
part of the world.   In 1524, Verrazano, under the flag of
France, and, a year later, Gomez, under that of Spain, undertook again the task of finding a westward route to Zipangu and
Cathay.   The Frenchman, apparently, coasted northward
from Carolina to Newfoundland, and the Spaniard seems to
have covered part of the same range, though the limits are not
known, nor even the direction in which he sailed.[3]

The three main contestants for empire in North America had
now appeared.   Spain, France, and England had all planted
their flags upon our shores, although their future struggles were
as yet hardly foreshadowed.   The fishing grounds, on the high
seas and far from the routes of Spain's gold-laden galleons, were
open to all, though the English seem early to have established
some sort of authority over the rough fishermen of the nations

[1] Cf. H. Harrisse, The Discovery of North America (London, 1892), pp. 180 ff.; and
C. de la Roncière, Histoire de la Marine Française (Paris, 1906), vol. II, p. 399.
[2] Cf. H. Stevens, Historical and Geographical Notes; New Haven, 1869.
[3] For the Verrazano voyage, vide B. Smith, An Enquiry into the Authenticity, etc.;
New York, 1864; J. C. Brevoort, Verrazano the Navigator; New York, 1874; H. C.
Murphy, The Voyage of Verrazano; New York, 1875; B. F. deCosta, Verrazano the
Explorer; New York, 1881.   The Gomez voyage is important but very obscure.
The statement by Fiske (The Discovery of America, vol. II, p. 491) is far too positive.
Harrisse (Discovery, pp. 229–43) gives new documents.

gathered there.[1]   The continent itself, however, was merely an unwelcome barrier, save the Spanish possessions in the south, with which, as yet, no other nation had thought of meddling. Nevertheless, a new era had opened, and commerce, which, from the dawn of history, had clung to the Mediterranean, now abandoned that enclosed sea for the open highways of the world's oceans.   The Oriental trade began to flow through new channels, and Spain, by the conquest of Mexico, in 1522, tapped unlimited sources of the precious metals.   The enormous import business from the East, formerly concentrated in the hands of the great mercantile cities of Italy, passed to the Iberian powers,[2] while men's horizons were widened by the new discoveries, and old established methods, routes, and connections had received severe shocks.   The example of Spain and Portugal was making other nations dream of gaining fabulous wealth by finding their way to the riches of the Orient, or gold in the wilds of America.

For the next four centuries, the civilization of Europe, which throughout the mediæval period had been hemmed within a narrow region by strong barbaric powers, was able to expand against almost negligible resistance, until, after having encircled the world, it is again faced in our own day by a "closed political system." [3]   At the very moment when new forces were being let loose by the social ferment following the Renaissance and the Reformation, the new lands offered vents through which those forces might in part escape, without causing such explosions as wholly to wreck the social system.   Their presence, or, to phrase it differently, the existence of a practically unlimited frontier, during the whole of our colonial period, was

[1] "The Englishmen, who commonly are lords of the harbors where they fish, and do use all strangers helpe in fishing if need require, accordinge to an old custome of the countrey."   Letter of Anthony Parkhurst, 1578, in Hakluyt, *Voyages* (Glasgow, 1904), vol. VIII, p. 10.   H. P. Biggar states that the English were so heavily interested in the American fisheries by 1522, that the Vice-Admiral sent several men-of-war to the mouth of the Channel to protect the returning vessels.   *Early Trading Companies of New France* (Toronto, 1901), p. 20.

[2] *Cf.* W. Heyd, *Geschichte des Levantehandels in Mittelälter* (Stuttgart, 1879), vol. II, pp. 514–40.

[3] H. J. Mackinder, "The Geographical Pivot of History," in *The Geographical Journal*, April, 1904, pp. 421–44.

one of the great formative elements in our institutions, and in the relations between the colonies and England.

We are so accustomed to think of that country as the great trading nation and mistress of the seas, that it is hard to conceive of a time when she had not even faintly dreamed that her destiny was to be upon the water, when her trade was still mainly in the hands of foreigners, and she herself was merely a producer of raw materials for the manufacturers on the continent. Such, however, was the situation at the opening of the sixteenth century. Men, indeed, began to talk of the new discoveries, which were even introduced into the rude theatre of the time; but, in the main, they stuck to their last, and fished and grew wool like their fathers. As yet, there was not the vaguest thought of a colonial empire — only dreams of gold and spices, and the silent fishermen catching cod.

The accession of Elizabeth opened the door to imperial ambition. Spain was, indeed, at the height of her power, whereas England's day was yet to come. Elizabeth's resources needed careful husbanding, and no open breach between the two countries could be allowed; but political interests were still European in the minds of statesmen, and peace, though many times in jeopardy, was not to be broken lightly for what English seamen might do "beyond the line." America was a means to European ends for Spain, and, until the depredations of the English became so great as to threaten those ends, murder, robbery, and the looting of cities passed with no action beyond protests, which Elizabeth met and parried.

We must pass by the doings of Hawkins, Drake, and the other sea-dogs, the whole pack of whom were soon in full cry after the hated Spaniards in their slow-moving galleons, laden with the treasure upon which their European power was nourished. This latter fact was now recognized, and wild and, perhaps, unlawful as were these English seamen, we must remember that, unlike common pirates, their depredations were not alone for private ends, but were blows struck for their religion, their country, and their queen. Had it not been for them, the Armada might indeed have been invincible, and the civilization of North America have been Latin instead of Anglo-Saxon.[1]

One of the outstanding characteristics of the later Tudor period was the remarkable development of individual initiative. Men were no longer content "ever like sheepe to haunte one trade," but in every field of human endeavor were striking across new paths. It was, moreover, an age of glorious amateurs. As in the best days of Greece, the bars that bound the individual within narrow limits of professionalism were broken asunder. It was as if to the nation's mature powers had suddenly been added the gift of youth. It was a cry of youth which Thorne uttered when he swept away all objections to the dangers of the Northwest Passage with his "there is no land unhabitable nor sea innavigable." Elizabeth's well-known methods, which perhaps temperament, necessity, and policy all had their share in fashioning, were admirably adapted to bring out, and to use to the utmost, these qualities in her subjects. Personal loyalty and individual initiative were largely fostered in place of taxation and governmental enterprise, and the patriotism of a united nation rose to new levels. "He is not worthy to live at all," wrote Sir Humphrey Gilbert, in 1576, "that for feare, or danger of death, shunneth his countries service, and his owne honour."[2]

This growing national feeling was strengthened by religious motives. The persecutions under Mary, and the tortures of the Inquisition, to which English sailors were so often subjected in the ports of Spain, both played their part in the drama now being enacted. Five thousand English volunteered for service against the Spaniard in the Netherlands, and the Queen's hand was being forced by the national feeling that she

---

[1] If "these thinges be sett downe and executed duelye and with speed and effecte, no doubte but the Spanishe empire falles to the grounde, and the Spanishe kinge shall be lefte bare as Aesops proude crowe . . . if you touche him in the Indies, you touche the apple of his eye; for take away his treasure, which is neruus belli, and which he hath almoste oute of his West Indies, his olde bandes of souldiers will soone be dissolved, his purposes defeated, his power and strengthe diminished, his pride abated, and his tyranie utterly suppressed." R. Hakluyt, "A Discourse concerning Western Planting"; *Maine Historical Society Collections*, vol. II, p. 59.

[2] Hakluyt, *Voyages*, vol. VII, p. 190.

herself had aroused. The conquest of Portugal by Spain, in 1580, nominally transferred to the latter all the colonial possessions of the entire world she did not already possess, leaving no room open for other nations, according to Spanish pretensions. The English government at last spoke, however, and in the same year, in answer to Spain's demand for the return of Drake's plunder, announced that Spain "by the law of nations could not hinder other princes from freely navigating those seas and transporting colonies to those parts where the Spaniards do not inhabit; that prescription without possession availed nothing." [1] The rights of other nations were definitely settled by the defeat of the Armada eight years later.

Business was beginning to improve somewhat after its long decline. The Muscovy Company had been chartered in 1555, and trade was seeking those new outlets which Sebastian Cabot had been recalled from Spain to find; but England felt the effects of the vast injection of American bullion into the currency system of Europe later than the continental countries. After the recoinage of the debased money in 1559, however, the advance in prices, which had already begun, was very rapid, with effects upon the country gentry and other classes, which were to have a marked influence upon American colonization.

In the meantime, while Drake was hastening home from the Pacific in the Pelican, loaded to the gunwales with the spoils of Spanish treasure-ships, another voyage, the first, except those of fishermen, since the ill-fated escapade of a London lawyer in 1536, was being made to the shores of Newfoundland. The motive was the old continuing one of a passage to the Orient by the northwest, although little is known of its details. The Queen, however, granted to its leader, Sir Humphrey Gilbert, a patent to colonize and rule such lands as he might choose from his new discoveries. This patent, which was issued in 1578, and marked a new epoch in England's American policy, followed in many respects the charters of the trading com-

---

[1] Cited by Alexander Brown, *Genesis of the United States* (Boston, 1890), pp. 9 *f.* The original source is not indicated.

panies granted by the Crown both previously and subsequently.[1] It had, however, a wholly novel feature in the clause which permitted Gilbert to transport a colony to his new possessions. It is probable that this first attempt to plant an English community beyond the seas was largely based upon the experience being gained at this very time in the efforts to colonize Ireland. Sir Humphrey himself, with other west-country gentlemen, had undertaken to plant colonies on the Crown lands in Ulster, eleven years before, and various plans and essays had been made, though unsuccessfully.[2] These colonizing schemes in Ireland were being considered and carried out during the whole period of the early efforts to plant colonies in America, and many individuals and city companies were interested in Irish and American lands at the same time. Both were almost equally wild and uncivilized, and both were rich and undeveloped.[3] The Irish Plantation Society, formed in 1613, was a serious rival to the Virginia Company, and diverted both funds and colonists at a critical time for the American scheme.[4]

The beginnings of the continental American colonies, indeed, are too apt to be considered as isolated events. Their unique importance from the standpoint of American history has tended to obscure their real nature. From that standpoint, they are naturally viewed as the founding of a great nation; but if they are considered solely in that relation, not only the planting of the colonies themselves, but the subsequent history of their relations with the mother-country, and the whole course of England's old colonial policy, are bound to be misunderstood. The American colonies, in their inception, were largely business ventures of groups of individuals or joint-stock companies, and, as such, were but episodes in the expansion of English commerce.

[1] It is given in Hakluyt, *Voyages*, vol. VIII, pp. 17–23.
[2] W. Cunningham, *The Growth of English Industry and Commerce* (Cambridge, 1892), vol. II, pp. 31–33.
[3] M. J. Bonn, *Die Englische Kolonisation in Irland* (Stuttgart, 1906), vol. I, pp. 265–373.
[4] Brown, *Genesis*, p. 860.

The patents and charters issued to companies for trade and discovery, prior to that of Gilbert, contained the germs of most of the provisions which subsequently found their way into the charters of American colonies, and the ideas of colonial administration. Monopoly of trade for a definite time was naturally granted, as recompense for the great expense and risk involved in opening new channels. The trades, moreover, were also justly regulated for the benefit of England rather than of the few individuals who were shareholders in the enterprises. Hence, we find stipulations such as that in the Cabot charter of 1496, requiring all business done under it to pass through the port of Bristol only; or that in the charter of 1566, to the Fellowship of English Merchants, requiring that all goods must be carried solely in English ships, manned for the most part with English sailors.[1] These and other restrictions were the germs of a domestic economic policy which, although reasonable enough in its inception, was to be pregnant with such fatal results when pursued consistently, and without taking into consideration the altered conditions brought about by the unexpectedly tremendous growth and political needs of those particular colonies planted by certain trading companies or individuals in America.

Under the system of international intercourse prevailing in the fifteenth and sixteenth centuries, it was found necessary to provide some sort of government and authority for the groups of English merchants, and their clerks, residing in foreign countries. The problem was met, in 1404, by Henry IV, who granted a charter to those resident in the Teutonic countries of northern Europe, permitting them to meet together to elect their own governors, and to make their own laws, the king ratifying and requiring obedience to such legislation in advance.[2] In 1462, Edward IV, in a charter to those resident in the Netherlands, appointed the governor, but allowed the merchants to elect twelve "Justiciers," who were to sit with

---

[1] Hakluyt, *Voyages*, vols. VII, p. 144, and III, p. 89.

[2] *Ibid.*, vol. II, p. 108; *cf.* also the earlier charter of Richard II (1391), cited by C. T. Carr, *Select Charters of Trading Companies* (Selden Society, London, 1913), pp. xi *ff.*

him as a court. The merchants were also to make their own laws, which, however, had to be approved by the royal governor. When it was no longer a question of trading in a civilized country, but of discovering new ones, unoccupied, or occupied only by heathen, the discoverer was naturally allowed to take possession in the name of the king, and was enfeoffed with the new land, the condition of tenure usually being a fifth of the precious metals found.

In these commercial charters, we thus find the germs of the commonwealth, royal, and proprietary colonies of the seventeenth century. There was no break at the beginning of American history. Nor was there any conscious intention upon England's part of founding an empire. The English colonies were by-products of British commercial activity, and English "colonial policy" was but a mere phase of her commercial policy. It is only by that light that the development of events can be rightly understood.

The lands conveyed to Gilbert were suitable for Englishmen to dwell in, and to be made valuable would require to be populated. This, however, raised a new question. Heretofore, men had lived as merchants in foreign but civilized countries, or fished or traded in others. If, now, they were to settle permanently in this barbarous land, would they cease to be Englishmen without becoming anything else? Elizabeth cut the knot by decreeing that such new countries should owe personal allegiance to herself, and, in that way, be united to her "Realmes of England and Ireland"; and, further, that any one born in the new lands, or emigrating thither from the old, should have all the privileges of a free-born native of the Realm.[1] These questions, now first arising, as to whether the settlers in new lands were within or without the Realm, and, if without, then whether they could be held as subject to the government that functioned for the Realm, were to become more and more

[1] Hakluyt, *Voyages*, vol. VIII, p. 20. Professor H. L. Osgood states that "by the realm was usually meant England, Wales, and Berwick on Tweed." *The American Colonies in the 17th Century* (New York, 1907), vol. III, p. 6. In Gilbert's charter, the words "realmes of England and Ireland" are used. Scotland, of course, was a separate realm.

insistent of answer in the days to come. But when Elizabeth granted her patent to Gilbert, little could any one have realized the size of England's future empire in America, or that that empire would be lost by civil war, in part because the answers to those questions could not be found. The main factor that gave rise to this distinction between the Realm and the Dominions, and that was to be primarily responsible for the failure satisfactorily to adjust the relations between them, was the physical distance, in terms of the sixteenth, seventeenth, and eighteenth centuries, by which they were separated.

Gilbert's efforts to colonize, however, like those of his half-brother, Raleigh, resulted only in failure. The time was ill chosen, as there was still work enough for enterprising spirits, and the employment of capital, in other directions. Under the stimulus of the defeat of the Armada, English seamen scoured the sea in search of Spanish prey, and it has been estimated that eight hundred Spanish vessels were lost in four years.[1] If in the light of such opportunities, colonizing seemed but a poor investment, voyaging and discovery, nevertheless, proceeded at a rapid rate. But New England, in spite of its being so near the field of English activities in the fisheries, was neglected, although its coast may occasionally have been visited by enterprising souls like Richard Strong, who sailed to "Arambec," in 1593, in search of "sea-Oxen."[2]

The land itself seems not to have been thought worth investigating until Bartholomew Gosnold made a clandestine voyage thither, to his own profit, and to Raleigh's annoyance, in 1602. Formerly, this little trading trip of Gosnold's, undertaken for the Earl of Southampton, Lord Cobham, and others, was thought to have been a serious attempt at colonization with the consent of Raleigh, the sphere of operations lying within the limits of his patent. The voyage thus secured more attention from historians than it deserved. Apparently some sort of permanent trading-post was, indeed, intended, as of the thirty-two persons who went to America, twenty were expected

---

[1] Brown, *Genesis*, p. 20.   [2] Hakluyt, *Voyages*, vol. VIII, p. 157.

to "remayne there for population." [1]   None did, however; and after having visited Massachusetts Bay, christened Cape Cod, and spent some time on the island of Cuttyhunk, where they built a fort, and loaded their ship with sassafras, the whole company returned to England, after an absence of four months. Raleigh, ignorant of the episode, but finding the "sassephrase" market taking a sudden drop, investigated, and the fact of the voyage came to light.   Although he confiscated the cargo, he became reconciled with both Gosnold and his own nephew, Bartholomew Gilbert, who also had had a hand in the business, and both were subsequently employed in Virginia. [2]

In the following year, Raleigh's consent was obtained by Hakluyt and some merchants of Bristol, to the sending out of another expedition, under Martin Pring, with some of Gosnold's men aboard, for the purposes of trade. [3]   The little company, in their two vessels, coasted along the shores of Maine, explored Massachusetts Bay and Plymouth Harbor, overlooked by Gosnold, and having loaded their ships with the much-desired sassafras, went back to England, to confirm Gosnold's good opinion of the country.   This was to receive still further confirmation from Weymouth two years later.

During these two years Elizabeth had died, and Raleigh had been convicted of treason.   Such rights as he may have possessed to the land of North Virginia were ignored, therefore, when the Earl of Southampton, Thomas Arundell, and others dispatched Weymouth to find a suitable place for colonizing in the parts visited by Gosnold and Pring.   This was the real intent of the expedition, although it was given out that it was for the discovery of the Northwest Passage. [4]   There is some

---

[1] S. Purchas, *Hakluytus Posthumus, or Purchas His Pilgrimes* (ed. Glasgow, 1905), vol. XVIII, p. 302.

[2] The clandestine nature of the voyage is proved by B. F. deCosta, "Gosnold and Pring," in *N. E. Historical and Genealogical Register*, 1878, vol. XXXII, pp. 76–80.

[3] Purchas, *Pilgrimes*, vol. XVIII, pp. 322–28.

[4] "We found the land a place answerable to the intent of our discovery, viz. fit for any nation to inhabit."   "Rosier's Relation," in Burrage, *Early English and French Voyages* (New York, 1906), p. 371. Sir F. Gorges, "A Briefe Narration of the Originall Undertakings, etc., 1658," in *Mass. Hist. Soc. Coll.*, Series III, vol. VI, p. 50.

evidence that the proposed colony was to be for Roman Catholics. At least, Sir George Peckham and Sir Thomas Gerrard, who claimed to be assignees of the Gilbert patent, had secured the privilege for Romanists of becoming colonists, and the Earl of Southampton and his leading associates in the present venture were of that faith.[1] Weymouth spent about a month on the coast, exploring the shores about the St. George's Islands and the river of the same name.[2]

The English, however, had not been the only explorers upon the New England coast, nor to them only had it begun to appeal as a possible place for colonizing. For the French, as well as the English, the sixteenth century in America had been a period of exploration, of staking out of vague claims, and of unsuccessful efforts to establish permanent settlements. The first decade of the seventeenth was to witness the success of both nations in the latter undertaking, the English at Jamestown in 1607, and the French at Quebec but one year later, so close was the race between them. In the territory of New England, however, both nations were to try, and fail, within the same period; and citizens of both countries had already, from time to time, received grants of undefined extension in that general part of the world, when finally a charter with definite bounds was assigned by the French King to the Sieur de Monts, in 1603. This grant embraced all the territory between the 40th and 46th degrees of latitude, or from Philadelphia to Montreal.

The issuance of this patent was immediately followed by an attempt at settlement, de Monts and Champlain, both of whom had previously been in Canada, sailing with a hundred and twenty men in the spring following the receipt of the grant. Buildings were erected, and the first winter passed on the island of St. Croix, in the mouth of the river of the same name, which empties into Passamaquoddy Bay.[3] It was thus the first

[1] *Calendar of State Papers, Colonial, America and West Indies, 1574–1660*, p. 695 (hereafter cited as *Cal. State Pap., Col.*); J. P. Baxter, *Sir Ferdinando Gorges and his Province of Maine* (Prince Society, Boston, 1890), vol. I, p. 65.

[2] The river was formerly thought to be the Kennebec. *Cf.* Burrage, *Early Voyages.* In Burrage's edition of *Rosier's Relation* (Gorges Society, Portland, 1887), there is an exhaustive survey of the literature.

[3] H. S. Burrage, *Beginnings of Colonial Maine* (Portland, 1914), p. 32.

authorized attempt to colonize any part of New England. The choice of a site had been unfortunate, and in the following spring, the colony removed to Nova Scotia, where it lasted two years more before the cancellation of the grant resulted in its abandonment. A lively and entertaining account of life in the colony was written by a genial lawyer, who was one of its members, and the attention with which American affairs were then being watched is indicated by the appearance of an English translation in the same year in which the original came out in Paris.[1] During the three years of his stay, Champlain was indefatigable in exploring the coast, making three principal voyages along the shores of New England, which he described and mapped as far south as the present settlement of Chatham, in Massachusetts.

The coast of Maine and the shores of Massachusetts Bay were carefully studied for sites for settlement, and the former was for long to form a debatable land between French and English. These years also saw the foundation laid of the friendship between French and Indian, which was to cost the English dear. De Monts's patent contemplated trade with the natives, rather than an agricultural colony; and the French empire in America, as has already been noted, consisted mainly of a series of trading-posts. It was to the interest of the French that the Indian should remain, as he himself wished, a hunter; whereas the growth of the English agricultural colonies denied him the possibility of continuing his savage life, without, on the other hand, absorbing him into civilization. It was not merely that the French, in the main, were tactful and friendly, accepting the Indian as he was, and even intermarrying, while the English were harsh and disdainful. It may be said that one Indian required to sustain his life approximately as many square miles as the English agriculturist, with his domestic animals, needed acres. On the other hand, the uses to which the French put the soil were identical with those for which it served the savage. The English, indeed, "bought" land, which the French never did; but the French and the Indian shared the soil to the profit

[1] Marc Lescarbot, *Histoire de la Nouvelle France*; Paris, 1609.

of both, while the English deprived the native of his means of subsistence, in exchange for coats and beads.[1] Not that they did so intentionally; but the consequence was inevitable. Nor was it the Indian alone who was to fall before the farmer and founder of towns. The French *coureurs des bois*, and traders in the scattered posts, were likewise to fall and, in part, for the same reason.

Nevertheless, at the time of the first authorized English attempt to colonize New England, the French were, if anything, ahead in the race. Champlain's knowledge of the coast and its possibilities was quite as accurate, probably, as that of Gosnold or Pring or Weymouth, though English writers usually give many pages to the latter trio while dismissing Champlain in a line or two. A definite grant of the territory had been made, and the first colony of their hereditary enemy was seemingly successfully started within the limits of the English patent, when King James affixed his signature to that document. A struggling little settlement in Virginia, however, was to prove the undoing of the French in the north, and win the New England coast for the English, though not without further effort on the part of its future settlers. But, whatever the local successes of French or English, it must not be forgotten that the colonies of both nations were mere pawns in the game of European policy, and that the allegiance of the colonist was to be determined in the last analysis, not by their own comparative strength on faraway shores, but by the strength which the two nations could put forth in their navies on the sea.

[1] Ellis, *The Red Man*, p. 242; J. Winsor, "The Rival Claimants for North America," *American Antiquarian Society Proceedings*, 1894, pp. 415-17.

CHAPTER III

THE RACE FOR EMPIRE

DURING the period upon which our story now enters, all of North America was claimed by the three contestants for empire — Spain, England, and France. The claims of the first covered the entire western world beyond the line established by the treaty of Tordesillas; while those of the other two are indicated, at least as to their minimum extent, by the patents granted. Adrian Gilbert, in his application to Queen Elizabeth, had asked leave to "inhabit and enjoy" all places discovered between the equator and the North Pole;[1] and although these limits are nowhere given in any single charter, those granted to various companies show English claims extending from at least 10° to 52° North Latitude, or from Panama to Labrador.[2] Following the difficulties of colonizing in Maine and Nova Scotia, mentioned in the last chapter, the French King granted to Madame de Guercheville all of the continent from Florida to the St. Lawrence, thus overlapping the Spanish and English claims.[3]

The title to newly acquired lands, originally deriving validity from Papal sanction, even in the eyes of Englishmen, had gradually come to rest upon the right of discovery.[4] This theory was based upon the principle of Roman Law that the finder could appropriate what belonged to no one. A heathen was considered as *nullus*, hence his property had no owner, and

[1] W. R. Scott, *Constitutions and Finance of English and Irish Joint-Stock Companies to 1720* (Cambridge, 1910), vol. II, p. 244.

[2] The southern limit was that of the Providence Company (Scott, *Joint-Stock Companies*, vol. II, p. 327); and the northern that of the Newfoundland Company, (D. W. Prowse, *History of Newfoundland* [London, 1895], pp. 122–25).

[3] F. Parkman, *Pioneers of France in the New World* (Boston, 1909), p. 303.

[4] Henry II asked and obtained the Pope's consent to conquer Ireland. W. B. Scaife, "The Development of International Law as to newly discovered Territory," in *American Historical Association Papers*, vol. IV, p. 269.

American soil could be appropriated by whoever first found it. Although it was agreed by all that discovery must be consummated by possession and use, there were two very difficult questions, as to which the law was silent, in connection with the new situations now arising. One of these was the length of time which might elapse between discovery and taking possession, before the claim should become invalid through failure to consummate the discovery; while the other was that of the extent of territory involved by the above acts.[1] The claims of the three contestants were preposterous, though no one more so than another, perhaps; and, in the absence of any superior authority, it is difficult to see how the matter could have been settled otherwise than by power of the sword, which thus replaced the Pope as arbiter. At the time we are now considering, it would seem as if, theoretically, England's claim to any part of the New World were the least valid of the three. Although it was necessarily based solely on the voyage of Cabot, she had made no effort to colonize for nearly ninety years, and as yet had failed to do so successfully. To the south, Spanish titles were, in part, unassailable;[2] while in the north, French claims were being made good by the struggling colony at Port Royal, and by scattered traders in furs.

The treaty of peace with Spain, in 1604, which followed almost automatically upon the accession of James to the English throne, changed the situation in important respects with reference to the success of English colonization. Privateering, which, in spite of many brilliant exploits, had become "a sordid and prosaic business," and decreasingly profitable, came to a legal end temporarily under the English flag. It is true that certain of the larger venturers in the trade merely flew the Dutch flag instead, and continued their depredations; but the

[1] Cf. B. A. Hinsdale, "The Right of Discovery," in Ohio Archeological and Historical Quarterly, vol. II, pp. 351–78; and Scaife, "International Law," pp. 269–93.

[2] The number of colonists living in Spanish possessions varies greatly in estimates. DeLannoy thinks that it may have been 152,000 by 1574 (DeLannoy and Van der Linden, Histoire de l'Expansion Coloniale des Peuples Européens [Paris, 1907], vol. I, p. 414); while Leroy-Beaulieu puts it as low as 15,000 in 1550. De la Colonisation chez les peuples modernes (Paris, 1898), vol. I, p. 5.

calling no longer offered its former opportunities, either for restless spirits or for the employment of capital. The more legitimate commerce with the Spanish possessions, such as the import of salt from Venezuela, which had grown to large proportions during the war, was also ended by the terms of the treaty, which completely surrendered English rights of trade with the Indies.[1]

Meanwhile, the amount of capital seeking investment had become large, and owing to the enormous increase of bullion, the changed feeling in regard to the taking of interest, and other causes, it was rapidly growing larger.[2] It was also becoming more fluid, as was labor, likewise. Contemporary, as well as many modern, authorities, have considered England as suffering from over-population at this time ; but it is doubtful if this were so; and it is probable that the material for colonization came rather from "the displacement and disturbance of population" than from its growth.[3] Not only the substitution, to a considerable extent, of sheep-grazing for farming, and the inclosure of the common lands, but the gradual breaking up of the whole mediæval system of trade and conditions of labor, had resulted in an extraordinary amount of idleness and vagabondage for several generations.[4] During the same period had occurred also the enormous rise in prices, and in the cost of living, with results very similar to those which we are now experiencing.[5] As to-day, they were severely felt by people with approximately fixed incomes; and the country gentry in particular, with their lands let on long leases, suffered greatly. During the war, younger sons, and the more enterprising of all classes, had had an opportunity to gain a living by embarking on a career in privateering or other warlike pursuits; but with the coming of peace, those openings

---

[1] A. P. Newton, *The Colonising Activities of the English Puritans* (Yale University Press, 1914), pp. 13–17.

[2] W. Cunningham, *English Industry*, vol. II, pp. 77 *ff*.

[3] E. P. Cheyney, "Some English Conditions surrounding the Settlement of Virginia," in *American Historical Review*, April, 1907, p. 526.

[4] F. Aydelotte, *Elizabethan Rogues and Vagabonds* (Oxford, 1913), pp. 3–20.

[5] *A Discourse of the Commonweal of this realm of England*, 1581; reprinted, Cambridge, England, 1893.

were for the most part closed to them. On the other hand, the scale of living had risen rapidly, and extravagance required a much greater outlay than in former days. "In a time wherein all things are grown to most excessive prices," wrote Harrison as early as 1577, "we do yet find the means to obtain and achieve such furniture as heretofore hath been unpossible." [1]

During the war, moreover, the older channels of legitimate trade had, for the most part, been closed to the English merchant, who found himself cut off "from Spain, Portugal, Barbary, the Levant, and, to a considerable extent, from Poland, Denmark, and Germany." [2] The seventeen years prior to the death of Elizabeth had been years of depressed business, now, in turn, to be followed by a like period of prosperity, while trade continued fairly good until 1636.[3] Although other elements entered into the problem, it may be noted that the efforts to colonize, whether near home in Ireland, or far off in the new world, had been failures when general business was poor, and successful when it became good.[4] Neither in Ulster nor in Munster, in Newfoundland, Virginia, nor Guiana, had the individuals or their associates, who had obtained grants, been able, as yet, to plant any permanent settlements.

The time, nevertheless, was evidently growing ripe for accomplishment. Apart from any political or religious motives, America was as certain to be colonized in the early part of the seventeenth century as it was to be discovered by Columbus, or someone else, in the latter part of the fifteenth. After the fall of Calais in 1557, England, though fearful of the future, had turned her back definitely and forever upon continental conquest and entanglements, and had embarked boldly upon those waves which it was to become her pride to rule.[5] With the seas safe for traffic, with a host of younger sons and other men suffering from the economic conditions of the time,

---

[1] Harrison's Introduction to Holinshed's *Chronicle*, reprinted as *Elizabethan England* (London, n. d.), p. 118.

[2] Scott, *Joint-Stock Companies*, vol. I, p. 98.   [3] *Ibid.*, pp. 465 *ff.*

[4] *Cf.*, however, Leroy-Beaulieu, who thinks that "la colonisation anglaise eut donc pour origine une nécessité réelle, une crise économique intense." *Colonisation*, vol. I, p. 91.

[5] A. B. Hinds, *The Making of the England of Elizabeth* (New York, 1895), p. 138.

with the growing need in England of many commodities found in the new world, with the great growth of capital seeking investment, and with the trade of practically every other portion of the earth already in the hands of corporate companies, English merchants and adventurers could not fail to turn again, with ampler resources and better methods, to the land where they had already tried and failed. The Muscovy Company controlled all trade with Russia, the Eastland that with the Baltic, the Levant that with Venice and the East, while another controlled the African west coast, and the East India Company held from the Straits of Magellan around to Africa again.[1] Although these companies, which were almost wholly owned in London, aroused the jealousy of Plymouth, Southampton, and the other provincial ports, which found themselves limited to a little nearby continental and coasting trade, they pointed the way to the corporate form and joint-stock undertakings as the successful method of handling large business enterprises, such as colonizing was now realized to be.

This was clearly brought out by an unknown author, who, probably toward the end of 1605, wrote the paper known as "Reasons for raising a fund." [2] The writer strongly advocated the raising of a "publique stocke" for "the peopling and discovering of such contries as maye be fownde most convenient for the supplie of those defects which the Realme of England most requireth." It is likely that this paper, which was intended for Parliament, had considerable influence in the granting of the Virginia charter, and it is, therefore, interesting to note that, at the very beginning of successful colonization, one of the leading points in future English colonial policy was thus touched upon. It is often lost to sight that practically the sole value of her colonies to England all through the sixteenth, seventeenth, and eighteenth centuries was the value of their trade, and the most important part of that trade, during nearly all of the period, was in supplying her with such materials as

[1] S. R. Gardiner, *History of England* (London, 1895), vol. I, p. 187.
[2] For discussion as to authorship and date, *vide* Brown, *Genesis*, pp. 36–42, where the document is printed in full.

she lacked at home. In this respect, her West Indian colonies became more important than her continental ones, though an exaggerated emphasis has been laid upon the contemporary importance of the latter, in part because they chanced to revolt, whereas the island colonies did not.

As one of the reasons for raising a public fund to assist in colonizing, our unknown author went on to say that "private purces are cowld compfortes to adventurers," and pointed to the "marvelous matters in traficque and navigacon" which the Hollanders had accomplished, in few years, by a "maine backe or stocke." Whether the paper was written in order to obtain the Virginia charter, it is impossible to say; but apparently it was, and, in any case, that charter was issued on the 10th of April, 1606. The great revolution in foreign trade, which had been going on for the past two centuries, was now complete, and the period of chartered companies, foreshadowed by the formation, in the latter part of the sixteenth century, of the few already noted, was well under way.[1] With the addition of the East India Company, chartered in 1600, the existing English companies covered practically all known parts of the world except America; and during the next generation about the only companies organized were for the new world — North and South Virginia in 1606, Guiana, 1609, Newfoundland, 1610, Northwest Passage, 1612, Bermuda, 1615, New England, 1620, and Massachusetts, 1629.

There was a very close connection between many of these great companies. The East India, for example, was practically an outgrowth of the Levant;[2] while of the two hundred and three members of the Virginia Company, one hundred and sixteen were members of the East India, and thirteen of the Muscovy, ten were to become interested in the Newfoundland, one hundred in the Northwest Passage, forty-six in the Bermuda, and thirty-eight in the New England companies. Members of the Virginia Company were also represented in the African, Levant, Guiana, Guinea, Eastland, Providence, Irish

---

[1] Cf. P. Bonnassieux, Les grandes Compagnies de Commerce (Paris, 1892), pp. 510 ff.
[2] W. W. Hunter, History of British India (London, 1899), vol. I, p. 244.

Plantation, and other stock enterprises.[1] To the noblemen and merchants thus brought into close working relations, America was but one of the many irons which they had in the fire, and by no means the most important. Their interest, as that of their successors, was naturally in British trade as a whole, and not in the success of any particular colony, much less in its religious bickerings or political aspirations. From the very beginning, the trade of the Empire was considered paramount to that of any unit, even in England itself. At this very time, King James, in pressing for the union with Scotland, expressed what was later to become the established policy. "It may be," he said, "that a merchant or two of Bristow or Yarmouth may have a hundred pounds lesse in his packe; but if the Empire gaine and become the greater, it is no matter." [2]

These two points thus early made, namely, that the value of colonies lay in their contributing to the empire products otherwise obtainable only from foreigners, and that the interests of the empire as a whole were paramount to those of any section, were well understood by those at the head of colonizing enterprises, and must have been understood also by the more intelligent of the early planters themselves. These views naturally would continue to be held by those who remained at the centre of the empire in England; while those who dwelt on its periphery, in many scattered settlements, would as naturally, in time, tend to lose sight of them, and to consider their own particular interests as greater than those of the empire. The struggle between these centripetal and centrifugal forces was bound to result in warping the imperial structure, though in one case only was it to end in the breaking away of a part of the system. Adjustments, continuing even to the present day, were to save the rest intact; but it is interesting to note the germs of conflict present from the very beginning. The forces which brought that conflict about were operative, in varying degrees, not only in North America, but throughout the entire empire, and extended back to its unconscious inception.

---

[1] Compiled from Brown, *Genesis*, pp. 811–1068.
[2] Cited by Scott, *Joint-Stock Companies*, vol. I, p. 132.

The charter granted in 1606 provided for the formation of two colonizing companies, one of which was authorized to plant anywhere on the American coast between latitudes 34° and 41° North, and the other between 38° and 45°, provided that, should either, or both, choose to settle in the overlapping strip of three degrees, they should not plant within one hundred miles of each other.[1] The patentees of the first company were residents of London, while those of the second were of Plymouth, the companies thus becoming known as the London and Plymouth companies respectively. Among the patentees of the latter, which embraced New England, were Thomas Hanham, Raleigh Gilbert and George Popham, although the names of the two who are thought to have been the prime movers in the whole enterprise, Chief Justice Popham and Sir Ferdinando Gorges, do not appear. Practically all those connected with it had seen service in the Spanish war, and many had already been interested in attempts to colonize in America and elsewhere. The charter, together with the instructions issued by the King some months later,[2] reveals a mixed organization, partly proprietary and partly royal. The patentees were to provide the capital and colonists, and to have control of the trade, which was to be carried on by means of "magazines," or joint stock; but the King, through the provision of a royal council appointed by himself, retained in his own hands the government of the entire province from 34° to 45°. Two local councils, one for each company's territory, were appointed by the royal council, with power to govern the affairs of each colony under the king's instructions. Land could not be granted to individuals by the patentees, but only by the king, upon application in their behalf by the local council for the colony in which it was located.[3]

Both companies at once took steps to plant their colonies, the Plymouth being the first in the field, although to the London Company was to accrue the earliest lasting success. The latter's expedition, including in its members Bartholomew Gos-

---

[1] Hazard, *Historical Collections* (Philadelphia, 1792), vol. 1, pp. 50–58.
[2] Brown, *Genesis*, pp. 64–75.   [3] Osgood, *American Colonies*, vol. 1, pp. 25–35.

nold, who had already been in New England, and Captain John Smith, who later was to become a factor there, sailed from London in three ships, on December 20, 1606. Arriving in Virginia the following spring, they established themselves at Jamestown, and so founded, what, in spite of many vicissitudes, was to be the first permanent English settlement in America.

Meanwhile, the Plymouth Company, mainly by virtue of the activity of Sir Ferdinando Gorges, who became indefatigable in his colonizing ardor, and of Chief Justice Popham, had also commenced operations. In 1600 had occurred Gorges's unfortunate connection with the revolt of Essex, which had blasted his character in the eyes of the Puritans, and so served, perhaps, to embitter his future relations with Massachusetts. He had been for some time reinstated as Governor of Plymouth, when Weymouth returned from his voyage in 1605; and from him Gorges obtained possession of the three natives whom the captain had kidnaped on the coast of Maine. Having learned much from them of the nature of the country and its inhabitants, he despatched a vessel under Captain Henry Challons, in August, four months after the granting of the charter, with strict instructions to take the northern route to Cape Breton, and then to follow the coast southward to the place the natives had described.[1] Challons disobeyed the order, went southward by the West Indies, and was captured by the Spaniards, some of the crew, with himself and the two natives, being carried to Spain, and others, by accident, to Bordeaux. The latter, after having filed claims with the authorities of the port, and left a "Letter of a Turnye," returned to England, as did also, after some time and difficulty, Challons himself.[2]

Although the little ship of fifty-five tons had carried only

[1] Gorges, "Briefe Narration," *Mass. Hist. Soc. Coll.*, Series III, vol. VI, pp. 51 f. Various members of the company were associated with Gorges, but he seems to have been the leader in this venture, as Popham was in the next. An account of the voyage, written by John Stoneman, the pilot, is in Purchas, *Pilgrimes*, vol. XIX, pp. 284–96.

[2] J. P. Baxter, *Sir Ferdinando Gorges*, vol. III, pp. 129–32, 168; *Cal. State Pap., Col., 1675–76*, p. 53.

twenty-nine Englishmen, it had been the intention to leave some of them for settling, "if any good occasion were offered"; and the Chief Justice had also dispatched a ship, under Captain Hanham, to meet and assist Challons in the enterprise. This, of course, he was unable to do; but he explored the shore, taking back with him to the company "the most exact discovery of that coast that ever came into their hands."[1] The reports were considered so encouraging that a much more considerable effort was next made by the adventurers.

On May 31, 1607, two ships, the Gift of God and the Mary and John, were dispatched from Plymouth under command of Raleigh Gilbert and George Popham, a relative of Sir John.[2] The vessels became separated on June 29, and did not meet again until August 7, among the St. George's Islands, off the coast of Maine.[3] Having reached the mouth of the Kennebec, then called the Sagadahoc, the colonists explored the stream, and finally chose for their place of settlement a point at its mouth, on the high ground of the peninsula of Sabino.[4] They landed on the 19th, when they had a sermon preached to them, and listened to the reading of their patent and laws. The next day they began the building of their fort, named St. George, followed by the dwellings and storehouse and the first boat built in America.

Meanwhile, the Spaniards were by no means oblivious of what was going on, both in North and South Virginia; and to the zeal of the Spanish ambassador in London in keeping his master posted as to the encroachments of the English upon his territories, we owe the preservation of a drawing of the fort in the infant colony, which he obtained from some one who had been there.[5] From the first discussion of the Virginia charter, Zuñiga had written frequently to the King, telling him of the

[1] Gorges, "Briefe Narration," p. 53. No account of this voyage has been preserved, although Purchas had one in his possession written by Hanham. *Vide* Purchas, *Pilgrimes*, vol. xix, p. 296.

[2] Always stated to have been his brother, until Brown threw doubt upon the point; *Genesis*, pp. 791, 968.

[3] "Relation of a Voyage to Sagadahoc," *Mass. Hist. Soc. Proceedings*, vol. xviii.

[4] H. O. Thayer, *The Sagadahoc Colony* (Gorges Society, Portland, 1892), pp. 167–87.

[5] Reproduced by Brown, *Genesis*, p. 190. *Cf.* also *Ibid.*, pp. 183 *ff.*

plans and doings of the English, and advising strong action to prevent their settling. For some years, Spanish spies were kept at Jamestown, who regularly sent home word of what was going on, by means of renegade English sailors, while evidently there was also a traitor at Sagadahoc, as even in the Royal Council itself.[1] A vessel was once dispatched by Spain to wipe out both the colonies; but the crew proved faint-hearted, and no attack was made upon either, the King, moreover, having some hope, apparently, that both would conveniently prove failures of themselves.

At first, however, all went well at Sagadahoc, and early in October the Mary and John was sent home to carry word of the colony.[2] The account brought back so pleased Gorges that he wrote a letter, "late at night," to Sir Robert Cecil, to tell him of the "greate newes." But he was doomed to disappointment. A couple of days later he had evidently heard more, and in a second letter wrote that the settlement was getting into trouble because of "childish factions, ignorant, timerous and ambitious persons." Popham, who had been made president of the colony, he described as "an honest man, but ould, and of an unwieldy body, and timerously fearfull to offend, or contest with others that will or do oppose him, but otherways a discreete, carefull man." Gilbert was declared, by hearsay, to be "desirous of supremacy, and rule, a loose life prompte to sensuality, little zeale in Religion, humerouse, headstronge and of small judgment and experience, other wayes valiant inough." [3] The next ship brought a letter from Popham to the King, but no better news for the company than the first, in spite of the president's enthusiastic belief in the presence of nutmegs, cinnamon, and "other products of great importance," in the imaginatively tropical climate of Maine.[4]

---

[1] Correspondence in Brown, *Genesis*, p. 117 and *passim;* also *The First Republic in America* (Boston, 1898), p. 91. *Cf.* I. A. Wright, "Spanish Policy toward Virginia," in *American Historical Review*, April, 1920, pp. 448 *ff.* and *Cal. State Pap., Col., 1675-76*, pp. 45 *ff.*

[2] *Cf.* note on the "Movement of the ships," Thayer, *Sagadahoc*, pp. 192 *ff.*

[3] Baxter, *Sir F. Gorges*, vol. III, pp. 154 *f.*

[4] *Maine Historical Society Collections*, vol. v, pp. 357-60.

During the winter, which was unusually severe, the store-house was burned, with most of the provisions; and before the arrival of the two supply ships sent out from England, Popham, the leader of the colony, died. The ships carried yet more serious news to the colonists in the death of the Chief Justice in England, which proved "such a corrosive to all, as struck them with despair of future remedy."[1] A later ship brought word of the death of Sir John, Gilbert's elder brother, which necessitated that leader's returning to England to look after his affairs. The colonists, in view of all these circumstances, resolved to quit the place, and return with Gilbert; and so all "former hopes were frozen to death," and, by October, the wilderness of Maine was abandoned by the English, as, five years before, it had been by the French.[2]

The character of the colonists, and, more particularly, the unusual sequence of accidents, were enough to account for the failure of the attempt, without invoking, with Gorges, "the mallice of the Divell" to explain it. The company at home became thoroughly discouraged, and no further efforts were made to plant a settlement, although Sir Francis Popham, son of the late Chief Justice, continued to send over vessels for some years for trade and fishing, and it is probable that no year now passed without the temporary presence of Englishmen upon the coast.[3] In connection with the obtaining of a new charter by the South Virginia Company, in 1609, the adventurers in the Northern Company were offered the opportunity to join with the Londoners on favorable terms, and to form with them "one common and patient purse," an opportunity of which some of them availed themselves.[4]

Although temporarily abandoned as a site for colonizing, the coast of North Virginia was by no means deserted, and the

[1] Gorges, "Briefe Narration," p. 55.

[2] Attempts have been made to magnify the importance of the colony, and even to insist upon its continued existence. Following the publication of the uncritical Popham Memorial, Portland, 1863, 98 pamphlets and articles appeared in six years. The literature is surveyed by Thayer, Sagadahoc, pp. 87–156.

[3] Gorges, "Briefe Narration," p. 56; "Briefe Relation," Purchas, Pilgrimes, vol. XIX, p. 271.

[4] Brown, Genesis, pp. 238–40.

events of the next few years there were of great importance to the future history of the territory. Hudson, an Englishman employed by the Dutch, coasted along its shores during the famous voyage on which he explored the river which bears his name;[1] and the following year, Argall and Somers, attempting to sail from Jamestown to Bermuda, were blown out of their course, and having made for the North Virginia coast, spent some time along it, fishing for cod.[2] Upon Hudson's voyage was based the Dutch claim to their portion of North America. The validity of such a claim to the country immediately about the Hudson would depend upon the interpretation of the two difficult points in connection with titles noted at the beginning of this chapter.[3] Any such claim extended by Holland to the coasts of the present eastern New England, however, could have no standing whatever, as French and English explorations in that exact locality had been both prior in date and far more thorough. The only real dispute there lay between the English and French, which was soon to be decided in the main by force. In fact, with three nations, to say nothing of Spain, claiming the same territory, all basing their claims upon discovery within a few miles of each other, even where explorations did not actually overlap, the points raised were too fine, in the then inchoate state of international law, to permit of any other arbitrament.

When, owing to the annulling of De Monts's patent, the French colony at Port Royal had been temporarily abandoned in 1607, de Poutrincourt, who still retained his rights, intended

[1] G. M. Asher, *Henry Hudson the Navigator* (Hakluyt Society, 1860), p. 63.

[2] Purchas, *Pilgrimes*, vol. XIX, pp. 73, 84.

[3] Leaving out of consideration the early coasting voyages, in which the Dutch had no part whatever, they had recently been preceded to within a reasonable distance of both the mouth and the source of the Hudson. The English had made a detailed discovery as far as the entrance of the Sound, while Champlain was within a few miles of the source of the river some months before the Dutch ascended it. If rights of discovery were to be limited only to the points actually visited, with no extension thence in any direction, the country would have become a veritable checker-board of warring nationalities. The Dutch themselves held no such view, and claimed all the land from Cape Cod to Delaware Bay, with indefinite limits toward the interior. Acknowledgment of any such claim would have to be based upon a theory of extension which would seem, therefore, equally to validate the claims of English and French, arising in both cases from discovery prior to the Dutch.

to return speedily, and to continue his settlement. Various
delays, however, kept him in France for three years, and it was
not until the spring of 1610 that he again set sail. The houses
and their contents, untouched by the friendly Indians, were
found intact, and life at the little colony, which had thus been
merely interrupted, was resumed. In the following year, a
certain Captain Plastrier, who had been fishing near the
Kennebec, complained to the Sieur de Biencourt, Poutrincourt's son, that he had been attacked and robbed by English,
who claimed title to the coast.[1] These may have been Captain Williams and his party, who were annually sent out by
Francis Popham, or Captains Harlow and Hobson, who were
on the coast, in 1611, on a voyage of discovery and Indian-
kidnaping, for the Earl of Southampton.[2] Thus obscurely,
off the New England coast, between a French fisherman and
English seamen, whose very names are unknown to us, began
that duel for empire between France and England, which was
to last a century and a half, and which was to decide the fate
of the vast continent of North America and the teeming
millions of India. Clive and Dupleix, Wolfe and Montcalm,
were the successors of these humble pioneers striving to assert
the claims of their rival nations to the empire of the world.

The significance of the attack by the English was not lost
upon the young Biencourt, who "represented very earnestly"
to his people how important it was to "every good Frenchman"
to prevent this usurpation by the English of lands claimed by
France, and occupied by her citizens "who had taken real
possession . . . three and four years before ever the English had
set forth" — which was quite true in so far as related to colonizing. In August, Biencourt made a trip along the shore of
Maine, stopping at St. Croix Island, where Plastrier had decided to spend the winter, and thence down to the Kennebec,
where he inspected the abandoned site of the Popham colony,

---

[1] Brown, *Genesis*, p. 534.

[2] The accounts of the latter voyage are slight. John Smith, in a page, gives us all
we know, and says nothing of Plastrier. *Works* (ed. Arber, Glasgow, 1910), vol. II,
p. 696. Purchas had a full account, which he did not print and which is now lost.
Pilgrimes, vol. XIX, p. 296.

and made a careful examination of the coast. At the island
of Matinicus, where the attack on Plastrier had taken place, he
found some Englishmen fishing; but although he was urged by
some of his party to burn their ships, he would not do so, as
they were peaceful civilians, and contented himself with erecting a large cross with the arms of France.[1]

A couple of years later, under the more aggressive régime of
Madame de Guercheville and the Jesuits, an extension of
French settlement toward the south was attempted by the
founding of a colony on Mt. Desert, which was named St.
Sauveur.[2] It was not, however, to remain undisturbed for
many weeks, for at a meeting of the Quarter Court of the
Virginia Company in London, in July, 1612, Captain Argall
had been commissioned to drive out foreign intruders from the
country claimed under English charters, and had sailed from
England for that purpose.[3] After wintering in Virginia, he
proceeded northward the following summer, to clear the
territory as far as 45°, and promptly ran across the newly established Jesuits on the Maine coast, being guided to them by
Indians, who were under the mistaken impression that the
English were friends.[4] The French, being taken wholly unaware, made practically no resistance, the only one among
their number who had presence of mind enough even to fire
their cannon, having forgotten to aim it. Argall easily over-
came such opposition, and having obtained possession of La
Saussaye's commission from the French King, proceeded to
break up the colony and dispose of his prisoners.[5] Fifteen of

---

[1] Brown, *Genesis*, pp. 534 *f.*

[2] *Cf.* E. C. Cummings, "Father Biard's Relation of 1616"; paper read before the
Maine Historical Society, in 1893; *Proceedings*, pp. 11–18. Biard's account, from the
Jesuit Relations, is reprinted by C. H. Levermore, *Forerunners and Competitors of
the Pilgrims and Puritans* (Brooklyn, 1912), vol. II, pp. 446, 522.

[3] Brown, *First Republic*, p. 176; *Genesis*, pp. 709–23.

[4] W. D. Williamson, *History of the State of Maine* (Hallowell, 1832), vol. I, p. 206,
states, but without giving any authority, that there had been Jesuits at Mt. Desert for
five years.

[5] The story of his having secretly rifled La Saussaye's trunks of his papers, and then
demanded them from him, seems hardly likely, in view of other facts. It rests on the
authority of Biard ("Relation," in Levermore, *Forerunners*, vol. II, p. 496). As to
Biard's character and credibility, *cf.* Biggar, *Trading Companies*, pp. 263–65.

them, including Biard and another of the Jesuit fathers, were
taken back as captives to Virginia, and the remaining thirty,
in two small boats, allowed to take their perilous way to rejoin
their countrymen to the northward.

Soon afterward, Argall, with three ships and the Jesuit Biard,
who, apparently out of personal rancor toward Biencourt, had
turned traitor to his former associates, again set sail from
Virginia, for the purpose of completely extirpating the French
settlements.   Revisiting St. Sauveur, he burned the buildings,
and tearing down the French cross, erected another.   Continuing his voyage, he put in at St. Croix, where he likewise
burned the buildings and confiscated the stores collected there.[1]
Arriving next at Port Royal, from which the inhabitants were
temporarily absent, a few miles off, after taking as booty even
the locks and nails from the buildings, as well as the food,
ammunition, and clothes of the unfortunate French, he burned
the whole settlement to ashes.[2]   It is difficult to conceive of a
more dastardly act than thus to rob a peaceful colony of its
stores, and then to render it homeless on the approach of
winter in a far northern country.

The action, however, if not the manner of it, fitted in with the
English temper of the time, which was becoming increasingly
aggressive in colonial matters.   On the shores of India, as on
those of North Virginia, the cannon's mouth was announcing
territorial decisions of vast import for the future.   Almost
simultaneously with the operations of Argall in Maine, Captain Best, off the Indian coast, was having a running fight,
lasting a month, with four Portuguese ships, attended by over
a score of galleys, against his own little fleet of only two vessels.
As a result of his brilliant victory against these overwhelming
odds, the English obtained their first permanent foothold in
continental India.[3]   The glorious battle of Swally, and the
petty raiding of Mt. Desert and Port Royal, were alike mere

[1] Biard, in Levermore, *Forerunners*, vol. II, p. 506.   *Cf.* also the English account in
Purchas, *Pilgrimes*, vol. XIX, pp. 214–16, 271.
[2] Biard and Purchas, *ubi supra;* also Biencourt's complaint, in Brown, *Genesis*, pp.
725 ff. and *Cal. State Pap., Col., 1574–1660*, p.15.
[3] Hunter, *British India*, vol. I, pp. 300–304.

incidents in the struggle of new forces let loose by the age of discovery, and the transformation of the European nations into world powers. The struggles between French and English in North Virginia and India; between English and Portuguese in the Gulf of Cambay; between Dutch and Spanish, or Dutch and Portuguese on many seas; between English and Dutch in Guiana and on the Amazon and in the Spice Islands of the East, must all be considered as but parts of one stupendous drama. Everywhere along the edge of the world, traders and settlers were being tossed on those stormy political waters, where met the new tides of imperial ambition, fast flowing to the farthest confines of the new-found seas.

In that portion of the drama with which we are particularly concerned, a new figure now appears upon the scene, whose services to North Virginia have been somewhat overrated by many, but whose personality remains a matter of fascinating interest. Around few names in American history has legend clustered more luxuriantly than around that of the South Virginian hero Captain John Smith; and as to the real merits of few men is opinion more diverse. Even though it must be frankly admitted that no one will ever again think as highly of the Captain as he thought of himself, yet much of the modern detraction from his character and services is so evidently biased as to be critically of little value. The main importance of his share in North Virginian colonization, unlike his labors in the south, was in his capacity as author, and his efforts to stimulate interest in the possibilities of the New World. He himself, however, wished for and endeavored to achieve a more active part in the settlement of the country to which he attached its present name of New England.

He first saw its shores, on his only voyage thither, off the island of Monhegan, in the spring of 1614, having been sent out by some London merchants "to take Whales and make tryalls of a Myne of Gold and Copper."[1] If those failed, he wrote, "Fish and Furres was then our refuge." It was soon evident that the refuge was needed, and it proved, fortunately,

[1] John Smith, *Works*, vol. 1, p. 187.

to be a goodly one, although along the New Hampshire and Massachusetts coasts, he found that the French had recently preceded him, and spoiled his market. While fishing for cod, and trading with the Indians, he also explored a considerable part of the shore, and, as a result of his observations, prepared a map, on which many of the names still familiar to us appear for the first time.[1]   In spite of all the explorers who had preceded him, Smith asserted that the shore was "still but even as a coast unknowne and undiscovered"; and historians formerly dated the beginning of modern New England cartography from the appearance of his chart. Without necessarily detracting from the excellence of Smith's field-work, however, his claim to be the first accurate cartographer of our coast has been dispelled by the discovery of the excellent map transmitted by the Spanish ambassador in London to King Philip in 1611, and found some years ago in the Archives at Simancas.[2]   This map, prepared for King James in 1610, shows that the New England coast was well known, and had been well drawn, before ever John Smith began his labors. It probably embodies the surveys made by Gosnold, Archer, Pring, Weymouth, Champlain, and, perhaps, others, and shows, for the first time, correctly drawn, such characteristic features as the peculiar hook of Cape Cod. This very point had hitherto been considered the distinguishing mark of excellence of Smith's map, drawn six years later.

However, if Smith's cartographical services cannot now be considered as important as formerly, his work as a popularizer remains unimpaired. Although the map of 1610, until published within the present generation, continued in the form of a single manuscript copy, and was seen in its day by few outside the inner circles of company promotion, Smith's was published in a large edition, and, together with his *Description*, which has not yet lost its charm, did much to spread a knowledge of New England among the people. Many a man in

---

[1] For various states of the map, *vide* J. Winsor, *Memorial History of Boston* (Boston, 1882), vol. I, pp. 52–56.

[2] Printed for the first time by Brown, *Genesis*, p. 456.

disgrace with fortune must have pondered his note for those "that have great spirits, and small meanes," and have read enviously of "the planters pleasures, and profits," as set forth by the plausible captain.

An act of cruelty, which occurred on Smith's voyage, was to bear unforeseen results in the future. One of the captains, a rascal named Hunt, kidnaped twenty-four savages, and sold them in Spain for slaves. One of these, who was subsequently returned to his native land, was the Squanto who so materially assisted the Pilgrims at Plymouth, as we shall see later.

Of more immediate influence were the fish and furs with which Smith reached London,— valued at £1500,— and which served to direct attention to the possibilities of the region. It was, it is true, a trifle compared with the £90,000 or more which the stockholders of the East India Company were receiving from the annual voyages of their fleet; but interest in colonizing as well as in trading was rapidly growing.[1] In Ireland, where colonization ran a course curiously analogous to that in America, settlement now proceeded rapidly.[2] In Newfoundland, two colonies were founded, and in Bermuda people were said to be beginning "to nestle and plant very handsomely."[3] Little Englanders of an early type, and opponents of chartered privilege, were not wanting, indeed, to inveigh against the growing imperialism of the times. As "for the Bermudas, we know not yet what they will do; and for Virginia, we know not well what to do with it," wrote one author; while Bacon compared the visionary possibilities of America with the solid results in Ireland.[4]

While Smith had been ranging our coast, getting informa-

[1] Hunter, *British India*, vol. I, p. 306.

[2] Cheyney, "English Conditions," pp. 514–21. For a report on a site for a colony in Derry, which might be mistaken for an American "prospectus" of the same period, *vide Cal. State Papers, Ireland, 1608–1610*, p. 318. The items are curiously familiar: "the goodness of the air and the fruitfulness of the land"; "the red deer, foxes, conies, martins, otters"; "the great plenty of timber for shipping"; "the commodious harbor"; "the infinite store of cods, herrings," etc.; "the sea-fowl in great abundance"; even the pearls.

[3] *Cal. State Pap., Col., 1558–1660*, p. 15.

[4] *The Trades Increase*, in *Harleian Miscellany* (ed. 1809), vol. III, p. 299; Brown, *Genesis*, p. 820.

tion, furs, and fish, another expedition, despatched by Gorges, under Captain Hobson, was seeking gold on Martha's Vineyard. Needless to say, he did not find it, and, as Smith laconically remarks, he "spent his victuall and returned with nothing." [1] The tangible cash results of Smith's own voyage pointed to him as the man whom the company needed, and by them he was made Admiral of New England for life, and started on another voyage, with two ships and Captain Thomas Dermer. He never again, however, saw America. Owing to damages to his vessel, received in a storm only a few days out, he was forced to return to Plymouth; and although Dermer went on, we know nothing of his trip. [2] On Smith's next attempt, he was taken prisoner by pirates; and on his fourth start, in 1617, for some reason he never got out of Plymouth harbor.

Voyages to New England now became frequent, however, and it is not necessary to mention them all. In 1615, Sir Richard Hawkins was exploring and trading for Gorges, whose agent, Richard Vines, probably spent the following winter in Maine, bringing back with him the first news of the great plague which was decimating the Indians, and which was to simplify the question of settlement. As Gorges speaks of the "extreme rates" at which he had to hire men to stay the winter quarter, it is probable that he had other parties there, in this or other winters. "This course I held some years together," he wrote in his old age, "but nothing to my private profit; for what I got one way I spent another; so that I began to grow weary of that business, as not for my turn till better times." [3] The surprising part is, not that he grew weary, but that he still continued the unprofitable business for a lifetime.

In 1618, he received a letter from Captain Dermer, in Newfoundland, saying that he had there found Squanto, one of Gorges's savages, and that the Indian's description of New England had made him desirous to "follow his hopes that

[1] Smith, *Works*, vol. I, p. 240.　　　　[2] *Ibid.*, vol. II, pp. 731 *ff.*
[3] Gorges, "Briefe Narration," pp. 57–62.

way." [1] The next spring, therefore, the indefatigable Gorges sent out Captain Rocroft to meet Dermer and coöperate with him. Dermer, meanwhile, had returned to England; so Rocroft failed to meet him, and after capturing a French barque off the New England coast, sailed to Virginia, contrary to orders, and was there killed in a quarrel. Gorges reimbursed the Frenchmen for the damages suffered, and, in other respects, made a heavy loss on the voyage, from which he recovered nothing.

As soon as possible after Dermer's unexpected arrival in England, he was again fitted out and sent to join Rocroft, who had meanwhile gone to Virginia. Having missed his associate in the enterprise, whom he had expected to find at Monhegan, Dermer sailed along the coast, making observations, from Sagadahoc to Martha's Vineyard, and then on to Virginia. Finding Rocroft dead, he wintered there, and went back to New England in the spring. [2] Apparently on this visit, he returned Squanto to his native Plymouth, where Dermer seems to have wished to plant. "I would," he wrote, "that the first plantation might hear be seated, if ther come to the number of 50 persons, or upward" — a desire which was to be fulfilled within a few months by the coming of the Pilgrims.

Meanwhile, the colony in South Virginia, at Jamestown, had been passing through a long series of troubles, which on more than one occasion had nearly ended its career. Those in its first years led the company to publish *A True and Sincere Declaration* as to the affairs of the settlement, in which the form of government was given as one of the roots of the evils which had "shaken so tender a body." [3] As a result of changes effected by the two subsequent charters, which they obtained in 1609 and 1612, the London patentees were incorporated as a joint-stock body, and their territory increased to a strip four hundred

---

[1] Gorges, "Briefe Narration," p. 62. He does not give the name of the savage. The identity is established by Bradford, *History of Plymouth Plantation* (Boston, 1861), pp. 96 *f.*

[2] This I take to be the explanation of the voyages, though he may have returned to England between them. It seems certain that he was on the coast in 1620. *Cf.* Dermer's letter in Purchas, *Pilgrimes*, vol. XIX, pp. 129 *ff.*; Gorges, "Briefe Narration," pp. 61 *ff.*; and Bradford, *Plymouth*, pp. 95–98.

[3] Reprinted by Brown, *Genesis*, pp. 338–53.

miles wide, extending from coast to coast, which they were empowered to grant to others.[1] The old Royal Council was replaced by one elected by the members of the company, thus becoming subject, not to the king, but to the fifty-six city companies, and to the six hundred and fifty-nine individuals, who formed the membership of the enterprise at the time of the 1612 charter. Governmental powers were also bestowed upon it, and the colony thus became a proprietary province, with a trading company as proprietor.[2]

The unfortunate results of the recent voyages in which Gorges had been interested, so far from dampening his ardor, had made him more anxious than ever to go on with his efforts. The governmental changes in the charter for South Virginia, together, perhaps, with the enlargement of its bounds, moved him to apply for a new charter for the northern plantation.[3] A dispute in which he had become involved with the southern company, regarding its rights to fish within the limits assigned to the North Virginia patentees, which rights he denied, had won for him the hostility of a part of the Virginia Company's membership. As the new charter for which he had applied contained a clause giving the New England Company a monopoly of the fishing along their entire section of the coast, it was bitterly attacked by the southerners, who had annually gone to the northern fishing-grounds for an important part of their year's supplies. The dispute was taken into Parliament, where Gorges defended himself with ability, and thence to the King. The factional fight then in progress between Smythe and Sandys, in the Virginia Company, led Smythe's party to support Gorges against their opponents in their own company; and as Gorges had also strengthened his cause by including among his associates many of the influential nobles of the court, an order in council was finally issued in his favor, on the 18th of June, 1621, for the delivery of the new charter.[4]

[1] Hazard, *Hist. Coll.*, vol. I, pp. 58–81.

[2] Osgood, *American Colonies*, vol. I, pp. 56 *ff.*

[3] Gorges, "Briefe Narration," p. 64.

[4] *Ibid.*, pp. 64 *ff.*; *Documents relating to the Colonial History of State of New York* (Albany, 1853), vol. III, p. 4; Thomas Pownall, *The Administration of the British Colonies* (London, 1777), vol. I, p. 49.

Thus was originated the "Council established at Plymouth in the County of Devon for the Planting, Ruling, and Governing of New England in America," which now became the proprietor of all the territory between 40° and 48° North Latitude, and extending from the Atlantic to the Pacific, in utter disregard of the French claims in Nova Scotia and Canada, and of the colonies planted there. The charter stated that there were no subjects of any foreign power in possession of any part of the territory, although Quebec had been settled for thirteen years, and French fishermen and fur traders were constantly being met by the English.[1] Upon the new company were bestowed rights of trading, colonizing, and governing. The members were allowed to elect their own officials in England, and to appoint those for ruling in the settlements. The members of the Virginia Company numbered nearly a thousand persons, who elected their council, and were responsible for the administration of the colony; but under the Gorges charter, the council was the whole company, limited to forty members, who were self-perpetuating, and whose relation to the colonists was thus direct and final.[2]

The new company was never either active or successful. The controversy which had marked its slow birth tended to keep people from investing; and from its narrow and monopolistic nature, it could make no appeal to popular support. While the passage of the charter was still pending, chance decreed that under it was to be made, even before its issue, the first successful planting within its granted limits, and without efforts of their own, the grantees, when they received the powers bestowed upon them by the King, were to find the Pilgrim colony already established at Plymouth.

[1] Charter in Hazard, *Hist. Coll.*, vol. I, pp. 103 *ff.*
[2] *Cf.* Osgood, *American Colonies*, vol. I, pp. 98 *ff.*

CHAPTER IV

SOME ASPECTS OF PURITANISM

THE history of the New England group of colonies was, in the main, shaped throughout the entire prerevolutionary period by the influence of three factors. These were the geographical environment, the Puritan movement in England, and the Mercantile Theory. The first of these has already been discussed, and the last will be more particularly referred to later. As the second was not only a continuing influence during the period, but was the chief determinant in the small settlement of Plymouth, and an element in the great migration to Massachusetts, it must be considered before entering upon the story of those two colonies.

The first difficulty in dealing with the problem of Puritanism is to define the term itself. The earliest appearance of the name seems to have been about 1566, and in the following year a certain London congregation was spoken of as "Puritans or Unspottyd Lambs of the Lord." The members of this congregation, which met secretly in Plumbers Hall, called their sect "the pure or stainless religion"; and the derivation of the name Puritan, for long a term of reproach, is sufficiently obvious.[1] Its application, however, is less so. Part of the confusion is due to the fact that, like "democratic" and many other such words, it has been applied to an attitude toward life, to a broad movement, and to a definite political party. Moreover, between the meeting of those "Unspottyd Lambs" in Plumbers Hall in 1567, and the overthrow of the Puritan Commonwealth of England in 1660, nearly a century elapsed, during which the meaning of the word underwent the changes

[1] C. Burrage, *The Early English Dissenters in the Light of Recent Research, 1550–1641* (Cambridge, 1912), vol. I, pp. 84, 93. Hinds, in *The England of Elizabeth*, p. 19, traces "the first whisper of that sound" to Calvin's letter of 1554.

which time always brings to words of its class, whereas it still continues as a living term in our social and religious vocabulary. Rigidly and briefly to define a word which has thus had a vague and changing content throughout a dozen generations is impossible. To attempt to confine its definition to only one of its former meanings is unhistorical, however desirable it may be that an author should define it as used by himself in his own writings. Not long ago it was fashionable to decry, as showing total lack of scholarship, any attempt to apply the name to the men who founded Plymouth, it being considered as applying solely to those who founded Massachusetts. It may be true that "the Separatists were not Puritans in the original sense of the word"; [1] but the word did not retain its original sense, and although Separatist and Nonconformist represent a real difference, the word Puritan may well be used to cover both. The pendulum, indeed, seems now to be swinging the other way, and several writers describe Puritanism broadly as an "attitude of mind," or as "idealism applied to the solution of contemporary problems." [2] As specific terms for the many sects and minor currents in the great movement, which for a time dominated the history of both the Englands, are by no means lacking, it would seem desirable to retain the use of the word Puritanism in its widest application, and it is so used in the present work.

The idea of unity seems to possess a peculiar fascination for the average human mind. Only a savage or a philosopher may be content with, or rise to, the conception of a pluralistic universe. Moreover, the desire to conform, and to force others to do so, is as typical of the average man as of the average boy.

It is in but few persons, and in rare periods, that the spirit of unrest, of dissatisfaction, of growth, manifests itself so strongly as to overcome the innate tendency toward static conformity. The mediæval period was essentially, for the most part, one of

[1] Burrage, *English Dissenters*, vol. 1, p. 34. *Cf.* E. Channing, *History of the United States* (New York, 1916), vol. 1, p. 272 *n.*

[2] Channing, *History*, vol. 1, pp. 271 *ff.*; G. B. Tatham, *The Puritans in Power* (Cambridge, 1913), p. 2; and R. G. Usher, *The Reconstruction of the English Church* (New York, 1910), vol. 1, pp. 244–46.

religious unity. For long, the two great ideas of the Empire and the Church had dominated men's minds. With the Renaissance and the Reformation, however, arose again, not only nationalities, but individualities. With the growth of the separate nations, developed simultaneously a new sense of individual responsibility in the face of the universe. For the average man during the Middle Ages, the moral, even more than the economic, life had been corporate. Outward conformity to the dogmas and usages of the only church which then represented Christ's Kingdom upon earth lulled his thoughts, and soothed his conscience. The necessity of belonging to the Church was not forced upon a man merely by fear of persecution or of the public opinion of his own little world. His belief in such a relation, and his ignoring the possibility of any other, had become as innate and instinctive as his belief in the physical laws of the universe by which he guided his daily life. It was not alone the historians of the period who were "content to be deceived, to live in a twilight of fiction," as "the atmosphere of accredited mendacity thickened." [1] The subtle poison had flowed through the veins of the entire social organism.

As the idea of nationality grew and rooted itself in the mind of the masses, it attracted to itself, by a sort of mental gravitation, the institutions and thoughts of the peoples. Everywhere, the religious reformation had been closely allied with secular politics, and the reformed churches became national. As universal empire had gradually given place to nations, so the universal church was in part broken into state churches, but without any loosening of the bond which bound the individual to them. The idea of *the* church persisted, and the average man considered separating himself from it almost as one would consider separating one's self from the civil state of to-day. It was almost as unthinkable and impossible to realize in practice. His life was so interwoven with it, his civil rights, as well as his religious duties, were so involved in his relations to it, that, even if he disagreed with its dogma, disliked its policy,

[1] Lord Acton, *Lectures on Modern History* (London, 1907), p. 5.

or strove within it to alter both, he had no thought of leaving it. To do so would have been to constitute himself a religious anarch. Not only were the mental inhibitions to the development of such an idea greater than those operating in the case of political anarchy to-day, but the pains and penalties attending the action, both from law and from public opinion, were also greater.[1]

One of the most dynamic ideas, however, which had come in with the Reformation, was that of the responsibility of the individual to God, both for his own life and for that of others. To those whose minds were open to receive it, the thought came with a force which was almost overwhelming. In the training of youth, it is well recognized that responsibility must be thrown upon them gradually if their characters are to grow normally, and not be warped or broken under sudden strain. But here were men, in many cases incredibly ignorant of the Christian story, to whom the very existence of such a book as the Bible had been unknown, and whose faith and conduct had been regulated for them for centuries. Suddenly they found themselves in possession of the original sources in their own tongues, and were told that the eternal salvation of their souls was no longer in the keeping of the institution upon which they had always leaned with the unconscious confidence of a child upon its parents. Inspired by a new sense of their importance as individuals, and, in the majority of cases, by a self-confidence born of ignorance, earnest men undertook to interpret the scriptures, and to revise the existing ritual, dogma, and government of the Church. Extreme individualism on all these points was the natural result. Sects, often counting only single congregations in their numbers, arose everywhere. Separatism was the logical end of these discontents and strivings; but men are not logical in their actions, and separatism formed but a small element in the Puritan movement. Where it did occur, the disintegrating force did not usually stop there, but continued to plague, with petty and ignoble quarrels, the little groups thus split off.

[1] Cf. Usher, *Reconstruction*, vol. I, p. 273

Not only were the Separatists logical, but their action required far more courage than that of the mere Nonconforming Puritans. Not only did the act itself call for a higher degree of intellectual daring, but the penalties attached to it were greater. In many cases, Nonconformity, so far from entailing loss or suffering, possessed a distinct money and social value; but no highly paid cure or easy berth in the household of a Puritan nobleman awaited the Separatist. Misguided as many of the latter may have been, and disappointing as were many of the Separatist movements, it would seem that, on the whole, the Separatists possessed more sincerity and loyalty to their ideas than the Puritans who remained within the Church. This the great majority of them did. The number of Separatists, like the number of Puritans generally, has usually been overstated in the past. The twenty thousand Brownists mentioned by Raleigh in 1593 have dwindled, under the light of modern critical research, to a mere five or six hundred at most.[1]

When the ordinary man gets a new idea, it does not necessarily dislodge the old ones that may be antagonistic to it, or even greatly modify them.[2] The tendency to cling to the established church was as strong in the minds of most Puritans as was their self-confidence in their own beliefs and superior sanctity, and their desire to alter the Church to suit them, whether in the earlier demands in the matter of vestments, or the later in matters of polity and doctrine. Thus the survival of the mediæval idea of the Church, coupled with the new one of individual judgment and responsibility, led the conservative Puritans to adopt a half-way policy as compared with the Churchmen and the Separatists.

Under Henry VIII there had been little change, save in the single fact of the break with Rome, and the substitution of King for Pope as the head of the Church. The ecclesiastical

[1] Burrage, *English Dissenters*, vol. I, p. 152.
[2] "Unless we allow for the innate capacity of the human mind to entertain contradictory beliefs at the same time, we shall in vain attempt to understand the history of thought in general and of religion in particular." J. G. Frazer, *Adonis, Attis, Osiris* [*The Golden Bough*] (London, 1907), p. 5 n.

property had, indeed, been largely confiscated and distributed among the laity so as to create a powerful economic interest in the maintenance of the King's supremacy. By the fact of that supremacy, religious questions had become political, and important changes would necessarily in time have to be made in church administration and discipline. Otherwise, however, there was little alteration, and apparently but two out of the King's subjects refused to conform to the new order.[1] Although further progress was made under Edward, the reign of Mary restored the union with Rome, and sent many exiles to Frankfort, Geneva, and other centres of the Protestant movement on the continent.[2]

On the accession of Elizabeth, the refugees flocked back to London, keen to work into the fabric of the English church the religious ideas which they had imbibed and developed during their exile. The bulk of the clergy, however, were not desirous of innovation, and seem hardly to have been affected by the controversies raging at the time.[3] Of the nine thousand four hundred serving the Church under the Pope in Mary's reign, fewer than one hundred and eighty, or less than two per cent, refused the Oath of Supremacy under Elizabeth.[4] Not only had the parish priests thus accepted with indifference the various changes,[5] but the laity in the country districts, especially in the north, had scarcely been touched by the Reformation. When Elizabeth came to the throne, the distracted country needed, above all else, peace and unity. The fifth of

[1] D. Neal, *The History of the Puritans* (New York, 1843), vol. I, p. 34.

[2] Hinds, *The England of Elizabeth*, pp. 6–68.

[3] H. Gee, *The Elizabethan Clergy and the Settlement of Religion, 1558–1564* (Oxford, 1898), pp. 1 ff.

[4] J. Brown, *The Pilgrim Fathers of New England and their Puritan Successors* (London, 1906), p. 26; Gee, in *Elizabethan Clergy*, p. 247, estimates that not many more than 200 were deprived between Nov. 17, 1558, and Nov. 17, 1564, for refusal to acknowledge the Elizabethan settlement. These were mainly Roman Catholics.

[5] One is reminded of the satirical verses on Richard Lee of Hatfield, on his conforming again in 1662:—

> Three times already I have turned my coat,
> Three times already I have changed my note,
> I'll make it four, and four-and-twenty more,
> And turn the compass round, ere I'll give o'er.

Cited by F. Bate, *The Declaration of Indulgence, 1672* (London, 1908), p. 30.

her house to reign in the period of about seventy-five years since the end of the long War of the Roses, she found a nation yet suffering from the severe economic effects of that protracted crisis, and a church rendered unstable in doctrine and almost impotent in discipline by the four alternations between Roman and Protestant allegiance which had occurred in less than a quarter of a century. The question of her own legitimacy, bound up as it was with the question of religious authority, and the extreme delicacy of international political relations, especially with Spain, France, and Scotland, added difficulties to the problem of church settlement.[1]

An established church was a necessity from all three standpoints, of religion, morals, and politics. Here and there, a few zealots might organize their own congregations and support a preacher; but any sort of congregational church government was out of the question for the overwhelming mass of the people, who were ignorant and indifferent, but still superstitiously devoted to the old Roman forms. The moral sanctions of the time were, moreover, far more closely involved with religion than they are to-day, and the church was far more essential as a prop to a government none too strong. The situation called for the opportunist policy which the Queen always favored in every difficulty. Whatever may have been her own religious beliefs or lack of them, which cannot now be known, she never cared for religious persecution, but she cared everything for a strong and united England. Although conformity was necessary to prevent the disintegration of the national life, the standards to which she required men to conform were purposely left so vague as to permit all but the most advanced of Protestant sectaries and most irreconcilable of Romanists to become members of the Church of England.

Opportunism may temporarily save a dangerous situation, but cannot be pursued successfully as a permanent policy. The course of events led extreme Catholics to feel that the Church had advanced so far that they could not follow it, and

[1] Cf. F. W. Maitland's chapter on "The Anglican Settlement and the Scottish Reformation," in *Cambridge Modern History* (New York, 1918), vol. v, pp. 550–99.

the ultra-Puritans to consider that it had stopped so short that they could not stay for it. To an opposition, all things, theoretically, seem possible. The practical difficulties are for those who have the responsibility of power. By the end of Elizabeth's reign, the Catholics realized that the most they could hope for would be toleration; and the real struggle for the control of the organization lay between the Puritans and those who wished the Church to continue its middle course. It must be pointed out, that this struggle of the Puritan Nonconformists was in no sense for toleration. They had as little thought of it as the Inquisition itself, nor did they exercise it when in power, either in old or New England   In that regard, the Separatist John Robinson, preaching to his little congregation in Leyden, was as far ahead of the Puritan leaders in England, as Roger Williams was of the leaders of Massachusetts.

As has already been seen, only two men failed to conform to the change under Henry in 1534, and less than two per cent were forced from their cures when Elizabeth introduced the Oath of Supremacy. In the great deprivations under James and Archbishop Bancroft, following the adoption of the Canons of 1604, the most careful sifting of all the records indicates that less than three hundred Puritan clergy were deprived of their livings.[1]   On the other hand, when the Puritans came into power, out of eighty-six hundred clergy of the Church, the livings of approximately thirty-five hundred, or over forty per cent, were sequestrated.[2]   The Nonconformist struggle was not for toleration, but for control. Indeed, the objection of the Puritans to the Court of High Commission itself, to which they sometimes voluntarily carried their own cases, and which had a certain popularity that has largely been lost to sight, was not so much that it was an instrument of oppression, as that at times it was turned against themselves.[3]

[1] Usher, *Reconstruction*, vol. II, pp. 3–14.
[2] Tatham, in *Puritans in Power*, pp. 91 f., gives from 3,000 to 3,500. In his monograph on *Dr. John Walker and the Sufferings of the Clergy* (Cambridge Univ. Press, 1911, p. 132), he states 3,500 as the probable number.
[3] R. G. Usher, *The Rise and Fall of the High Commission* (Oxford, 1913), pp. 72, 105, 329.

One of the claims made for them is that they constituted a large percentage of both the clergy and the laity, and embraced a great part of the learned men of the church, and were therefore entitled to guide the organization. This claim does not stand the test of rigid criticism. As exhaustive a list as possible, giving every doubtful name to the Puritans, shows not over three hundred Puritan clergy in the church between 1600 and 1610, or about three per cent of the establishment.[1] There are no figures available for the laity, but computations based on various methods of estimating the numbers yield totals equivalent to from two to six per cent of the population. These figures may be too low, but it must be considered that the common people, particularly in the country districts, were inert to a much greater degree even than to-day, and their normal attitude toward the clergy might well have been summed up in the dictum of the choir in Hardy's "Under the Greenwood Tree," that "there 's virtue in a man's not putting a parish to spiritual trouble."

On the other hand, again, as tending unduly to swell the estimated number of Puritans, it must be remembered that the great landlords possessed the gift of many livings, and if one of them, from any motive whatever, turned Puritan, all of his livings could be bestowed upon Puritan clergy, and the congregations would be nominally counted as Puritan. For example, to cite by no means the most influential of a group which included such men as the Earl of Warwick, we may note that Sir Robert Jermyn controlled ten livings in one archdeaconry, while nine other laymen controlled sixty-five more.[2] Thus these ten men—chosen somewhat at random—owned seventy-five livings; and, upon their declaring themselves Puritans, not only would seventy-five clergy have to become Puritans, to be acceptable, but, if we place their congregations as low as two hundred each, we would have fifteen thousand laity thus attending Puritan churches as a result of the religious or other motives which had moved ten landlords to number

[1] Usher, *Reconstruction*, vol. 1, pp. 249–51.
[2] *Ibid.*, p. 270.

themselves with the Saints. This indicates how impossible it is to calculate the number of Puritans who were such by sincere conviction.

As to the learning of the Puritan clergy, the latest researches also fail to bear out the earlier controversial claims on their behalf. Of the two hundred and eighty-one men whose names are known, one hundred and seventy-six had no university degree, while of the remainder, only thirty-one were higher than Masters of Arts.[1] There were, indeed, Puritan divines eminent for learning, but the proportion of university men among them was no higher than is known to have been the case among the Conformists.

Hence the Puritans were but a small minority, both of the clergy and of the laity. The instinct of fair play, which leads a man to side with the under-dog, without stopping to consider whether the upper-dog may be not only upper, but justified, induces us to lay great stress on the rights of minorities, on the theory that a majority can take care of itself. Minorities, however, are usually vocal, organized, and zealous, while the majority is dumb, unwieldy, and but little inclined constantly to resist the attacks of all the various minorities in the field. If there is reason to condemn the Church in England for requiring the Puritan minority to conform, then the Puritans themselves must be condemned just as strictly for their oppression of the minorities in New England. There cannot be two canons of judgment for the same act; and, in fact, as we shall see later, the Puritans there in power were, if anything, the more guilty of the two.

There is much truth, however, in the doctrine of the saving remnant; and, in the low condition of morals in the early seventeenth century, it may well be that the Puritan element was that remnant by which England was saved, as well as New England founded. For morality had sunk to a low ebb, and, even if the reality was not as black as it was painted by Puritan writers, we know enough to realize that there was sore need of a reforming zeal which should cleanse society of its rapidly

[1] Usher, *Reconstruction*, vol. i, p. 251.

accumulating filth. That zeal was provided almost wholly by the Puritans. Not but that there were plenty of moral and able men in the other party, who were striving with the problems of the day as well as the Unspotted Lambs and Saints — striving, perhaps, with better understanding and more breadth of view. But that was not what the moral situation called for. Luckily the more extreme of the Puritans were thorough-going fanatics; for nothing less than a good dose of fanaticism seemed likely to purge England of its social evils. But that is a different matter from fanaticism erected into a permanent compulsory system, or from the attempt to control an organization by three per cent of its membership; and it must be admitted that there was much to be said on the side of Archbishop Bancroft and the Church. Not only was the small number of the Puritans known to him, and also their methods, which were by no means above reproach, but their refusal to coöperate in an effort to reform one of the worst abuses confirmed his belief that their real desire was not for reform but to force their views on the other ninety-seven per cent of the clergy and the nation, and to gain control of the ecclesiastical machinery of the State Church.

He was thoroughly familiar with the facts that modern research has brought to light in regard to the methods of securing signatures to the various petitions presented to the King, and knew how much less they represented than they purported to.[1] Very real abuses in the Church, which were undoubtedly largely responsible for the low spiritual state of the people at large, were those of pluralities, non-residence, and lack of properly qualified preachers, although the number of clergy holding more than one living has been exaggerated. To a very great extent, the reason for the practice, as well as the cause of the great number of inferior, and even immoral, men, who were to be found in the Church, was economic. As we noted in an earlier chapter, the period had been one of an unexampled rise in prices, and in both the cost and scale of living. The tithes,

---

[1] Usher, *Reconstruction*, vol. I, pp. 45, 291, 294, 412. On the unreliability of Puritan petitions in other cases also, *cf.* Tatham, *Puritans in Power*, pp. 59 *ff.*

which supported the clergymen, had originally been paid in kind, but had gradually been commuted into money payments at a time when prices were low, and the general manner of living far inferior to that of the later Elizabethan period. In 1585, over one half of all the clergy received salaries of less than £10 each;[1] of these, approximately three thousand received less than £5, and one thousand but £2 annually, or less.[2]

Pluralism and ignorant preachers were the only possible spiritual fruits of such an economic system, though the use of pluralities was abused by some of the higher clergy. Bills were introduced in the Parliament of 1604 for the increase of the incomes of the parish priests, thus striking at the root of the trouble; but they were shelved by the Puritan Commons, though the Puritans were loud in their denunciation of these very evils.[3] By means of contributions, however, they increased the pay of their own clergymen, so that a Puritan incumbent might expect from two to three times what a Conformist might be paid in a similar cure. At a time when over half of the clergy were receiving less than £10, one Puritan of the Dedham Classis received £50, several others from £30 to £70, a Mr. Dalby £40, another £50, yet another £73, a Puritan assistant £33, and one Puritan congregation which offered over £46 had difficulty in finding any reformer who was willing to accept so small an amount.[4] Here at any rate, was a very tangible reward for those who felt that they could remain in an institution which they condemned, while they drew pay from both sides. Many a poor devil of a sincerely conforming parish priest, struggling along on two or three pounds a year, must have wondered whether it were not worldly-wise to turn Puritan; and a Separatist had to console himself with a logical position and a comfortable conscience.

Advocates of the Puritans, in an effort to prove that their minds were not absorbed by squabbles over petty details of

---

[1] J. Strype, *Life and Acts of Archbishop Whitgift* (Oxford, 1822), vol. I, p. 371.

[2] Usher, *Reconstruction*, vol. I, p. 219.

[3] *Ibid.*, p. 352; It was said that three quarters of the House was Puritan, but this is doubtful. S. R. Gardiner, *History*, vol. I, p. 178.

[4] Usher, *Reconstruction*, vol. I, pp. 274 f.

vestments and symbols, have explained at length the importance of such matters in that age; and they are quite right.
The Puritan attack, however, was not merely against the sur-
plice, or minister who did not preach, or immorality in private
life, as it certainly was not for liberty of conscience.   It was
obvious to those in authority that what the reformers desired
was a change of the established church government into the
Presbyterian form, with themselves in control.   Masson claims
that between 1580 and 1590 there were not less than five hundred beneficed clergy who practically maintained a Presbyterian organization within the body of the Church.[1]   Although
these numbers may be somewhat too large, evidence was continually cropping out which showed that the Puritans wished
not only to gain control of the Church, but to substitute the
Presbyterian discipline in its place.[2]   Marsden, like many other
writers, has raised the questions whether the points at issue
were really vital, and whether more "Christian meekness and
moderation" should not have been shown "even to the obsti-
nate."[3]   From the standpoint of the administration of a great
organization, upon which rested the responsibility of maintaining what it believed to be essential both to the Church and
to the State, it must be admitted that these things did seem
vital, just as they seemed so to the small Puritan minority.   If
they were not vital, then we must impugn either the good faith
or the intellectual ability of the entire mass of Puritans who
fought for them so bitterly; and if they were, then it must be
conceded that they were quite as much so for the majority in
power as for the minority in opposition.

The ecclesiastical struggle between the Nonconforming Puritans and the Church, then, was fundamentally administrative.
It came down to the question whether a powerful organization,
which thoroughly believed in itself and its own importance, as
all powerful organizations and vested interests come to do,

[1] D. Masson, *Life of Milton* (London, 1875), vol. II, p. 532.
[2] Usher, *Reconstruction*, vol. I, pp. 42 *ff.*, 347 *ff.*; J. B. Marsden, *The History of the
Early Puritans* (London, 1853), pp. 78 *ff.*
[3] Marsden, *Early Puritans*, p. 168.

should allow itself to be turned out of control by a small minority, whose attitude it considered detrimental, not only to itself, but to religion and the State. There could be only one answer. Had it not been for the survival of the mediæval idea as to the necessity of belonging to the Church, it is possible that those Puritans who were actuated purely by spiritual motives would have followed the more consistent Separatists, and merely have withdrawn from the body with whose government and usage they were no longer in accord. In that case, the way would have been cleared for the great moral influence which the Puritans exerted, without the embittering results of the struggle, and the reaction of 1660 against Puritanism as it showed itself when in political power. On the other hand, political liberty might have been the loser.

In theological dogma, the Puritans had, at least until the later period, but little quarrel with the Church. Both were largely under the influence of Calvinistic doctrine, although there was considerable latitude of belief among individuals of both parties. The central pivot of their creed was the absolutely unconditioned will of God.[1] The system, which is strongly tinged with legal doctrine, acknowledges no law but that of his untrammeled will. From this flow two consequences. One is that there is no room for a non-moral sphere of activity, for actions which, belonging merely to the domain of nature, are untinged by moral obligation. The other is the doctrine of predestination, by some considered the central point of the Calvinistic theology. "God not only foresaw the fall of the first man, and the ruin of his posterity in him," wrote Calvin, "but also arranged all by the determination of his own will."[2] The decree involved both election and reprobation. Except for this decree, all human beings, including those to whom the gospel had never been preached, and the baby who died at his first breath, were condemned to hell forever. God, however, chose certain individuals as his elect to

[1] W. Walker, *John Calvin* (New York, 1906), pp. 409-29; *cf.* also P. Schaff, *Creeds of Christendom* (New York, 1877), vol. I, pp. 451 *ff.*

[2] John Calvin, *Institutes of the Christian Religion*, translated by J. Allen (Philadelphia, 1844), vol. II, p. 170.

be saved, foreordained from all eternity by "his gratuitous mercy, totally irrespective of human merit." The rest He condemned eternally, by "a just and irreprehensible but incomprehensible judgment."[1]

Although this decree, being eternal and immutable, could not be altered by anything that the individual could do, as he was forever blessed or damned irrespective of his character or conduct, yet, since the wills of those chosen as the elect were in harmony with God's will, by careful observation of one's own actions it might be possible to lift the veil and discover whether one were, perhaps, of the elect or not. Hence all those torturing self-examinations and searchings of heart, which fill so much of the early Puritan letters and diaries. Such doctrine, though apparently stripping God of every shred of what we consider moral character, would be of profound influence upon that of those who truly believed it; and the Puritan believed with extraordinary tenacity. His imagination was wholly concentrated on questions of religion, and that religion was a "narrow Hebraism" which "kept open its windows toward Jerusalem, but closed every other avenue to the soul."[2] His creed must not be considered as merely a series of logical deductions from the Bible, which appealed to him solely through the intellect. Heaven and hell were as vividly visualized by him as external facts.[3] In the early seventeenth century this doctrine was a living thing, the word-pictures not having lost their reality by long familiarity and much repetition.

If it be asked how people who believed that no efforts that they could make would save them from everlasting damnation, if not of the elect, could possibly face life with any cheerfulness, the answer is that the Puritans considered themselves as elected. Now and then a poor wretch did torture himself

---

[1] Calvin, *Institutes*, vol. I, p. 149.

[2] J. F. Jameson, Introduction to *Johnson's Wonder-Working Providence* (New York, 1910), p. 16.

[3] *Cf.* S. N. Patten, *The Development of English Thought* (New York, 1904), p. 121; and B. Wendell, *The Temper of the 17th Century in English Literature* (New York, 1904), p. 227.

with the belief that he was damned, and occasional qualms were experienced by the staunchest; but, on the whole, the terrible doctrine seems to have lost its greatest sting for the individual in the comfortable assurance that, although the bulk of his neighbors were going to hell, he himself was one of the everlasting Saints.   Such belief naturally fostered, too, that smugness of self-assurance that has always been character- istic of Puritan reformers in all ages, and also a hard intolerance. Those who did not believe as the Puritans believed were not of the elect, and so were condemned by God to eternal torment. No act of intolerance shown toward them by the Puritans could thus compare with the almost unthinkable intolerance displayed toward them by the author of their being.   To show toleration or mercy toward such was, logically, to exalt human- ity above the deity.

To the Puritan, the reign of law was merely the reign of God's will, but it was universal.   No act was indifferent, either in the universe or in the individual.   John Winthrop's consid- eration of the special providence of God, in permitting the discovery of a spider in some porridge before it was eaten, was not merely Puritanical.[1]   It was scriptural, and it was to the Scriptures that every Puritan turned to ascertain the will of God upon every detail of daily life.   This obviously opened the way to the most far-reaching tyranny to which men could be called upon to submit, should those fanatically holding the view be in possession of the civil power to enforce it.   The tyranny of political despotism had left untouched the whole vast field of private conduct, save in so far as the acts of in- dividuals might minister directly to the despot's pleasure, wealth, or power.   The conformity forced upon individuals by established churches had left to the individual his whole free- dom outside of the limited relations to the establishment and its doctrines.   But the Puritan left no such free spaces in life. Nothing was so small as to be indifferent.   The cut of clothes, the names he bore, the most ordinary social usages, could all be regulated in accordance with the will of God.   For him,

[1] R. C. Winthrop, *Life and Letters of John Winthrop* (Boston, 1869), vol. 1, p. 69.

that will was expressed once for all, and only, in the Bible, and of that Bible the Puritan believed that he alone had the key, and was the valid interpreter for the rest of mankind. The more extreme of the sects, indeed, occasionally remind one of those hill tribes of the northern Himalayas, who consider themselves so holy that no one is allowed to touch their persons, while they alone are allowed to approach the symbol of their god.[1]

In a trial before the High Commission, in 1567, of certain Puritans who had hired a hall ostensibly for a wedding, and had then held an illegal prayer meeting in it, one of them claimed that he should be tried only by the word of God. "But," said the dean, "who will you have to judge of the word of God?"[2] The obvious answer, which every Puritan, from then to now, has made, is that he alone is such an interpreter, not merely for himself, but for the entire community. It was natural, with the Puritans' idea of God, that they should take special delight in the Old Testament. From it, almost exclusively, they drew their texts, and it never failed to provide them with justification for their most inhuman and bloodthirsty acts. Christ did, indeed, occupy a place in their theology, but in spirit they may almost be considered as Jews and not Christians. Their God was the God of the Old Testament, their laws were the laws of the Old Testament, their guides to conduct were the characters of the Old Testament. Their Sabbath was Jewish, not Christian. In New England, in their religious persecutions and Indian wars, the sayings of Christ never prevailed to stay their hands or to save the blood of their victims.[3]

From this attitude toward the Bible the doctrine developed, as Milton wrote, that in that book God had once for all revealed all true religion, "with strictest command to reject all other traditions or additions whatsoever."[4] It was upon this belief

---

[1] Frazer, *Adonis*, etc., p. 137.　　　　[2] Usher, *High Commission*, p. 58.

[3] This did not, however, imply any love for living Jews. *Cf.* D. deS. Pool, "Hebrew Learning among the Puritans of New England prior to 1700," in *American Jewish Historical Society Publications*, vol. xx, p. 57.

[4] John Milton, *Of true Religion, Heresy, Schism, Toleration, etc.* (*Works*, London, 1806, vol. iv, p. 259.)

that the Puritan took his stand in opposition to the Church. For him, truth had been revealed once for all, in its entirety. Nothing could be added, nothing could be taken away. To this deadening doctrine, the Church opposed the idea of growth and development. Combine this theory of the absolute finality of the truth, as revealed in books written centuries before, with the Puritan habit of literal interpretation, and the verbal application of sayings, torn from their context, to every occasion of domestic and public life, and we have, not merely an engine of spiritual and moral despotism, but one which was calculated to stultify all liberty of thought. Once allow the body of men professing such doctrine to dominate public opinion, or control the machinery of government, and there would evidently be no limit to their deadly influence upon freedom of intellect as well as of action. It is not a question of the personal morality of its professors or of the nobility of their motives. Without the vital idea of development, both would slowly harden into mere forms and empty professions, while the human mind would lie shackled, debarred from seeking new truth, or from making those experiments which alone bring about healthy growth. The attempt was made, both in old England, with its ancient civilization, and in the New, untrammeled, as far as is ever possible, by any vestige of the past. It is one of the elements that give unique interest to the history of New England as compared with that of the other colonies on our coast. Had they all alike failed, no interest would attach to the others, above that of scores of other attempts to settle a wilderness. But in New England there was an effort, under the most favorable conditions possible,— numbers, economic resources, untrammeled freedom,— to found and govern a state solely by the self-confessed elect of the community.

Puritanism was essentially a movement of protest, and so was largely negative. In fact, to such a degree was it a matter of protest and negation, that the Puritan became absolutely fascinated in his contemplation of that first great protestor and protagonist of negation, the devil himself. It has frequently been pointed out that, in the one great poem which the movement has given us, the "Paradise Lost" of Milton, the real hero is Satan, and that it is upon him that the poet's interest centres. The Puritan's relations with the Deity were not merely fatalistic, but were expressed in the legal form of a covenant in which God and the individual were the contracting parties. Drama, or melodrama, was supplied only by the devil, who, from that standpoint, may almost be said to have been the saving grace of the Puritan doctrine. Men become eloquent over what appeals to their interest; and it is noteworthy that not only did the finest English Puritan poem centre about the devil, but the finest American Puritan prose was to be devoted to the horrors of hell, and that Jonathan Edwards was to find the last touch to the felicity of Heaven in the saints' contemplation of the tortures inflicted upon the damned by the Archfiend in the depths below.

It was, as we have said, natural sympathy that attracted the Puritans to the Old Testament, that long protest against paganism, with its "thou shalt nots." The positive side of the New Testament seems to have left them singularly cold. Indeed, so little appeal did the words of even Christ himself make, that, for once, they abandoned their literalism in the quoting of texts, and doubted whether the use of the Lord's Prayer should be permitted, as it savored too much of ritualism. The Puritans' virtues were thus mainly negations. Their ideals were based almost wholly upon mere avoidance of sin. They sought complete surrender of will. Humanity, in their eyes, was so utterly an evil thing, that only by an undeserved act of the grace of God was it possible that even a few human beings could possibly do anything pleasing in his sight.

This is not an ideal which can permanently satisfy man's whole nature or exert complete influence over him. It is a far cry back to the Greek picture of the perfect life as the fullest development of the entire man, body and soul. Whether that may not properly be a Christian ideal also is not to be discussed here, but it is toward some such ideal of self-expression that the ordinary man strives. His history is that of the fuller and fuller development of his dual nature, in all its varied aspects. Sometimes the emphasis is placed here, sometimes there, but it is difficult to see what other subject can really be the central theme of his earthly striving, and the history of it. Education, economic struggles, law, government, liberty, "emancipation from superstition and caste," all must be traced through their long careers, but none are ends in themselves. They are but the beginnings of opportunity, of no value save in so far as they secure for man the most balanced development and most perfect self-expression of which his nature is capable. To this natural desire, the Puritan opposed the utter surrender of one's own will to the divine will as expressed in minuteness of detail, applicable to every need, even to the style of hats for a minister's wife, in the old Semitic writings. At the time of the Puritan movement, there was much rank growth in society. That growth needed a severe pruning, and for that service the Puritan deserves all praise. But the pruning-knife, after all, is only one of the garden implements, and a tree is pruned that it may grow more abundantly.

This system of negation and protest might have done its needed work and passed, had it not had the misfortune, from the moral and intellectual sides, to come to dominate the power of government. At first Puritanism claimed nothing that could really be termed a party. It may be compared to the Labrador current, cold and invigorating, flowing through the ocean of national life. As it proceeded, however, it met and united with another great current, and the sweep and impetuosity of the two combined carried with them the whole life of the nation, as neither could have done alone. Much had been borne by the people during the reign of Elizabeth, which it had become increasingly evident toward her end that they would not submit to under any successor. The early years of the Stuart dynasty indicated that a constitutional struggle, far transcending the religious, was in preparation. It was by no means true that all of those who were opposed to the King's views as to his prerogative agreed with the Puritan views as to prelacy; but in the case of many individuals, the two revolts were merged into one; and in any case, the two movements, being both directed against the government, would tend to unite, in order to make common cause against the same enemy, though to attain their several ends.   It is true that, in the long run, the leading ideas of the Reformation led toward liberty and equality, especially through the influence of that widely diffused education which was a corollary of the new attitude toward the Bible.   It is a fallacy, however, to believe, because certain results have followed certain causes, that, therefore, those results were striven for by the men who endeavored to put those causes into motion, for the purpose, perhaps, of securing results of quite another sort.   The Puritan, at least, was no more a believer in the political rights of an individual as such, or in democracy, than in religious toleration, and the leaders in Massachusetts denounced both with equal vehemence.   Calvin himself, who most fully represents the political philosophy of the movement, was inconsistent and confused in his thought on the subject; and, as Borgeaud has said, "modern democracy is the child of the Reformation, not of the Reformers." [1]   The Reformation was much broader than the Puritan groupings, and so was reform in the state; but the political leaders realized the great force to be added to the struggle for civil liberty, and welcomed the burning zeal of the religious malcontents.   Thus arose the Puritan party, strong alike in numbers and in purpose, and composed, like all parties, of men infinitely varying in views and character. Their united forces helped at once to create civil liberty under the law and to establish a tyranny of public opinion.

We have already seen some of the incentives that induced men to become Puritans.   As the movement grew, worldly motives, aside from the purely religious or purely patriotic, would tend to influence an increasing number.   We have noted above how the financial sacrifice was frequently made by the Churchman and not by the Puritan.   Indeed, "many of wit and parts," wrote one of the most attractive of English Puritan

[1] Charles Borgeaud, *The Rise of Modern Democracy* (London, 1894), p. 2.

women, "who could not obtain the preferment their ambition gaped at, would declare themselves of the puritan party," while "others, that had neither learning, nor friends, nor opportunities to arrive to any preferments, would put on a form of godliness, finding devout people that way so liberal to them, that they could not hope to enrich themselves so much in any other way." [1]

Moreover, there had for some time been growing up into prominence a new class, which we now call the middle, and which had had no assigned position under the feudal form of society. In the Stuart period, this class was, for the first time, to impress its character deeply upon national affairs. The activities by which, during the preceding two centuries or more, its members had been gradually rising into their new position had given a marked quality to their minds and characters. Looked down upon by the noble, and disliked by the peasant, they returned these feelings with interest. When the noble disdained their birth and breeding, they in turn condemned the immorality of those above them in both. Again the element of negation entered, and the Puritan fostered an ideal which was the reverse of the lives of those who looked down upon him. Puritanism became the "reasoned expression of the middle-class state of mind," [2] which it has always remained.

Among the leaders, however, as among the middle class and country gentry, there was a group which had a very great influence, not only upon the party in England, but upon colonization in America, and which will concern us more directly. We must now turn to examine the settlement of those two colonies in the New World which represented, in the main, the earlier religious, and the later economic and political, aspects of the English Puritan movement.

[1] L. Hutchinson, *Memoirs of Col. Hutchinson* (Everyman's Library, 1913), p. 65.
[2] C. L. Becker, *Beginnings of the American People* (New York, 1915), pp. 81-85.

CHAPTER V

THE FIRST PERMANENT SETTLEMENTS

In 1606, in the obscure English village of Scrooby, in Nottinghamshire, a little group of men, which included John Robinson, William Brewster, and William Bradford, had for some years been meeting together in Brewster's house for worship, and had formed themselves into an Independent church. Robinson was a graduate of Cambridge, and had been a Church of England clergyman in Norwich.[1] Brewster, after a short attendance at Cambridge, had become connected, in some capacity, with Davison, then Secretary of State, and had accompanied him to the Low Countries in 1585. When Davison fell from power, Brewster's career at court was ended, and at the time of the formation of the church in Scrooby, he had, for some years, been occupying the position of postmaster there, living in the old manor-house which had attracted the covetous eyes of James the First.[2] A spiritually minded man of some culture but of modest means, he was the most influential layman in the little congregation, which, for the most part, was composed of the untutored farmers and farm-hands of that remote rural district. With little or no education, without even that sharpening of wits which comes from mere contact in the more populous ways of life, they were, as their own historian has said, only such as had been "used to a plaine countrie life and the innocent trade of husbandry."[3] That historian, William Bradford, was himself of yeoman stock, and a mere

[1] O. S. Davis, *John Robinson, the Pilgrim Pastor* (Boston, 1903), pp. 62–74. *Cf.* also C. Burrage, *A Tercentenary Memorial;* Oxford, 1910; and W. H. Burgess, *The Pastor of the Pilgrims;* New York, 1920.

[2] Bradford, *History of Plymouth Plantation*, ed. by C. Deane (Boston, 1861), pp. 409 *ff.*; H. M. Dexter, *The England and Holland of the Pilgrims* (Boston, 1905), pp. 216–320. Scrooby was a halting place on the great northern post-road, and the duties of "postmaster" were more varied and important then than now.

[3] Bradford, *Plymouth*, p. 11; Dexter, *England and Holland*, pp. 379 *ff.*

lad of sixteen or so, when the Scrooby church was formed.[1] Already one of the leaders in the practical affairs of the church when scarcely more than a lad, he developed into a man of sound judgment, as well as morals, and one whose counsel was to be invaluable to the little colony in the New World, the fortunes of which he was to share and chronicle. A student, and a writer of a singularly pure English style, he seems also to have made himself familiar with Dutch, French, Latin, Greek, and Hebrew, if we may believe Cotton Mather's statement, which is, in part, borne out by other evidence.[2]

The persecution that the little band underwent before the year of their attempt to emigrate to Holland was, in the main, from neither church nor state, but only such as they had to suffer from the scoffs and jeers of their more easy-going and more commonplace neighbors and companions. In 1607, however, some one or more of these latter, possibly from a neighborly desire to pay off a grudge, apparently laid a complaint before the ecclesiastical authorities, of which the Commissioners of the Province of York had to take note; and in November, Neville, Brewster, and seven others were cited to appear. Neville, who did so, was allowed to testify without taking the usual oath, and, after a short confinement, was released without further trial. Fines were imposed upon the others for non-appearance, but beyond that no action seems to have been taken, nor were any efforts made to apprehend them.

According to the standards of the day, they were treated with leniency, and there is little to indicate that they were "harried from the land," or that either the civil or ecclesiastical authorities were anxious to interfere with them.[3] Justly dreading, however, what might happen, rather than what had happened, and, perhaps, partly influenced by some of the

---

[1] J. Hunter, *The Founders of New Plymouth* (London, 1854), pp. 101-15.

[2] Cotton Mather, *Magnalia Christi Americana* (ed. Hartford, 1855), vol. i, p. 113.

[3] R. G. Usher, *The Pilgrims and their History* (New York, 1918), pp. 19 *ff*.; F. J. Powicke, "John Robinson and the Beginning of the Pilgrim Movement," *Harvard Theological Review*, July, 1920, pp. 261 *f*. This article contains a criticism of Usher's somewhat extreme position.

motives which induced them to leave Holland later, they decided to flee from England secretly, and to establish a church in Amsterdam, whither a neighboring congregation had already gone. To take their departure legally, it would have been necessary to get the consent of the authorities—a matter having nothing more to do with religion than the granting of passports to-day. Neither money nor goods were allowed to leave England without governmental permit; and, as the Scrooby group intended to take both without such authorization, they had to leave clandestinely. About one hundred of them made the attempt, but were betrayed to the customs officers by the captain of the ship that was to transport them. A certain amount of the discomfort and unpleasant notoriety to which these simple and modest folk objected was undoubtedly of necessity incidental to the simultaneous arrest of so large a body of law-breakers. They were temporarily placed in confinement, for this purely secular offense, and were well treated by the magistrates, who "used them courteously, and showed them what favour they could." [1] The Privy Council, which had to be advised of the attempt to evade the customs laws, acted promptly; and, in spite of the slow communication in those days, within a month all but seven, who were considered the ringleaders of the fugitives, were released and sent to their homes. The seven, of whom Brewster was one, were also freed later, apparently without even having been tried.

Some of the party reached Holland safely that autumn, and others made another attempt some months after. At the very moment of embarking from an out-of-the-way place, they were surprised by some of the country people, who notified the authorities, and such of the passengers as had not got on board were again taken into custody. Although they were known to be breaking the laws, apparently no justice or court could be found to punish them; and, when again set at liberty, they finally reached Holland in safety. Neither the Privy Council nor the ecclesiastical authorities had taken any notice of the matter. Not only had there been little or no religious

[1] Bradford, *Plymouth*, p. 12.

persecution, but even when the refugees had obviously committed civil crimes these were officially condoned.[1]

After about a year in Amsterdam, owing to the quarrels that marred the life of the church earlier established, the newcomers decided to remove to Leyden, where they remained until the eventful year 1620.[2] Their life in the old university town, although hard in many ways, seems to have been singularly peaceful, and wholly unmarred by any of those petty bickerings and contentions so curiously characteristic of the ultra-godly of the period. They seem, indeed, to have valued "peace and their spirituall comforte above any other riches whatsoever," and to have lived together in "love and holiness," as Bradford wrote. Robinson was their minister, and Brewster their elder, the latter eking out his income by teaching English and printing Puritan books. The company generally set to trades and handicrafts, by which "at length they came to raise a competente and comforteable living," and won the deserved respect of their Dutch hosts.[3] They seem, however, to have lived a life apart, and to have been but little influenced by the nation with which they had cast their lot. In spite of extravagant claims to the contrary, direct Dutch influence in New England, as derived through the Pilgrims' sojourn in Holland, can be traced in but one particular, that of marriage by a civil magistrate instead of a clergyman.[4] At that time, Holland was, in almost all respects, far ahead of England intellectually. In the matter of religious toleration she was immeasurably in advance of the rest of Europe. Dutch influence would have been a noble one, indeed, in New England's history, but there is virtually nothing to indicate its presence.[5]

[1] Bradford, *Plymouth*, pp. 13–15; Usher, *Pilgrims*, pp. 27–31; E. Arber, *The Story of the Pilgrim Fathers* (London, 1897), p. 93.

[2] Bradford, *Plymouth*, pp. 16 *ff*.

[3] *Ibid*., pp. 17, 19, 412; Arber, *Pilgrim Fathers*, p. 195. Brewster taught in Latin.

[4] Bradford, *Plymouth*, pp. 101, 330.

[5] The claims put forward by Douglass Campbell, *The Puritan in Holland, England and America*, are now generally considered as thoroughly unsound. *Cf*. the article by the Dutch historian, H. T. Colenbrander, "The Dutch Element in American History," in *Annual Report of the American Historical Association*, 1909, pp. 191–203. Also, in the same report, Ruth Putnam, "The Dutch Element in the United States," pp. 203–19.

Although there were other English in Leyden, and, therefore, the size of Robinson's congregation is difficult to determine accurately, it seems to have numbered about two hundred at the time that its members were considering their third emigration, and had decided to leave Holland.[1] The reasons for this decision, as given by Bradford, were the difficulty, for many, of making a living, and the unlikelihood of attracting others; the possibility that they would themselves disperse in time; the temptations which beset their children; and their desire to spread the gospel in the new world.[2] To these, Winslow, who had joined the group about 1617, added their wish to remain Englishmen; the inability to give their children as good an education as they themselves had received; and the somewhat ambiguous reason, "how little good we did or were like to do to the Dutch in reforming the sabbath."[3] Their motives were, therefore, partly patriotic, partly economic, and partly religious, the same which, in shifting proportions and embodied in a very varied assortment of personalities, we find as mainsprings of colonization from the beginning. The one constant factor is the economic. No matter what other motives may have induced any one, from John Cabot to the last arrival at Ellis Island, to turn his face westward, added to them has ever been the hope of bettering his economic condition. America has always offered comparative material prosperity to the most idealistic as well as to the most sordid. When this factor ceases to operate, as in time, perhaps a short time, it must, American history will enter upon a new phase.

The little group of Englishmen in Leyden, who thus desired to emigrate, were without means for any such undertaking. Whatever their motives might be, it was evident that no colony could be planted, in which they were concerned, unless monied men, from the same or other motives, could be induced to risk capital in what, so far, had constantly been proved a very unprofitable business. English merchants and capital-

---

[1] Usher, *Pilgrims*, pp. 293–304; Dexter, *England and Holland*, pp. 601 *ff*.
[2] Bradford, *Plymouth*, pp. 22–24.
[3] Winslow, in Young, *Chronicles of the Pilgrim Fathers* (Boston, 1844), p. 381.

ists had already spent vast sums in the attempt to turn America to account, with but little success. The English-American balance-sheet showed a colossal amount spent in exploration and attempted development on the one page, and but a handful of people in Virginia, a feeble beginning in Bermuda, and the Newfoundland fishing fleet, on the other.

At first, the Pilgrims did not seem to realize how inadequate their resources were for such a project. Apparently, the question which they discussed most was where they should go, rather than how they should get there. Some of the more substantial and important members advocated Guiana, as they might there grow rich with little labor — which was a very human ambition.[1] Fear of tropical diseases and the Spaniard negatived this otherwise alluring plan. Thought of possible persecution vetoed the next proposition also, which was to settle somewhere near the colony already established in Virginia. The final decision was to live under the government of that company, but as a distinct body by themselves, after a grant of religious freedom should have been procured from the King. It is rather odd, in view of the persecution which they thought they had undergone, and that which they constantly seemed to fear, that they should have been so confident that the King would consent in writing to an act so far in advance of English thought. The fact that they had escaped any rigorous attack in England, and that their illegal acts on leaving had been condoned by the authorities, may have added to their hope of being so tenderly treated, which was unreasonably held out to them by "some great persons of good rancke and qualitie."[2]

In the fall of 1617, John Carver and Robert Cushman were dispatched to London to confer with Sir Edwin Sandys about the matter. Sandys was a brother of Sir Samuel Sandys, at that time lessee of the Scrooby Manor, in which Brewster had lived, and was favorably disposed toward the Leyden people. He was also a member of the East India, Bermuda, and Virginia companies, the last of which he was virtually

[1] Bradford, *Plymouth*, p. 27.   [2] *Ibid.*, pp. 28*f*.

managing at the time of the emissaries' arrival, owing to the
illness of that Company's treasurer.[1] The "Seven Articles
of the Church at Leyden," which the Pilgrims had carefully
worded in the somewhat naïve expectation that they might
satisfy the authorities without committing themselves, were
privately submitted to some of the members of the Virginia
Council, and approved; so that Sandys wrote hopefully of the
prospects to Robinson and Brewster.[2] The upshot of the
matter, however, was what might have been expected, or was
perhaps even more favorable than should reasonably have
been hoped for under the circumstances. The King would
not grant them toleration under his "broad seale, according to
their desires," which would naturally have got him into serious
difficulties politically; but, apparently, he did agree to "con-
nive at them, and not molest them, provided they carried
themselves peaceably."[3] They wisely decided that, if this
were not enough, nothing would be, for, if the King meant to
wrong them "though they had a seale as broad as the house
floor, it would not serve the turne, for ther would be means
enow found to recall or revers it."[4] With this and, perhaps,
the vain regret that they had not let sleeping dogs lie, they
had to be content.

The next step was to secure a patent, and find "adventurers,"
— as men were still called who invested in such enterprises,—
who would supply the necessary money. Owing to the dissen-
sions in the Virginia Company, which now became acute, the negotiations were delayed; but on April 19, 1619, that company
elected Sandys treasurer; and a patent, taken out in the name
of John Wincob, "comended to the Company by the Earle of
Lincolne," received its seal June 9.[5] This was never made use

[1] Brown, *Genesis*, pp. 991–94.

[2] Correspondence in Bradford, *Plymouth*, pp. 31–38. The articles are reprinted by
E. D. Neill, *History of the Virginia Company of London* (Albany, 1869), pp. 123 *f.*;
Arber, *Pilgrim Fathers*, pp. 280 *f.*; and elsewhere.

[3] Bradford, *Plymouth*, pp. 29 *ff.*

[4] *Ibid.*, p. 30.

[5] *Records of the Virginia Company of London* (Washington, 1906), vol. I, pp. 221,
228. Its date was not known when Palfrey wrote. Bradford gives few dates, and
the exact sequence of events is much a matter of inference. The Wincob patent has
not been preserved, and its terms are unknown.

of, and apparently the one they intended to utilize was that previously granted to John Pierce, on February 2, antedating a later one to the same person.[1]

During the following months, their efforts to raise money became known both in Holland and in England. The Dutch, now become the most important colonizing power, tried to induce them to settle either in Zealand or on the Hudson River; and they also received offers from an English merchant, Thomas Weston, who ran over from London on the scent of business. He finally prevailed upon them to make an agreement with himself and his associates. His own motives, as amply proved by events, were wholly mercenary, as were those of most of the other outsiders who financed the enterprise. The planting of the first permanent colony in New England was due to the desire for gain on the part of these ordinary business men, who risked a large sum, and made heavy losses, as well as to the higher motives of some of the actual emigrants, whose character, sense, and patience rescued the enterprise from disaster. The infant colony was the child of two parents, and the share of each in its creation must be recognized, even if one were vulgar and sordid, and subsequently disinherited its offspring.

The agreement, which became the subject of bitter controversy, created a joint stock, divided into shares of £10 each. Every person, over sixteen years of age, who went as an emigrant received one share free, and a second if he fitted himself out to that amount, or paid for his transportation. On the one hand, the results of the entire labor of the colonists were to go to this joint fund, and, on the other, all their food, clothing, and other necessities were to be provided for them out of the stock. At the end of seven years, the entire fund, with its accumulations, including houses, lands, and cash on hand, was to be divided, pro rata, among all the shareholders, the expectation being that the profits would accrue mainly from fishing and the Indian trade.

[1] *Records of the Virginia Company*, vol. 1, p. 303. On Feb. 16, it was stated at a meeting of the Company that Pierce's colonists did not intend to sail for two or three months. *Ibid.*, p. 311. This early patent is connected with the Pilgrims by inference only, which, however, seems reasonable.

The emigrants had anticipated that two days a week would be allowed them for their own profit, and that, at the end of the seven-year period, they would retain individual possession of their houses and improved lands. Indeed, it was only after they were so far committed to the scheme that many of them could not well turn back, that they found this was not to be the case.[1] The merchants, however, can hardly be blamed for refusing to allow so large a vent for possible profits to slip through. It was the general custom at the time for any one going to the colonies, who could not pay his way, to become an indentured servant for seven years in exchange for his transportation.

The suggestion of the emigrants that one third of their working time, and the permanent improvements, as well as the land on which they lived, should accrue to themselves, and in no part to those who were providing the means, must have seemed as grasping to the Adventurers as their attitude, in turn, seems to have been considered by the Pilgrims. The exact amount put into the venture by the capitalists, during their connection with it, cannot now be determined accurately; but according to Captain John Smith, there were about seventy of them, and the joint stock invested up to 1624 was about £7,000.[2] The greater part must have been subscribed by the Adventurers, not by the emigrants; so that, making all due allowances for the share contributed by the latter, and for returns made subsequently by their efforts in America, the final loss on the part of the capitalists was very heavy. Their judgment as to the risk their money was running was thus unpleasantly justified. They were not subscribing to foreign missions, but employing their capital in a purely business venture, and the terms, as business was conducted at that time, cannot be considered as at all harsh. Cushman, in London, who was acting as agent for the Leyden people, fearing the failure of the entire enterprise if the merchants' terms were not accepted, exceeded his authority, and agreed

[1] The text of agreement and objections is in Bradford, *Plymouth*, pp. 45 *ff*.
[2] Smith, *Works*, vol. II, p. 783.

to them, to the great resentment of his principals, who refused to sign the revised contract.

Meanwhile, a small ship, the Speedwell, which it was intended to take to Virginia and keep there, had been bought in Holland, and a larger one, the Mayflower, chartered in London to carry the major part of the colony.[1] The two vessels were to meet at Southampton, and make the passage together. It had been decided that, if a majority of the congregation voted to remain in Leyden, Robinson should stay with them, Brewster becoming the spiritual leader of those who should go. As this proved to be the case, the members of the little party which at last sailed from Delft Haven there took their final leave of their beloved pastor.[2] Their debt to him had been great. His gentle spirit, humble seeking of ever more light, and broad tolerance of mind, shone almost alone in that period of intolerant dogmatism and persecuting zeal, alike of Churchman and Puritan. "We ought," he wrote, "to be firmly persuaded in our hearts of the truth, and goodness of the religion, which we embrace in all things; yet as knowing ourselves to be men, whose property it is to err and to be deceived in many things; and accordingly both to converse with men in that modesty of mind, as always to desire to learn something better, or further, by them, if it may be."[3] He recognized that "men are for the most part minded for, or against toleration of diversity of religion, according to the conformity which they themselves hold, or hold not, with the country, or kingdom, where they live. Protestants living in the countries of Papists commonly plead for toleration of religion: so do Papists that live where Protestants bear sway:

---

[1] The captain was Christopher Jones, and not the Captain Thomas Jones of unsavory memory. J. R. Hutchinson, "The Mayflower, her Identity and Tonnage," *New England Historical and Genealogical Register*, vol. LXX, pp. 337–42. Also Usher, *Pilgrims*, p. 72. The ship is thought to have been in the wine trade for several years; and as a wine ship was known among sailors as a "sweet" ship, this may have had something to do with the remarkable health of the Pilgrims on the voyage. For disease on shipboard during that period, *cf.* Oppenheim, *Administration of the Royal Navy*, vol. I, p. 136. Drake on his famous voyage lost 600 out of a crew of 2,300.

[2] Bradford, *Plymouth*, pp. 42, 60.

[3] John Robinson, *Works* (Boston, 1851), vol. I, p. 39.

though few of either, *specially of the clergy*, as they are called, would have the other tolerated, where the world goes on their side." [1] In his farewell address to his flock shortly before their leaving, he dwelt particularly upon the need of their being open-minded, for "he was very confident that the Lord had more truth and light yet to break forth out of his holy word," and so his followers should "follow him no further than he followed Christ." [2] It is unlikely that such doctrines were wholly grasped by all his humble followers, but the influence of his life and teaching were felt long after in the little church of Plymouth; and the spirit which, in general, animated that colony must have been derived in large measure from the rare spirituality of its first pastor in the Old World.

In the latter part of July the Speedwell reached Southampton, where the Mayflower had already arrived, and whither Weston had also gone for a final conference. On finding it impossible to make the Pilgrims accept the changes in the agreement, he left them, telling them "they must then looke to stand on their own leggs," and even refused to pay £100, which was necessary to adjust matters in Southampton before their sailing. Provisions were sold to settle the debt, and both ships cleared for America early in August. Owing to the leakiness of the small Speedwell, it was necessary to put back to Dartmouth, where repairs were made. After a second start, the Speedwell still giving trouble, both vessels put into Plymouth, where it was decided to leave some of the company behind, and proceed in the Mayflower alone.[3] One hundred and two passen-

---

[1] Robinson, *Works*, vol. 1, p. 40. The italics are mine. *Cf.* Buckle, *History of Civilization*, vol. 1, p. 337: "In every Christian country where it [toleration] has been adopted, it has been forced upon the clergy by the authority of the secular classes."

[2] Winslow, in Young, *Chronicles*, p. 397. Dr. H. M. Dexter has vigorously attacked the idea of Robinson's having been broad-minded in the modern sense, and thinks his words refer only to church discipline and not to belief. *Congregationalism in the last 300 Years*, pp. 400 *ff*. From a study of Robinson's writings, I cannot agree with him. *Cf.* Davis (*John Robinson*, pp. 241–65), who also disagrees with Dexter; and the very just estimate by H. H. Henson, *Studies in Religion in the 17th Century* (London, 1903), pp. 234 *ff.*; and W. W. Fenn, "John Robinson's Farewell Address," *Harvard Theological Review*, July, 1920, pp. 236 *ff*.

[3] Bradford, *Plymouth*, pp. 68 *ff*.

gers crowded into the little vessel, the company being made up of thirty-five of the Leyden congregation and the remainder from London.[1] Cushman stayed behind; but, on the other hand, an invaluable accession was made in the person of Captain Myles Standish. This little "Captain Shrimp," as Morton of Merry Mount nicknamed him, although not a Puritan, remained a staunch friend to the colonists, and with his little "army" of a dozen or less, stood as a shield between them and their enemies, white and red. He was short in stature and in temper. "A little chimney is soon fired," Hubbard wrote of him. But he could also be as gentle as he was valiant; and the first service he rendered the infant colony was not in fighting the Indians, but in tenderly nursing his new friends through the sickness of the first winter.

Finally, their "troubles being blowne over, and now all being compacte togeather in one shipe, they put to sea againe with a prosperous winde," heavily laden with passengers, a vast amount of ghostly furniture, and the first consignment of the New England conscience. After falling in with Cape Cod, on the 19th of November, they ran among dangerous shoals in their effort to pass southward to reach Hudson's river, and so resolved to put back, casting anchor two days later in the harbor of Provincetown.[2] Much speculation has been indulged in as to their reasons for not going farther; but the obvious ones would seem as good as any, and there is no cause to suspect treachery on the part of Captain Jones of the Mayflower, the Dutch, or others.[3]

As has been noted, only about one third of the company were of the Leyden people. The other sixty-seven were evidently a very mixed lot, comprising undesirable characters, as well as some excellent ones. As it was now decided to settle in the nearest suitable spot, they knew that they would be outside

[1] The list is in Bradford, *Plymouth*, pp. 447-55; *cf.* also Dexter, *England and Holland*, p. 650.
[2] Bradford, *Plymouth*, p. 77.
[3] First suggested by Nathaniel Morton in his *Memorial*, 1669 (ed. Boston, 1855), p. 22. The statement is now generally discredited, though frequently repeated. Dr. Ames, *The Mayflower and her Log*, pp. 100 *ff.*, attempted to revive it by identifying Christopher Jones with the now discarded Thomas.

the jurisdiction of the Virginia Company, and, therefore, also outside the bounds of their own patent. Some of the London element, taking advantage of that fact, boasted openly that they did not intend to be ruled by anyone, but "would use their owne libertie." [1] It was evident to the more substantial members that, if order were to be maintained on shore, some responsible government would have to be created, backed by sufficient show of public opinion and force to keep the unruly in subjection. Before anyone was permitted to land, therefore, the famous Mayflower Compact was drawn up, by which the signers agreed to combine themselves into a "civill body politick" for their order and preservation, and by virtue of it to enact necessary laws and to elect officers. [2] This short document, the body of which is but seven lines, was not intended to be a new departure in state constitutions, but was a perfectly simple extension of the ordinary form of church covenant, with which they were familiar, to cover the crisis in their civil affairs which they now faced. As events developed, however, it came about that the Compact remained the only basis on which the independent civil government in Plymouth rested, as the colonists were never able to get a charter conferring rights of jurisdiction. It was the first example of that "plantation covenant" which was to form the basis of the river towns of Connecticut, of New Haven, and of so many other town and colony governments in that land of covenants, ecclesiastical and civil. [3] From the exigencies of the case, rather than from any preconceived philosophical notions, the first settlers thus established a pure democracy, which was subsequently modified. At first, however, the entire male population met in a body which constituted a General Court, and was the source of all local political power and judicial decisions.

The document was signed by forty-one men, of whom only seventeen were from Leyden. It may here be noted that the

[1] Bradford, *Plymouth*, pp. 89 *ff*.

[2] The compact is in Bradford, *Plymouth*, pp. 89 *f.*; the list of signers in Morton, *Memorial*, p. 26.

[3] *Cf.* Osgood, *American Colonies*, vol. I, p. 291.

usual historical method of approach to the settlement of Plymouth, which is by way of Scrooby and Holland, is, to a certain extent, misleading. The capital, which made the enterprise possible, was practically all subscribed in London. Of the first emigrants but a third belonged to Robinson's congregation, and, in the entire Pilgrim movement to America, only a dozen or so persons, at most, can be even remotely traced to the neighborhood of Scrooby.[1]   It is true that the Scrooby leaven, in the persons of Brewster and Bradford, and the influence of Robinson, leavened the whole Plymothean mass; but, if we had the documents, which we have not, it would be instructive to hear the story from the standpoint of the Londoners, both capitalists and colonists.

The first few weeks were occupied in searching for a site for settlement; and it was only on the third expedition in their little shallop that the exploring party finally landed at Plymouth, on December 21.[2]   Having found the harbor fit for shipping, and the site possible for a settlement, they decided to search no farther.   "It was the best they could find, and the season, and their presente necessitie, made them glad to accepte of it," wrote Bradford, somewhat unenthusiastically.[3]

Five days later, the Mayflower herself arrived from Provincetown, and the people began the erection of the first common house for themselves and their goods — a log hut about twenty feet square, with a thatched roof.   Soon, however, they abandoned building in common, and "agreed that every man should build his own house, thinking that by that course men would make more haste," so promptly did human nature and winter's cold assert themselves over theory.   The season, though stormy, happily proved unusually mild.   Fortunately, also, the great sickness which had recently decimated the Indians, had killed off almost the entire native population about Plymouth and Massachusetts bays, and completely

[1] Dexter, *England and Holland*, p. 650.
[2] The celebration of "Forefathers Day," for many years, on Dec. 22, was due to a mistake in transposing Old-Style dates into New.   In any case, there was, of course, no such "landing" of the whole company as appears in popular tradition.
[3] Bradford, *Plymouth*, p. 88.

broken the spirit of the remainder, though this was as yet unknown to the settlers, who lived in constant fear of attack.[1]
They occupied but a clearing on the edge of the vast and
unknown wilderness. Mysterious and unexplored, it stretched
interminably before them, while the midwinter North Atlantic
tossed as endlessly behind them. In the woods, Indian yells
had been heard, and an occasional savage had been seen skulk-
ing behind cover. John Goodman, going for a walk one evening with his dog, suddenly found the small beast taking refuge
between his legs, chased by two wolves. He threw a stick at
them, whereupon "they sat both on their tails grinning at
him a good while."

Soon, owing to exposure, many of the settlers fell ill; and so
quickly did the disease spread, and so fatal were its effects,
that by the end of March forty-four, or nearly one half of the
little company, were dead. Sometimes two or three died in
a day, and but six or seven were well enough to nurse the
living and bury the corpses. Their kindness and courage
under these trials were beyond all praise. Before the arrival
of the first supply ship, in the following autumn, six more
had died, including the governor, Carver, so that only one half
the company remained. But the little colony was not to be
crushed.

Bradford was elected in Carver's place, and in March, in
spite of the terrors which encompassed them, in spite of the
graves of the dead, which far outnumbered the homes of the
living, Winslow could yet note that "the birds sang in the
woods most pleasantly."

Suddenly, toward the end of that month, at the very moment
when they were debating questions of defense, an Indian
walked boldly into the settlement, and bade them welcome in
English. The savage, Samoset by name, proceeded to give
them much useful information about the natives, and from
him, apparently, the settlers first learned of the great mor-

[1] The nature of the disease is unknown. It was evidently neither yellow fever nor
smallpox, as some have thought, and white men were not affected, even when they
slept in the same huts with the Indians. *Cf.* C. F. Adams, *Three Episodes in Massachusetts History* (Boston, 1893), vol. i, pp. 1-4.

tality among them. After spending the night, he was dismissed with gifts, promising to bring others of the natives with him on his return. This he did a few days later, the savages bringing with them some tools which they had stolen a while before, and which they now restored. A week later, Samoset and another Indian, named Squanto, who was the only survivor of the group which had dwelt where the Pilgrims had settled, came to announce the arrival of the great sachem himself, Massasoit. With him, the settlers made a treaty of peace and friendship, which was honorably maintained on both sides for over half a century, the Indian proving himself a loyal friend to the English until his death in 1662.[1]

The sachem's visit was returned in July, Winslow and Hopkins making the journey of forty miles, with the ever-useful Squanto as guide. During the summer, the colonists were joined also by another Indian, Hobomack, who made his home with them, and continued faithful during his life. In spite of some minor troubles, due to the childish jealousy and desire to appear important on the part of the two savages, the debt that the settlers owed to them cannot be overestimated. They not only served as interpreters and intermediaries with the other Indians, but taught the colonists how to plant and manure the native corn and where to catch fish, acted as guides about the country, and made themselves generally invaluable. These services were not regarded wholly with favor by some of the Indians who were opposed to the whites, and the settlers had to teach the sachem Corbitant a sharp lesson, to make them leave their two Indian friends alone.[2]

The Mayflower, having been detained by the sickness of her crew, as well as by that prevailing on shore, until the middle of April, had then sailed for home, none of the planters abandoning the enterprise to sail with her. Needless to say, there had been no opportunity to gather cargo to send to the merchants in England before her sailing. With the summer, however,

[1] The treaty is in Bradford, *Plymouth*, pp. 94 *ff*. The minor incidents in connection with Plymouth in this chapter, when references are not given, are all taken from Bradford, or Bradford and Winslow, the latter as given in Young's *Chronicles*.

[2] Bradford, *Plymouth*, pp. 102 *ff*.; Young, *Chronicles*, pp. 202–14, 218–23.

health had returned, and there had been a moderate degree
of comfort, as well as abundance of food, at Plymouth; so that
in September, under the guidance of Squanto, the Pilgrims
undertook their first trading voyage, sailing to Massachusetts
Bay. Their plan had been both to explore the country and
to make peace with the Indians of that district, as well as to
"procure their truck." Although gone only four days, the
little party of thirteen, under command of Standish, were
eminently successful in all three objects, making the first beginning, on any large scale, of that trade which was to prove
their financial salvation. In fact the Bible and the beaver
were the two mainstays of the young colony. The former
saved its morale, and the latter paid its bills; and the rodent's
share was a large one. The original foundations of New York,
New England, and Canada all rest on the Indian trade, in
which the item of beaver-skins was by far the most important
and lucrative.

Having thus got together a good store of pelts and some
clapboards, they were able to despatch the Fortune, which
had arrived in November, back to England within a fortnight
after her arrival, with their first consignment, worth £500, all
of which was lost to them by the capture of the ship by the
French.[1] A long letter from Weston, brought from England
by Cushman, complained bitterly and unreasonably of their
having returned no cargo in the Mayflower, and also brought
word that a new patent had been obtained for them from the
Council of New England, in the name of John Pierce and his
associates.[2]

There had also arrived on the Fortune thirty-five persons to
remain in the colony, evidently sent by the merchants, and
with practically no supplies of any kind. They were made
welcome by the Pilgrims, who were ever hospitable, not alone
to those who differed from them in doctrine, but even to their
avowed enemies, so long as either needed their help. Bradford noted that they were glad of this addition to their strength,

[1] Bradford, *Plymouth*, pp. 105 *ff.*; Young, *Chronicles*, pp. 234 *ff.*
[2] *Mass. Hist. Soc. Coll.*, Series IV, vol. II, pp. 158 *ff.*

though he "wished that many of them had been of better condition, and all of them better furnished with provisions."
The colonists, who had but recently been congratulating themselves on having ample food for the coming winter, due to their
own efforts, had now to be put on very short commons; and
it was not until the gathering of the crops in the autumn of
the following year that they again had a sufficient supply.

The addition to their numbers, however, must have increased
their feeling of security in the Indian troubles which soon
threatened them. The powerful Narragansetts, who were hostile both to the Pilgrims and to their native allies, and who
had suffered but slightly from the plague, sent them a challenge
in the form of a bundle of arrows tied in a snake-skin. Squanto
having interpreted the message, they returned the skin stuffed
with powder and shot, with word to the natives that "if they
had rather have warr then peace, they might begin when they
would." Nevertheless, in spite of their "high words and lofty
looks," Winslow wrote, they were not a little anxious, and took
all the precautions possible, including the building of a palisade about the village. Nothing came of the episode, however, except the anxiety of the settlers, which was increased
the following summer by the receipt of a letter telling them of
the great and sudden massacre at Jamestown.[1] So greatly
were they then worried that they faced another winter of short
rations more willingly than they did the savages, and took
much valuable time from the tilling of their crops for the building of a fort.

Until the great immigration into Massachusetts Bay, in
1630, Plymouth continued to be the largest single settlement
in New England; but, from 1622 onward, there were scattered
beginnings at other points along the coast, many of which
proved permanent. Gorges endeavored to put new life into
colonization, and in that year published his "Briefe Narration"
of the efforts he had made heretofore.[2] In less than two months

---

[1] The letter was sent to them by a stranger, John Hudlston, whose name deserves
to be remembered for his thoughtful kindness. It is in Bradford, *Plymouth*, pp. 124 *f.*

[2] Reprinted in *Mass. Hist. Soc. Coll.*, Series II, vol. IX, pp. 1–25.

after the granting of Pierce's patent for the benefit of the Pilgrims, another grant was made to Captain John Mason of all the lands lying between the Naumkeag and Merrimac rivers, and extending from their heads to the seacoast, thus including the shore from Salem to Newburyport.[1] In August, a third grant was passed, to Mason and Gorges jointly, of the coast from the Merrimac eastward to the Kennebec, extending sixty miles inland, and including all islands within fifteen miles of the shore, to be called the Province of Maine.[2] Other grants were also made in the same year,[3] and a small settlement may have been begun at Nantasket.[4]

Of more immediate interest to the people of Plymouth than paper principalities or small fishing stations, of which there were probably many along the coast, used annually at certain seasons, was the attempt made by their own financial backer, Thomas Weston, to establish a private and rival trading colony almost at their very door.   Profits not having come in as rapidly as he had anticipated, he had sold out his holdings in the enterprise to his associates, and now intended to plant and trade for his own account, getting all he could from the Pilgrims.   Although he attempted to misrepresent the new relation which he now bore toward them, it was not long before they learned the truth from their friends at home.   Toward the end of May, a small shallop arrived with seven of his men, whom he had detached from a fishing vessel of his at Damaris Cove, near Monhegan, and sent to Plymouth to be cared for.   Soon followed word of his having broken with the company, and of his having procured a separate patent for himself.   By the vessel which brought this news arrived also sixty more of his colonists, who were set ashore at Plymouth, by the Charity, which then proceeded to Virginia.   Well and sick, the whole

[1] Printed in C. W. Tuttle, *Capt. John Mason* (Prince Soc., Boston, 1887), pp. 170–77. *Cf. Ibid.*, pp. 45–52.

[2] *Ibid.*, pp. 177–83.

[3] For list of grants *cf.* S. F. Haven, "History of Grants under the Great Council for New England," in *Lowell Lectures*, Boston, 1869; also the two volumes of the *Farnham Papers*; Maine Historical Society, Portland, 1901–2.

[4] S. G. Drake, *The History and Antiquities of Boston;* Boston, 1856. *Cf.* Winsor, *Memorial History*, vol. 1, p. 79.

sixty-seven remained a burden upon the Pilgrims, until, the Charity having returned, they sailed in her to Wessagusset, now Weymouth, where they seated themselves. An unruly crew, with no leadership, and utterly unfitted for colonizing, they were soon short of provisions. A joint voyage to the southward, made by some of them and of the Pilgrims, resulted in securing but little corn, the expedition having had to be abandoned on account of the death of Squanto, who, as usual, was serving as guide.

As the winter passed, the Wessagusset men slowly starved. Their attitude toward the natives was the height of folly, and the somewhat hostile Massachusetts Indians, perceiving their plight, formed a plot to exterminate both settlements at once. This was revealed to the Pilgrims by Massasoit, who, at this most opportune moment, had been cured by them of what his followers had thought a deadly sickness. The crisis was a serious one, and the Pilgrims acted promptly. Feigning a trading voyage, Standish and eight men went to Wessagusset, inveigled the ringleaders into one of the houses, and there slew them. Pecksuot, who had personally insulted Standish, was killed with his own knife, which the captain snatched from around his neck; and, in all, six savages were slain on the expedition. Three of Weston's men, who, in spite of warnings, had gone to stay with the Indians, were murdered by them in retaliation. Most of the remainder, refusing the Pilgrims' offer to care for them at Plymouth, sailed for Monhegan, in the hope of finding passage to England.[1] Weston himself, arriving soon after, found his colony deserted, and himself ruined. On reaching Plymouth, after having been robbed and stripped by the Indians, he unblushingly borrowed capital from the compassionate Pilgrims in order to set himself up as a trader.

Another of the capitalists also gave the Pilgrims trouble by trying the same plan of planting a colony of his own. On the 30th of April, 1622, Pierce, in whose name their patent stood, obtained another, which, on the same day, he exchanged for

[1] Young, *Chronicles*, pp. 314-45.

a deed-pole, by which he became the owner of the lands on which Plymouth was settled. Having thus cut the ground from under the Pilgrims' feet, he proceeded to send out a hundred and nine colonists for his own account. The ship was forced to turn back, however; and finally, the Pilgrims, on making complaint to the Council for New England, had their original rights confirmed, upon payment to Pierce of £500.[1]

These troubles, which occupied their minds in the early summer of 1623, were soon followed by the arrival of Captain West, who had been commissioned Admiral of New England, and sent to collect license fees from the fishermen along the coast. These proved to be "stuborne fellows," however, and the only result of West's brief attempt at authority was to bring up anew in Parliament the fight for free fishing and the opposition to the monopoly created by the New England Council. Robert Gorges also came over as Governor of New England, accompanied by the Rev. William Morell, who was to superintend ecclesiastical affairs in the interest of the Church of England; but, although Gorges spent the winter at Weston's abandoned site, nothing more came of this high-sounding scheme to govern the wilderness.

Among the passengers in the Anne, which arrived at Plymouth in the same summer of 1623, were some few who were not to belong to the general body, or be subject to the rules of joint trading, but came on "their perticuler," as Bradford describes it. An agreement was soon made with them, debarring them from the Indian trade until the period of joint trading should end, and otherwise defining their status in the community. Such an anomalous group within the body politic naturally tended to trouble, nor were leaders lacking who endeavored to fan the sparks into a blaze. Among the "perticulers" was a rough-and-ready trader named John Oldham, a man of considerable practical ability, but heady, self-willed, and of an ungovernable temper. In the following spring appeared also a canting hypocritical clergyman, John Lyford

---

[1] Bradford, *Plymouth*, pp. 138–41; Records of Council for New England, *Proceedings American Antiquarian Society*, April, 1866, pp. 91–93.

by name, who seems to have been a sort of lascivious Uriah Heep. Pretending great humility, he was honorably received by the Pilgrims, as they thought befitting a clergyman, and was given a seat in the Governor's Council. Soon, however, he and Oldham joined forces, and gathered together the various malcontents of the colony, without any very clear idea, apparently, beyond that of fishing in troubled waters, in the hope of making some profitable catch. The waters were troubled enough at this juncture, for the factions among the Adventurers at home were then at their height. To the party there adverse to the Pilgrim interest, Oldham and Lyford dispatched letters, containing matter distinctly inimical to the established order. These were read and copied by Bradford, in the cabin of the ship which was to bear them, unknown to the senders. The latter, indeed, had some suspicions, and "were somewhat blanke at it, but after some weeks, when they heard nothing, they were as brisk as ever," like boys relieved from the fear of having been caught in mischief. In fact, they became so brisk that Oldham, when called upon to do his turn of guard duty by Standish, refused and raised a tumult.

The grotesque effect of their next stroke was naturally lost upon people who, with all their excellent qualities, were, unhappily for themselves, very obviously lacking in the saving grace of humor. The curiously assorted couple decided to set up a church of their own. The thought of Oldham, "a mad Jack in his mood," and the sniveling clergyman, whose innumerable light loves had brought so many heavy sorrows, reforming the Pilgrims' church is one of the bits which lighten the somewhat sombre recital of those frontier days. A General Court was convened, and the two were brought to trial. Both of them were sentenced to banishment, Oldham to go at once, and Lyford to have six months' grace, although the former seems to have been rather the more respectable, as he was much the more masculine, of the two. Oldham went, but, having nursed his wrath, he suddenly returned in March, for the sole purpose, apparently, of exploding it upon the yet unreformed Pilgrims, who, however, merely "committed him till he was tamer." Lyford, meanwhile, had utilized his reprieve to write home again, criticizing the government of the colony, and making some just complaints, on the part of the large minority, of the required conformity of worship. The sentence of banishment was then enforced, and both rebels betook themselves temporarily to Nantasket.[1]

In the same summer in which the Pilgrims had acquired Lyford and Oldham, an addition of about sixty other persons had also been made to the colony, some of them "very usefull" to the settlers, and some of them "so bad, as they were faine to be at charge to send them home againe the next year."[2] Other settlements, too, continued to be planted along the coast. Robert Gorges, who had received a grant of some three hundred square miles on the northeast side of Massachusetts Bay, but who had settled his men at Wessagusset, left some of them there when he returned to England, and the permanent occupation of that section was begun.[3] In 1623, David Thompson established himself at the mouth of the Piscataqua; while Edward and William Hilton may soon after have settled some miles up the river, thus founding the modern towns of Portsmouth and Dover. Christopher Levett, who was one of Robert Gorges's Council, made a short-lived plantation at York, and a permanent colony was effected on Monhegan.[4] For the greater convenience of their fishing operations, which were never successful, the Pilgrims had secured a grant of land at Cape Ann, and erected a fishing stage there, although the grant, which was derived from Lord Sheffield, was of questionable validity.[5] A fishing company was formed of Dorchester men in England, who made a little settlement on the Cape, holding

[1] Bradford, *Plymouth*, pp. 183 *ff*.   [2] *Ibid.*, p. 142.

[3] Haven, *Lowell Lectures*, p. 154; Adams, *Three Episodes*, vol. I, p. 144; Hazard, *Historical Collections*, vol. I, p. 391. In regard to the settlement by Thompson, we have documentary evidence in *New Hampshire State Papers*, vol. xxv, pp. 715, 734; but there is no such proof of the traditionary settlement by Hilton, until 1628, although it is accepted by the earlier historians. *Cf.* W. H. Fry, *New Hampshire as a Royal Province* (New York, 1908), pp. 18, 32. Also, J. G. Jenness, *Notes on the First Planting of New Hampshire* (Portsmouth, 1878), pp. 4, 14 *ff*.

[4] Burrage, *Colonial Maine*, pp. 169–75; J. P. Baxter, *Christopher Levett of York*, Gorges Society, Portland, 1893; Bradford, *Plymouth*, p. 154.

[5] J. W. Thornton, *The Landing at Cape Anne* (Boston, 1854), pp. 31 *ff*.

it of the Plymouth people.[1] Although the undertaking was unprofitable, and always a source of trouble to the Pilgrims, it is of interest owing to the connection with it of some of those who were later influential in England in organizing the Massachusetts colony.

About 1625, individuals also seem to have established themselves at Shawmut, at Noddle's Island, and on the Mystic River; and, a year later, Thompson removed from the Piscataqua, and settled on the island which has since borne his name in Boston Harbor.[2] Farther eastward, John Brown, by 1625, had founded a settlement at New Harbor, on the eastern shore of Pemaquid; and in the next five years, eighty-four families had located there, on St. Georges River, and at Sheepscot.[3] A station had also been established at Old Orchard Bay, while the importance of Monhegan as a centre for Indian trading is proved by large transactions there as early as 1626.[4]

Thus, the inhabitants of Plymouth, after the middle of the first decade of their settlement, were evidently outnumbered by the other permanent settlers, who were likewise founding New England. Some of these we know to have been of the established Church, as were Gorges and Mason, the proprietors of a large section of the territory; while of the majority, we know only that they were traders and planters, who were quite evidently in New England to make their fortunes, and for no other reason.

In 1625, there sailed into Boston Bay and New England history, a certain "man of pretie parts," by name Captain Wollaston, a convivial sport named Thomas Morton, and "a great many servants, with provisions and other implements for to begine a plantation." Among the implements was obviously a prodigious supply of strong waters. They "pitched them-

[1] Smith, *Works*, vol. II, p. 783; Bradford, *Plymouth*, pp. 168 f.; John White, *The Planter's Plea* (Force Tracts, Washington, 1838), vol. II, pp. 38 ff.; Wm. Hubbard, *History of New England* (Cambridge, 1815), pp. 102 ff.

[2] J. Winsor, *Memorial History*, vol. I, pp. 78, 83; C. F. Adams, "Old Planters about Boston Harbor," *Mass. Hist. Soc. Proceedings*, Series I, vol. XVI, p. 206.

[3] Burrage, *Colonial Maine*, pp. 78, 83. [4] *Ibid.*, pp. 183, 199.

selves in a place" within the present town of Quincy, calling
their settlement Mt. Wollaston, after their leader. He, however, like some others before and since, did not find life in New
England to "answer his expectations," and carried off a number of his servants to Virginia, where he sold them at a good
figure, and took his exit from the stage of history.

Thomas Morton, of Cliffords Inn, Gent., whose literary portrait has come down to us in the somewhat unreliable form of
an appreciation by himself, supplemented by sundry exceedingly unflattering sketches by his enemies, now proceeded to
take control of the situation in a manner entirely satisfactory
to himself, the rest of the stranded Quincy band, and, it was
darkly rumored, the less virtuous of the Indian squaws. He
suggested to the remaining servants that, instead of allowing
themselves to be transported to Virginia, they should stay
with him as copartners, he having had a share in the enterprise;
and that, together, they should thrust out Wollaston's lieutenant. To this they willingly agreed, and matters proceeded
merrily. Morton, who, whatever his failings, was a thorough
sportsman and passionately fond of outdoor life, became a
great favorite with the Indians, and trade was brisk. It must
have been, if Bradford's report that they sometimes drank
ten pounds' worth of liquor in a morning is to be credited,
as the liquor certainly was not. "They also set up a May-
pole," wrote the scandalized Pilgrim, "drinking and dancing
aboute it many days togeather, inviting the Indian women,
for their consorts, dancing and frisking together like so many
fairies or furies" and revived "the beasley practicses of the
madd Bacchinalians." [1]

The joy of life had, indeed, made one other feeble effort to
acclimatize itself in the frosty New England air on Christmas
Day, in Plymouth, four years before. Most of the then recent
arrivals, constituting, perhaps, a third of the entire community,
had had the hardihood to wish to refrain from work on that
day, and to celebrate it "in the streete at play, openly" with

[1] Bradford, *Plymouth*, pp. 237 *ff.*; Morton, *New English Canaan* (Force Tracts),
vol. II, 89 *ff.*

such ungodliness as pitching a bar and playing ball.[1] That, however, with a certain show of grim humor, had been successfully repressed, as was the May-pole of Merry Mount, on the arrival of Endicott in Massachusetts.

When the echoes of Morton's mad songs died for the last time among the pines of Quincy, rigid conformity to the Puritanical code of manners and morals had won its second victory. Repression and conformity, the two key-notes of Puritan New England, were to continue to mould the life of her people throughout the long "glacial age" of her early history. They did not, indeed, produce universal morality, but they produced the outward semblance of it, and a vast deal of hypocrisy. If they must revel, Bradford told the ball-players, let them do it out of sight, "since which time nothing hath been attempted that way, at least openly." Twenty years later, as he meditated upon the extraordinary amount of crime of unnamable sorts, which, as he wrote, had developed in New England "as in no place more, or so much, that I have known or heard of," the possibility did, indeed, occur to him that, among other reasons, it might be "as it is with waters when their streams are stopped or damed up, when they gett passage they flow with more violence."[2]

In spite of the good which Puritanism did as a protest against the prevailing immorality, it must be admitted also, that, in taking from the laboring classes and others so much of their opportunity for recreation of all sorts, it undoubtedly fostered greatly the grosser forms of vice, and helped to multiply the very sins it most abhorred. Those who lacked the taste or temperament to find their relief from the deadly monotony of long hours of toil in theological exposition, and who were debarred from their old-time sports, turned to drunkenness and sexual immorality, both of which were frequent in Puritan New England.

The attempt to erect the moral opinion of a minority into a

[1] The colony numbered about 85. The newcomers were 35, and Bradford says (*Plymouth*, p. 112), "the most of this new-company" were guilty of the attempt.

[2] Bradford, *Plymouth*, p. 385.

legal code binding upon all was not, by any means, confined
to that section alone at the beginning of the seventeenth century.   It was, and is, a characteristic of Puritanism wherever
found.   At the very time that Bradford was condemning the
Christmas sports of Plymouth, the authorities in Bermuda, for
example, were passing laws requiring that there should be
haled to court all "Sabath breakers" who were such "by
absenting themselves from church, or leaving during service,"
or "by using any bodily recreation by gaminge, sportinge, or
by doing any servile work as travelling, fyshinge, cuttinge of
wood, digginge of potatoes, carryinge of burdens, beatinge of
corne," together with a long list of other misdemeanors.   New
England Sabbatarian legislation never went further.   Even
that petty spying upon one another, to detect sins to be reported to the church, which must have been such an unpleasant
form of keeping one's brother in New England, was by no
means indigenous there.   The "churchwardens and sydes-
men," continued the Bermudian law, "shall dailie observe the
carriage and lives of the people, and shall forthwith informe
the ministers of all such scandalous crymes as shall be comitted
by any of them." [1]   Such quotations from the statute books
of the other colonies could be multiplied almost indefinitely.

The Puritan seed was sown on many soils, and if it took root
and flourished so abundantly in New England as there to
crowd out the flowers of the field to a greater extent than elsewhere, it was due in part to the nature of the actual soil which
the Puritan himself had to till.   We have already noted how
the geographical features of the region fostered the classes of
fishermen, small traders, subsistence farmers, and townsmen;
how it prevented the growth of a large land-owning or slave-
owning population; how, in a word, it produced a society
which was largely democratic and almost wholly middle-class.
Moreover, in the discussion of Puritanism, we noticed how that
movement was strongest, struck its roots deepest, and assumed
its most uncompromising form, in the very class which thus

[1] J. H. Lefroy, *Memorials of the Discovery and Early Settlements of the Bermudas*
(London, 1877–79), vol. II, p. 320.

became almost synonymous with the New England population.

To return to Merry Mount, however, it must be conceded that there were more serious things wrong there than merely heavy drinking and loose living. Morton, led by cupidity, had made the fatal error of selling fire-arms to the Indians. Needless to say, the profits, in beaver, of such a trade, were enormous; but it threatened the life of every white man on the coast, and residents of the scattered settlements asked Plymouth to join with them in suppressing the deadly mischief. Morton, after a brief struggle, of which he gives an amusing account, was taken into custody, and shipped to England with a complaint to the Council for New England.

The cost of the expedition, which had been led by Standish, amounted to a little over £12, borne by eight settlements, of which the inhabitants of Plymouth outnumbered all the other seven together.[1] That colony, however, contributed but one sixth of the money spent, for which several reasons might be suggested. During the years of its existence, it had received practically no help from the capitalists at home, subsequent to the first fitting out, and the really great achievement of its leaders had consisted in maintaining, for the first time, the existence of a plantation in a wilderness by its own unaided efforts. The three main points of interest in that connection were the abandonment of the common-stock theory, the growth of trade, and the buying out of the interest of the capitalists, which latter transaction foreshadowed the transfer to America of the Massachusetts charter.

The theory of a common-stock as a necessity for the profitable operation of colonies was the accepted one of the day, in spite of repeated failures due to human nature. That failure had been as evident in Plymouth as elsewhere. Young unmarried men objected to having the fruits of their toil go to support other men's wives and children. Married men disliked having their wives sew, cook, and wash for the others. Hard-working men thought it unfair that they should support

---

[1] Bradford, *Plymouth*, pp. 240 *ff.*; *cf.* also Bradford, *Letter Book*, in *Mass. Hist. Soc. Coll.*, Series I, vol. III, p. 63.

the more idle or incapable. The older men, or those of the better class, declined to work for the younger or meaner. The pinch of hunger, in 1623, finally decided the colonists to set aside their agreement, in the interests of the capitalists as well as their own, in the one particular of raising food. The immediate result was a greatly increased production, so that many had a surplus and trading began among themselves, with corn as currency. The following year, one acre of land was confirmed to each individual in severalty.[1]

There was, however, no surplus of food for export, and lumber and beaver were the only available commodities.[2] But the site that had been chosen for the colony was in a poor location for the Indian trade, which required access to the interior along some waterway; and the Pilgrims were therefore forced to resort to coasting voyages for their main supply of skins.

Not only had the London merchants received almost no interest upon their investment, but it began to seem evident to them that the principal itself was lost. Quarrels among themselves over the character of the colonists sent out, and mutual recriminations, completed the break-down of the company. Finally, in December, 1624, some of them wrote to Bradford and others that they had decided to abandon the venture and lose what they had already expended rather than risk any more, suggesting that the Pilgrims send over what they could to pay special debts, amounting to £1400. Those writing the letter also sent out, on their own account, some cattle and various useful commodities, to be sold to the settlers at seventy per cent advance, to cover the profits and risks. The latter were indeed great, insurance alone, at that time, consuming about twenty-five per cent for the round trip;[3] and the following year, Standish, who had been sent to

[1] Bradford, *Plymouth*, pp. 134, 167. The list of lots, with their owners, is in *Plymouth Records*, vol. xii, pp. 1-6.

[2] In 1626, it was decreed that no corn, beans or peas could be exported without license from the governor and council. *Plymouth Records*, vol. xii, p. 8.

[3] Gerard Malynes writing in 1622, quotes rates of insurance to various ports. He does not give New England, but quotes San Domingo as 12 per cent each way, and the East Indies at 15 per cent. *Cf.* his *Consuetudo vel Lex Mercatoria* (London, 1636), p. 108.

London for the purpose, could not borrow money, for the purchase of trading goods, at less than fifty per cent. Goods and
capital they must have, however, and the profits, when made,
were correspondingly great. While Standish was in London,
Winslow made a trip to the Kennebec, in a small vessel, laden
only with a little of that surplus corn which they had raised,
and there secured seven hundred pounds weight of beaver,
besides other furs. In 1626, hearing that the trading station
at Monhegan was going out of business, Bradford and Winslow, accompanied by Thompson from Piscataqua, went to
attend the sale, at which the Pilgrims bought goods to the
value of £400. An additional stock, amounting to £100, was
bought from the wreck of a French ship in the ill-fated Damaris
Cove, the purchases being paid for with the beaver which they
had accumulated the winter before. The following spring,
Allerton arrived from London with £200 more, which he had
succeeded in raising at thirty per cent; so that their capital
was now ample.[1]   The greatest advance which they made in
their trade with the Indians, however, was due to the friendly
Dutch, who sold them some wampum, and taught them its
great value in dealing with the savages. This appearance of
the ubiquitous Dutch, helping a struggling colony to achieve
economic strength by valuable advice or yet more valuable
trading in needed goods, was a frequent one in the early seventeenth century, and in all quarters of the globe. The Pilgrims
at Plymouth, the French at St. Christophers, and innumerable
other little settlements on secluded bays or on lonely islands,
owed their prosperity or preservation to the timely arrival of
a "Dutch trading captain." It would be interesting to trace
how many little bands of people, abandoned by their own
companies or governments, were thus nursed into strength
by the Holland traders, who sought them out, and knew
their needs.[2]

Assured now of sufficient food, and with the Indian trade
well established, the settlers felt that their position in these

[1] Bradford, *Plymouth*, pp. 198, 204, 209, 222, 234.
[2] *Cf.* S. L. Mims, *Colbert's West Indian Policy* (Yale Univ. Press, 1912), pp. 20 *f.*

respects was secure. There were, however, two matters which gave them cause for anxiety. One was the interference by outsiders with their trade on the Kennebec, and the other was their ill-defined situation in regard to the Adventurers in London. In spite of the abandonment of the enterprise by the latter, their claims would continue in existence unless legally extinguished; and it was essential for the settlers to come to some agreement with them, in order that their property and goods should not be liable to seizure in the future. Negotiations, begun by Allerton in 1626, were completed by him on a second trip the year after, when he not only secured a patent for a definite tract on the Kennebec from the Council for New England, but consummated the deal with the Adventurers by which all claims of every description were to be canceled by the payment to them of £1800, in annual instalments of £200 each. The payment of this sum, together with £600 of additional debt, was undertaken by Bradford, Brewster, Standish, and Winslow, with four others in the colony and four friends in England, in exchange for a monopoly of the colony's trade for six years.[1]

By their purchase of all the Adventurers' interest, the Pilgrims had thus practically eliminated the proprietary elements that had existed in their organization, and the settlement became what, for all practical purposes, it had been from the start — a corporate colony.[2] A new patent for Plymouth, granted them in 1630, in the name of Bradford and certain associates, assigned them a definite territory, which the earlier ones had not done, and a confirmation of the Kennebec holdings also straightened out boundary matters there. Their title-deeds, therefore, were now secure. Their powers of government, however, continued to rest solely upon the compact signed in the cabin of the Mayflower ten years before; for, in spite of their efforts, they were never able to obtain a royal charter with privileges similar to those enjoyed by Massachusetts. But in four of the most important elements in that

---

[1] Bradford, *Plymouth*, pp. 212, 221, 226.
[2] *Cf.* Osgood, *American Colonies*, vol. I, p. 290.

larger migration,— the bringing of families to form permanent homes, the peculiar form of church government, the individual ownership of freely acquired land, and the severing of business and legal relations with any company in England,— the Massachusetts leaders but followed the ways laid out by the simple founders of Plymouth.

CHAPTER VI

NEW ENGLAND AND THE GREAT MIGRATION

During the years that the Pilgrims had thus been struggling to found a tiny commonwealth on an inhospitable bit of the long American coast-line, events had been moving rapidly on the more crowded stage of the Old World. In France, the power of the Huguenots had been hopelessly crushed by the fall of Rochelle in 1628; while in England, affairs were evidently approaching a crisis, due to the incompetence of the government of Charles, with its disgraceful military failures abroad, and its illegal financial exactions at home. No one was safe from the ruin of his fortune or the loss of his freedom. The nobility and gentry, subject to the imposition of forced loans, faced imprisonment if they refused to pay; and those below the rank of gentleman were the unwilling hosts of a horde of ruffians, the unpaid and frequently criminal soldiery returned from unsuccessful foreign ventures, and billeted upon them by the government. The laws against Catholics were largely suspended to please the Queen, who was of that faith, and the prospects were daily growing darker for the Puritan and patriot elements, both within and without the Church. Religious toleration as an avowed governmental policy was not, as yet, seriously considered by any considerable body of men outside of Holland, the notable example of which country had failed to influence England, where the control of the church was evidently passing into the hands of Laud and his party. The time had thus come when the King must face a united opposition of the soundest men in the country — of those who feared alike for their property, their liberty, and their religion.

The formation of the Puritan party, drawing into its fold men animated by any or all of these motives, in varying proportions, coincided with the beginning of the great increase in emigration to Massachusetts, which was to carry twenty thousand persons to the shores of New England between 1630 and 1640. But if attention is concentrated too exclusively upon the history of the continental colonies in North America, and, more particularly, of those in New England, the impression is apt to be gained that this swarming out of the English to plant in new lands was largely confined to Massachusetts and its neighbors, and to the decade named. The conclusion drawn from these false premises has naturally been that Puritanism, in the New England sense, was the only successful colonizing force. We do not wish to minimize the value of any deeply felt religious emotion in firmly planting a group of people in a new home. Such value was justly recognized by one of the wisest practical colonizers of the last century,[1] who was not himself of a religious temperament, but who, to secure the firm establishment of his colony, would "have transplanted the Grand Lama of Tibet with all his prayer wheels, and did actually nibble at the Chief Rabbi." [2] The Puritan colonies, nevertheless, not only were far from being the only permanent ones, but themselves were not always equally successful; and it is well to point out that many elements, besides peculiarity of religious belief, entered into the success of the New England colonies, as contrasted with the conspicuous failure of the Puritan efforts in the Caribbean.

At the beginning of the increased emigration to Massachusetts, colonizing, indeed, had ceased to be a new and untried business. To say nothing of the numerous large and small French, Dutch, and Spanish settlements firmly established in the New World, and the English already planted on the mainland, the latter nation had successfully colonized the islands of Bermuda in 1612, St. Kitts in 1623, Barbadoes and St. Croix in 1625, and Nevis and Barbuda three years later. By the time John Winthrop led his band to the shores of Massachusetts Bay, besides the five hundred Dutch in New

[1] Gibbon Wakefield. *Cf.* pp. 156–163 of his *View of the Art of Colonization;* Oxford, ed. 1914.

[2] Dr. Garnett, cited by H. E. Egerton, *Origin and Growth of Greater Britain* (Oxford, 1903), p. 107.

Amsterdam, ten thousand Englishmen were present, for six months of each year, in Newfoundland, engaged in the fisheries there; nine hundred had settled permanently in Maine and New Hampshire; three hundred within the present limits of Massachusetts; three thousand in Virginia; between two and three thousand in Bermuda; and sixteen hundred in Barbadoes; while the numbers in the other colonies are unknown.[1] The figures are striking also for the year 1640, or slightly later, at which date the tide is too often considered as having flowed almost wholly toward the Puritan colonies of New England for the preceding ten years.   The number in Massachusetts at that time had risen to fourteen thousand, in Connecticut to two thousand, and in Rhode Island to three hundred.   Maine and New Hampshire however, contained about fifteen hundred, Maryland the same number, Virginia nearly eight thousand, Nevis about four thousand, St. Kitts twelve to thirteen thousand, and Barbadoes eighteen thousand six hundred. There are no contemporary figures for Barbuda, St. Croix, Antigua, Montserrat, and other settlements.[2]   At the end, therefore, of what has often been considered a period of distinctly Puritan emigration, we find that approximately only sixteen thousand Englishmen had taken their way to the Puritan colonies, as against forty-six thousand to the others; which latter figure, moreover, is undoubtedly too low, owing to the lack of statistics just noted.   Nor does the above statement take into account the thousands of Englishmen who emigrated to Ireland during the same period, and whose motives were probably similar to those animating the emigrants to the New World, however different their destinations may have been.   There had, indeed, been a "great migration," resulting in an English

[1] *Cal. State Pap., Col., 1574–1660*, p. 26; *A Century of Population Growth* (Census Bureau, 1909), p. 9; C. P. Lucas, *Historical Geography of the British Colonies* (Oxford, 1905), vol. II, pp. 13, 179.

[2] *Century of Population*, p. 9; F. B. Dexter, "Estimates of Population in American Colonies," *American Antiquarian Society Proceedings*, 1889, vol. v, pp. 25, 32; Lucas, *Historical Geography*, pp. 142 f. 181.   In 1645, there were 18,300 effective men in Barbadoes, which would indicate a much larger population. The population is given as 30,000 whites in 1650. F. W. Pitman, *Development of the British West Indies* (Yale Univ. Press, 1917), p. 370.

population in America and the West Indies, by 1640 or thereabout, of over sixty-five thousand persons; but it is somewhat misleading to apply the term solely to the stream of emigrants bound for the Puritan colonies, who were outnumbered three to one by those who went to settlements where religion did not partake of the "New England way." Although young John Winthrop might write of his brother that it "would be the ruine of his soule to live among such company" as formed the colony of Barbadoes in 1629,[1] nevertheless, the population of that island had risen to nearly nineteen thousand in another decade, whereas that of Massachusetts had reached only fourteen thousand.

If, in addition, we recall the fact that, approximately, not more than one in five of the adult males who went even to Massachusetts was sufficiently in sympathy with the religious ideas there prevalent to become a church member, though disfranchised for not doing so, we find that in the "great migration" the Puritan element, in the sense of New England church-membership, amounted to only about four thousand persons out of about sixty-five thousand. In the wider sense, indeed, Puritanism, in its effect on legal codes and social usages, is found present, in greater or less degree, in almost all the colonies, island and mainland, but the influence of the form that it took in New England was to be wholly disproportionate upon the nation which evolved from the scattered continental settlements.

If, however, we shift from our usual point of view and, instead of studying the English emigration of the time in the light of the leaders who reached New England, consider the great body of those who left the shores of England, we shall have to account for those fourteen emigrants out of every fifteen, who, although willing to leave their homes and all they had held dear, yet shunned active participation in the Bible Commonwealths. It is evident that other causes, besides the quarrels in the Church and the tyranny of Laud, must have been operative on a large scale, to explain the full extent of the

[1] Winthrop Papers, *Mass. Hist. Soc. Coll.*, Series V, vol. VIII, p. 22.

movement. It seems probable that the principal cause that induced such an extraordinary number of people, from the ranks of the lesser gentry and those below them, to make so complete a break in their lives as was implied by leaving all they had ever known for the uncertainties of far-off lands, was economic. They came for the simple reason that they wanted to better their condition. They wanted to be rid of the growing and incalculable exactions of government. They wanted to own land; and it was this last motive, perhaps, which mainly had attracted those twelve thousand persons out of sixteen thousand who swelled the population of Massachusetts in 1640, but were not church members; for the Puritan colonies were the only ones in which land could be owned in fee simple, without quit-rent or lord, and in which it was freely given to settlers.[1]

The local sources in England of the great migration, and the relations of that movement to local economic conditions, have not received adequate treatment as yet, and the subject is somewhat obscure; but apparently it was the eastern and southeastern counties that furnished the main supply of immigrants for the New World. It was in these counties that the artisans from Flanders had sought refuge, when driven abroad by Alva, as well as the Huguenots from France. In these counties, also, the enclosures, which were of such far-reaching economic influence, had taken place earlier than elsewhere, while wages there showed a lower ratio to subsistence than in the north.[2] The special area in which the inhabitants were most disposed to seek new homes was that around the low country draining into the Wash; and throughout the early seventeenth century economic and agrarian agitation was not-

[1] B. W. Bond, Jr., *The Quit-rent System in the American Colonies* (Yale Univ. Press, 1919), pp. 15, 35.

[2] Cunningham, *English Industry*, vol. II, pp. 36, 38; W. A. S. Hewins, *English Trade and Finance, chiefly in the 17th Century* (London, 1892), p. 108; R. H. Tawney, *The Agrarian Problem, in the 16th Century* (New York, 1912), p. 405; W. J. Ashley, *Introduction to English Economic History and Theory* (London, 1893), vol. II, pp. 286–88; G. Slater, "The Inclosure of Common Fields considered geographically," *Geographical Journal* (London), vol. XXIX, pp. 39 f.; M. Aurosseau, "The Arrangement of Rural Populations," *Geographical Review*, vol. X, pp. 321 f.

ably constant in that particular region,[1] the period of heaviest emigration — that between 1630 and 1640 — marking, perhaps, its years of greatest economic readjustment and strain. The rise in rents and land-values had, indeed, been enormous during the preceding half-century.[2] But this agricultural prosperity had been so closely bound up with the great expansion of the cloth industry, that in this section it may be said to have been wholly dependent upon it.[3] From 1625 to 1630, however, the business of the clothiers suffered a very severe decline, which continued for some years, and the effects of which were very marked in the agricultural industries as well.[4] In Norwich, for example, the Mayor and Aldermen complained that, owing to the dearth of food, and to the great increase of unemployment due to bad trade conditions, the amount necessary for poor relief had to be doubled.[5] Moreover, as is always the case in periods of great economic alteration, the change had not affected all classes in the community alike. The yeomanry, who were less influenced by the rapidly rising scale of living, and so could save a much larger proportion of their increased gains from the high agricultural prices, were improving their position at the expense of the gentry.[6] Enterprising traders, in the cloth and other industries, who had acquired fortunes, but who naturally were not of the old families, were pushing in and buying country estates, and, like all *nouveaux riches*, were asserting their new and unaccus-

[1] Newton, *Puritan Colonisation*, p. 79.

[2] *Victoria History of County of Lincoln* (London, 1906), vol. II, p. 334.

[3] *Victoria History of County of Suffolk* (London, 1911), vols. I, pp. 661, 676, and II, p. 268.

[4] *Ibid.*, vol. II, p. 266.

[5] *Cal. State Pap., Domestic, 1629–31*, p. 419. *Cf.* also, *Ibid.* pp. 8, 403, 419. A few years earlier, Sir Wm. Pelham, writing to his brother-in-law, said: "Our country was never in that wante that now itt is, and more of munnie than Corne, for theare are many thousands in thease parts whoo have soulde all thay have even to theyr bedd straw, and cann not get worke to earne any munny. Dogg's flesh is a dainty dish," etc. *Lincolnshire Notes and Queries*, vol. I, p. 16.

[6] "Our yeomanry, whose continuall under living, saving, and the immunities from the costly charge of these unfaithfull times, do make them so as to grow with the wealth of this world, that whilst many of the better sort, as having past their uttermost period, do suffer an utter declination, these onely doe arise, and doe lay such strong, sure, and deep foundations that from thence in time are derived many noble and worthy families." Robt. Reyce, *Suffolk Breviary*, 1618 (ed. London, 1902), p. 58.

tomed position by raising the scale of living.[1]   Many of the
gentry, on the other hand, unable to adjust themselves to the
new economic conditions or to take advantage of them, and
yet unwilling to give up their comparative position in the
county, found themselves "overtaken," as a contemporary
writer says, "with too well meaning and good nature," and so
were "inforced sometimes to suffer a revolution" in their
domestic affairs.[2]   About the years of the emigration, however,
there seem to have been financial difficulties and economic
unrest among all the classes, due to the immediate crisis in
the cloth trade, as well as to the more general conditions of the
time.

The district in which these economic changes were at work
was also the one in which Puritanism had taken its strongest
hold, and the leaders both of the Puritan movement at home
and of colonization abroad "formed a veritable clan, intimately
bound together by ties of blood, marriage, and neighborhood,
acting together in all that concerned colonization on the one
hand and autocratic rule on the other."[3]   We have already
seen, in an earlier chapter, how the trading companies had
brought into working contact the great nobles, city merchants,
and country gentlemen, and accustomed them to act together
as, perhaps, nothing else could have done, thus paving the way
for the formation of the Puritan party.

In addition to this foundation, the leaders were united by
ties based upon social and blood-relationship, many of which
were of great importance in the affairs of both Old and New
England.   Among many such, we may note that John Endicott
was a parishioner of the Reverend John White, who was
interested in the Cape Ann fishing company with John Humphrey.   Humphrey, in turn, was a brother-in-law of the Earl

[1] *History of Suffolk*, vol. 1, p. 673.   [2] Reyce, *Breviary*, p. 60.
[3] C. M. Andrews, Introduction to Newton, *Puritan Colonisation*, p. viii.   Robert
Reyce, writing of the gentry, in 1618, says: "So againe what with the enterlacing of
houses in marriage (a practise at this day much used for the strengthening of families
therby) such is the religious unity wherewith in all good actions they doe concur, that
whatsoever offendeth one displeaseth all, and whosever satisfieth one contenteth all."
Breviary, p. 60.

of Lincoln, one of the most earnest of the Puritan peers, and son-in-law of Viscount Say and Sele.   Lincoln's other brothers-in-law were Isaac Johnson and John Gorges, the latter a son of Sir Ferdinando.   Lincoln's steward, Thomas Dudley, was a parishioner of John Cotton.   The Earl of Holland was a brother of the Earl of Warwick, who was the leader of the Puritans.   The latter's interests in Parliament were attended to by Lord Brooke, while his man of business was Sir Nathaniel Rich.   The Riches and the Barringtons were neighbors and close friends.   Lady Joan Barrington, who was a correspondent of many of the New England emigrants, was an aunt of John Hampden and Oliver Cromwell, and Roger Williams at one time applied for the hand of her niece.   Many of these were deeply interested in the attempt to found a Puritan colony in the Caribbean, as were also Gregory Gawsell, John Gurdon, and Sir Edward Moundeford, who were all three country neighbors and intimate friends of John Winthrop and his family circle.[1]

At the time that our story has now reached, there were two projects for Puritan settlement in which members of this clan were particularly interested, that of the island of Old Providence in the Caribbean Sea, and that of the remnants of the Cape Ann fishing attempt, which was mentioned in the preceding chapter.   The latter somewhat ill-judged effort, in 1623, to combine as a single enterprise an agricultural colony on land and a fishing business at sea, had been abandoned two years later, with a loss of £3000.[2]   Most of the men had been withdrawn, but Roger Conant, with a few others, decided to remain in America, transferring their homes to the location of what was in a few years to be known as Salem.   Thinking that something might still be saved from the wreck, a few of the Adventurers in England plucked up courage, and having interested fresh capitalists, including Thomas Dudley, secured the services of John Endicott as local governor, and, in 1628,

---

[1] Newton, *Puritan Colonisation*, pp. 61 *ff.*; E. J. Carpenter, *Roger Williams* (New York, 1909), pp. 16–21.

[2] J. White, *The Planter's Plea* (Force Tracts), p. 39.

were granted a patent from the Council for New England.[1]
The Puritan character of the new undertaking would be sufficiently evidenced by the names of White and his parishioner
Endicott, Humphrey, and Dudley, did we not know also that
the Earl of Warwick, who seven years before had secured the
patent for the Pilgrims, now acted in obtaining that for the
New England Company.[2] Sir Ferdinando Gorges, to whom
Warwick applied, gave his consent, provided that the new
patent should not be prejudicial to the interests of his son
Robert, and distinctly stated that the new colony was to
found a place of refuge for Puritans.[3] The grant, which extended from three miles north of the River Merrimac to three
miles south of the Charles, conflicted with that bestowed on
Gorges and Mason in 1622, as well as with that of Robert
Gorges of similar date. As the same limits were confirmed
in the royal charter to the Company of Massachusetts Bay
in 1629, the seeds of future discord were sown in these conflicting titles.[4]

Endicott was at once dispatched, with a few followers, to
take possession, and to prepare the way for a larger body to
be sent in the succeeding year. The little band, with which
he arrived in September, 1628, together with the old settlers
already on the spot, made up a company of only fifty or sixty
people, most of whom seem to have done little but "rub out
the winter's cold by the Fire-side," "turning down many a
drop of the Bottell, and burning Tobacco with all the ease
they could," while they discussed the progress they would
make in the summer.[5] There was, however, much sickness
among them, which may have accounted in part for their

[1] White, *Planter's Plea*, p. 43; T. Dudley, "Letter to the Countess of Lincoln,"
in Young's *Chronicles of the first Planters of Massachusetts* (Boston, 1846), p. 310;
cf. Osgood, *American Colonies*, vol. 1, p. 130.

[2] There was no uniform designation until the issue of the charter of 1629, the
company being variously styled "the New England Company," "the Company of
Adventurers for New England in America," etc. Thornton, *Landing at Cape Anne*,
p. 57 n.

[3] Gorges, *Briefe Narration*, p. 80 (written many years later).

[4] Haven, *Lowell Lectures*, pp. 153 f.

[5] White, *Planter's Plea*, p. 43; E. Johnson, *Wonder-working Providence of Sions
Saviour in New-England* (ed. New York, 1910), p. 45.

close hearth-keeping. From what we know of Endicott's harsh manners and lack of wisdom in dealing with delicate situations, it may be assumed that his superseding of Conant in the office of local governor was not made more palatable by any grace in his announcement of the fact; and, in any case, ill-feeling developed between the old and new planters. This, however, was smoothed over by Conant's own tact, and affairs were adjusted "so meum and tuum that divide the world, should not disturb the peace of good christians."[1] Morton, owing to his unsympathetic neighbors, the Pilgrims, was temporarily in England, and so absent from his crew at Merry Mount; but Endicott promptly visited that very un-Puritan and somewhat dangerous settlement, and having hewn down the offending May-pole, "admonished them to look ther should be better walking."[2] It is possible that, before winter set in, preparations may have been made for a second settlement at Charlestown to forestall the claims of Oldham in that locality.[3]

Endicott's whole mission at this time, indeed, seems to have been merely to prepare the way for others; and in the following year, six ships were dispatched, carrying over four hundred people, with cattle and additional supplies.[4] Four clergymen, including Skelton and Higginson, were also sent, for the spiritual welfare of the colony, and the conversion of the Indians, which latter object, at this stage of the enterprise, was officially declared to be the main end of the plantation.

Meanwhile, the number of those in England interested in the venture continued to grow, and a royal charter, under the broad seal, was granted March 4, 1629, in the names of Sir Henry Rosewell, Sir John Younge, Thomas Southcott, John Humphrey, John Endicott, and their associates, the total

[1] W. Hubbard, *History of New England* (1815), p. 110.

[2] Bradford, *Plymouth*, p. 238.

[3] The Robert Gorges claim had been sold in two parts, one to Sir Wm. Brereton and one to John Dorrell and John Oldham. J. G. Palfrey, *History of New England* (Boston, 1859), vol. I, p. 294; *cf.* T. Prince, *Chronological History of New England* (Arber reprint, London, 1897), p. 483; and Cradock's instructions in Young, *Chron. Mass.*, pp. 147 *ff.*, 171.

[4] Prince, *New England*, p. 489; Young, *Chron. Mass.*, pp. 132, 216. The number included 35 of the Leyden congregation bound for Plymouth.

membership of the company being about one hundred and ten.[1]   The grant followed somewhat closely that received by the Virginia Company in 1609, the patentees being joint proprietors of the plantation, with rights of ownership and government similar to those enjoyed by the earlier London Company.   A General Court, to meet quarterly, was provided for, and annually, at the Easter session, this court was to elect a governor, deputy governor and a board of assistants, consisting of eighteen members.   By an important clause, six of the latter, together with the governor or his deputy, constituted a quorum, and were therefore required to be present at the sittings of the court.   The General Court, consisting of the members of the Company, known as freemen, was also given the power to add to its number, and to make such necessary laws and ordinances as should not be repugnant to the laws of England.   The first governor was Mathew Cradock, with Thomas Goffe as deputy, the Assistants including Sir Richard Saltonstall, Isaac Johnson, John Humphrey, John Endicott, Increase Nowell, Theophilus Eaton, and John Browne.   It was this charter of a proprietary company, skillfully interpreted to fit the needs of the case, and constantly violated as to its terms, which formed the basis of the commonwealth government of Massachusetts for over half a century.

The company, so organized, proceeded to arrange for a local government in Massachusetts, confirming Endicott as governor, and associating with him a council of thirteen.   This was to include the three clergymen then there, the two Brownes, and two of the old planters, if the latter group should desire such representation.   Efforts were made to conserve as equitably as possible the rights of those former settlers, and other instructions for the conduct of the company's affairs were forwarded to Endicott a few weeks after the grant of the charter.[2]

---

[1] *Records of the Governor and Company of the Massachusetts Bay in New England* (ed. N. B. Shurtleff, Boston, 1853), vol. i, p. 5 (hereafter cited as *Massachusetts Records*).   The charter is given on pp. 1-20.   S. F. Haven, prefatory chapter to the Company's Records, in *Archeologia Americana*, 1857, vol. iii, pp. cxxxiv-cxxxvi.

[2] Young, *Chron. Mass.*, pp. 141-71.

Writing home, at the end of the first summer, Higginson stated that, on their arrival, they had found "aboute a half score houses, and a fair house newly built for the Governor," and that, including the newcomers and old settlers, about three hundred people were planted in the colony, of whom two thirds were at Salem and the remainder at Charlestown.[1] "But that which is our greatest comfort and means of defence above all others," he continued, "is that we have here the true religion and holy ordinances of Almighty God taught amongst us. Thanks be to God, we have here plenty of preaching, and diligent catechising, with strict and careful exercise."

As we noted in an earlier chapter, many writers have insisted greatly upon the rigid distinction between the Pilgrims, as Separatists, and the Puritans, as mere Nonconformists. Not only, however, were the members of the several communities by no means agreed as to what constituted Separatism and Nonconformity, but, in the American wilderness, such distinctions rapidly ceased to have any but a disputatious value, with, at intervals, political reverberations in England. The Pilgrims, at the time of their emigration from Holland, may have been strict Separatists or on the way to becoming mere non-Separatist Independent Puritans;[2] and the leaders of the churches of Massachusetts for many years denied any Separatism on their own part or that of the Pilgrims. John Cotton wrote categorically, in 1647, that "for New England there is no such church of the Separation at al that I know of."[3] On the other hand, many, of all shades of religious belief, refused to acknowledge this view of the matter. They found it impossible to answer Roger Williams's query as to "what is that which Mr. Cotton and so many hundreths fearing God in New England walk in, but a way of separation?"[4]

[1] F. Higginson, *New England's Plantation;* Young, *Chron. Mass.*, pp. 258 f.
[2] C. Burrage, *English Dissenters*, vol. 1, p. 357.
[3] *Master John Cotton's Answer to Master Roger Williams* (Narraganset Club Publications, Providence, 1867, vol. 11, p. 203).
[4] R. Williams, *Mr. Cotton's Letter examined and answered* (Narraganset Club Publications, vol. 1, p. 109).

Indeed, in view of the open and patent facts, the only possible answer was the casuistical one of Cotton and the other leaders, that they had separated, "not from the Churches in Old England, as no Churches, but from some corruptions found in them." [1] As these corruptions were held to include the polity and ritual of the English Church, and as members of the New England churches, though they might listen to its preaching, were not allowed to be in communion with it, and as no Church of England services were permitted on New England soil, the point as to whether or not the New England Puritans were Separatists is a mere matter of terms. It depends upon the question how far a minority of any organization, social, political, or religious, can go in denying the validity of its ideas, in refusing to conform to its practices, and in not allowing them to be used, and still consider themselves as being in the organization. Opinions will always differ, and it is as impossible to decide to-day whether the Puritans became Separatists as it was for themselves and their critics to decide at the time.

The question of terms is not especially important, but the question of polity, as it was developed in the little church at Salem, is immensely so, for it undoubtedly gave a very great impetus to the growth of Congregationalism in Massachusetts, and, indeed, has been called "the chief point of departure in the ecclesiastical history of New England," which was so inextricably interwoven with its political history. In no other part of the country has a more distinct and persistent type of thought and character been developed than in that section; and in this regard we have already noted the important influences of the geographic environment. But the impress of its institutional life was no less effective upon the minds of its people. It was not Puritanism alone that developed the type; for, we repeat, the Puritan strain may be traced in the legislation and social life of many of the English settlements, and the Puritanism of any individual to-day may derive quite as directly from an ancestral Bermudian, Georgian, Jamaican Commonwealth man, Carolinian Scotch Covenanter, or

Pennsylvanian Ulsterite, as from a settler in Salem or Plymouth. But wherever we find Congregationalism, town government, and the village school, we may trace the triple influence straight to New England.

It is impossible to say what may have been the precise ideas as to church government held by the groups which emigrated with Endicott and in the following year, but the evidence seems clear that, at least as far as Endicott was concerned, they were identical with those of the Pilgrims, or were unconsciously derived from them after arrival. Dr. Fuller, who visited Salem during the sickness of the first winter, was not only a physician but a deacon of the Plymouth church. With him Endicott discussed the question of church polity, and, as a result, wrote to Governor Bradford that "I am by him satisfied touching your judgments of the outward forme of Gods worshipe. It is, as farr as I can gather, no other than is warranted by the evidence of truth, and the same which I have proffessed and maintained ever since the Lord in mercie revealed him selfe unto me."[1] A few weeks later, after the arrival of Skelton and Higginson, the Salem church was organized, with the former as pastor, and the latter as teacher, the members being united by a church covenant, which became one of the essential features of the New England church system.[2] In that system, every local church was independent, choosing and ordaining its own pastor, teachers, and ruling elders, and was composed of such Christians only as could satisfy the other church members of their converted state.[3] "The stones that were to be laid in Solomon's temple," wrote Cotton, with characteristic far-fetched use of Old Testament texts, "were squared and made ready before they were laid in the building . . . and, wherefore so, if not to hold forth

---

[1] Bradford, *Plymouth*, p. 265; Burrage thinks the Pilgrim influence slight, differing from most authorities. *English Dissenters*, vol. I, pp. 360 ff. Cf. W. Walker, *History of Congregational Churches in U. S.* (New York, 1894), pp. 101 ff.

[2] Bradford, *Plymouth*, pp. 265 f. The covenant of 1629 and the enlarged one of 1636 are in W. Walker, *Creeds and Platforms of Congregationalism* (New York, 1893), pp. 116 ff. Cf. C. Burrage, *The Church Covenant Idea* (Philadelphia, 1904), pp. 88 ff.

[3] Cf. T. Lechford, "Plain dealing or Newes from New England"; *Mass. Hist. Soc. Coll.*, Series III, vol. III, pp. 63–75.

that no members were to be received into the Church of Christ, but such as were rough-hewn, and squared, and fitted to lie close and levell to Christ and to his members?"[1]

Although the church government was democratic in form, and thus of influence in fostering democratic beliefs as to government in general, it must be remembered that at probably no period during the life of the charter, did the number of church members include more than a very distinct minority of the population. Lechford's statement, that three quarters of the people were outside the pale of the church in 1640, seems borne out by other testimony, and this proportion appears not to have been greatly changed till near the end of the century.[2] The influence of this democratic form of church organization, however, was clearly foreseen by King James in his dictum, "No bishop, no king"; and of even greater effect in its logical political consequence was the employment of the covenant. In defending its use in the church, Cotton, in the volume already quoted, was forced onto broader ground. "It is evident," he wrote, "by the light of nature, that all civill Relations are founded in Covenant. For, to passe by naturall Relations between Parents and Children, and violent Relations between Conquerors and Captives; there is no other way given wherby a people (sui Juris) free from naturall and compulsory engagements, can be united or combined together into one visible body."[3]

It is difficult to overestimate the influence which, in time, these two ideas, of a democratic church polity and a voluntary covenant as the only basis for a civil government, would come to exert upon those holding them; but for the moment, the result was the forcible expulsion from the community of two members who did not hold them. John and Samuel Browne, both men of good estate, the one a merchant and the other a lawyer, and both original patentees of the Company, had

[1] John Cotton, *The Way of the Churches of Christ in New England* (London, 1645), p. 54.
[2] Lechford, *Plain Dealing*, p. 143; A. E. McKinley, *Suffrage Franchise in the Thirteen English Colonies* (University of Pennsylvania Publications, 1905), p. 313.
[3] Cotton, *The Way of the Churches*, p. 4.

left England for Salem in the spring of 1629, with high recommendation to Endicott from the Company at home, as men much trusted and respected.[1] When the Salem church was organized, the two brothers, who were both on the council, objected, accusing the ministers of having become Separatists, which they denied. As the Brownes refused to give up the use of the prayer-book, and held private services with their followers, Endicott, either from personal feeling or from a real fear that the trouble would disrupt the colony, took a strong stand, and shipped them back to England.[2] There is no contemporary account of the details, and it is therefore as unwise, perhaps, to condemn Endicott, as it is unjustifiable to speak of the Brownes as "anarchical," or, with an odd lack of humor, as "Schismatical."[3] Endicott was mildly censured by the Company in England, who wrote that they conceived that "it is possible some undigested councells have too sudainely bin put in execution, wch may have ill construccion with the state heere;" while the ministers were asked to clear themselves if innocent, or else to look back upon their "miscarriage wth repentance." In time the Brownes seem to have been settled with satisfactorily on a cash basis.[4]

While progress was thus being made in the establishment of the Massachusetts Bay colony, another project for a Puritan settlement was rapidly taking form. After the dissolution of the Virginia Company, the quarrel between the Sandys and Warwick factions was continued in the courts of the Somers Islands, or Bermuda Company, and its affairs were going from bad to worse, largely owing to the frequent changes in the person of the governor as the two factions succeeded each other in power at home. In April, 1629, Sir Nathaniel Rich received a long letter from Governor Bell, in regard to various matters, in the course of which he described two islands lying in the Caribbean, in either of which he thought one year would

[1] T. Hutchinson, *History of Massachusetts* (Salem, 1795), vol. 1, p. 19; Young, *Chron. Mass.*, p. 168
[2] Hutchinson, *History*, vol. 1, p. 19; Morton, *New England's Memorial*, pp. 100 *f.*
[3] Young's epithets, in *Chron. Mass.*, p. 160 *n.*
[4] *Massachusetts Records*, vol. 1, pp. 409, 407, 52, 54, 61, 69.

"be more profitable than seven years here," and placed the disposition of both islands in Warwick's hands.[1]

It was a momentous time. Hardly more than a few days before, Parliament had been angrily dissolved by the King, not to meet again for eleven years. Eliot, Selden, and seven other of the popular leaders had been committed to the Tower. In every direction, Puritans of distinction, and even such lesser men as John Humphrey and John Winthrop, were made to feel the hostility of the court. The recent successful colonization of St. Kitts and Barbadoes by the Earls of Carlisle and Marlborough, both members of the court party, and hostile to the Warwicks and Riches, combined with the flattering report of the new-found islands by Bell, induced Warwick, whose affairs had not been going well, to make an immediate counter-move. With Rich, Gawsell, and others, he provided £2000, and dispatched two ships for the Caribbean under letters of marque. They arrived at Providence about Christmas, the company beginning to make ready for the larger body which was to arrive in the spring, precisely as Endicott had done at Salem. "The aim and desire above all things," wrote the promoters of the enterprise, "is to plant the true and sincere Religion and worship of God, which in the Christian world is now very much opposed." At first, the utmost secrecy was maintained as to the real aims of Warwick and his associates; and it was only in December of the following year, after the main body of the colonists had already been planted, that letters-patent for the islands were procured from the King.[2]

There can be no doubt, however, that the matter was well known to Winthrop and others of those who were contemplating emigration in the summer of 1629. Not only was Gawsell a neighbor and friend of Winthrop, but all steps taken by the Massachusetts group seem to have been talked over with Warwick and Rich.[3] John Winthrop, now in his forty-third year, who was living the life of a country squire at Groton, in

[1] Newton, *Puritan Colonisation*, pp. 32 f.
[2] *Ibid.*, pp. 48, 50, 53, 95, 86. This island had been confused, until recently, with New Providence in the Bahamas.
[3] *Ibid.*, p. 47.

Suffolk, and was a small office-holder under government, had been anxiously watching the course of affairs. Of a sensitive and deeply religious nature, strongly attached to the Puritan cause, he could not but regard the future with the greatest anxiety. "The Lord hath admonished, threatened, corrected and astonished us," he wrote to his wife in May, 1629, "yet we growe worse and worse, so as his spirit will not allwayes strive with us, he must needs give waye to his fury at last. ... We sawe this, and humbled not ourselves, to turne from our evill wayes, but have provoked him more than all the nations rounde about us: therefore he is turninge the cuppe toward us also, and because we are the last, our portion must be, to drinke the verye dreggs which remaine. My dear wife, I am veryly persuaded, God will bringe some heavye Affliction upon this lande, and that speedylye." [1] In addition to his fear that all hope of civil, as well as of even a moderate degree of religious, liberty was rapidly fading, Winthrop was also much troubled by the prospects for his personal social and financial position. A few months earlier, he had written to his son Henry, at that time a settler in Barbadoes, that he then owed more than he was able to pay without selling his land; and throughout all his letters and papers of the period runs the same strain of anxiety over money matters. [2] Although possessed of a modest estate, which, when subsequently sold, realized £4200, [3] the demands of a large family, and the increased cost of living, were more than he could meet. In June, he was, in addition, deprived of his office under the Master of the Wards, and wrote to his wife that "where we shall spende the rest of or short tyme I knowe not: the Lorde, I trust, will direct us in mercye." [4]

With the discussion then going on in Puritan circles as to Endicott's settlement at Salem, and with his neighbors actively interested in the colony at Providence, it was natural that

---

[1] R. C. Winthrop, *Life and Letters of John Winthrop* (Boston, 1869), vol I, p. 296.
[2] *Ibid*, vol. I, p. 286.
[3] Letter from J. Winthrop, Jr.; *Mass. Hist. Soc. Coll.*, Series V, vol. VIII, p. 28. Winthrop had appraised it at £5760. R. C. Winthrop, *J. Winthrop*, vol. II, p. 78.
[4] *Ibid.*, vol. I, pp. 214 *ff.*, 301 *f.*

Winthrop should seriously consider the thought of emigrating. Just at this time, a paper consisting of arguments for and against settling a plantation in New England was being circulated among the group of Puritans mentioned earlier in this chapter. The reasons given in favor of it were mainly religious and economic. The first dwelt upon the glory of opposing Anti-Christ, in the form of the French Jesuits in Canada, and of raising "a particular church" in New England, while the second referred to the supposed surplus population at home, and to the standard and cost of living which had "growne to that height of intemperance in all excesse of Riott, as noe mans estate allmost will suffice to keepe saile with his aequalls." [1]

The document, which has come down to us in at least four different forms, was possibly drafted by Winthrop himself, though the evidence is only inferential, and it has also been attributed to the Reverend John White and others.[2] It is interesting to note that John Hampden wrote to Sir John Eliot, then in prison, for a copy of it.[3] Whether or not Winthrop was the author, several copies, one of them indorsed "May, 1629," contain memoranda of "Particular considerations in the case of J. W.," in which he wrote that the success of the plan had come to depend upon him, for "the chiefe supporters (uppon whom the rest depends) will not stirr wthout him," and that his wife and children are in favor of it. "His meanes," moreover, he wrote, "heer are so shortened (now 3 of his sonnes being com to age have drawen awaie the one half of his estate) as he shall not be able to continue in that place and imployment where he now iss, his ordinary charg being still as great almost as when his meanes was double"; and that "if he lett pass this opportunitie, That talent wch God hath bestowed uppon him for publicke service is like to

---

[1] R. C. Winthrop, *J. Winthrop*, vol. I, pp. 308, 328.
[2] The editor of this life of Winthrop (vol. I, pp. 308, 318) naturally claims it for his ancestor. Channing thinks it probable (*History*, vol. I, p. 327); but Doyle does not (*Puritan Colonies*, vol. I, p. 85). *Cf. Mass. Hist. Soc. Proceedings*, Series I, vols. VIII, pp. 413–30, and XII, pp. 237 *ff.*
[3] Letter of Dec. 8, 1629; *Ibid.*, vol. VIII, p. 427.

be buried."[1] "With what comfort can I live," he added in one version, "wth 7 or 8 servts in that place and condition where for many years I have spent 3: or 400 li yearly and maintained a greater chardge?"[2] The prospects in England, for his wife and children, lay heavily on his mind. "For my care of thee and thine," he wrote to the former, after the die was cast, "I will say nothing. The Lord knows my heart, that it was one great motive to draw me into this course."[3]

His judgment regarding the ending of the opportunity for a public career for such as himself in England was obviously wrong, as events developed there. The England which retained a Pym, a Hampden, an Eliot, and a Cromwell, may well have offered scope for the talents of a Winthrop. As our eyes are usually fastened on this side of the water, we are apt to think of the Pilgrims, Puritans, and other immigrants as starting their careers by coming here. We rarely consider them in the light of leaving behind them other possible careers in England. It is no disparagement of the courage with which they faced the wilderness, to think of them, for a moment, as Englishmen, abandoning their place in the struggle at home, and to consider the type of mind which thus preferred to exchange the simplifications of unpeopled America for the complexities of the situation in England. Is it, perhaps, altogether fanciful, to attribute, in slight part, that deeply ingrained feeling of Americans, that they wish to have nothing to do with the problems of the world at large, to this choice of the founders in abandoning their place in the struggles of Europe for a more untrammeled career on a small provincial stage?

Winthrop's reasons have been thus dwelt upon, because, in the motives given by him who was the purest, gentlest, and broadest-minded of all who were to guide the destinies of the Bay Colony, we presumably find the highest of those which animated any of the men who sought its shores. As we descend

---

[1] *Mass. Hist. Soc. Proceedings*, Series I, vol. VIII, p. 420. The wording is slightly different in the version in R. C. Winthrop, *J. Winthrop*, vol. I, p. 327.

[2] *Mass. Hist. Soc. Proceedings*, Series I, vol. XII, p. 238.

[3] Letter of Jan. 15, 1630; R. C. Winthrop, *J. Winthrop*, vol. I, p. 366.

the scale of character, the religious incentives narrow and disappear, as does also the desire for honorable public service, and the economic factor alone remains.

In July, a few weeks after Winthrop lost his office, Isaac Johnson, a brother-in-law of the Earl of Lincoln, wrote to Emanuel Downing, a brother-in-law of Winthrop, asking them to meet at Sempringham, the Earl's seat in Lincolnshire, whither they both went on the 28th.[1]   There they undoubtedly met Dudley, Johnson, Humphrey, and others of that family and social group.   All those gathered there, so far as we know, were keenly interested in the project for Massachusetts.   As they were also in close touch with Warwick, Rich, and others of those who were just at the moment planning to send out the colony to Providence in September, it is probable that both places were considered, and Warwick continued for years to urge Winthrop and his group to move to the southern colony. The decision, however, was in favor of Massachusetts; and, a few weeks later, on August 26, Saltonstall, Dudley, Johnson, Humphrey, Winthrop, and seven others, signed an agreement by which they bound themselves to be ready, with their families and goods, by the first of the following March, to embark for New England, and to settle there permanently.[2]

There was one clause in the agreement, of incalculable importance.   "Provided always," so it read, "that before the last of September next, the whole Government, together with the patent for the said plantation, be first, by an order of court, legally transferred and established to remain with us and others which shall inhabit upon the said Plantation." [3] Possibly as a result of consultation with the Cambridge signers, Governor Cradock, at a meeting of the court of the Company a month earlier, had read certain propositions, "conceived by himself," which anticipated this condition.   They seem

[1] *Mass. Hist. Soc. Coll.*, Series IV, vol. vi, pp. 29 f.   Sempringham is a tiny hamlet, and of the beautiful house of the Earls of Lincoln, only the garden wall remains. W. F. Rawnsley, *Highways and Byways in Lincolnshire* (London, 1914), p. 38.   The house is mentioned in Camden's *Brittania* (ed. London, 1806), vol. ii, p. 334.

[2] R. C. Winthrop, *J. Winthrop*, vol. i, pp. 344 f.

[3] *Ibid.*, p. 345.

to have struck those present as serious and novel, and of such importance in their possible consequences as to call for deferred consideration in great secrecy. The matter was brought up at a number of successive meetings, and it was only after much debate, objections on the part of many, and the taking of legal advice, that the court finally voted that the charter and government might be removed to America.[1] By such transfer, and the use made of the charter in New England, what was intended to be a mere trading company, similar to those which had preceded it, became transformed into a self-governing commonwealth, whose rulers treated the charter as if it were the constitution of an independent state. Such an interpretation could not legally be carried beyond a certain point, and the attempt was bound to break down under the strain.

The step, in its far-reaching consequences, was one of the most important events in the development of the British colonies, but its story remains a mystery. It was a completely new departure, but may have been suggested to the leaders by the act of the Pilgrims in buying out their English partners and thus in effect, though without any legal authority, constituting themselves a self-governing community. There has been much discussion as to whether the absence in the original charter of any words indicating that the corporation was to remain in England was due to accident or design. It is impossible to prove the point either way, for Winthrop's statement, of somewhat uncertain application and written many years later, does not seem conclusive against the other facts and probabilities.[2] The proceedings at the meetings of the court show clearly, at least, that many of the most active patentees had had no inkling of any such conscious alteration of the document at the time of issue, nor does it seem likely that Charles I would have knowingly consented. If the

---

[1] *Massachusetts Records*, vol. I, pp. 49–52, 55.

[2] R. C. Winthrop, *J. Winthrop*, vol. II, p. 443; C. Deane, in *Mass. Hist. Soc. Proceedings*, Series I, vol. XI, pp. 166 *ff.*; Mellen Chamberlain, *Ibid*, Series II, vol. VIII, p. 110; J. Parker in *Lowell Lectures*, pp. 365 *ff.*; and Osgood, *American Colonies*, vol. I, pp. 145 *ff.*, 183.

charter were intentionally so worded as to create "the Adventurers a Corporation upon the Place," [1] for the purpose the wording was later made to serve, then such of the leaders as arranged the matter consciously hoodwinked both the government and many of their own associates.

At length, however, the consent of the patentees was obtained, after their counsel had approved the legality of the step; and in October, in contemplation of the removal of the government to America, Winthrop was elected Governor, and Humphrey, Deputy, in place of those who were to remain behind.[2] Eight months later, in the early summer of 1630, Winthrop and a band of between nine hundred and a thousand immigrants landed in America, and settled what were later known as the towns of Charlestown, Boston, Medford, Watertown, Roxbury, Lynn, and Dorchester.[3] Eighty of the inhabitants already planted at Salem under Endicott had died during the winter, and of those who formed the present settlements, about two hundred succumbed between the time of leaving England and the end of December, including Johnson, his wife the Lady Arbella, the Reverend Mr. Higginson, and other important members of the colony.[4]

The settlers, apparently, did not have time to house themselves properly before winter came on, and many, particularly of the poor, had to face the icy winds of a New England January with no better shelter than a canvas tent.[5] Provisions, even in England, were exceedingly scarce and dear that year, partly, some claimed, because of the large quantities taken out by emigrants to New England and the other plantations.[6] Massachusetts had evidently not received her share,

---

[1] Decision of the English Chief Justices in 1677; *Acts Privy Council, Colonial,* vol. I, p. 724. *Cf. Ibid,* p. 841.

[2] *Massachusetts Records,* vol. I, pp. 59 *f.* At the last moment, as Humphrey's sailing was delayed, Dudley was elected in his place. *Ibid,* p. 70.

[3] The ships did not all arrive together. Some were delayed until the first week in July. John Winthrop, *History of New England* (ed. Boston, 1853), vol. I, p. 34. *Cf.* Young, *Chron. Mass.,* pp. 310 *ff.*

[4] Dudley's Letter, in Young, *Chron. Mass.,* pp. 311, 319.

[5] J. Winthrop, *History,* vol. I, p. 52.

[6] *Cal. St. Pap., Dom., 1628-9,* p. 266; *Acts Privy Council, Colonial,* vol. I, p. 154.

if such had been the case, and famine soon faced the settlers, who were forced to live partly on mussels and acorns.[1] Even upon their arrival in the summer, food had been so scarce that they had been forced to give their liberty to a hundred and eighty servants, entailing a loss of between three and four hundred pounds.[2] The cold, which had held off until December 24, suddenly came on in extreme severity, and "such a Christmas eve they had never seen before." The contrast with the Christmas Day which the Warwick settlers were passing at Providence, in the Caribbean, was complete; and Humphrey and Downing, who were in frequent conference with the earl and with Rich, kept writing to advise Winthrop to move the colony farther south, if only to the Hudson River.[3] At a critical moment, the ship Lion, which Winthrop had had the foresight to send at once to England for provisions, arrived with a new supply; but so deep was the discouragement, that many returned in her to the old home, never to come back. Others, however, were of sterner stuff, and took passage in the same boat to fetch their families.[4]

At last the winter passed, and with the summer came renewed hope. The public business had been temporarily managed by the Assistants only, and the first General Court was not held until October. At that session the charter was violated in an important point, in that the freemen relinquished their right to elect the governor and the deputy. Thereafter, it was ruled, these were to be elected by the Assistants only, with whom they were to have the power of making laws and appointing officers.[5] The extent of this limitation of the right of election, which was revoked, however, at the next General Court, is evident from the fact that in March, in contemplation of the probability of there being less than

---

[1] R. Clap, Memoirs, in Young, *Chron. Mass.*, p. 352.

[2] Dudley's Letter, *Ibid.*, p. 312.

[3] Letters in *Mass. Hist. Soc. Coll.*, Series IV, vol. vi, pp. 3, 8, 38.

[4] Hutchinson, *History*, vol. i, p. 29. For details of the first winter, as noted by one of the poorer emigrants, *cf.*, Letter to Wm. Pond from his son, *Mass. Hist. Soc. Proceedings*, Series II, vol. viii, pp. 471 *ff.*

[5] *Massachusetts Records*, vol. i, pp. 73, 78, 79.

nine Assistants left in the colony, it was agreed that seven should constitute a court.   In fact, the charter was continually violated in that regard, as the number of Assistants, for over fifty years, was never more than about one half of the required eighteen.[1]

The Assistants, into whose hands the control of the government now passed, were probably a majority of the entire voting population of the colony.   According to the terms of the charter only members of the Company, or the so-called freemen, had the right to vote at its meetings.   After the "sea-change" which was presumed to have altered that document into "something rich and strange" in the way of political constitutions, those meetings became the political assemblies of the colony, and the freemen of the Company became the only enfranchised voters of the state.   While two thousand persons were settled in Massachusetts about the time of that October meeting, it is probable that not more than sixteen to twenty members of the Company had crossed the ocean, of whom a number had returned or died.[2]   If the charter were indeed the written constitution of a state, it was unique among such instruments in that it thus limited all political rights, in a community of two thousand persons, to a tiny self-perpetuating oligarchical group of not more than a dozen citizens. Ninety-nine and one half per cent of the population was thus unenfranchised and unrepresented, and even denied the right of appeal to the higher authorities in England.

Such was the situation, brought about with full knowledge and intention, and as long as possible persisted in, by the Puritan leaders.   Those leaders, as we have such clear proof in the case of the noblest of them, John Winthrop, seem to have come to Massachusetts with three distinct and clearly understood objects.   They wished, first, to found and develop a peculiar type of community, best expressed by the term Bible-Commonwealth, in which the political and religious ele-

---

[1] *Massachusetts Records*, vol. I, p. 84; Hutchinson, *History*, vol. I, p. 293 *n.*   *Cf. Acts Privy Council, Colonial*, vol. I, p. 842.
[2] Palfrey, *History*, vol. I, pp. 313, 323.

ments, in themselves and in their relations to one another, should be but two aspects of the same method of so regulating the lives of individuals as to bring them into harmony with the expressed will of God, as interpreted by the self-appointed rulers. Secondly, both as religious zealots, who felt that they had come into possession of ultimate truth, and as active-minded Englishmen, desirous of an outlet for their administrative energies, they considered themselves as the best qualified rulers and the appointed guardians for the community which they had founded. Lastly, having been largely determined by economic considerations in venturing their fortunes in the enterprise, they looked with fear, as well as jealousy, upon any possibility of allowing control of policy, of law and order, and of legislation concerning person and property, to pass to others.

In such a church-state, no civil question could be considered aside from its possible religious bearings; no religious opinion could be discussed apart from its political implications. It was a system which could be maintained permanently only by the most rigid denial of political free speech and religious toleration. Fortunately, however, it contained within itself the seeds of its own dissolution. Apart from other factors, the church-covenant idea, brought by the Pilgrims, accepted by Endicott, and indorsed by the three churches formed by the Winthrop colonists, in 1630, at Dorchester, Charlestown, and Watertown, was the seed of a democratic conception of the state, which grew so persistently as to defy all efforts of its own planters to destroy it. The attitude of the two most influential Massachusetts leaders, lay and ecclesiastical, is not a matter of inference. "Democracy," wrote Winthrop, after stating that there "was no such government in Israel," is "amongst civil nations, accounted the meanest and worst of all forms of government." To allow it in Massachusetts would be "a manifest breach of the 5th. Commandment." [1] "Democracy," wrote John Cotton to Lord Say and Sele, "I do not conceive that ever God did ordeyne as a fit government eyther for church or commonwealth. If the people be gover-

---

[1] R. C. Winthrop, *J. Winthrop*, vol. II, p. 430. I have modernized the spelling.

nors who shall be governed?"[1]   We have already quoted Borgeaud's statement that "democracy is the child of the Reformation, not of the Reformers." The democracy of Massachusetts, slow in developing, was the child of the church-covenant and of the frontier, not of the Puritan leaders.

While the latter were thus attempting to found and maintain an aristocracy or oligarchy to guard a church polity which was unconsciously but implicitly democratic,[2] their position was rendered precarious at the very outset, and increasingly so as time went on, by the necessary presence in the colony of that large unenfranchised class which was not in sympathy with them. As we have seen, even under strong social and political temptation, three quarters of the population, though probably largely Puritan in sentiment and belief, persistently refused to ally themselves with the New England type of Puritan church.   Their presence in the colony was undoubtedly due to economic motives, more especially, perhaps, the desire to own their lands in fee.   It must also have been due to economic considerations on the part of the Puritan rulers. The planting of a Bible-Commonwealth might have been possible without these non-church members, but the creation of a prosperous and populous state was not, as was evidenced by statistics throughout its life.   Even of the first thousand who came with Winthrop, it is probable that many were without strong religious motives; that few realized the plans of the leaders; and it is practically certain that the great bulk of them had never seen the charter.

Many of the more active soon wished to have some voice in the management of their own affairs; and at the October meeting of the General Court, one hundred and eight, including Conant, Maverick, and Blackstone among the old planters, requested that they be made freemen.[3] It became evident to the dozen or so men who alone possessed the governing power, that some extension of the franchise would be necessary

[1] Hutchinson, *History*, Appendix, vol. i, p. 437.

[2] *Cf.* H. L. Osgood, "Political Ideas of the Puritans"; *Political Science Quarterly*, vol. vi, p. 21.

[3] *Massachusetts Records*, vol. i, pp. 79, 80.

if the leading spirits among their two thousand subjects were not to emigrate again to other colonies, or to foment trouble at home. On the other hand, the extension of the franchise was, in their minds, fraught with the perils already indicated. The decision to extend the franchise, but to limit its powers, and to violate the terms of the charter by placing the election of the governor and deputy in the hands of the Assistants instead of the freemen, was probably the result of an effort to solve this problem. Before the next meeting of the General Court in the following May, at which the new freemen were to be admitted, further thought had evidently been devoted to the question, and another solution arrived at. Winthrop was chosen Governor, not by the Assistants, as voted at the preceding meeting, but by "the general consent of the Court, according to the meaning of the patent"; and the momentous resolution was adopted that "noe man shall be admitted to the freedome of this body polliticke, but such as are members of some of the churches within the lymitts of the same." [1] The first attempt on the part of its unenfranchised subjects to secure a larger share of political liberty had resulted merely in establishing, more firmly than before, the theocratical and oligarchical nature of the government.

[1] *Massachusetts Records.* vol. I, p. 87.

CHAPTER VII

AN ENGLISH OPPOSITION BECOMES A NEW ENGLAND OLIGARCHY

In an earlier chapter, in discussing the problems which confronted Elizabeth, we spoke of an established church as a necessity in her day from all three standpoints — of religion, morals, and politics. We also touched upon the simplicity of problems as they appear to those in opposition, as contrasted with their aspect to those who bear the responsibility of power. In England, in the earlier part of the seventeenth century, in spite of the example of Holland, the doctrine of the necessity of a state church, to which all men must conform, in their capacity of citizens as well as of Christians, was still held, although the influence of the "dissidence of dissent," as the logical outcome of individual interpretation of the Bible, was beginning to be felt. Voices were being raised in many quarters denouncing the intolerance of the various sects, both Anglican and Puritan; and, although the Protestants might consider that the religious glacier which held all men in its embrace was as rigidly frozen as ever, the ice was, in truth, rapidly melting beneath the surface. To Englishmen in tolerant Leyden, John Robinson was preaching that "magistrates are kings and lords over men properly and directly, as they are their subjects, and not as they are Christ's," and that by "compulsion many become atheists, hypocrites, and Familists, and being at first constrained to practise against conscience, lose all conscience afterwards."[1] In England, Chillingworth, through the doctrine of the innocence of error, was elevating toleration into a principle of justice and a practicable rule of government.[2] In the New World, Roger

[1] Robinson, *Works*, vol. II, p. 41.
[2] Cited by A. A. Seaton, *The Theory of Toleration under the later Stuarts* (Cambridge Univ. Press, 1911), p. 56.

Williams was soon to begin his life-long struggle against what he vehemently denounced as "that body-killing, soule-killing, and State-killing doctrine" of religious persecution by the arm of the civil power.[1]

We cannot, perhaps, blame men for not being in advance of their age, or even for being behind it. The founders of the Bay Colony were but little qualified, by reason of the narrowness of their views and the intensity with which they were held, to lead men to any higher ground than that which they had been accustomed to tread. Moreover, having changed their place from members of an opposition to members of a government, their new responsibilities would tend to foster even more strongly that fear of innovation which is nearly always characteristic of the middle-class man in power. The exercise of authority is apt to prove an intoxicating draught, even to the best-intentioned men who have been unaccustomed to it; and, of the tiny group who now claimed absolute sway over two thousand subjects, rapidly increasing to sixteen thousand, none had held any position of administrative importance in the old country. Some of them had, indeed, occupied offices, but they were rather of a nature to encourage that intolerance of contradiction, and tendency to arbitrary action upon a small stage, which are apt, in time, to become characteristic of the petty judge, the schoolmaster and the clergyman. Of Endicott's whole career in England, for example, we know only that his rector spoke of him as "a man well knowne to divers persons of good note,"[2] which, in reference to a parishioner in a small country town, more probably referred to his moral character than to any administrative experience. Winthrop had held an unimportant position in a law court. Dudley had managed the estate of a nobleman. Cotton was the rector of a large provincial parish. The work which they and the other leaders did was done honestly; and although the course they pursued, in regard both to the religious qualification for the franchise, and to the later persecutions for

---

[1] *Mr. Cotton's Letter examined; Narr. Club Pub.*, vol. 1, p. 44.
[2] White, *Planter's Plea*, p. 43.

religious beliefs, was, in the long run, to hamper the growth of the colony and to be partly responsible for the eventual loss of the charter, they should not be too severely condemned, perhaps, for the illegal and unjust, as well as politically unwise, course, upon which they now entered. It must be said, however, that, when the great opportunity was offered them of advancing the cause of religious liberty, they turned aside. To the new voices being raised on behalf of justice and humanity, the Massachusetts leaders were as deaf as Laud and the Anglican hierarchy. Equally, and for the same reason, each party solidly and consciously blocked the path to toleration in so far as lay in its power.

The problems of government in the new country soon came thick upon the little group from the opposition in the old. The notorious Morton, for example, was once more singing and trading in "his old nest in the Massachusetts," in the autumn of the year in which Winthrop landed. There were valid reasons, notably his selling fire-arms to the Indians, which might have served adequately as warrant for his arrest by the authorities; but when that action was decided upon, the alleged grounds bore a curiously trumped-up appearance. In the official order for his apprehension, no crime was mentioned; and in his sentence the only matters cited were the "many wrongs he hath done" the Indians, and the theft of a canoe from them.[1] Whatever the moral nature of his intercourse with the natives, it was not likely that, from their standpoint, there had been any very serious crime committed against them by a man living almost isolated in their midst, and whose sole business was trading with them. The convenient, but apparently unfounded, suspicions of a murder committed by him in England, and a warrant procured from the Chief Justice for his shipment thither, could not have served as a basis for any sentence inflicted in Massachusetts.[2] The probable truth is that the Puritans either wanted to teach the discontented "old planters" a lesson, for which purpose Morton offered himself as an easy victim, or they suspected, what was

---

[1] *Massachusetts Records*, vol. I, pp. 74 *f*.   [2] Bradford, *Plymouth*, p. 253.

indeed the fact, that he was in communication with Gorges.[1]
Obviously, neither of these could be openly alleged as a cause
for the punishment they inflicted, which was extraordinarily
severe. He was put in the stocks and deported to England;
his entire property was confiscated, and his house burned
to the ground. Set at liberty in England with little delay,
he got into communication with Gorges, and was soon joined
by two other victims of colonial methods.

Gorges, though a stanch supporter of the Church of England,
was in close relations with the Puritan peers. He and Warwick were having constant dealings, as both were active in
the Council for New England, and his son John was a brother-
in-law of the Earl of Lincoln, in whose house, as we have seen,
the Massachusetts project took shape. There is nothing to
indicate any hostility upon his part to the Massachusetts
colony until 1632; and the several emissaries whom he secretly
sent there were probably dispatched for the sole purpose of
seeing whether or not the settlers were encroaching upon the
lands claimed by himself and his son Robert, whose rights,
it will be recalled, he specifically reserved when he consented
to the granting of the Massachusetts charter. The grantees
of that instrument, however, denied that the Gorges rights
had any legal validity, and claimed and occupied the disputed
land as their own. A quarrel was, therefore, inevitable, and
as the Puritans, it must be confessed, had little respect for
legality themselves, they could, when need required, be counted
upon to take such steps as they might see fit to oppose any
action of Gorges.

Winthrop had been scarcely a month on the shores of the
Bay, when another newcomer arrived in the shape of one of
the most picturesque and mysterious characters who were
ever to stroll on Boston Common. Sir Christopher Gardiner,
Knight of the Sepulchre (somewhat whited), suddenly appeared, with no ostensible business, but with that unexpected

---

[1] C. F. Adams, *New English Canaan of Thomas Morton* (Prince Soc., Boston,
1883), p. 41. For a fair and full account, *cf.* the same author's *Three Episodes*, vol.
I, pp. 240–50. Morton's own account is in his *New English Canaan*, pp. 108 *ff.*

phenomenon in the Puritan colony, a pretty young mistress. To be sure, he called her cousin, but it was soon suspected, as Bradford somewhat quaintly wrote, that "she (after the Italian manner) was his concubine."[1]   In spite of the fact that a late defender has claimed that "he was unfitted for the quiet pleasures of domestic life,"[2] he seems to have made some efforts in that direction; for the authorities soon received word from London to the effect that he had two wives there, who were then in conference, and of whom one was calling loudly for his conversion, and the other for his destruction.[3] On the first of March, 1631, it was ordered by the Massachusetts court that he and seven others should be sent prisoners to England by the good ship Lyon;[4] but the knight, getting word of what was proposed, fled to the Indians.[5]   Some weeks later he was taken into custody by the Plymouth people, who asserted that they had found on his person evidence that he was a Roman Catholic.[6]   While he was lodged in jail in Boston, letters addressed to him by Gorges, as well as one to the absent Morton, came into the hands of Winthrop, who opened them, and decided that they indicated a design on the part of Gorges to regain possession of his land — an ambition not wholly unnatural.[7]   Whether or not the authorities decided that it was wiser that Gardiner should not appear in England to add his testimony to that of Morton, nothing further seems to have been done to carry into effect the order for his deportation, and he was soon set at liberty.

Meanwhile a lonely settler from Maine had appeared in Boston, and had looked with favor upon Gardiner's fair companion. He decided to marry the lady and to take her back to the Eveless Eden of the Androscoggin. Gardiner himself accompanied them, and the curiously assorted trio spent the winter together at Brunswick, from which season there was an

---

[1] Bradford, *Plymouth*, p. 294.
[2] P. Oliver, *The Puritan Commonwealth* (Boston, 1856), p. 35.
[3] Dudley's Letter, in Young, *Chron. Mass.*, p. 333.
[4] *Massachusetts Records*, vol. 1, p. 83.
[5] J. Winthrop, *History*, vol. 1, p. 65.
[6] Bradford, *Plymouth*, p. 295.   [7] J. Winthrop, *History*, vol. 1, p. 68.

odd echo in the Maine law courts nine years later, when Gardiner's host, and not himself, was properly sued for a warming-pan stolen by the knight during his chilly stay. In the summer of 1632, Gardiner landed in England just in time to add his witness to that of Morton and Ratcliffe in Gorges's attack upon the Massachusetts charter.[1]

Ratcliffe, who was a mentally unbalanced servant of Cradock, had apparently talked loosely about the government and the Salem church. For these "mallitious and scandulous speeches," as the crime was designated in his sentence by the court, he was whipped, had both his ears cut off, was fined the impossible sum of £40, and banished from the colony.[2] He was not long in joining Morton and Gardiner in England, and becoming one more arrow in Gorges's quiver.

These cases, moreover, though they proved more important individually, in their reaction upon the colony, by no means stood alone. A certain Thomas Gray, for an unspecified crime, was banished, his house was pulled down, and all Englishmen were enjoined from giving him shelter, "under such penalty as the Court shall thinke meete to inflicte." Thomas Dexter, for saying, "This captious government will bring all to naught," adding that "the best of them was but an atturney, &c.," was put in the stocks, fined £40, and disfranchised. Henry Lynn, "for writeing into England falsely and mallitiously against the government and execuccion of justice here," was ordered whipped and banished; while Thomas Knower was put in the stocks for saying that, if punished, he would have the legality of his sentence tried in England.[3]

The course of justice, if no worse than in contemporary England, was evidently but little improved by its passage overseas, or by being administered by those who had been so loud in their denunciations of the summary methods of Laud and the High Commission. It seemed to many, as to the "old planter" Blackstone, that the tyranny of the "Lord-Bishops"

[1] C. F. Adams, *Mass. Hist. Soc. Proceedings*, Series I, vol. xx, p. 80.,
[2] *Massachusetts Records*, vol. I, p. 88; J. Winthrop, *History*, vol. I, p. 67.
[3] *Massachusetts Records*, vol. I, pp. 77, 101, 103, 104, 102.

had merely been exchanged for that of the "Lord-Brethren"; and it was evident also that the fixed policy of the leaders was to allow no appeals from their decisions to the home courts of England. All the colonists, therefore, who would not, on the one hand, wholly refrain from criticizing the policy and acts of the leaders, and, on the other, prove themselves acceptable to the clergy, and so secure the franchise by being elected free-men, were wholly without representation, without voice in the making of their laws, and without recourse to the courts and king at home.

As the charter was that of a trading corporation, the levy-ing of taxes was a mere development of the right to assess shareholders, and, therefore, extended only to freemen. But no such legal restriction was observed, and from the beginning, the authorities taxed the non-freemen equally with themselves, though denying them the political rights which they them-selves possessed.[1] Indeed, not only their property was thus subject to enactments in which they had no voice, but their time and the work of their hands as well; for the General Court passed a law that all except members of the court, and officers of the church and commonwealth, were liable to be impressed for manual labor on all public works.[2] The town meeting, indeed, seems to have been the only place in which the great majority of the colonists could legally make their voice heard at all, and there only upon questions concerning the most trivial local matters.

The New England town, already noted as one of the three typical institutions in the development and influence of that section, may be considered in its origin as "the politically active congregation," bound together, in addition to its church ties, by a peculiar agrarian policy.[3] Originating at Plymouth,

[1] H. L. Osgood, "New England Colonial Finance in the 17th Century"; *Political Science Quarterly*, vol. xix, p. 82.

[2] *Massachusetts Records*, vol. i, p. 124.

[3] M. Eggleston, *The Land System of the New England Colonies*, Johns Hopkins Univ. Studies, Baltimore, 1886. *Cf.* also C. M. Andrews, *The River Towns of Conn.*, J. H. U. S., 1889; W. E. Foster, *Town Government in Rhode Island*, J. H. U. S., 1886; A. B. Maclear, *Early New England Towns*, Columbia Univ. Studies, 1908; H. L. Os-good, *American Colonies*, vol. i, pp. 424 *ff.*; and for English towns on Long Island, J. T. Adams, *History of the Town of Southampton* (Bridgehampton, 1918), pp. 94–103.

it became universal throughout the Puritan colonies on the mainland, and was reproduced with extraordinary fidelity of detail wherever New Englanders migrated. The New England colonies, for the most part, neither sold nor rented their land, but granted it freely in fee to actual settlers, in rough proportion to their present ability to use it.[1] In general most of it was granted primarily to towns, which owned it in their corporate capacity; and by them it was allotted to individuals in the form of home-lots or arable land and meadow. The remainder formed the "common," for the use of all, under certain restrictions. The whole land-system, as well as the methods of cultivation, exhibited many striking resemblances to those of our early Teutonic ancestors; and, some years ago, these coincidences were largely insisted upon as cases of genuine survival.[2] It is more probable that a return to favorable wilderness conditions merely strengthened those primitive elements still remaining in the manorial system, with which the settlers were familiar in England. As we have already pointed out, the geographical environment in New England, as contrasted with that of the other colonies, tended strongly to develop the type of compact settlement. This was further reinforced by the form of emigration, which was distinctly of neighborhood groups, and by the type of church government.

The exigencies of the situation, when the settlers first landed, had necessitated their dispersal in various communities, whose members at once found it needful to manage their local affairs to some extent by meeting together among themselves. The charter made no provision for any but a general government; nor, under it, did the company have any legal right to incorporate other bodies. These more or less informal local governments were, therefore, extra-legal both before and after the passage of a township act by which it was attempted specifi-

---

[1] The occasional few and unimportant exceptions do not affect the general statement.

[2] *Cf*. H. B. Adams, *The Germanic Origin of New England Towns*, J. H. U. S., 1882; Id., *Village Communities of Cape Anne and Salem*, J. H. U. S., 1883; G. E. Howard, *Local Constitutional History of the U. S.*, J. H. U. S., 1889. Too enthusiastic believers should read "The Survival of Archaic Communities," in F. W. Maitland, *Collected Papers* (Cambridge Univ. Press, 1911), vol. II, pp. 313 *ff*.

cally to give them certain rights of local administration. At the town meetings, which at first were spontaneous, and afterward regulated, all the inhabitants had the right to be present and to take part in the discussion of public affairs, although only the freemen were entitled to vote, except upon a few questions of minor importance. The distinction was somewhat similar to that in the churches, which all could attend, but in the management of which only church members had a voice. The town meeting, therefore, was a completely democratic institution in only one of its aspects, although it came to have great influence upon both political theory and practice.

A further development brought these local communities into working relations with the General Court. Owing to the distance of the scattered settlements from Boston, and the danger of all the freemen being absent at once from their homes, it was enacted, in 1634, that every town should elect two or three deputies, who should have the power of the whole, and who should act as their representatives in the General Court.[1] As the charter provided that seven of the eighteen Assistants must be present in the Court in order to constitute a quorum, that body was now composed of a small number of Assistants and a steadily growing number of Deputies. As the Virginia House of Burgesses had been established in 1619, and the Bermuda Assembly in 1620, the representative government provided for in Massachusetts was the third in the colonies.[2]

Owing to the close alliance maintained between the clergy and the Magistrates, as the Assistants soon came to be called, the body of deputies grew to be considered the more popular element in the Court. It was clear that real grievances and the democratic influences at work in the town meeting were likely to develop into attacks upon the arbitrary power of the very limited body of freemen. The form that the struggle assumed was that of a contest, lasting twenty years, between the deputies and the magistrates, with the influence of the

[1] *Massachusetts Records*, vol. i, p. 118.
[2] *Cf.* J. H. Lefroy, *On the Constitutional History of the Bermudas* (Westminster, 1881), p. 6.

clergy constantly on the side of the latter. The freemen themselves were, indeed, not all in favor of the arbitrary exercise of power by the small oligarchical group which for so long remained in control. As early as 1631, the people of Watertown, when taxed for fortifying Newtown, declared that "it was not safe to pay moneys after that sort, for fear of bringing themselves and posterity into bondage." [1] Although legally in the right, they accepted Winthrop's interpretation of the charter, which is interesting as showing how completely the unjustified transformation from a company into a commonwealth had already been effected in the minds of the leaders.

Although the people, until well into the eighteenth century, probably had little thought of becoming independent of England, it seems clear from all the acts of the leaders, especially the transfer of the charter itself, that it was their intention, even before leaving England, to govern in as complete independence of that country as future circumstances might permit. They wished, it is true, to found a state for the glory of God and the establishment of true religion, but in which, nevertheless, they themselves should constitute the supreme power. Every encroachment upon it, from any direction, was grudgingly yielded to; and it is not unlikely that, even then, some of them dreamed of an actual political independence. "We are not a free state," wrote Pyncheon to Winthrop, in 1646, evidently with this in mind; "neither do I think it our wisdom to be a free state; though we had our liberty, we cannot *as yet* subsist without England." [2]

The political history of Massachusetts under the charter was thus made up of two separate elements. The first was the resistance of the governing group to any effort of England, legal or illegal, to assert her rights, even justly, over her colony; and the second was the struggle of a part of the colonists themselves, for toleration and liberty, against the governing class. Even had the colony never separated from England, we should, in all probability, have come to possess the same

[1] J. Winthrop, *History*, vol. I, p. 84.
[2] *Mass. Hist. Soc. Coll.*, Series IV, vol. VI, p. 383. The italics are mine.

measure of civil liberty and religious toleration that the English have to-day; but that separation having taken place, had the Puritan oligarchy retained and extended their power, we should have but little of either. It is, therefore, the second conflict which, although less dramatic, is the more vital in the history of human freedom. We must now turn to consider the earliest important attacks from both of the quarters indicated.

Of those from across the water, the first was launched, as could well have been foreseen, by Sir Ferdinando Gorges, and was brought upon the colony directly through the policy pursued by its leaders. The untiring interest of Gorges in the affairs of New England, and his hope of yet creating a profitable settlement there for himself, were both well known to the Puritans. The old knight had spent vastly greater sums in the effort to plant the wilderness than had been contributed by any individual among themselves. He had attempted the colonization of Maine at a time when the men who were now engaged in banishing his agents were hardly more than children.[1] He had made no effort to disturb the Pilgrims during their ten-years' stay at Plymouth, and would probably have left the Massachusetts settlers also in peace, had it not been for their denial of the rights he claimed in a part of the soil they had preëmpted, and for their treatment of his emissaries. The Massachusetts authorities, by throwing down the gauntlet, had created a powerful enemy who was not slow in picking it up.

In 1632, Gorges and Mason, with the assistance of Gardiner, Morton, and Ratcliffe, prepared a petition, which was presented to the Privy Council in December.[2] Winthrop stated that among many false accusations and "some truths misrepeated," it accused the colony of separating from the Church of England, and of threatening to cast off its political allegiance.[3] Supporters of the company in England hastily put

---

[1] Winthrop was a lad of 19 in 1607, and Endicott but 16.
[2] *Acts Privy Council, Colonial*, vol. I, p. 183.
[3] J. Winthrop, *History*, vol. I, p. 122.

into motion those unseen agencies that were most efficacious in doing business at the court of Charles; and, in spite of what seemed overwhelming odds against them, in courtly influence, won an unexpected victory, even gaining a word of commendation from the King.[1] Their success is involved in a mystery, which, however, we suspect might be unlocked by that same "golden key" which the Pilgrims were using contemporaneously at another of the royal doors. Meanwhile, the Council for New England had requested that the Company's charter be presented for examination, and Humphrey had been forced to confess that it was in New England, stating that, though he had often written for it, he had been unable to obtain it.[2]

The demand, however, was repeated from a more powerful source two years later. In 1633, Laud had become Archbishop of Canterbury, and had declared war upon the Puritans. Colonial affairs, which had heretofore been considered, when considered at all, by the Privy Council, were now put into the hands of a body styled "the Lords Commissioners for Plantations in General," which was headed by the Archbishop, and given almost royal powers in both civil and ecclesiastical matters, including that of revoking all charters and patents unduly obtained.[3] Gorges utilized this new opportunity, and at once began to work upon the Archbishop's hatred of Puritanism, in order to recover his own legal claims. On February 21, 1634, the Board, having taken into consideration the great numbers of persons "known to be ill-affected and discontented, as well with the Civil as Ecclesiastical government," who were daily resorting to New England, ordered that Cradock produce the Massachusetts charter.[4] Upon receipt of Cradock's first letter requesting its return, the authorities at Boston decided to return an evasive answer, ignoring

---

[1] J. Winthrop, *History*, vol. I, p. 123 *n.*

[2] Records Council for New England; *American Antiquarian Society Proceedings*, 1866, p. 107.

[3] C. M. Andrews, *British Committees, Commissions, and Councils of Trade and Plantations, 1622–1675*, J. H. U. S., 1908, pp. 16 *f.*

[4] *Acts Privy Council, Colonial*, vol. I, p. 199. The order is given in Hubbard, *History*, p. 153.

the Council's demand. After the first communication had been followed by an official copy of the order itself, word was returned by Winslow, who was acting as agent for both Plymouth and Massachusetts, that the charter could not be sent except by a vote of the General Court, which body would not meet until September.[1]

Meanwhile, Gorges was plying the English authorities with letters advising that a governor, "neither papistically nor scizmatically affected," be appointed for New England, modestly suggesting that he himself was an eminently proper person for the office, and urging that the Massachusetts charter be repealed.[2] His wish was gratified as to the first two points, and it looked as if he was at last to see the shores of that land which had been the chief object of his thoughts for thirty years. Winslow, whose suit, at first, had seemingly prospered, was suddenly and dramatically confronted, in the presence of Laud, with his old enemy Morton of Merry Mount, and, as a result of the latter's accusations, was temporarily committed to prison.[3]

The grandiose scheme that Gorges had conceived contemplated the division of all New England among certain members of the old Council, and the validating of the individual assignments by legal sanctions. It was also arranged that the charter should then be resigned by that body, which had only too truly become, as the declaration read, "a Carcass in a manner breathless."[4] This was done in April, and in the following month a writ of *Quo Warranto* was entered, to deprive the Massachusetts company of its own charter, as the final step in the transformation of New England. Aside from the play of conflicting influences involved, the leaders, by their handling of affairs, had, without question, violated the terms of that instrument, and so had given their adversaries a reputable cause to plead. The verdict was adverse to the Company, judgment was entered against such of the patentees as ap-

[1] J. Winthrop, *History*, vol. 1, pp. 161, 163.
[2] Baxter, *Gorges*, vol. III, pp. 261–75.
[3] Bradford, *Plymouth*, p. 330.   [4] Hazard, *Hist. Coll.*, vol. 1, p. 391.

peared, and the remainder were outlawed. The patentees, however, refused to acknowledge the action of the courts, and the charter was not returned, though again demanded two years later.[1] Meanwhile, Gorges's new-risen hopes had been wholly dashed. Though he had been appointed governor, the King had provided him with no funds from the empty treasury, and Gorges's own resources were always inadequate for his undertakings. Mason, who was aiding him, suddenly died. The ship which was to have carried the knight to his new province broke as it was being launched, and delay followed delay, while the aspect of public affairs was rapidly changing.

This favorable turn, however, was not foreseen in the colony, and immediately upon receipt of the news of the appointment of the new Commission for Plantations, the Massachusetts government prepared for armed resistance. A sentry was posted on a hill near Boston, to give notice of the arrival of any hostile ships; £600 was raised for the completion of the fortifications on Castle Island; a military committee was appointed; and, a few weeks later, the clergy were consulted as to what should be done if a general governor were sent out from England. Their unanimous answer was that "We ought not to accept him, but defend our lawful possessions (if we are able), otherwise to avoid or protract."[2] It must be recalled that the Massachusetts settlers were as yet Englishmen, and not independent Americans; and the home government, whose subjects they were, could hardly regard these acts and utterances otherwise than as rank rebellion, however different an aspect they might come to wear in the eyes of ourselves as heirs of a subsequent and successful revolution. Political events in England soon developed in such a way as to prevent any very serious consideration of colonial affairs for another

[1] Hutchinson, *History*, vol. 1, p. 85; Hutchinson, *Papers* (Prince Soc., Albany, 1865), vol. 1, p. 119.

[2] *Massachusetts Records*, vol. 1, pp. 136–39; J. Winthrop, *History*, vol. 1, pp. 170, 183. They were also asked whether it was lawful to retain the cross in the royal ensign, Endicott having chosen this inopportune moment to give an example of his blundering fanaticism, by cutting it out. *Massachusetts Records*, vol. 1, pp. 136, 147; J. Winthrop, *History*, vol. 1, pp. 175, 183, 199.

quarter of a century, and the policy of "avoid or protract," seemed temporarily to serve all purposes.

The colonial government, which had thus assumed what was practically a position of avowed independence of the king and courts of England, next decided to take up a stronger line in regard to its own subjects in the colony itself, for the spirit of the Watertown freemen against taxation had evidently spread. Just prior to the meeting of the General Court in the spring of 1634, every town deputed two men to consider such matters as might come up; and after consultation, a demand was made upon the governor to allow them to inspect the charter. Having found upon examination that the General Court was the only legal body entitled to legislate, they apparently inquired why that power had been usurped by the magistrates. Winthrop replied that it was because the General Court had become unwieldy in size; and he made the suggestion that, for the present, "they might, at the general court, make an order, that, once in the year, a certain number should be appointed, (upon summons from the governor) to revise all laws, etc., and to reform what they found amiss therein; but not to make any new laws, but prefer their grievances to the court of assistants; and that no assessments should be laid upon the country without the consent of such a committee, nor any lands disposed of." [1]   It is difficult to conceive of a more complete abrogation of the rights of even the very limited body of freemen; and, though Winthrop does not tell us how this astonishing offer was received, the records leave us in no doubt. At the meeting of the General Court, it was immediately voted that there should be no trial for life or banishment except by a jury summoned by themselves; that there should be four such courts a year, not to be dissolved without their own consent; that none but the General Court had power to make laws or to elect and remove officials; and that none but the General Court had power to dispose of lands or to raise money by taxation. [2]

[1] J. Winthrop, *History*, vol. I, p. 153.
[2] *Massachusetts Records*, vol. I, pp. 117 *ff.*

Another incident, of less importance, but interesting as showing the feeling abroad and the means by which it might, for a time, be suppressed, occurred at a meeting of the inhabitants of Boston later in the year, to choose some men to divide additional town-land. The voting was by secret ballot, for the first time, and Winthrop, Coddington, and the other leaders failed of election. The first stated in his account of the affair, that the electors chose mostly men of "the inferior sort," fearing that the richer men would give the poor an unfairly small proportion of land, the policy, he added, having been to leave a large amount undivided for newcomers and commons.[1] The argument, which was sound, might perhaps have been considered sounder by the discontented, had the governor himself, for example, not acquired by that time above eighteen hundred acres, Saltonstall sixteen hundred, and Dudley seventeen hundred.[2] After Winthrop had made a speech, and the Reverend Mr. Cotton had "showed them that it was the Lord's order among the Israelites to have all such businesses committed to the elders," a new vote was ordered and the magistrates were elected.[3]

It was evident that, if the little group of leaders, lay and ecclesiastic, were to retain power permanently, in view of the spirit evinced by the people, and the extremely rapid growth of the population, it could be only by securing a firmer hold upon the body of magistrates and the election of freemen. A few months previously, Cotton had preached a sermon arguing that the magistrates, who were annually elected under the charter, were entitled to be perpetually reëlected, except for "just cause"; and he compared their rights to office with those of a man in his freehold estate.[4] This suggestion seems to have borne fruit something more than a year afterward, when, it having been shown "from the word of God, etc., that the principal magistrates ought to be for life," it was voted that a council should be created, to have such powers as the

---

[1] J. Winthrop, *History*, vol. 1, p. 181.
[2] Adams, *Three Episodes*, vol. 1, p. 365.
[3] J. Winthrop, *History*, vol. 1, p. 181. [4] *Ibid*, vol. 1, p. 157.

General Court should grant them, and not to be subject to removal except for crimes or "other weighty cause." This, of course, was again a violation of the charter, and, like so much of the reactionary legislation, was due to the direct influence of the clergy.[1] Though Winthrop, Dudley, and Endicott were elected to the new offices, the council was never granted any powers, and the plan failed.[2]

Of somewhat more practical service, in view of the fact that church membership was an indispensable qualification for the franchise, was the law, passed at the same court, that no new churches could be organized without the approbation of the magistrates and a majority of the elders of the preëxisting churches, and that no man could become a freeman who was not a member of a church so approved of. By this means a degree of control, at least, could be maintained over the great numbers of newcomers now arriving.

We do not wish to convey the impression that the leaders of the colony were animated by mere love of power or a vulgar ambition, strong though the former was in most of them. But the danger to the liberties of their subjects was no less great because Winthrop and Cotton were wholly convinced of the divine nature of their mission. It is too frequently assumed that despotic acts are necessarily those of a self-conscious despot; whereas, in most cases, they are merely the readiest means employed for reaching ends which authority may think itself rightly privileged, or morally bound, to attain. Charles and Laud were no less certain than the rulers of Church and State in Massachusetts, that their mandate was a heavenly one. Liberty cannot mean one thing in old England and another in New, nor can intolerance be condoned in the one and condemned in the other. The King and the Archbishop were no more closely allied, nor more bent upon forcing their own will upon that of the people, than were the civil and ecclesiastical powers of the little American commonwealth, however

[1] R. C. Winthrop, *J. Winthrop*, vol. II, p. 271.

[2] J. Winthrop, *History*, vol. I, p. 220; *Massachusetts Records*, vol. I, pp. 167, 174, 195, 264.

worthy or unworthy the motives of each may have been. Pride in the valiant work that the Massachusetts leaders did in subduing the wilderness, and in the sacrifices that they made for their religious beliefs, has tended to make their descendants, in the words of the old English saw, "to their faults a little blind, and to their virtues very kind"; but if the nations of the world are to grow in mutual understanding and brotherly feeling, their histories must be written from the standpoint of justice to all, and not from that of a mistaken national piety.

We now come to the case of the first, and perhaps the most conspicuous, individual who was to fall under the discipline of both Church and State in New England. Roger Williams had arrived in Boston as early as 1631. Added to a most winning nature and a personality that ever exerted a charm over friends and enemies alike, he brought with him a reputation for being a godly minister, and within a few months after his arrival, was invited by the church at Salem to become their teacher. He had also, apparently, within only a few weeks of his landing, been chosen to the same office by the Boston congregation, but had refused to join with them because they would not acknowledge themselves to be separated from the Church of England.[1] He had also, thus early, declared his doctrine that the power of the magistrates should be limited to civil matters, and that they had no authority to punish the breach of the Sabbath or other religious offenses.[2] For these reasons, the General Court wrote a letter to Endicott, expostulating with the Salem church for accepting Williams, which that church apparently ignored.[3] He did not, however, remain long, but removed to Plymouth, where he stayed preaching until again called to Salem in 1634.[4]

Meanwhile, he had not only so extended his doctrine of the separation of church and state as to deny that a magistrate

[1] Letter to John Cotton, Jr., 1671 (*Narr. Club Pub.*, vol. VI, p. 356).
[2] J. Winthrop, *History*, vol. I, p. 63.
[3] The evidence is somewhat conflicting. *Cf.* citations of authorities in H. M. Dexter, *As to Roger Williams* (Boston, 1876), p. 5.
[4] Bradford, *Plymouth*, p. 310.

had power to require an oath, but had added a new and, it is needless to say, fundamentally dangerous doctrine for the legal foundation of the colony, in his declaration that, the Indians being the true owners of the soil, the King had had no right to grant a charter, and the colony should repent of having received it. The authorities might, perhaps, fear the expression of such opinions, and his subsequent banishment, the motives for which have always been the subject of heated dispute from his own day to this, may have been caused by his denial of the legal basis of the colony, as much as by his theory of religious toleration. It was without doubt the latter, however, which brought down upon him the special hostility of the clergy. Winthrop, who like Bradford and Winslow, had an affectionate regard for the young clergyman, specifically stated that the ministers rendered their judgment "that he who should obstinately maintain such opinions, whereby a church might run into heresy, apostacy, or tyranny, and yet the civil magistrate could not intermeddle," should be removed.[1]

The civil power was at once brought into play. Williams was cited to appear, and the town of Salem was denied title to certain lands which it claimed as its own, until it should discard its teacher.[2] Williams then endeavored to have the Salem church separate from all the others, and the congregation addressed a sharp letter of reproof to the magistrates. The final triumph was, of course, on the side of the established authorities. Williams, after what seems to have been a fair trial, was ordered to be banished,[3] the decree being subsequently revised to take effect in the spring, provided Williams would refrain from attempting to spread his opinions, which, apparently, he was unable to do. The authorities, having heard that he was planning to lead a colony to Narragansett, and fearing that the "infection" would spread from there throughout the churches, undertook to ship him back to England; but he escaped in the middle of January, making

[1] J. Winthrop, *History*, vol. 1, p. 194.   [2] *Ibid*, vol. 1, p. 195.
[3] *Massachusetts Records*, vol. 1, p. 161.

his way through the snow-filled forests to the safe confines and hospitable savages of Rhode Island.[1]

His subsequent prominence as the founder of that state, and his written advocacy of the principle of toleration, have tended to overemphasize the contemporary importance of the proceedings just described.[2] The authorities had a fair basis for their action, on civil grounds alone; and although the religious aspect undoubtedly entered largely into the case, it marked, in that respect, no new departure in policy.[3] It merely showed somewhat more clearly, perhaps, that, in any case which threatened to weaken the established relations of church and state or to question the right of the latter to require the most rigid conformity to the doctrines and practices of the former, the magistrates and clergy could be counted upon to act rigorously together. Although personally popular, Williams had acquired few adherents who were willing to follow him beyond a certain point in his struggle, and the victory of the court created but a slight disturbance. The colony, however, in order to avoid even the possibility of strife, had lost what it could ill afford to spare — a mind of wider vision than its own.

If Williams's expulsion had caused no tumult, that was not to be true of another case with which the authorities soon had to deal. Ann Hutchinson, who had been a parishioner of John Cotton in England, had come to Massachusetts with her husband, later followed by her brother-in-law, John Wheelwright, and had been in Boston about two years at the time of Williams's banishment. She had acquired a considerable influence among the women, due more, perhaps, to her kindly

---

[1] J. Winthrop, *History*, vol. I, p. 209.

[2] Besides his works already referred to, his doctrine of religious liberty found expression in *The Bloody Tenent of Persecution*, 1644, and *The Bloody Tenent yet more Bloody*, 1652, reprinted as vols. III and IV of the *Narr. Club Pub.*

[3] *Cf.*, however, besides the standard histories, J. L. Diman, Preface to *Narragansett Club Publications*, vol. II, pp. 1–8; and Dexter, *As to Roger Williams*. The latter is strongly biased against Williams, and contains some untenable views as to the founders' attitude toward the charter, but is useful as citing almost all known references to the case. It was critically reviewed by H. S. Burrage, *American Historical Association Report*, 1899, vol. I, pp. 10–12.

spirit and helpfulness in sickness, than to her brilliant mind, which seems to have impressed itself upon many of the ablest men in the colony. The New England of that day, as for long after, offered almost no opportunity for the play of such a restless intellect as hers except upon religious questions, and Mrs. Hutchinson was, in addition, a sincerely religious woman. After some time, during which we hear nothing of her, she appeared as holding Thursday meetings in her house for those women who had been unable to attend church on the preceding Sunday, and to whom she rehearsed the sermons preached. She soon passed on to comparing those of various clergymen, and gradually evolved the doctrine that, while Mr. Cotton and her brother-in-law preached a "Covenant of Grace," all of the others preached a "Covenant of Works" — a theological distinction which has often been considered so baffling as to elude understanding. Even at the time, Winthrop wrote that "no man could tell (except some few, who knew the bottom of the matter) where any difference was."[1] It may be inferred, however, that by a "Covenant of Grace" she meant a religion based upon a direct revelation in the individual soul of God's grace and love, while by a "Covenant of Works" was intended a religion founded upon a covenant between God as judge and man as fallen, which men had merely to obey unquestioningly, as they obeyed the civil law, and of which the minister was the official interpreter.[2]

It is needless to point out that the latter accorded with the whole doctrine and polity of the Massachusetts church and state, while the former would have undermined both as constituted. To many, the preaching of a religion of love, as contrasted with the harsh tenets of the established doctrine of law and judgment, brought a joy and peace they had sought in vain in the latter, and Mrs. Hutchinson's followers grew

---

[1] J. Winthrop, *History*, vol. I, p. 255.
[2] The modern literature regarding the Antinomian controversy is large. *Cf.* C. F. Adams, *Antinomianism in the Colony of Massachusetts Bay;* Prince Society, Boston, 1894; also his *Three Episodes*, vols. I, pp. 363, and II, 533–81. A very lucid account is given by R. N. Jones, *The Quakers in the American Colonies* (London, 1911), pp. 4–25.

rapidly in number. Among them were included Mr. Cotton himself,— who, however, drew back in the succeeding turmoil, — and the new young Governor of the colony, Sir Harry Vane.

Vane, as yet but twenty-three years old, high-born and brilliant, but immature, had arrived in the autumn of 1635 in the ship that brought the Reverend Hugh Peter and John Winthrop, Jr. He had come over, as had the younger Winthrop, in connection with the plantation project of Lords Say, Brook, and others; but he remained in Boston, and was soon admitted a member of Cotton's church. During the preceding years there had been from time to time various disagreements between Winthrop and Dudley, both of whom had occupied the office of governor, the troubles arising largely from Dudley's touchy and overbearing nature. Reconciliations had been effected by the kindly and patient Winthrop, and the petty quarrels are of practically no historical importance, save in that the people had taken sides to a certain extent. Vane and Peter had been but a few months in the colony, when, for reasons best known to themselves, they undertook to arrange a meeting between Governor Haynes, the two ex-governors, the three clergymen, Cotton, Hooker, and Wilson, and themselves. The discussion finally centred upon whether the mildness of Winthrop or the severity of the fanatical Dudley was the wiser in governing the colony. The question, as usual, was referred to the ministers for their opinion, who gave it in favor of "strict discipline" for the honor and safety of the gospel. Whereupon, Winthrop acknowledged that he had been too lenient, and promised a stricter course thereafter, and Massachusetts took one more step backward.[1] The following spring Vane was elected governor.

Meanwhile, Mrs. Hutchinson had won over practically all the Boston church, except Wilson, Winthrop, and a few others, who, however, were strong enough to defeat the proposal to install Wheelwright as teacher.[2] The strife was gradually spreading, and Vane, who had allied himself with the Hutchinson party, made a flimsy excuse to resign the governorship.

---

[1] J. Winthrop, *History*, vol. 1, pp. 211 *ff.*   [2] *Ibid.*, vol. 1, pp. 241 *ff.*

The Boston church and the Court both refused to consider his reasons valid, and the resignation was withdrawn. A conference of the ministers, called by the Court, was held in December, to try to compose the differences, but accomplished nothing except to increase the bitter feeling between the parties. A day of fasting was proclaimed, and although Wheelwright had removed to Mt. Wollaston, he attended the Boston church on that occasion, and preached his famous "fast-day sermon." [1] For expressions contained in it, as falsely interpreted by the authorities, he was declared by the Court to have been guilty of contempt and sedition, the same body condemning Stephen Greensmith to a fine of £40 for saying that all the ministers, except Cotton, Wheelwright, and, possibly, Hooker, taught a covenant of works. [2]

Wheelwright having next been summoned to appear before the General Court, a petition was presented, signed by nearly all the members of the Boston church, asking that the hearings should be open to freemen, and that cases of conscience might be first dealt with by the churches. [3] This was declared to be "a groundless and presumptuous act." Wheelwright's examination was begun in private, and the authorities stated that it would proceed *ex officio*. This raised loud complaints among the people, who avowed that it was but one of those High Commission proceedings which they had left England to escape. Wheelwright refused to answer the questions put, and the hearings were finally allowed to be open. The clergy were then asked by the Court whether they did teach a covenant of works. All but Cotton replied in the affirmative, and the verdict was thus foreshadowed. Nevertheless, it took two days of further struggling, again behind closed doors, before the sentence of sedition and contempt could be agreed to, and the party of the priests and magistrates secure their victory. [4] A petition, denying that any of Wheelwright's utterances had

---

[1] It is reprinted by C. H. Bell, *John Wheelwright* (Prince Society, Boston, 1876), pp. 153 *ff*.

[2] *Massachusetts Records*, vol. I, p. 189.

[3] J. Winthrop, *History*, vol. I, p. 256.

[4] Adams, *Three Episodes*, vol. I, pp. 444 *f*.

been seditious, was presented to the Court, signed by sixty members of the Boston church, for which they were rebuked by Winthrop.[1]

The majority of the Court, however, evidently feared the next election, and secured the passage of a resolution requiring that the elections should be held at Newtown, and not, as had always been customary, at Boston.[2] At the election, in May, Vane and Winthrop were the opposing leaders, and although the former attempted some ill-judged political manœuvres, the ecclesiastical party was wholly successful. Winthrop was elected governor, Dudley deputy-governor, and Endicott, apparently as a reward for his share in the proceedings, was made a member of the unconstitutional life council, while all the Boston Antinomians were defeated for the magistracy. When, in answer to this, that town next day returned Vane, Coddington, and Hoffe as deputies, the Court "found a means to send them home again," claiming that two of the Boston freemen had not been notified of the election. The next morning, Boston held a new election, and returned the same deputies, and "the court not finding how they might reject them, they were admitted." [3]

The victory over Boston, however, was evidently not considered sufficient, and the Court proceeded to pass an immigration law, to the effect that no town could receive any person for a longer time than three weeks without permission of one of the council or two of the magistrates. In other words, no Englishman could settle in Massachusetts without personal permission from Winthrop, Dudley, or Endicott, or two of their eight associates. The law had evidently been framed to prevent any accession to the ranks of the Hutchinson party, and was promptly put into execution on the arrival of a considerable body of newcomers, including a brother of Mrs. Hutchinson, who were forced to leave the colony after having reached its shores.[4] Feeling naturally ran high, and

[1] Adams, *Antinomianism*, pp. 133 *ff.*; J. Winthrop, *History*, vol. I, pp. 183 *f.*
[2] *Massachusetts Records*, vol. I, p. 191.
[3] *Ibid.*, vol. I, pp. 195 *ff.*; J. Winthrop, *History*, vol. I, pp. 261 *ff.*
[4] *Ibid.*, p. 278.

Winthrop defended, while Vane attacked, the validity and justice of such an enactment.[1]   With the law already alluded to, placing the whole control of the franchise in the hands of the magistrates and the clergy, and with this new law, which gave the right of admission to the colony wholly to the former, the control of the oligarchy would seem to have been fairly complete.

The Court, however, even as constituted as a result of the May election, did not move rapidly enough in the prosecution of Wheelwright, and was summarily dissolved in September. Sixteen members were dropped, and the new Court, comprising forty-two members, contained twenty-two new names.[2]   Even this purge was not enough, and two deputies were expelled, one for declaring that the Boston petition was lawful, and the other for declaring that he believed Wheelwright was innocent and was being persecuted for the truth.

Meanwhile, Vane had returned to England, and a synod of all the clergy had met and declared that there were eighty-two erroneous or blasphemous opinions involved in the controversy.[3]   Mr. Cotton, who had no taste for that banishment which he claimed was no hardship, now went over to what was evidently to be the winning side.   With a broader mind and wider vision than any of the other clergy of the colony, he had not the courage to stand alone, beyond a certain point, against their unanimity in intolerance.   The higher promptings of his nature were crushed by the united voice of the priest-hood, as Winthrop's had been so short a time before, and the noblest of the colony's leaders, lay and clerical, from that time tended to sink to the lower level of their fellows.

Events now moved more swiftly.   At the November Court, Wheelwright was sentenced to be disfranchised and banished, and was refused the privilege of an appeal to England.[4]   He was given fourteen days in which to settle his affairs, and at

---

[1] The documents are given in the Hutchinson *Papers*, vol. i, pp. 79–114.

[2] *Massachusetts Records*, vol. i, pp. 204, 205.

[3] They are given in full by Adams, *Antinomianism*, pp. 95–124.   J. Winthrop, *History*, vol. i, pp. 284 *ff*., gives an account of the meeting, but mentions only 80.

[4] *Massachusetts Records*, vol. i, p. 207; J. Winthrop, *History*, vol. i, p. 294.

the beginning of winter was on his way to New Hampshire. One of the expelled deputies was disfranchised and threatened with banishment should he "speake anything to disturbe the publike peace." Another was also disfranchised and banished. Two weeks later, seven of the signers of the petition were disfranchised, and ten more, who acknowledged their "sin" in having signed, were pardoned. The following week, seventy-five men, in the towns of Boston, Salem, Newbury, Roxbury, Ipswich, and Charlestown, were condemned to have all their arms and ammunition taken from them unless they would likewise acknowledge their "sin." A law was passed that any one who should "defame" any Magistrate or Court, or any of their acts or proceedings, should be fined, imprisoned, disfranchised, or banished.[1]

In the meantime, Mrs. Hutchinson had been brought to trial. When, at its beginning, she asked what law had been broken, the Court answered, "the fifth commandment," which enjoined her to honor father and mother, whereas she had brought reproach upon the "fathers of the commonwealth." [2] When the trial was over, and the sentence given that she should be "banished from out of our jurisdiction as being a woman not fit for our society," she said, "I desire to know wherefore I am banished." "Say no more," answered the Governor; "the Court knows wherefore and is satisfied."

It was evident now that no voice could be raised in criticism of any acts of the civil or ecclesiastical authorities, and that the minds and lives of the ten thousand or more inhabitants of Massachusetts had come wholly under the control of their rulers. One man, who with a group of people undertook to organize a church without having secured the permission of the magistrates and clergy, was fined £20 and imprisoned "during the pleasure of Court." Hugh Buet, being found guilty of "heresy," was condemned to leave the colony within three weeks or be hanged. Two others were imprisoned for criti-

---

[1] *Massachusetts Records*, vol. I, pp. 207-13.

[2] Adams, *Antinomianism*, pp. 165, 237. Two reports of the trial are given in that volume, pp. 157-284.

cizing the government and clergy; and, for the same offense, Katherine Finch was ordered to be whipped.[1]   In 1635, a law had been passed making church attendance compulsory for all inhabitants, under pain of fine and imprisonment.   Three years later, it was enacted that every resident, whether a freeman and church member or not, should be taxed for the support of the ministers.   In the Old World, the churches had been satisfied with excommunication, but in Massachusetts, a law was now passed that, if any person was excommunicated by the church, he must endeavor to have himself restored within six months, under penalty of "fine, imprisonment, banishment, or further."[2]   That ominous "further" was evidently intended to mean death, and it is difficult to conceive of a measure more conducive to the rearing of a race of conforming hypocrites.

The policy so ruthlessly followed by the leaders can hardly be excused by attributing it to the spirit of the age or to the necessity of maintaining civil order.   They were all familiar with the example of religious toleration in Holland; and in neither Plymouth, Rhode Island, nor Connecticut was church membership a legal requisite for the franchise.   Moreover, Massachusetts, only a few years later, in annexing the northern settlements, permitted their inhabitants to vote without being church members, although denying that privilege to her own citizens.

Criticism of the leaders' actions was severe and constant, even from their best friends in England.   The real father of the colony, the Reverend John White, wrote to Winthrop in alarm, saying that he desired him "to have an eye to one thinge, that you fall not into that evill abroad, which you labored to avoyd at home, to binde all men to the same tenets and practise."   Stansby, in a letter to the Reverend Mr. Wilson, complained that, on account of their strictness, over one half of the people were not admitted to church membership, and that this would do them much harm.   Stephen Winthrop, temporarily in London, sent home word to his brother John, that

[1] *Massachusetts Records*, vol. I, pp. 252, 312, 262, 269, 234.
[2] *Ibid.*, pp. 140, 240, 242.

"here is great complaint against us for our severity against Anabaptists. It doth discourage any people from coming to us for fear they should be banished if they dissent from us in opinion." Sir George Downing, a cousin of the younger Winthrop, in a letter retailing English opinion of the colony, speaks of that "law of banishing for conscience, which makes us stinke everywhere." [1]

Nor must the standpoint of the English citizen be neglected. England's American possessions, in spite of monopolies and charters, were coming more and more to be looked upon as the heritage of the English people, as the land of opportunity for those who fell by the wayside in life's race at home, as well as for religious exiles. Yet here was one of the best parts of the whole continent being monopolized by a band of people who rejected, oppressed, and banished others, or at the least deprived them of all political rights, not because they were undesirable citizens, not because they were immoral, but because they refused to conform to the peculiar church polity and doctrine, neither Church of England nor English Puritan, which the first settlers had evolved in the American wilderness.

Winthrop, in his controversy with Vane over the immigration law, and apologist historians since, have made much of the possible technical rights under the charter possessed by the company members, and their successors in perpetuity, to choose their fellow citizens according to any standard, however fanatical, however unjust, of which they might approve. These rights were questionable, and the controversy has usually ignored those of the potential English colonist at home. But our interest does not lie in legal technicalities: it is concerned with the influences that moulded New England; and from that standpoint, we can only point to the results of the policy of the first leaders and to its baneful effects. As we noted above, Winthrop's finer impulses had been permanently checked, while Cotton, who might have made a noble leader, was now content to follow natures lower than his own.

[1] *Mass. Hist. Soc. Coll.*, Series V, vol. I, p. 252; Series IV, vol. VII, p. 11; Series V, vol. VIII, p. 200; Series IV, vol. VI, p. 537.

The voices that had pleaded for religious toleration, for civil liberty, and for a religion of love, were silenced. The intellectual life of the colony ceased to be troubled and entered into peace, but it was the peace of death. The struggle for civil freedom did, indeed, go on, and in that alone lay the sole contribution of the colony to the cause of human progress; for the almost complete suppression of free speech and free inquiry surrendered the intellectual life of Massachusetts to the more and more benumbing influence of a steadily narrowing theology.[1] For two centuries, from the day that Winthrop pronounced that verdict, "the Court knows wherefore and is satisfied," the social and religious life of New England as a whole conformed to the rigid lines of Calvinism in its harshest and least attractive aspects. In England, Puritanism had been grafted upon a national stock of abundant sturdiness and health. In the forests of America, uncultured and ungrafted, the wild fruit grew steadily more gnarled and bitter.

[1] *Cf.* C. F. Adams, *Massachusetts, its Historians and its History;* Boston, 1898.

CHAPTER VIII

THE GROWTH OF A FRONTIER

In the first chapter we called attention to the importance of the Appalachian barrier in long confining the process of colonizing within bounds, and preventing that wide dispersion which rendered so precarious the hold of France upon its far larger American empire. The relation of area to barrier, in that section chosen by the English, was, indeed, almost ideal for the formation of colonies, and, subsequently, of a nation through their union. While the mountains kept the original settlements within bounds until their population and institutions had both had opportunity to develop and take strong root, the extent of the continental mass behind, simple in its physiographic features, was sufficient for the growth of almost unlimited numbers and a unified state, and, so, for the effective influence upon the world of whatever form of culture might there arise. The West Indian colonies, on the other hand, in spite of their rapid growth, could not fail, eventually, to become politically unimportant, merely from their limited area and resulting limited population. Barbadoes, for example, comprised only one hundred and sixty-six square miles, the equivalent of one seventh of the land-surface of Rhode Island, or one fiftieth of that of Massachusetts. Within a century from its settlement, it contained no ungranted or uncultivated land — a condition which must have been approximated long before.[1] The possibility of growth, beyond a certain point, was, therefore, lacking in the islands, and, from the same cause, their development was to a great extent uninfluenced by another factor, which was of marked importance in the continental colonies and the nation for two centuries and a half.

[1] Worsley to Board of Trade, cited by Pitman, *Development of British W. I.*, p. 70.

This factor was the constantly advancing frontier, with its radical reactions upon the thought and institutions of the also constantly expanding older settlements.

American political thought has been moulded, to a very great extent, by the two ideals, of unrestricted competition in exploiting the resources of the continent, and of a democracy fostered by the semi-isolated and self-reliant life of the frontier, with its comparative equality of opportunity and of economic status.   Both these ideals, until a recent period, were developed by the presence of free land, in which they had largely had their origin.[1]   As we have already pointed out, land in New England, in the earliest period, was to be obtained without either purchase price or rent, to which fact, perhaps, had been due the large non-Puritan immigration that mingled with the religious stream from 1630 to 1640.

It is also to the influence of the frontier that the American intellect owes some of its most marked characteristics: its restlessness, its preoccupation with the practical, its lack of interest in the æsthetic and philosophical, its desire for ends and neglect of means, its preference of cleverness to training, its self-confidence, its individualism, and its extreme provinciality.   The influence, moreover, has been a continuing one, for almost every decade in American history, until 1890, witnessed the creation of a new frontier, which lay just a little beyond the settled regions, and reacted upon them.[2]

In describing the first expansion of the New England frontier, therefore, we are concerned with the earliest manifestation of one of the most potent forces in American history. The fringe of little settlements along the coast had been, indeed, the frontier of Europe; but with the planting of settlements farther inland, an American frontier came into existence, to react upon what, with the rapid movement of time characteristic of a new country, soon became the conservative, older

[1] *Cf.* F. J. Turner, "Social Forces in American History"; *Magazine of History*, vol. XIII, p. 117.

[2] *Cf.* the very suggestive article by F. J. Turner, "The Significance of the Frontier in American History," *Proceedings of State Historical Society of Wisconsin*, 1894, pp. 79-112.

East. That frontier has always been the refuge of the restless and the discontented, of those who have desired a freer, if not greater, economic opportunity, as well as of those who have been unable to adjust themselves to the prosaic life of a settled community, with its penalties of one sort or another for such as will not yield at least lip-service to its social, religious, or political beliefs. In Massachusetts there was no more room — if, indeed, there were as much — for those who disagreed with the authorities in any particular, than there had been at home; and those who came to that colony in the hope of enjoying any larger degree of religious toleration or civil liberty than in England were promptly disillusioned. About the time of the last events described in the preceding chapter, the prospects for freedom of thought or action must have looked as dark to the dwellers in Massachusetts not wholly in sympathy with the rulers' policy, as it had looked to those same rulers in the old country, when they met at the Earl of Lincoln's, and decided to remove to the wilderness. The opposition having become the government, it was now forcing a new opposition to follow the same course, involuntarily by banishment or voluntarily by free migration. Before continuing the story of that movement, however, we must allude briefly to that portion of the European frontier which lay northward of the Puritan settlements, and which, like them, had been formed by immigration from the Old World.

During the period we are now discussing, the history of Maine was the story of confused grants of territory and of the planting of small isolated farming, fishing, and trading communities. The existence led by the inhabitants, in their solitary shacks or little villages, was that of a rough border life in which the monotony of the hard, bitter winters, and the routine of planting, fishing, or bargaining for furs, was punctuated by an occasional murder among themselves, and by quarrels, sometimes bloody, with the Indians and the French.

In 1629, the Province of Maine, as granted to Mason and Gorges seven years previously, was divided between them, Mason accepting as his share that portion lying between the

Merrimac and the Piscataqua,— which received the name of
New Hampshire,— while Gorges retained the balance, extending from the Piscataqua to the Kennebec.[1]   Mention has previously been made of the small beginnings at Pemaquid, Sheepscot, and Monhegan to the eastward, and of Portsmouth and
Dover in what now became Mason's particular province.   The
settlements next planted, at Richmond's Island, Pejebscot,
around Casco Bay, and elsewhere, were the work of servants for
English merchants or of individual emigrants, and were hampered by the conflicting claims arising from the carelessly drawn
patents.[2]   Gorges himself became interested in a new attempt
to colonize, and his nephew, William, was sent over as governor of a little colony planted at York, which later was to
become the subject of one of those grandiose schemes of government to which the old knight was so uncontrollably ad-
dicted.[3]   All of these early plantings, however, were of slight
historical importance.

Although settlement was proceeding slowly and painfully,
the vast forests and many rivers of the province offered a rich
field for the exploitation of the fur trade, which was the main
object of the French in the north, and one of the principal
resources of the English settlements as well.   The traffic, indeed, had been the means by which the Plymouth Pilgrims
had bought their freedom from their merchant partners, and
we have already noted that colony's activities on the Kennebec.   A tragic incident that occurred at their little post on
that stream, located at what is now Augusta, is of interest
mainly as revealing the aggressive attitude which was later to
become the settled policy of the Massachusetts colony in relation to its neighbors.   Early in 1634, one Hocking, a fellow

---

[1] *Farnham Papers* (Maine Historical Society, Portland, 1901), vol. 1, pp. 96 *ff.*
For the numerous grants of this period, *cf.* H. S. Burrage, *Colonial Maine*, pp.
197–226.

[2] The patents may be found in the *Farnham Papers, passim.*   The most accurate
narrative account is that of Burrage, *Colonial Maine.*   The Trelawney and Cammack
patents, and an extremely valuable correspondence relating to conditions at this
time, are in the *Trelawney Papers;*   Maine Historical Society, 1884.   *Cf.* also, J. P.
Baxter, *George Cleeve of Casco Bay* (Gorges Society, Portland, 1885), pp. 27 *ff.*

[3] *Farnham Papers,* vol. 1, p. 159; Gorges, *Briefe Narration,* p. 79; Burrage, *Colonial
Maine,* pp. 216 *ff.*

employed in an enterprise of Lords Say, Brook, and others, on the Piscataqua, tried to poach upon the Pilgrims' patented lands, and even to pass the trading station, in order to intercept the Indians carrying their furs. The Pilgrims' agents acted with restraint; but in the course of the dispute, Hocking wantonly killed one of their men; whereupon a companion of the slain man, "that loved him well," as Bradford records, shot Hocking dead.[1]

Although the Plymouth men had been entirely in the right, a garbled version of the affair was sent to England and also to Massachusetts. Needless to point out, that colony had absolutely no jurisdiction whatever in the quarrel, which had occurred far outside its bounds, and not even in the unclaimed wilderness, but within the legal limits of its older neighbor. Nevertheless, the authorities at Boston arrested John Alden, one of the Plymouth magistrates, who happened to be there at the moment, and who had been at the Kennebec when the affray occurred.[2] This was naturally resented, even by the peace-loving Pilgrims, and letters requesting Alden's release were dispatched by the Plymouth government to Dudley. One of these, at least, that governor tried to suppress, but "Captaine Standish requiring an answer thereof publickly in the courte," he was forced to produce it.[3] Alden was released, but Standish, who had been the bearer of the letter, was bound over to appear at the next Massachusetts court, to testify to the Pilgrims' patent. Finally, after Winslow and Bradford themselves had gone to Boston and conferred with Winthrop, the matter was adjusted, and Dudley and Winthrop wrote to the Lords in England the true version of the murder; but it was not likely that the other settlements would soon forget the high-handed proceedings of the Bay Colony in an affair so obviously beyond its jurisdiction.[4]

But the trading post on the Kennebec was not the sole concern of the Pilgrims in Maine, nor was that province the scene

[1] Bradford, *Plymouth*, p. 317.
[2] J. Winthrop, *History*, vol. 1, p. 156; *Massachusetts Records*, vol. 1, p. 119.
[3] Dudley's reply, in Bradford, *Plymouth*, p. 320.
[4] J. Winthrop, *History*, vol. 1, pp. 162, 174.

merely of contentions arising from conflicting English land-grants, or from rival colonial jurisdictions. It had been the stage on which the curtain had first risen in the struggle for empire between England and France, and was now to wit-ness new episodes in that long drama. Still farther north the contest had recently become acute. Sir William Alexander, by virtue of an English grant, had claimed a large portion of French America, and Sir William Kirk had seized Port Royal and Quebec. By the treaty of St. Germain, however, in 1632, England agreed to restore "all places occupied in New France, Acadia, and Canada by the subjects of the King of Great Britain," although the boundaries of those vaguely localized regions were not specified, and remained matters for conten-tion, which meant raiding and Indian warfare, for over a cen-tury to come.[1]

Meanwhile, several more places had been occupied by the Pilgrims and those associated with the Plymouth colony. In 1630, a "very profane young man," Edward Ashley by name, had started a trading post on the Penobscot, which the Pil-grims feared might injure their fur business on the Kennebec.[2] In spite of scruples, therefore, they joined with Ashley, and that person having been drowned at sea, after being released from the Fleet prison in London, they came into sole posses-sion.[3] They did not long enjoy it in peace, however, for the following year the French descended upon them and carried away all their goods, valued at nearly £500, leaving word with the agents that "some of the Isle of Rey gentlemen had been there." Allerton, who had broken with the Pilgrims, had also begun to trade, at Machias; and, a couple of years later, suffered in like manner from the French, who killed two of his men, and carried off all the others, as well as the whole stock of goods, which, as Bradford says "was the end of that projecte."[4]

In spite of their own heavy loss, the Pilgrims had clung

---

[1] The section of the treaty relating to America is in the *Farnham Papers*, vol. 1, p. 176.

[2] Bradford, *Plymouth*, pp. 258 ff.

[3] *Acts Privy Council, Colonial*, vol. 1, p. 172; Bradford, *Plymouth*, p. 275.

[4] Bradford, *Plymouth*, pp. 293 f.; J. Winthrop, *History*, vol. 1, pp. 139, 184.

to the Penobscot until, in 1635, d'Aulnay, acting under orders from the French King to clear the coast of the English as far as Pemaquid, seized the post, and shipped the local agents back to Plymouth. The Pilgrims hired a vessel, and dispatched an armed force to try to regain possession; but, owing to the conduct of the man whom they had engaged to effect the enterprise, it failed miserably, and they merely entailed upon themselves a heavy additional loss. Massachusetts, when called upon for help, though she realized the danger to herself from the increasing aggressiveness of the French, refused aid unless the infinitely poorer Plymouth colony would bear the entire expense. That colony was, therefore, obliged to desist, and Bradford bitterly complained that not only did the Bay people thus do nothing to defend the common frontier, but that, owing to their cupidity, they even sold food and ammunition to the French, and so increased the menace both from them and their Indian allies.[1]

In Mason's province of New Hampshire, settlement, though more peaceful, was also proceeding but slowly beyond the Dover and Portsmouth plantations already noted. As the settlers of those two places were Episcopalians, and as an opportunity was offered to buy out the Hilton interest in the former, the Massachusetts leaders urged some of their friends in England to acquire it, with the result that Lords Say and Brook, Sir Richard Saltonstall, and others came into possession, and sent out additional colonists.[2] This pouring of new wine into the old Dover bottle produced a series of explosions, which subsequently prepared the way for annexation by Massachusetts. Mason died in 1635, and bequeathed his province to his family.[3] Two years later occurred the Antinomian controversy in Massachusetts, and the expulsion of Wheelwright, whom, when discussing that episode, we left on

[1] Bradford, *Plymouth,* pp. 332 *ff.;* J. Winthrop, *History,* vol. I, pp. 198, 200, 246; *Mass. Hist. Soc. Coll.,* Series III, vol. VIII, p. 192; *Massachusetts Records,* vol. I, pp. 160 *f.*
[2] *New Hampshire Provincial Papers* (Concord, 1867), vol. I, p. 157.
[3] C. W. Tuttle, *Captain John Mason;* Prince Society, Boston, 1887. The will and notes are on pp. 391–408.

his way to New Hampshire. He succeeded in making the winter trip to the settlements on the Piscataqua, and the following spring, with a few associates and the help of his new hosts, he founded the town of Exeter, the inhabitants entering into a written compact for their self-government.[1] That the Massachusetts authorities would have preferred that he should die alone in the winter's snow is hardly a charitable supposition; but just what they did wish for is uncertain; for they wrote a letter of remonstrance to the New Hampshire people, saying that they "looked at it as an unneighborly part" that they should help any one expelled by themselves.[2]

One of these northern towns, from its first settlement, had been considered by Massachusetts as under its own jurisdiction. In March, 1637, the General Court had ordered that a plantation should be started at Wenicunnett,— the name being later changed to Hampton,— a little more than three miles north of the Merrimac.[3] It was thus slightly outside of the bounds of the patent, if that were construed, as it had been construed to that time, to include only such land north of the river as lay within three miles of it.[4] The project may mark, however, the first tentative step toward the colony's later, and wholly unwarranted, interpretation of that instrument, so as to include all the territory lying south of a line drawn due east from a point three miles north of the most northerly part of that stream, to the ocean, thus including practically all of New Hampshire and a large part of Maine. About a year and a half after the "bound house" was built, a group of colonists went to take possession of the new site. The Exeter men at once objected to this encroachment of Massachusetts on their neighborhood; but the General Court

---

[1] *New Hampshire Provincial Papers*, vol. 1, pp. 131 f. The Indian deed, formerly thought to have been obtained by Wheelwright for the land, is now generally considered spurious. *Ibid.*, pp. 136 f. *Cf.*, however, Bell (*John Wheelwright*, pp. 79 ff.), who contends that it was genuine.

[2] J. Winthrop, *History*, vol. 1, p. 350.

[3] *Massachusetts Records*, vol. 1, pp. 167, 271; J. Dow, *History of Town of Hampton* (Salem, 1893), vol. 1 , pp. 7 f.

[4] It is noteworthy that in 1633, in a letter to Secretary Coke, Emanuel Downing asked that the charter limits be extended a little to the north, where were the best firs and timber. *Cal. State Pap., Col., 1675–76*, p. 74.

replied that the new settlement was within their patent, and that they looked upon the protest as "against good neighborhood, religion and common honesty." They did, however, quietly send out a surveying party, and having found that the part above Pennacook was north of the line of 43½ degrees, they phrased a new answer to Exeter's renewed protest, saying that, while they relinquished none of their rights, nevertheless, as the Exeter men did not profess to claim anything which might fall within the Massachusetts patent, the matter would be allowed to rest. The way was thus left open for future aggression, and the Court immediately proceeded to erect the new settlement into a legal town.[1]

The frontier north of Massachusetts had thus, for the most part, come into being without any action on her part, except in the two settlements last noted. Owing to the location between the French and English, and the uncompromising geographic factors of soil and climate, the vast forested area, comprising over two thirds of all New England, increased but little in population throughout the century; and by 1700 New Hampshire had but six thousand souls, or less than that of the Bay Colony at the time that Wheelwright left it. The northern provinces, unhappily for themselves, were destined to play the part of buffer states between the French, with their savage allies, and the more safely located colonies in the south.

In tracing the foundations of the latter, we find the influence of Massachusetts far more potent, for they were being laid mainly by men who found scant room in that increasingly reactionary commonwealth. The founders of Rhode Island and Connecticut alike condemned the religious and political policy that the Bay Colony had now definitely made its own; and the more democratic and tolerant forms of government, which developed in the two former, "represented more nearly the principles which underlie the government of the United States to-day than any other of the British colonies."[2] The seeds of both political and religious liberty had been brought

[1] J. Winthrop, *History*, vol. I, pp. 349, 365; *Massachusetts Records*, vol. I, p. 259.
[2] C. M. Andrews, *The Colonial Period* (New York, 1912), p. 28.

to America by the Massachusetts colonists; but the leaders, partly from a dread of losing their own influence, and partly from a genuine fear of noxious weeds, had done their best to interfere with their growth. The founders of Rhode Island and Connecticut, with less desire for personal power, and greater courage as to tares in the wheat, watered and nursed the seeds of liberty, which bore an abundant harvest. In Rhode Island, indeed, the weeds flourished riotously; but the faith of the founders was justified in both colonies, and their commonwealths marched with Holland at the head of those struggling for human freedom, while England and Massachusetts yet lagged and nagged.

The lands around Narrangansett Bay had been known for some time to be attractive as sites for colonizing, when Williams made his way thither after his banishment, in the winter of 1636. In spite of frequent trading with the Indians, however, only one settler had as yet located there permanently. William Blackstone, who had left England because he disliked the tyranny of the Lord-bishops, and who had, as we have seen, an equal aversion for that of the Lord-brethren, had quietly left his plantation in Massachusetts, and betaken himself to the wilderness north of Providence.[1] A lover at once of peace, of books, and of freedom, there is something singularly attractive in his little known personality. He called his new home "Study Hill"; and there in his orchard grew the first "yellow sweetings" ever known, which, later, when he occasionally preached to the newcomers, he handed around, "to encourage his younger hearers."

Thus, while, owing to the great services Williams was to render the colony, he is entitled to the name of its founder, he was not its first settler, nor was the little band that planted Providence with him in 1636 the only one to lay the foundations of the future commonwealth. Nor had he himself, apparently, any intention of doing so. "It pleased the most

---

[1] Lechford, *Plain Dealing*, p. 97. *Cf.* Adams, *Three Episodes*, vol. 1, p. 328 *n.* Some time before Blackstone settled, Winter, Trelawney's agent in Maine, thought of settling about Narragansett, and claimed that he had Warwick's permission to plant a colony. *Trelawney Papers*, vol. 1, p. 20.

high," he wrote, many years afterward, "to direct my steps into this Bay, by the loving private advice of that very honored soul Mr. John Winthrop the Grandfather, who, though he was carried with the stream for my banishment, yet he personally and tenderly loved me to his last breath. It is not true, that I was imployed by any, made covenant with any, was supplied by any, or desired any to come with me into these parts."[1] The others came, however, and the leading idea of the settlement was reiterated four years later in the proposals for a form of government, when the "arbitrators" noted that they agreed "as formerly hath bin the liberties of the town, so still, to hould forth liberty of conscience."[2]

In 1638, another group, of eighteen persons, including William Coddington, settled the town of Portsmouth; and in the following year, that little hamlet planted an offshoot at Newport, while a few individuals from both Providence and Portsmouth organized Warwick.[3] These four towns were absolutely independent of each other, and of any superior government of any sort, except England. Although Newport and Portsmouth partially combined in 1640, it was not until seven years later, when the charter of 1644 finally went into effect, that there was any colony of Rhode Island, or a united government over the several settlements.[4] It thus offered a great contrast to the Massachusetts colony, in which the towns were the creatures of the General Court; and it was this extreme looseness of organization, combined with religious toleration, which formed the leading characteristic of the Rhode Island political experiment. Although the settlers at Providence had signed an agreement to unite for purposes of government, there were no town officers, and practically no organization, until four years later. The agreement was merely to yield obedience to such orders "as shall be made for public good of the body in an orderly way, by the major consent of the pres-

---

[1] Williams's answer to the charges of Harris, in Rider, *Rhode Island Tracts*, No. 14 (Providence, 1888), p. 53. But Williams's statements are often contradictory.

[2] *R. I. Records* (Providence, 1856), vol. I, pp. 14, 28.

[3] *Ibid.*, pp. 45 *ff.*, 87, 129.

[4] *Ibid.*, pp. 100 *ff. Cf.* Foster, *Town Government in Rhode Island*, pp. 10 *ff.*

ent inhabitants, masters of families, incorporated together in a Towne fellowship, and others whom they shall admit unto them only in civil things." These masters of families met once a fortnight, discussed their common affairs, and decided them by majority vote.[1] The government was thus almost a pure democracy, only women, minors, and bachelors being excluded. Even when the towns were united, and a more elaborate governmental machinery was set up, the extremely democratic trend of thought was evidenced in the remarkable provision that the General Assembly could not initiate legislation, but that laws were first to be considered in each town, and that only after all four had considered them, were they to be sent to be acted upon by the Assembly, all legislative initiative thus being retained in the hands of the people.[2]

With such looseness of organization, and extreme individuality of thought and action, another characteristic was bound to be lack of harmony, with frequent bickerings and disputes. These were soon in evidence, and it was found also that a pure democracy and absence of restraint were not compatible with orderly living. As the commonwealth grew, the difficulties were met in the spirit of men who, believing in liberty and toleration, were yet forced to make concessions to human nature; while, on the other hand, the Massachusetts authorities met their difficulties in the spirit of men who honestly disbelieved in democracy and toleration, and whose concessions were forced by a growing demand for things in which they had no faith. In Connecticut, also, the leaders were, happily, on the side of that part of the people, important in all the colonies, who were struggling upward toward a larger liberty, and who, even in Massachusetts, were slowly bringing it into being.

Knowledge of the existence of the Connecticut River, and of the advantages of its rich bottoms as sites both for trading and for planting, seems to have been first acquired by the English through information given to the Pilgrims by the

---

[1] *R. I. Records*, vol. I, p. 14; Letter from Williams to Winthrop; *Mass. Hist. Soc. Coll.*, Series IV, vol. VI, pp. 186 f.

[2] Foster, *Town Government*, p. 19.

Dutch. Friendly intercourse between Plymouth and New Amsterdam had been opened by the latter as early as 1626; and the Dutch not only taught the Pilgrims the value of wampum in the Indian trade, but, seeing how barren a site they had chosen for their settlement, told them of the Connecticut, and "wished them to make use of it." However, "their hands being full otherwise, they let it pass" until, having been solicited by Indians who had been driven from their homes there by invading Pequots from the West, they dispatched several exploring and trading expeditions in 1633.[1] The same Indians had also earlier requested the Massachusetts people to make a settlement, but they had declined.[2] The Pilgrims, having made up their minds to erect a permanent trading post on the river, also asked the Bay people to join them; and when the latter refused, alleging their poverty, they even offered to provide the capital for both if Massachusetts would assume half the responsibility. This, likewise, being refused, the Pilgrims went on with the project alone, after telling the Bay authorities that they could have no cause to complain, as they had now had ample opportunity to join; to which they assented.[3] This was in the middle of July, and although the Massachusetts leaders had done their best to discourage the Pilgrims, by telling them the place was "not fit for plantation," and by picking other flaws in the project, nevertheless, four weeks later, they had themselves dispatched a bark to Connecticut to trade, and John Oldham, going overland, had also spied out the resources of the place, and trafficked with the Indians there.[4] In view of all their actions, then and subsequently, it would seem difficult to avoid the conclusion that the Massachusetts authorities,

[1] Bradford, *Plymouth*, pp. 222, 233, 311.

[2] In 1631. J. Winthrop, *History*, vol. 1, p. 62.

[3] Bradford, *Plymouth*, pp. 312 f.; J. Winthrop (*History*, vol. 1, p. 125) gives as reasons for refusal that the place was not fit for habitation on account of the Indians, the bar across the river, and the closing of navigation in winter. Even his admiring editor, Savage, was "constrained to remark" that these "look to me more like pretexts, than real motives," and that the Pilgrims' subsequent complaints of their treatment by Massachusetts "appear very natural, if not unanswerable" (p. 125 *n.*).

[4] J. Winthrop, *History*, vol. 1, p. 132. Doyle (*Puritan Colonies*, vol. 1, p. 151), by a slip, wrongly dates the negotiations in 1634, making it appear that they followed the Massachusetts expeditions instead of preceding them.

having been offered by their neighbors a chance to share in a profitable opportunity, deliberately tried, by fraud and force, not only to obtain all the profits for themselves, but to prevent the very people whose enterprise it was from retaining any share in it. Not possessing the interpretative advantages of a New England ancestry, one is, perhaps, limited to remarking that the business dealings of ultra-religious people are often peculiar.

The Dutch, meanwhile, seem to have repented of their former hospitality, probably because of the warnings that the English had early sent them of their encroachment upon English territory, and of the rapid growth of the eastern colonies, which might threaten even their occupation of the Hudson.[1] Hearing of the projected settlement by Plymouth, a party was sent from New Amsterdam in January to buy land from the Indians,[2] and some of the Dutch were already ensconced in a little fort, on the present site of Hartford, when the English arrived in the late summer. In spite of Dutch protests, however, the Pilgrims, in their "great new barke," sailed past the fort, and, passing north of the bounds of the Hollanders' Indian purchase, settled at what is now Windsor, buying the soil from its savage occupants. A later attempt by the Dutch to dislodge them by threatened violence proved unavailing.[3]

---

[1] Bradford, *Letter-book*, pp. 51 *ff.* The Dutch territorial claims were noted (*supra*, Chap. III). The English grant of this territory preceded Dutch discovery by three years, but the question was one of time between discovery and settlement, and of extension of territory from points discovered. There was no established international law by which this particular dispute could be settled. Individual opinion may differ as to the ethics of the case. To me, with no desire to make out a case either way, the legal points seem to be impossible of dogmatic answer.

[2] Bradford, *Plymouth*, p. 313; Acts of the United Colonies, vol. II, p. 65 (*Plymouth Records*, x). These Acts, vols. I and II, form vols. IX and X of the *Plymouth Records*, and are hereafter cited as *Acts United Colonies*. J. R. Brodhead, *History State of New York*, vol. I, p. 204, gives the month as June; but the Records say January. Various Dutch documents, all of a later period, state that a settlement was contemplated, and possession taken, in 1623. *Cf. Documentary History State of New York*, vol. III, p. 50; *N. Y. Colonial Docts.*, vols. I, pp. 286, 360, and II, p. 133. There is, however, no contemporary documentary evidence of it; and it is certain, at least, that there was no settlement actually made until that designed to forestall the English in 1633.

[3] Bradford, *Plymouth*, pp. 313 *f.* The Dutch side of the case is given in *Act. United Colonies., ubi supra.*

Meanwhile, on the same day on which Winthrop recorded in his Journal the results of the Massachusetts expedition to Connecticut, he also entered the arrival of the ship Griffin, eight weeks from England, with John Cotton, Thomas Hooker, Samuel Stone, and John Haynes among her passengers. Cotton, as we have seen, remained in Boston, but the others immediately went on to Newtown, where a body of Hooker's English congregation had preceded him by a year.[1] Of this transplanted body, Hooker and Stone now became pastor and teacher. It is not likely that Hooker, with the political views he possessed, could have found the Massachusetts atmosphere congenial; and a year later, he and his congregation applied to the General Court for permission to remove to Connecticut. The reasons they gave were the lack of land for expansion at Newtown, the fear that otherwise Connecticut might fall into the hands of other English or the Dutch, and, lastly, "the strong bent of their spirits to remove thither." The Court, however, refused the petition, alleging many reasons, which, in the main, came to the fear that such a defection would weaken the colony, and tend to draw away future emigrants from it.[2] In the debates on the subject, a majority of the deputies were in favor of allowing Hooker and his party to leave if they wished, while a majority of the magistrates opposed it. This raised the question whether the magistrates could veto a vote of the more numerous body of deputies, which was the more popular and democratic of the two. As the result of a sermon preached by Cotton the contest, which had promised to become bitter, was postponed, and the Newtown settlers were granted additional land in their present neighborhood.[3] The incident is interesting, not only as marking the beginning of the political struggle between the two elements in the legislature, which we shall have occasion to follow later, but also as an early example of that fear which the East has always had of the growth of its western frontier and its desire to check it. Owing to continued pressure, however, the legislature with-

---

[1] J. Winthrop, *History*, vol. 1, p. 104. [2] *Ibid.*, vol. 1, p. 167.
[3] *Ibid.*, vol. 1, p. 168; *Massachusetts Records*, vol. 1, p. 129.

drew its opposition the following year, and in 1635 permission was granted the towns of Watertown, Roxbury, and Dorchester to move anywhere, provided that they would continue subordinate to the Massachusetts government — a condition which that government had no legal right to impose. A few months later it went further, indeed, and passed a law that no one could leave the colony without permission of a majority of the magistrates.[1] As, under a previous law, no one could settle in Massachusetts without the consent of the half-dozen or more men mainly in control, so now no one, however uncongenial his surroundings or urgent his need, could leave without permission from the same little group.

Parties from Dorchester at once availed themselves of the Court's consent to leave, and by July were arriving daily on the Connecticut. On that river no spot would suit them except that already bought and occupied by the Pilgrims, from which the Massachusetts people now tried to oust them. In reply to a protest from Governor Bradford, the Dorchester men had the effrontery to answer that, as to the land settled by the Pilgrims, God "in a faire way of providence tendered it to us." Upon this bit of fraud and hypocritical cant, Bradford caustically commented that they should "abuse not Gods providence in such allegations." Massachusetts, however, was strong, and the Plymouth people were weak; and although the latter did finally wring a reluctant acknowledgment that the right was on their side, nevertheless they were forced to yield fifteen sixteenths of their land, and were allowed only one sixteenth and a little money, in an enterprise which was wholly theirs, in which they had courteously tendered Massachusetts a half interest, and which was located entirely outside any territory to which that colony had any legal title. There was good reason for Bradford's note in his diary, that the controversy was ended, "but the unkindness not so soone forgotten."

The winter was very severe, and many of the new settlers were obliged to return to Boston; but in the spring, Hooker, with most of his congregation, emigrated to the river, travel-

[1] *Massachusetts Records*, vol. 1, pp. 146, 148, 167.

ing overland, with their herds of cattle, the precursors of an endless western stream. These newcomers, Bradford carefully notes, as we also are glad to do, treated the Pilgrims more fairly. By the end of 1636, there may have been eight hundred people in Connecticut, settled mainly at Hartford, Windsor, and Wethersfield, while the little settlement of Springfield, within the legal limits of Massachusetts, had also been planted.[1]

These settlements, at first, were merely plantations and not organized towns. They apparently had no officers, except constables,—who, Massachusetts tried to require, should be sworn by one of her own magistrates,—and the body politic consisted of the inhabitants, who met together, as we have found them doing in Rhode Island, to decide upon their common interests. The territory, however, in which they were located, was also claimed at the time by a group of patentees, including Lords Say, Brook, and others, who had been granted the lands by the Earl of Warwick in 1632, but who had made no attempt to enter upon them until three years later, when they sent John Winthrop, Jr., to act as governor, and took other action looking toward settlement. Winthrop, who had come to Boston in the ship with young Vane, was there at the time that the emigration from Massachusetts took place, and Hooker and the other emigrants consulted him concerning such rights as his principals might claim. As a result, an agreement, to last one year, was entered into between Winthrop, acting for Say, Brook, and their associates, and Hooker and his, which provided that a court of eight magistrates should be created, with power to summon a General Court, until further advices could be received from England. This agreement, for purposes of record, was ratified in the Massachusetts General Court, but was not a "commission" from that colony, as often stated.[2]

[1] Bradford, *Plymouth*, pp. 341 *f.*; J. Winthrop, *History*, vol. 1, pp. 216, 223; B. Trumbull, *History of Connecticut* (New Haven, 1818), vol. 1, p. 68.

[2] *Massachusetts Records*, vol. 1, pp. 170 *f. Cf.* W. DeL. Love, *The Colonial History of Hartford* (Hartford, 1914), pp. 70 *ff.* The earliest records of the three Connecticut towns are lost, but by using those of Springfield, Mr. Love has thrown much light upon the disputed points as to the origin of the Connecticut "constitution."

On May 31, 1638, when a new form of government was under consideration, Hooker preached his famous sermon, in which he laid down the doctrines that "the choice of public magistrates belongs unto the people by Gods own allowance," and that "they who have the power to appoint officers and magistrates, it is in their power, also, to set bounds and limitations of the power and place unto which they call them," because "the foundation of authority is laid, firstly, in the free consent of the people." [1]   Neither to Hooker, nor to his fellow colonists of Connecticut, was this last principle new, either in theory or in practice.   He was arguing, not for a democratic government, which they already possessed, but for a fixed code of laws to rule the magistrates in their actions.   The following year, the constitution of the new government was adopted by the residents of the plantations of Hartford, Wethersfield, and Windsor. [2]   That constitution provided for a General Court, in which each of the three original plantations should be represented by four deputies, and which should have the authority to incorporate towns.   It was only subsequent to the creation of this general government by the inhabitants of the commonwealth, that the towns, as political entities, came into being.   Freemen were merely required to be passed upon by the General Court, no religious qualification being attached to the franchise.   It is noteworthy that the governor was not allowed to serve for two successive terms, and that no reference was made to any external authority, not even to that of the king.

While the descent of the "Fundamental Orders" of Connecticut can be traced in every step from the earliest charters of the trading companies, the transition was now complete. From such as we saw Tudor monarchs granting to merchants in the fifteenth century, past all those which we have noted as milestones by the way, the progress had been as steady as it

---

[1] The text of the sermon has not survived.   The notes, by some hearer, which are all we have, are in G. L. Walker, *Thomas Hooker* (New York, 1891), p. 125, and elsewhere.

[2] *Public Records of Colony of Connecticut* (Hartford, 1850), vol. I, pp. 20 *ff*.   (Hereafter cited as *Conn. Col. Records.*)

was unperceived, from the privileges possessed by a few ex-patriated English traders and their clerks, dwelling among foreigners, to the self-governed commonwealth of a people in a land which they had made their own. While the charters, however, served as the framework of their government, the foundation of their political philosophy was found in the church covenant, which the Separatists had used in Europe for forty years before the Mayflower sailed; and the constitution of Connecticut was thus equally descended from religious theory and from the practice of trade.

Although there was little in the Fundamental Orders, as settled in 1639, which cannot be found in previous custom or legislation in Massachusetts or Plymouth, nevertheless, only those elements which were of a democratic tendency were put into the new constitution, and there was distinctly a more democratic attitude on the part of the leaders and people than in the Bay Colony. Such provisions as that making the governor ineligible for immediate reëlection, and the franchise independent of religious qualification, probably show a reaction from the rule of Massachusetts.

The contrasted influences which the new colony and its parent were bringing to bear upon the development of American thought at this time may best be illustrated by the theories of their several leaders. Perhaps the two most influential men in New England in 1640, and the two who most deserved the positions assigned them, were John Winthrop, the leader in Massachusetts, and Thomas Hooker, the leader in Connecticut. Winthrop's opinion of democracy as "the worst of all forms of government," we have already noted, and may contrast with Hooker's belief that the complete control of their rulers "belongs unto the people by Gods own allowance." In the important question whether judges should render arbitrary decisions wholly according to their personal views, or be limited by a fundamental body of laws, the two leaders were equally far apart. "Whatsoever sentence the magistrate gives," wrote Winthrop, who opposed any such limitation, "the judgment is the Lord's, though he do it not by any rule prescribed by civil authority." [1]   "That in the matter which is referred to the judge," asserted Hooker, on the other hand, "the sentence should lie in his breast, or be left to his discretion, according to which he should go, I am afraid it is a course which wants both safety and warrant. I must confess, I ever looked at it as a way which leads directly to tyranny, and so to confusion, and must plainly profess, if it was in my liberty, I should choose neither to live nor leave my posterity under such a government." [2]

The aristocratic and oligarchical tendencies at work in Massachusetts there received enormous additional strength from the fact that the clergy were almost a unit in their support of reactionary ideas. This was a defect which was, to a certain extent, inherent in the Calvinistic ministry; and the failure of the contemporary Puritan colony in the Caribbean was, in considerable measure, due to the outrageous claims of the Puritan ministers there upon the civil power. [3]   The influence of the Puritan clergyman upon his more devout followers could be equaled only by that of the Catholics, and it is difficult for the modern layman to realize its full extent. It came about in part from the Puritan doctrine already noted, that nothing in life was untinged with a religious aspect. If no one dreams now of any necessity of consulting the clergy, as such, with reference to the fashion in clothes or the economic and social policy of the nation, it is partly because those matters are no longer considered as religious, but purely temporal. The opinion of a clergyman, therefore, is of no more value than that of the well-informed layman, with his broader practical experience of life, if, indeed, of as much. One does, however, have recourse to a specialist, and a banker's opinion is sought on finance, and a doctor's on health. As, according to Puritan theory, there was no act which was not of a religious or moral character, the clergyman was, so to say, a specialist on

---

[1] *Connecticut Historical Society Collections*, vol. I, p. 17.

[2] Letter to Winthrop, *Ibid.*, p. 11.

[3] Newton, *Puritan Colonisation*, pp. 160 *ff*. *Cf.* similar conditions in Bermuda, where the ministers went to such lengths as to "make a man quite out of love with the government of the clergy." *Cal. State Pap., Col., 1574–1660*, p. 323.

one aspect of everything, and from that standpoint his advice must be sought in every detail of life, and his influence was correspondingly great.

The individuals who emigrated to Rhode Island and Connecticut were mainly those who were dissatisfied with the restrictions imposed by Massachusetts. That process of secondary selection had now begun which was to continue to winnow out from every new community the most adventurous and independent, and to plant them again to the westward in still newer settlements, where, in turn, the process would again be repeated. In the colonies now forming, therefore, there was a freer opportunity for the seeds of liberty to grow than in the old Bay. The new commonwealths had, in addition, the great advantage that in them, at least at their beginning, the influence of the clergy was wholly upon the side of freedom; and in estimating the results of priestly power in New England, it is only just to recall that Roger Williams and Thomas Hooker were clergymen, as well as the narrower divines of Boston and her sister towns.

The westward movement of New England was to continue until her sons and her institutions were to be found in a continuous chain of communities from Portland on the Atlantic to Portland on the Pacific, and the influence of New England thought upon the life of the nation cannot be overestimated. In so far as the origins of that thought can be traced back to any definite leaders, or individual colonies, it was evidently the ideas of Williams and Hooker, rather than those of Winthrop, with all his high qualities, which were to dominate the American people, and to be absorbed into their very being.

At the same time that these new communities and influences were coming into existence, there was the possibility of another experiment being tried, in colonial matters, of a radically different sort.

The group of Puritan leaders, Warwick, Say, Brook, and others, whom we noted earlier as being interested in promoting Puritan colonization both in New England and in the Carribean, had continued to be actively engaged in colonizing the latter; while by their acquisition of the Hilton patent in New Hampshire, and the grant in Connecticut, they were still in possession of large tracts in the former. Since the emigration of Winthrop in 1630, affairs in England had not improved politically, though they had distinctly done so economically. About 1634 or 1635, nearly all of the group of leaders with whom we are particularly concerned suffered in one way and another from the influence of the Court party. Warwick, who had been forced out of the Council for New England three years earlier, was attacked under the forest laws, and also made to divide his lord-lieutenancy of Essex. Pym was sued by the Attorney-General, and Barrington, Say, and Brook suffered in their estates.[1] In July, Humphrey, the Earl of Lincoln's brother-in-law, arrived in Massachusetts with "propositions from some persons of great quality and estate," who were thinking of emigrating if satisfactory arrangements could be made.[2] In October, the younger Winthrop went to England, returning a year later with his commission as governor of a projected colony at the mouth of the Connecticut.[3] At the end of November, 1635, twenty men arrived there, and under the direction of Lyon Gardiner, a fort was erected at Saybrook. Saltonstall, one of the patentees, had also, a few months earlier, attempted to plant some men higher up the river; but they had been driven out by the same lawless Dorchester party that had fallen on the Pilgrims, causing Saltonstall a loss of £1000.[4]

Among the proposals made by Say, Brook, and the others to Massachusetts, as conditions of their emigrating to New England, it was stipulated that there should be two ranks in the commonwealth — gentlemen and freeholders; that the power of making and repealing laws should belong to both ranks, but that the governor should always be chosen from the higher. To these and the other proposals the authorities in

[1] Newton, *Puritan Colonisation*, p. 175.   [2] J. Winthrop, *History*, vol. I, p. 160.
[3] The commission and agreement are in Trumbull, *Connecticut*, vol. I, pp. 497 ff. The Warwick patent is given in vol. I, pp. 495 f. Cf. C. J. Hoadly, *The Warwick Patent* (Acorn Club, Hartford, 1902), pp. 7 ff.
[4] *Mass. Hist. Soc. Proceedings*, Series IV, vol. VI, pp. 579 f.

the colony wholly agreed, but with the proviso that the church-membership qualification for the franchise must be retained.[1] The theocracy of Massachusetts, under the guidance of its ministers, had drifted far from the current of English life. Englishmen have always had a thoroughly healthy hatred of ecclesiastical rule in civil affairs, and, whatever country squires, noblemen's factors, or tradesmen and mechanics, might be willing to do, it could not be possible that such men as Warwick, Say, Brook, and Pym could place their political rights and careers wholly in the hands of the narrow-minded ministers and congregations of the little Massachusetts town churches. On that account, and because of the turn of affairs in England, the project was given up, and when, three years later, Warwick, Brook, Say, and Darley announced definitely that they were going to emigrate, it was not to New England but to their island in the Caribbean. Although they were not permitted to do so, the fact marks the distinct breach which had now taken place between the rulers of Massachusetts and the leaders of the Puritan party in England. The mistaken policy of the colony, which earlier had brought alarmed protests from her less powerful friends at home, had now definitely alienated her most influential ones. The selfish attitude toward her neighbors, already shown upon the Penobscot, the Piscataqua, and the Connecticut, and which, unfortunately, was to become more aggressive and unscrupulous, also lost her the friendship of her sister colonies. The result was that, when the real struggle came with the English government, a generation later, Massachusetts, although, thanks to her geographical position and aggressive acquisitiveness, she had become the most powerful of the New England group, found herself with hardly a friend in the old country or the new.

The work of extending the frontier was not a mere matter of discussions or of peaceful penetration into an untenanted wilderness. Owing to the great plague, which had so nearly annihilated the natives in the regions where the settlers had first planted, the Indian danger had never been a serious one,

[1] The proposals and Cotton's answer are in Hutchinson, *History*, vol. I, pp. 433 ff.

and no such massacre as almost wiped out the Virginia colony need have been apprehended. The savage, however, had been an important element in the life of the settlements. As friend or spying enemy, he was as constantly in and out of the little villages as he is of the pages of the early records. Although there was, unluckily, little that the white man could teach him that was of any service, he, on the contrary, taught the colonists many a useful lesson. He showed them how and where to plant, trapped their game and gathered in their stock of furs, guided them through the almost trackless forests, and, in a multitude of ways, gave them knowledge of the land which they had entered and of the products it might yield. In the background, nevertheless, always lurked the danger that the natives might grow tired of being slowly dispossessed, that they might decide to make an end of a situation which the more far-sighted among them could not fail to see would inevitably more and more narrow the free range for their savage life. In the fifteen years since Bradford and his little band had landed in an almost deserted spot, the white population had grown alarmingly. Moreover, their increasing numbers and desire for expansion would naturally lead the settlers to adopt a more aggressive attitude toward the natives in any dispute occurring between them. There was more and more probability of trouble, arising from individual outrage on the part of an unscrupulous or ruffianly white, or of some aggrieved or drunken Indian, of which the organized power of the former would but too likely take full advantage. The Old Testament texts on dealing with those outside the pale of God's chosen people offered little comfort to the Indian, should the Puritan divines ever start on the war-path.

At the beginning of 1633 word was received in Boston that a certain Captain Stone had been murdered by the Pequots, or Indians allied to them, after having landed at the mouth of the Connecticut. The exact truth of what occurred is not known. Stone, who was a trader from Virginia, was a drunken, dissolute, and thoroughly worthless character, and very likely provoked the natives by some act. On the other hand, their stories of what happened did not agree, and were not above suspicion.[1] The Massachusetts authorities reported the matter to Virginia, and no further action was taken until the following year, when an embassy from the Pequots arrived at Boston. That tribe had become embroiled in a quarrel with the Narragansetts on the east, and the Dutch on the west, and were, therefore, anxious to smooth their relations with the English. They agreed to deliver up the two men who had killed Stone, to surrender their rights to Connecticut, and to pay damages in furs and wampum. A few days later a number of Narragansetts appeared, who had come to waylay the Pequots on their way home; but the Massachusetts authorities purchased the safety of the savages and promise of peace between the two tribes, by offering the Narragansetts some of the Pequot wampum. Although the Bay Colony had thus bought the Pequot title to Connecticut with the blood of the slain Virginian, the natives had no idea, apparently, of observing the terms of the bargain, nor did the English take further steps in the matter until two years later, when the younger Winthrop, then at Saybrook, was commissioned to treat with the savages regarding rumors of recent outrages, and to declare war if he could not obtain satisfaction.[2]

A fortnight later news came of the murder of John Oldham, and the capture of two boys, in his small boat, while off Block Island on a trading voyage. The natives of that island, who were subordinate to the Narragansetts, were the guilty parties, but the crime seems to have been committed with the connivance of the Narraganset sachems, except Canonicus and Miantanomo. Through the intercession of Roger Williams, the latter sachem secured the release of the two youngsters, while emissaries of Massachusetts, who went to treat with Canonicus, returned home fully satisfied. So far, matters had been conducted reasonably and patiently. Suddenly, however, on the advice of the Massachusetts magistrates and

---

[1] J. Winthrop, *History*, vol. I, pp. 132, 146; Bradford, *Plymouth*, pp. 323 *ff.*
[2] J. Winthrop, *History*, vol. I, pp. 176 *ff.*; *Mass. Hist. Soc. Proceedings*, Series III, vol. III, pp. 130 *f.*

ministers, the policy was completely changed, and a course of blundering stupidity and criminal folly was entered upon. John Endicott, with about a hundred volunteers, was ordered to proceed to Block Island, where he was instructed to put all the men to death, without making any effort to distinguish between guilty and innocent. The women and children were to be carried off, and possession taken of the island. Thence he was to go on to the Pequots, demand the murderers of Stone and Oldham, and a thousand fathoms of wampum, and to secure, by consent or force, some of the children as hostages.[1]

Endicott possessed none of the qualities of a military leader, and although his lack of knowledge prevented this bloody decree from being carried out, he managed to do just enough to enrage the savages without intimidating them. The party, after two days' searching, failed to find the island Indians, who were in hiding in the underbrush, but burned their wigwams, mats, and provisions, staved their canoes, and valiantly slew their dogs. They next proceeded to Saybrook, where Lyon Gardiner, who, in his little outpost, was responsible for the lives of twenty-four men, women, and children, did his best to warn Endicott of his folly. The corn-fields of the Saybrook people were two miles from the fort, and if the Indians, who had shown themselves suspiciously unfriendly of late, should be stung to revenge by Endicott, starvation and massacre would confront the settlement. "You come hither to raise these wasps about my ears," said Gardiner, "and then you will take wings and flee away." In spite of the dictates of common sense and humanity, Endicott proceeded to do just that. At Pequot Harbor he killed two Indians, burned many wigwams, staved the canoes, and then sailed away to the safety of Boston, leaving Saybrook and the towns on the Connecticut at the mercy of the savages, whom Massachusetts had now roused to fury.[2]

The Pequots immediately made peace with the Narragan-

[1] J. Winthrop, *History*, vol. I, pp. 229 f.

[2] *Ibid.*, vol. I, p. 232; John Underhill, "Newes from America," *Mass. Hist. Soc. Coll.*, Series III, vol. VI, pp. 6-11; L. Gardiner, "Relation of the Pequot Wars," *Ibid.*, vol. III, pp. 138 ff.

setts, urging them to a common war against the English. Such a combination, under the circumstances, would have meant a disaster of the first magnitude, and Massachusetts was now forced to ask the help of the only man who could avert it, but whom she had already driven from her company — Roger Williams. In response to most urgent appeals sent from the Governor and Council, he at once started, "all alone in a poore canow, and to cut through a stormie wind with great seas, every minute in hazard of life, to the Sachem's house." There he remained three days, and by means of his friendship with Miantanomo, he won the Narragansetts back to the side of the English, and broke up the proposed alliance between the savages. In consequence of this inestimable service, Winthrop and some of the Massachusetts council, Williams wrote, "debated whether or no I had not merited, not only to be recalled from banishment, but also to be honored with some mark of favor"; but neither the authorities nor the contemporary historians, except Winthrop, had the generosity to say a word of the man who had saved New England.[1] In the fall, Miantanomo and other Narragansett sachems went to Boston, and signed a treaty with the English, which included an offensive alliance against the Pequots.

Meanwhile, the results of the folly that Massachusetts had perpetrated, and against which Plymouth as well as Saybrook had formally protested, now made themselves felt.[2] Three men were killed at Saybrook, another was roasted alive, a trader was murdered at Six-mile Island, then two more at Saybrook, and another on his way up the river. At Wethersfield, nine men were slaughtered, and two young girls carried into captivity.[3] The horrors of Indian warfare became the hourly dread of every inhabitant along the frontier, thanks to the Massachusetts magistrates and ministers. Having, as Gardiner predicted, raised the wasps about his ears and those of all

[1] Williams's Letter to Mason, *Mass. Hist. Soc. Coll.*, Series I, vol. 1, p. 277. J. Winthrop, *History*, vol. 1, pp. 234, 237. Even Palfrey dismisses Williams's services in three lines; *History*, vol. 1, p. 460.

[2] J. Winthrop, *History*, vol. 1, p. 238.

[3] Gardiner, "Relation," pp. 143, 144, 148.

the English along the river, Massachusetts now asked help of Plymouth, as she had before turned to Williams.   That colony agreed to lend aid, but in doing so, recalled to her stronger neighbor how she had refused help against the French when the Pilgrims were the petitioners; how she had interfered with their trade on the Kennebec; and how she had deprived their Connecticut pioneers of their lands.[1]

But the settlers on the latter river could not await the slow movements of the Bay Colony, if the lives of their wives and children were to be saved.   At the Connecticut General Court of May 1, 1637, war was declared against the Pequots, and ninety men, from the three plantations, were levied for immediate service.[2]   The expedition, under command of Captain John Mason, with some Indian auxiliaries under Uncas, immediately proceeded to Saybrook, where they were joined by Underhill, who happened to be there, and a few additional men.[3]   A skirmish, in which the Indians, whose fidelity had been doubted, acquitted themselves loyally, encouraged them not a little.   The original plan had been to sail down the coast to the Pequot River and to attack the enemy directly, but this was wisely changed at the suggestion of Mason.   According to the new plans, the party set sail for Narragansett Bay, with the design of then returning overland, and making a surprise attack on the Pequots, who were expecting it from the water.   After landing on the shore of the Bay, and being reinforced by several hundred Narragansetts, Mason marched his band from eight in the morning until an hour after dark, when they camped about two miles from the Pequot fort. It had been decided to attack only the larger of the two villages, a palisadoed enclosure of an acre or two.[4]   About one o'clock, the English were on the march again, but were deserted by all the Indians, Narragansetts and Mohegans alike, before reach-

---

[1] Bradford, *Plymouth*, pp. 352 *ff.*; J. Winthrop, *History*, vol. 1, pp. 260 *ff.*

[2] *Conn. Col. Records*, vol. 1, p. 9.

[3] The accounts do not agree. *Cf.* Mason, "A brief History of the Pequot War," *Mass. Hist. Soc. Coll.*, Series II, vol. VIII, p. 134; Underhill, "Newes from New England," p. 16; Gardiner, "Relation," p. 149.

[4] Mason, "Brief History," p. 137; P. Vincent, "A true Relation," *Mass. Hist. Soc. Coll.*, Series III, vol. VI, p. 38.

ing the fort.   The palisade having two entrances, opposite
one another, it was agreed that two parties, led respectively,
by Mason and Underhill, should make simultaneous attacks
upon them.   In spite of the fact that the Indians had been
warned, by the barking of their dogs, of the approach of the
enemy, Mason boldly jumped over the brush piled at the entrance, and was followed by his men.   The other party also
entered at the opposite side, and the slaughter of the dazed
and half-awakened savages began.   Seeing, however, that the
resistance might prove too much for his men, Mason snatched
a torch from a wigwam and set fire to the village, which,
owing to the strong wind blowing, was soon ablaze.   The
English now had only to withdraw, and to shoot any wretched
savage who attempted to climb over the palisade.   In the
early dawn of that May morning, as the New England men
stood guard over the flames, five hundred men, women, and
children were slowly burned alive.[1]   Not over eight escaped,
and there were but seven captives.   The English lost two
killed and twenty wounded.   It is difficult to imagine what
thoughts must have been in the minds of the Puritans as they
slowly roasted the Indian women and children. Mason merely
notes that, by the providence of God, there were one hundred
and fifty more savages than usual in the village that night.

The English, carrying their wounded, retreated to the ships,
— which fortunately had come into Pequot Harbor,— as the
savages from the smaller village were hampering their movements.   With the vessels had also arrived Captain Patrick
and forty men from Massachusetts, that colony having voted
one hundred and sixty, and Plymouth sixty, although too late
to take part in the expedition.   The bulk of the Pequot nation
was now destroyed, and it remained only to make an end of
the few hundred who had thus far escaped.   Sassacus, the
sachem, being repudiated by his own followers, fled with seventy warriors to the Mohawks, and the English indefatigably

---

[1] Mason says 600 to 700 ("Brief History," p. 141);   Underhill, 400 ("Newes from
New England," p. 25);   Gardiner, 300 ("Relation," p. 150).   Mason's account throughout is the most accurate.

ran down detached parties. In a swamp twenty miles from the Dutch line, eighty of the Pequots' "stoutest men," with two hundred old people, women, and children, made a last stand. After being subjected to the fire of the English for some hours, the two hundred non-combatants surrendered, while the warriors fought to the last man, twenty finally escaping through the surrounding lines. The other savages turned against the all but annihilated Pequots, and "happy were they," wrote Mason, "that could bring in their heads to the English: Of which there came almost daily to Windsor or Hartford." In all, during the campaign, over seven hundred were killed or made captive.[1]

Of the prisoners some were divided between Uncas and the Narragansetts, while the rest were kept by the English, or sold into bondage in the West Indies.[2] In the division of this human spoil, the clergy took its part. "Sir," wrote the Reverend Mr. Peter to Governor Winthrop, "Mr. Endecot and myself salute you in the Lord Jesus. Wee have heard of a dividence of women and children in the bay and would bee glad of a share viz: a young woman or girle and a boy if you thinke good. I wrote to you for some boyes for Bermudas, which I thinke is considerable."[3] Fifteen boys and two women were sent thither as slaves, but whether for the profit of the Reverend Peter, Winthrop does not say. Roger Williams pleaded over and over again, but in vain, with the Massachusetts authorities for a more lenient course. "Since the Most High delights in mercy, and great revenge hath bene allready taken," he advised incorporating the survivors among the friendly Indians; but though, only a short time before, the Massachusetts authorities had been pleading with Williams to save themselves, they now turned a deaf ear to his intercession for the natives.[4] The Narragansetts and Mohegans

[1] *Massachusetts Records*, vol. I, p. 192; *Plymouth Records*, vol. I, p. 60; Mason, "Brief History," pp. 141, 148; J. Winthrop, *History*, vol. I, p. 279.

[2] *Ibid.*, vol. I, p. 279.   [3] *Mass. Hist. Soc. Coll.*, Series IV, vol. VI, p. 95.

[4] *Ibid.*, p. 225. Other quotations from Williams and others are conveniently gathered in G. H. Moore, *Notes on the History of Slavery in Massachusetts* (New York, 1866), pp. 1–10.

were both anxious to adopt the few survivors of their powerful enemies, according to Indian custom, so that Williams's suggestions were as practicable as they were merciful. Two hundred were finally so allotted by Connecticut, when the last remnants of the Pequots submitted and the River plantations entered into a treaty with Uncas and Miantanomo.[1] From the end of the Pequot war, all the New England colonies adopted not only Indian but negro slavery, and it was wholly due to economic, and not ethical, causes that the institution did not take root. In the one small locality in all New England where it proved profitable, it did so root itself, and the importing of slaves for use in the other colonies long constituted an important part of Puritan trade.[2]

The contest between the English and the Indians had been inevitable from the start. The murders of the two traders were but the sparks that touched off the explosive material which had long been accumulating. The struggle, with varying details and proximate causes, but based upon the unchanging fundamental conflict of the natures and economic interests of the two races, was to be repeated over and over again as the American frontier advanced. Endicott's stupid campaign, and, perhaps the too thorough absorption of Old Testament examples, had made the struggle almost inhumanly bloody in the first advance of that frontier in New England. The effect, however, was complete. It was to be nearly forty years before the savages regained sufficient strength, and found a leader to attempt again to dispute the relentless advance of the Puritan planters

[1] Text in E. R. Potter, "Early History of Narragansett"; *Rhode Island Historical Society Collections*, vol. III, pp. 177 *f*.

[2] E. Channing, *The Narragansett Planters* (J. H. U. S., 1886), p. 10; W. E. B. DuBois, *The Suppression of the African Slave Trade* (Harvard Univ. Press, 1916), pp. 27 *ff*.

CHAPTER IX

ATTEMPTS TO UNIFY NEW ENGLAND

As a result of the complete crushing of the power of the Pequots their whole country was opened to peaceful settlement, and the extension of the frontier in that direction became rapid. Within about two years from the signing of the treaty with the savages, the foundations were laid of Guilford, New Haven, Milford, Stratford, Fairfield, Norwalk, and Stamford along the Sound, and of Southampton and Southold on the eastern end of Long Island, thus making a continuous line of English settlement up to the Dutch boundary, if not, indeed, within it.[1]

For its size, New Haven was undoubtedly the wealthiest colony in New England, its assessed valuation, the year after it was planted, having been £33,000, or the present equivalent of, perhaps, $700,000.[2] Its founders, under the leadership of the Reverend John Davenport, a Nonconformist London clergyman, and Theophilus Eaton, a schoolmate of his, had arrived in the early summer of 1637, just in time to take part in the Antinomian controversy and the taxes for the Pequot war. Mr. Davenport was requested to contribute to the former, and Mr. Eaton to the latter.[3] Their company was a distinguished one, including several other wealthy London merchants besides Eaton; five ministers; four school-teachers, among whom was the first president of Harvard; the father of Elihu Yale, the founder of Yale University; and Michael Wigglesworth, the "lurid morning star" of New England

[1] The Southampton settlers at first tried to plant well within it, but were forced out by the Dutch. *Cf. N. Y. Col. Docts.*, vols. II, pp. 145 *ff.*, and XIV, pp. 30 *ff.*; Adams, *History of Southampton*, pp. 48 *ff.*

[2] Estimated from entry in *Records of the Colony and Plantation of New Haven* (Hartford, 1857), p. 25. Hereafter cited as *New Haven Records*.

[3] J. Winthrop, *History*, vol. I, pp. 271 *ff.*; *Massachusetts Records*, vol. I, pp. 210, 225.

verse.[1]   Both Davenport and Eaton had been, for some years, members of the Massachusetts Bay Company, and that company's colony made great efforts to retain the new body of settlers within its own bounds.   While the leaders took under consideration the various offers made to them, they either found them unsatisfactory, or had already determined to establish an independent colony of their own.[2]   After Eaton had examined the country around Quinnipiack, it was decided to plant there, and seven men were left to guard the site during the winter, the whole company following in the spring. Not only were the resources of the colonists unusually ample, but their preparations seem to have been exceptionally complete, and the little town soon contained the most stately dwellings in all New England.   Some idea of their scale may be gained from the reputed presence in Davenport's of thirteen fireplaces, and of nineteen in Eaton's.[3]   The intention, apparently, was not only to found a Puritan state, but to have it become the chief mercantile centre of the New World, which accounts for their having built, as one of their Massachusetts critics wrote, "as if trade and merchandize had been as inseparably annexed to them as the shadow is to the body, in the shining of the sun."[4]   One disaster followed another in their business ventures, however, and the dreams of the merchant-founders were never realized.

Davenport and most of his company were not only Puritans, but of the strictest sect, and the Bible Commonwealth which they proceeded to form was of the most extreme type.   Like the Connecticut and Rhode Island people, they were without a charter, and were mere squatters upon the soil; but in June, 1639, a meeting was held of the "free planters," to discuss a frame of government to replace a previously signed plantation covenant, now lost.   We have no knowledge of what constituted a "free planter," but the term undoubtedly ex-

[1] C. H. Levermore, *Republic of New Haven* (J. H. U. S., 1886), p. 8; E. E. Atwater, *History of Colony of New Haven* (New Haven, 1881), pp. 112 *ff.*

[2] J. Winthrop, *History*, vol. I, p. 283; letter from Davenport and Eaton to Massachusetts, *Bulletin New York Public Library*, 1899, pp. 393 *f.*

[3] Atwater, *New Haven*, pp. 393 *f.*   [4] Hubbard, *History of New England*, p. 334.

cluded a large number of males in the settlement. The proceedings took the form of queries put by Mr. Davenport, upon which those present voted by raising hands. As a result of unanimous votes at this meeting, the fundamental agreement provided that the franchise should be restricted to church members, and that the free planters should choose twelve men, to whom should be intrusted the sole right of selecting from among the rest of the colonists those who should become church members and freemen, and who were to have the power of appointing magistrates from among themselves, of making and repealing laws, and, in fact, of performing all public duties.[1] This was legalizing the most extreme claims of the Massachusetts oligarchy. Only one voice, apparently that of Eaton, was raised to protest "that free planters ought not to give this power out of their hands"; but he was, of course, overruled. Four months later, at the October court, it was further voted that "the worde of God shall be the only rule to be attended unto in ordering the affayres of government in this plantation."[2] As had been the case in Connecticut, no mention had been made of allegiance to England; but in this additional step, the new colony swept away all obligation to observe the common and statute laws of the mother-country. The conflicting texts of the Bible, as arbitrarily chosen and interpreted by the small self-perpetuating group of rulers, became the only laws that might safeguard, or hazard, the rights of dwellers in New Haven and the affiliated church-towns which soon sprang up. The reactionary thought of the framers of these fundamental orders, however, was to be without appreciable influence upon the growth of colonial political theory as then developing; for New Haven was to have only a quarter of a century of independent but unimportant life before being absorbed by Connecticut, while a more and more democratic tendency was manifesting itself in all the colonies, even in Massachusetts.

The effects of the frontier life, and of the distance separating England from her colonies, were already beginning to

---

[1] *New Haven Records*, vol. I, pp. 11 ff.   [2] *Ibid.*, p. 21.

show themselves strongly. The semi-independent communities which had been established in Rhode Island, Connecticut, and New Haven were entirely without legal authority; and the two latter, in their "constitutions," had utterly ignored the existence of any power outside of themselves. The situation was not wholly overlooked in England, but as the crisis in public affairs there was rapidly drawing near, the authorities were helpless to interfere. A new demand for the return of the Massachusetts charter, when flatly refused by that colony in 1638,[1] could not be followed by any show of force; and during the next twenty-two years — which were those of the Civil War, the fall of the Stuart monarchy, and the reign of Cromwell — the New England colonies pursued their way almost wholly without reference to the power of England.

The influence of the frontier was being felt in their domestic concerns as well. Although the most aggressively radical of the inhabitants of Massachusetts had, perhaps, gone to the other colonies, there to establish themselves in greater freedom, the struggle of the citizens continued, nevertheless, against the arbitrary power of their government. From the first, the body of magistrates had acted in a judicial, as well as an executive, capacity. The only rule by which they were guided is indicated by a resolution in the General Court of 1636, which provided that they should "determine all causes according to the lawes nowe established, and where there is noe law, then as neere the lawe of God as they can."[2] As English law, in many cases, was not justly applicable, and as, in others, it was largely neglected, this really meant the comparatively few laws already enacted in the colony, and the same arbitrary selection and interpretation of Old Testament texts that we have just noted in New Haven. As the magistrates acted as both attorneys and judges, and as no appeals were permitted from their decisions, no accused person had any protection

[1] J. Winthrop, *History*, vol. 1, p. 324; *Acts Privy Council, Colonial*, vol. 1, pp. 217, 227 f.; Hutchinson, *History*, vol. 1, pp. 84 ff., 442 ff.; Hazard, *Historical Collections*, vol. 1, pp. 432 f.
[2] *Massachusetts Records*, vol. 1, p. 175.

against them.   Anyone, therefore, who might be obnoxious to the ruling powers on account of his views, could not hope for justice; and the so-called trials of Mrs. Hutchinson, Wheelwright, and other notable offenders, were, in reality, not trials at all, but "relentless inquisitions used by the government for the purpose of crushing opposition."[1]   That condition was not, indeed, peculiar to Massachusetts, and was probably just as true of contemporary England.   It was Hooker's glory in Connecticut to have raised his voice, as the leader of that colony, to plead for a legal restraint upon this arbitrary exercise of the judicial power of government, and for the creation of a body of fundamental law.   In 1639, a committee was appointed in that colony for the purpose of drawing up such a code.   The same had been formally demanded in Massachusetts even earlier, but there the wishes of the people had been steadily opposed by their leaders.

While the Massachusetts trials of the type just noted were exceptional, and in general, when passions were not aroused, the ordinary course of justice was fairly equitable, nevertheless, the entire absence of any restraint upon the unbridled will of the magistrates was a source of apprehension to the more serious thinking and liberty-loving residents of Massachusetts, outside the ring of authority.   Not only was any opposition to the course pursued by the government liable to result in banishment, with the complete uprooting of a man's life, and perhaps the financial ruin of himself and his family, but in trivial matters all the inhabitants, and more particularly, of course, the four fifths who were not church members, were liable to constant interference by the authorities.   Such a law, for example, as that declaring that whosoever should "spend his time idly or unproffitably" should suffer such penalty "as the court shall thinke meete to inflicte"[2] was typical, both in its utter lack of definition of the nature of the crime, and in its failure to specify the penalty to be incurred by the criminal.

---

[1] Osgood, *American Colonies*, vol. I, p. 189.
[2] *Massachusetts Records*, vol. I, p. 109.

In spite of the demands of the people in Massachusetts, however, it was not until 1640 that a draft of a fundamental law seems to have really been considered. The clergy and most of the magistrates had been opposed to any limitation of arbitrary authority, and had fought the requests with what their modern defender has called the weapon of "a good-natured procrastination," but which may have worn another aspect to some at the time.[1] Finally, in 1641, an Abstract of Laws, or Body of Liberties, was passed, which marked a distinct step forward, though by no means assuring full protection. One draft, which was not, however, accepted, was based entirely upon Bible texts, of which, characteristically, but two were drawn from the New Testament and forty-six from the Old.[2] Additional safeguards were required, and four years later, the whole discussion as to specific penalties for specific offenses was again reopened. The clergy and Winthrop still opposed any limitation upon judicial authority, the Governor, indeed, going so far as to say that God had made specific penalties only in certain cases, and as "judges are Gods upon earth," their power should not be more limited than his — which might be denominated strong doctrine.[3] In spite of all opposition, however, a new code, based in part upon the Body of Liberties, was finally secured and printed in 1648, twenty years after the first demand, and ten after Hooker's famous sermon at Hartford.[4]

The antagonism to the power of the magistrates was manifested also by new episodes in the struggle between them and the more democratic deputies, which we noted as beginning at the time of the Connecticut emigration. A dispute over the ownership of a sow, between a poor widow and a rich man

[1] Palfrey, *History*, vol. II, p. 22. For earlier efforts to secure its passage, *cf. Massachusetts Records*, vol. I, pp. 174, 222, 279, 292; J. Winthrop, *History*, vol. I, pp. 191, 240.

[2] *Cf. Mass. Hist. Soc. Coll.*, Series I, vol. V, pp. 171 *ff.* The Body as passed is in *Ibid.*, Series III, vol. VIII, pp. 216 *ff.*

[3] *Massachusetts Records*, vol. II, pp. 92 *ff.*; "Arbitrary Government Described," in R. C. Winthrop, *J. Winthrop*, vol. II, p. 448. *Cf.* also J. Winthrop, *History*, vols. I, pp. 388 *ff.*, and II, pp. 67 *ff.*

[4] *Massachusetts Records*, vol. II, pp. 61, 168, 262.

notorious for his unjust business dealings, was finally brought
to the General Court for decision.   The evidence was by no
means convincing, and the Court was divided, with a majority
of the magistrates in favor of a verdict for the rich Keaynes,
and a majority of the deputies in favor of the poor widow.
The point was thus raised again as to whether the small number
of magistrates, by a negative vote, could block the will of the
much larger body of deputies.[1]   Winthrop wrote a treatise on
the question, appealing to certain English precedents and the
Old Testament, and stated that, if the magistrates were not
allowed to veto the action of the deputies, the colony would
be a democracy and "there was no such government in Israel." [2]
So implacably did the grim shades of Moses and Aaron block
the paths of Boston Common.   The magistrates, in view of
the strong opposition that developed, offered to leave the
matter to the clergy, and to give way if the decision were
adverse.   They knew, of course, that it would not be so, and
Winthrop records that it was "their only care to gain time,"
until the people could be brought to the heel of their clerical
leaders as usual.   As part of the plan, the members of the
Court were asked to take advice before the next meeting; and
it is interesting as showing the normal danger for the ordinary
citizen in discussing public matters, that a special act should
be thought necessary making it "no offence for any, either
publicly or privately, to declare their opinion in the case, so
it were modestly." [3]   The following year, a compromise was
effected, which, however, was distinctly in favor of the magistrates; and thereafter the deputies and the magistrates sat as
two separate houses, each with a negative vote on the other.[4]

Another incident in the struggle, which soon occurred, involved both the question of the power of the local government
over the colonists, and the relations of the colony to the home
government in England.   In 1644, it was suggested to the
General Court that the condition of the large number of un-

---

[1] J. Winthrop, *History*, vols. I, pp. 377 *ff*., and II, pp. 83 *ff*., 142 *ff*.

[2] The essay is given in R. C. Winthrop, *J. Winthrop*, vol. II, pp. 427 *ff*.

[3] J. Winthrop, *History*, vol. II, p. 143.   [4] *Massachusetts Records*, vol. II, pp. 58 *f*.

represented inhabitants be improved by increasing the civil privileges that a citizen might possess without being a church member, such privileges then being limited, apparently, to a small share in local town business.[1] Nothing, however, was done, and two years later, a petition signed by a Dr. Robert Child, Samuel Maverick, and five others was presented, reciting that there were many thousands in the colony who were debarred from all participation in government, although they paid taxes and were subject to military and other duties. Child was a newcomer, "a gentleman and a scholar," and a graduate of the University of Padua. Maverick was the richest of the "old planters," and the only freeman who was not a church member — a privilege which he owed to the circumstances connected with the first planting of the colony, as already related. Thomas Fowle, another of the signers, was a merchant; while yet another, David Yale, was a man of property, and both a stepson of Theophilus Eaton of New Haven and a brother-in-law of Governor Hopkins of Connecticut. At this very time, he was acting as attorney for the Earl of Warwick.[2] The motives of the signers may not have been wholly disinterested, but the effort to make out that they were persons of no importance in the colony has been overdone.[3]

The petitioners desired that "members of the church of England, not scandalous in their lives and conversations," be admitted to the churches, and that "civil liberty and freedom be forthwith granted to all truly English, equall to the rest of their countrymen, as in all plantations is accustomed to be done, and as all freeborne enjoy in our native country." [4] Other reforms were demanded, and although some of the charges were overdrawn, nevertheless, the main point was not fairly met in the lengthy reply prepared by Winthrop, Dudley,

[1] J. Winthrop, *History*, vol. ii, pp. 193, 349.

[2] *Cal. State Pap., Col., 1574–1660*, p. 327.

[3] J. Winthrop, *History*, vol. ii, pp. 320 *n*., 358. *Cf.* Winslow, "New England's Salamander," in *Mass. Hist. Soc. Coll.*, Series III, vol. ii, pp. 117 *ff.*

[4] Hutchinson, *Papers*, vol. i, pp. 216 *ff.*; *New England's Jonas cast up in London*, Force Tracts, vol. iv, pp. 8 *ff.*

and others of the court.[1]   That point was that in an English colony, and upon English soil, the great majority of the inhabitants were debarred from a share in the government because of beliefs which would not have so disfranchised them in the home country.   No amount of legal casuistry expended upon the charter, and no amount of sophistry employed in explaining the relations between the colony and England, could alter that fact, nor the additional one that Massachusetts was a colony and not an independent nation.   As the request of the petitioners was for such liberties only as they would have possessed at home, and not for general religious toleration, an appeal to England was natural, and was set on foot as soon as the reply of the magistrates was received.   Winthrop, however, declared that he would not tolerate such an appeal, and the petitioners were heavily fined by the court, and two of them imprisoned.[2]   Child, and some of the others insisting upon going to England, they were seized just before the ship sailed, their baggage and houses were searched, and they themselves imprisoned.   As some of the magistrates had not agreed to the earlier proceedings, they were not consulted in the present one, which was distinctly of a Star-Chamber sort.   Among the papers of Dand, another signer, was found one suggesting the appointment of a royal governor, for which he also was promptly put in jail.   Vassall and Fowle finally reached England; but the political situation there by 1647 had become such as to preclude any consideration of colonial matters.

[1] Hutchinson, *Papers*, vol. 1, pp. 223 *ff*.; J. Winthrop, *History*, vol. 11, pp. 348 *ff*. Prof. G. L. Kittredge has recently written an elaborate account of Dr. Child — "Doctor Robert Child the Remonstrant," reprinted from *Publications, Col. Soc., Mass.*, 1919. It is a strong brief in defense of the action taken by the Massachusetts authorities, and contains the fullest and most accurate account of the Petition and the subsequent trials yet written.   Prof. Kittredge is a firm supporter of the old theory that Child was plotting to overthrow the government in the interests of Presbyterianism.   While this may be so, it seems not to cover the cases of the other remonstrants.   The main interest of the affair for our present work, however, lies in the evidence afforded of discontent with the Puritan régime, and in that connection, Prof. Kittredge, after showing the extreme diversity of views held by the signers on most matters, speaks of "their discontent with the administration which was the sole binding element common to all the Remonstrants" (p. 29).   He also states (p. 52), that "there was more or less public sentiment in favor of the defendants."

[2] *Massachusetts Records*, vol. 11, pp. 196, 199, 205, 241.

The tide of popular rights in the colonies was rising, however, and "all the troubles of New England" were "not at the Massachusetts," as Winslow wrote to Winthrop, nor were high-handed proceedings wholly limited to that commonwealth. In Plymouth, a written proposal, favored by many of the inhabitants and of the deputies, was presented to the General Court, "to allow and maintaine full and free tollerance of religion to all men that would preserve the civill peace and submit unto government." "You would have admired [wondered] to have seen," wrote Winslow, "how sweet this carrion relished to the pallate of most of the deputies." "Notwithstanding it was required, according to order, to be voted," the Governor would not permit any vote to be taken; and the effort thus to extend to others the same freedom that the leading founders of the colony had availed themselves of for twelve years in Holland was summarily suppressed.[1]

During the decade we have been considering, the struggle of Englishmen at home for the preservation of their liberties against the incompetent and reactionary rule of the second Stuart, had left that ruler but little leisure to consider the American colonies. Except for occasional and ineffectual efforts to retain some control over them by the home government, they had been left free to work out their own theories, untrammeled by any higher power. By 1640, the scattered settlements in Maine, the towns in New Hampshire, the Bay Colony, Plymouth, the four separate towns in what is now Rhode Island, Saybrook, the affiliated towns of New Haven, and the river settlements of Connecticut, were pursuing their several ways virtually as independent states, preëmpting lands, erecting governments, treating with the natives, with each other, and with the French and Dutch, as if they were sovereign powers. Nor was there anything to prevent innumerable other petty states, each with its few square miles of territory, and ruling according to its own ideas, from arising over all New England, save as restrained by the jealousy of those already in existence. If this tendency had not been restrained,

[1] Letter of Winslow to Winthrop, in Hutchinson, *Papers*, vol. 1, p. 174.

New England might have come in time to be a checker-board
of tiny republics, engaged in constant disputes over boundaries
and other relations at home, and, should the shield of England
cease to protect them, the prey of foreign foes abroad.

There were three possible methods of preventing this development of a Puritan Balkans. England might assert her
rights legitimately, and endeavor to bring some sort of uniformity and order out of what might otherwise become an
impossible situation; one or another of the colonies might,
by force of greater strength, subdue its weaker neighbors,
and thus create one or several greater states; or, finally, a
confederation might be formed of all of them. Under the
circumstances, the legal and logical method would have been
some sort of imperial control by the mother-country, but that
was out of the question unless the English government was
strong and united enough to enforce her will, and wise and
experienced enough to make it acceptable to the colonists.
For the present, that solution was impossible. Of the other
two, the first would naturally appeal to a strong and aggressive colony like Massachusetts, while a confederacy would
be favored by her weaker but no less independent neighbors.
Both the latter plans were tried, and the intercolonial relations of the next quarter of a century were largely the result
of these two conflicting methods of unifying New England
being pursued simultaneously.

Owing to the death of Mason, and the failure of Gorges's
plans for Maine, the settlements north of Massachusetts were
without a settled government, and the inhabitants do not
seem to have had the ability to create a stable one for themselves, which was so marked a characteristic of those in Massachusetts and Plymouth, Connecticut and New Haven. We
have already seen how Massachusetts, by an unwarrantable
construction of her charter, had begun to lay claim to all the
land of New Hampshire and Maine lying eastward of the most
northerly source of the Merrimack, although the whole course
of the Crown and Council for New England at the time of the
grant showed that such a claim was absolutely untenable.

Nor, in the beginning, had the Massachusetts leaders dreamed of making it,[1] and it was, in fact, as Professor Osgood says, "more clearly an usurpation than was any later act of the crown which affected New England."[2] The decision, otherwise favorable to Massachusetts, of the English Chief Justices in 1677, declaring the interpretation claimed to be utterly without warrant, and reassigning the lands to the heirs of the two original patentees, seems entirely just.[3]

Early in 1641, a dispute between church factions in Dover, headed by two contending clergymen, gave Massachusetts a chance to intervene. Captain Underhill, who had been banished from that colony at the time of the Hutchinson controversy, was then on the Piscataqua, and, perhaps with an idea of once more ingratiating himself with the home authorities, sent a petition to the Massachusetts Court, asking aid for himself and his party. Massachusetts at once dispatched a magistrate and two clergymen, and the Underhill party were victorious, the clergyman heading the opposing faction having opportunely turned out to be a personally immoral character.[4] The Dover patentees, Warwick, Say, and the others, who had purchased the patent in the interests of Massachusetts some years before, now passed the grant, with slight reservations, to that colony, which at once annexed the town.[5] A temporary government was installed, and, two years later, it was agreed that the inhabitants should have the privilege of freemen to manage their local affairs, and to elect deputies, even though they were not church members.[6] Thus a right not yielded to four fifths of her own citizens was granted to

[1] *Cf.* letter of Emanuel Downing, already cited, asking for an extension of the charter limits northward, in 1633. *Cal. State Pap., Col., 1675–76,* p. 74.

[2] Osgood, *American Colonies,* vol. I, p. 377.

[3] *Acts Privy Council, Colonial,* vol. I, pp. 723 *ff.* Palfrey's statement that the charter, "literally interpreted," endowed Massachusetts with the lands claimed is hardly borne out by the facts. *History,* vol. I, p. 587. *Cf.,* however, Burrage, *Colonial Maine,* p. 364.

[4] J. Winthrop, *History,* vol. II, pp. 33 *f.*

[5] *Massachusetts Records,* vol. I, p. 332; J. Winthrop, *History,* vol. II, p. 50. Apparently Strawberry Bank (Portsmouth) was also annexed. *Cf. New Hampshire Provincial Papers,* vol. I, p. 192.

[6] *Ibid.,* pp. 183 *ff.,* 168.

those in her new possessions, and imperial ambition seems to have won the first victory over Israelitish polity. This provision not only disproved her former claim that civil order could not be maintained without forced religious conformity, but, combined with the further provision that the settlers in the newly annexed territory should be subject only to local, and not to general, taxation, it tended to show that she herself did not believe the claims she made as to the interpretation of the charter.[1] If she really considered that the territory now being seized under pretext of ownership was as indubitably hers as that south of the Merrimack, why did she thus deprive herself of the right of religious and fiscal control?

She next claimed and absorbed the town of Exeter, and her new claims, extending to Maine, there came into conflict with those of Gorges and the Pilgrims. The latter, indeed, had lately heard her state that she was entitled to a part of the town of Plymouth itself, and she did encroach upon the Plymouth territory.[2] A further enlargement of her power to the south, and one obviously outside her jurisdiction, was next made within the present limits of Rhode Island.

Samuel Gorton, from his heretical notions in religion, according to the Gospel of New England, and his somewhat explosive efforts to defend persons he thought oppressed by the colonial authorities, had led a troubled and troubling life in Massachusetts, Plymouth, Portsmouth, and Providence. Indeed, in his wandering course through the Puritan heavens, he seems to have been as fatally followed by trouble as a comet by its luminous tail. As he punctuated his career by denominating the Massachusetts magistrates "a generation of vipers," the Governor of Plymouth, "Satan," and the justice of Portsmouth, "a just-ass," he can hardly be said to have had an ingratiating way with the authorities, although no crime could be laid at his door. The people of that day had an insatiable passion for ploughing in the theological field, which was always proving as full of unexploded shells as any

---

[1] *New Hampshire Provincial Papers*, vol. I, pp. 182, 184.
[2] Bradford, *Plymouth*, pp. 367 *ff.*

on the modern battle-front of France, and Gorton seems to have had a fatal facility for turning these up. He had already been blown out of three colonies, when, after some experience with him, the men of Providence decided that he or they must leave. Finally banished, he made an Indian purchase, and settled some miles to the south.

This, however, was not far enough for his former neighbors, who, in 1641, asked assistance from Massachusetts in ridding them of Gorton. That colony refused to consider the request, unless Providence would place herself under her jurisdiction.[1] The matter became complicated by a dispute between Miantanomo and two other sachems, arising out of Gorton's purchase, and the sachems also applied to Massachusetts. Both they and the Providence men were received under her jurisdiction, and the next move was to send a force of forty armed men to take Gorton and his party into custody.[2] Even those opposed to him in Providence suggested arbitration; but the Massachusetts clergy advised the magistrates that this was not an "honorable" course, as the Gorton party "were no state, but a few fugitives living without law or government," and "their blasphemous and reviling writings" could be "purged away only by repentence and public satisfaction." [3] The case was, therefore, prejudged without a hearing, and the more summary method was taken of trying to set fire to the log fort in which Gorton and his company had taken refuge.

It must be presumed that the ministers of Christ considered this as a more "honorable" course than arbitration with "a few fugitives" from their vindictiveness. The attack was made on a Sabbath morning, and even the heretical Gorton was naturally surprised.[4] In receiving the Indians under their jurisdiction, Massachusetts had required that the savages should not profane that day by doing any work upon it, and that they should not kill any man but upon just cause and

---

[1] J. Winthrop, *History*, vol. II, pp. 69 *ff.*; *Rhode Island Historical Society Collections*, vol. II, pp. 191 *f.*
[2] J. Winthrop, *History*, vol. II, pp. 144 *ff.*; *Massachusetts Records*, vol. II, pp. 26 *f.*, 40.
[3] J. Winthrop, *History*, vol. II, pp. 168 *f.*
[4] Gorton, *Simplicities Defence*; Force Tracts, vol. IV, pp. 58 *ff.*

authority.[1]   The attempt, immediately following, on the part
of that colony's expedition, to burn their fellow white men
alive during church hours, because they were too impatient
to wait, may have struck their new savage subjects as a little
incongruous.   Nine of the Gortonists were captured, taken to
Boston, and imprisoned.   The clergy called for blood, and
gave their written opinion that all nine of the prisoners "deserved death by the law of God."   In this unjust and inhuman
decision, all the magistrates but three concurred, and it was
prevented from passing only by the people's representatives
among the deputies.   Finally, the prisoners were condemned
to be distributed among seven towns, there to be "kept to
worke for their living, and wear irons upon one leg, and not
to depart the limits of the town, nor by word or writing maintain any of their blasphemous or wicked errors upon pain
of death."[2]   The sentence was executed and the prisoners
were kept in irons until the following year; when the growing
popular disapproval of the clergy's actions caused their victims
to be suddenly released and banished.[3]

The Massachusetts authorities had thus utilized the request
of one faction in a settlement wholly outside their own limits,
to extend their jurisdiction.   They had attempted, upon a
charge of heresy directed against persons living in another
colony, to murder the entire body of the opposing faction,
after refusing the arbitration proposed by that faction's own
enemies.   When the decree was finally softened to banishment,
this was held to include exclusion of the prisoners from their
former homes, now considered as part of the Bay Colony.
They had seized and sold the cattle and goods of the unfortunate people, to pay the expenses of their so-called trial and
illegal detention.   In all this, there had not been even the
fallacious plea, as in the case of Williams and Mrs. Hutchinson,
that the civil peace of Massachusetts had been endangered.

---

[1] J. Winthrop, *History*, vol. II, p. 147.
[2] *Ibid.*, vol. II, pp. 176 f.; *Massachusetts Records*, vol. II, pp. 51 *ff.*; Gorton, *Simplicities Defence*, pp. 66 *ff.*
[3] J. Winthrop, *History*, vol. II, pp. 188 f.; Gorton, *Simplicities Defence*, p. 83.

The outcome showed, however, that the cruel and immoral power of the clergy and magistrates was coming to be opposed by a growing body of healthy and liberal opinion. The bloody sentence demanded by them had been refused by the people's leaders, and public opinion had finally secured the reversal, within a year, of the milder one that had been executed. The confusion of Gorton's own religious views, and his incoherence in expressing them, could in themselves have won him little popular support.[1] What the people were groping after was the right of the individual to think and act for himself, so long as the state was not endangered, as had been clearly expressed in the Plymouth petition. The road was to be long and bloodstained, but there was now no doubt that the people of Massachusetts intended to travel it, and that their feet were at last set in the right direction.

By 1640, although new arrivals had not been coming in so rapidly of late, the population of the New England settlements had grown to about eighteen thousand. Moreover, they had, on the whole, been prosperous. We have already seen how even Plymouth, with its slender resources, its poor soil, and its ill-chosen site, had yet achieved more than economic independence, and we have noted the financial resources of New Haven. The capital and numbers of Massachusetts were, of course, far larger than those of either of the others, and it was estimated that that colony had spent, in its first dozen years, nearly £200,000, or in our day, perhaps, five million dollars, in making its settlement.[2] Possessed of the unrestricted resources of a continent, and having suffered no losses from Indians or foreign foe, New England was apparently in a sound economic condition, when suddenly the crash came. "Merchants would sell no wares but for ready money," Winthrop wrote in 1640; "men could not pay their debts though they had enough, prices of lands and cattle fell soon to the one-

---

[1] Most of Gorton's writings are as incoherent as they are vituperative. Age, however, seemed to clear his mind and style, and his letter to Morton, in 1669, defending himself from the charges in the latter's book, was clear and dignified. It is given in Hutchinson, *History*, vol. 1, pp. 467 *ff*.

[2] Jeremiah Dummer, *A Defence of the New England Charters* (London, 1721), p. 9.

half, yea to a third, and after one-fourth part." [1] The Massachusetts General Court was soon called upon to pass special legislation to assist debtors, as the suffering became general.

In spite of their enormous natural resources, the colonies, like all new countries, lacked capital in the form of money. They borrowed heavily from England and imported from her still more heavily in food, clothes, and manufactured goods, without as yet having developed sufficient export trade to enable them to meet their foreign bills.[2] The inherent unsoundness of the position had been concealed, temporarily, by the effects of the continued influx of new settlers on a large scale, which had created a demand for all the colonists' surplus in the shape of everything required by a planter during his first years. Prices of both goods and lands advanced steadily, as a fire is blown into flame by a forced draught. Suddenly the tide of immigration stopped entirely; the exceptional demand, which had come to be regarded as normal, ceased; English merchants naturally required payment on overdue accounts; and all the familiar phenomena of an economic crisis became evident.

It is usually stated that emigration from England stopped because the prospect there had become so much brighter for the Puritans that there was no longer reason for leaving home.[3] This, however, by no means meets all the requirements of the case. We have already seen that the great majority of the people who had been coming to New England had not joined the churches there, although in the main of Puritan stock. Nor, at the time in question, did the Puritan leaders in England, in spite of altered conditions, by any means relax their efforts to plant Puritan colonies. In fact, such men as Say and Pym were more enthusiastic than ever in their plans. These efforts, however, were no longer directed toward New England, but in quite other directions.[4] By her religious per-

---

[1] J. Winthrop, *History*, vol. II, p. 21; *cf.* also pp. 8, 29, 37.

[2] A very complete list of imports could be made up from the bills of lading of the ships arriving in 1640, given in *Acts Privy Council, Colonial*, vol. I, p. 268.

[3] This was Winthrop's version: *History*, vol. II, p. 37.

[4] Newton, *Puritan Colonisation*, pp. 287 *ff.*

secutions and peculiar church-membership requirement for the franchise, Massachusetts had, little by little, antagonized all her old friends at home, from the Earl of Warwick down, who had been constantly calling the attention of her leaders to the fact that no more people, not even Puritans, would go to her if she did not discontinue her career of persecution. By that course she had already virtually excluded from her portion of the English Empire all Englishmen not acceptable to her clergy and a dozen of her leading laymen. This closed her ports to almost the entire stream of English emigration, which continued large, although somewhat changed in character, while the labor of her former friends was now expended in diverting what remained of the Puritan element itself in that stream away from, instead of toward, Massachusetts.

In this connection, Winthrop wrote bitterly to Lord Say, complaining of his efforts to induce settlers to go out from England to the Caribbean instead of to New England. To this, Say made a long reply, rebuking the authorities in the colony for their misuse of Scripture texts to further their own views, and ended with the admonition that "for what you say of the church not compatable with another frame of government, I pray putt away that error . . . the church beinge wholly spirritual, can subsist with any forme of outward government." [1]

Not only, however, did immigration to Massachusetts stop, but there threatened to be an emigration from that colony to the English leaders' Caribbean settlement. John Humphrey, one of the most influential of the original planters, who had not prospered in the Bay, was made Governor of the West Indian Puritan settlements, and, in 1641, sailed thither with several hundred Massachusetts people.[2] Many others removed to other colonies, and Winthrop relates, with evident relish, the misfortunes which befell them as God's judgment

---

[1] *Mass. Hist. Soc. Coll.*, Series V, vol. I, p. 302; J. Winthrop, *History*, vol. I, pp. 399 *f*.

[2] *Manchester Papers*, p. 424, cited by Newton, *Puritan Colonisation*, p. 292; J. Winthrop, *History*, vol. II, p. 15. There was also some movement the other way: 1200 persons are said to have gone from Barbadoes to New England from 1643 to 1647. *Cal. State Pap., Col., 1661–68*, p. 529.

upon them for leaving.[1] That the influences checking the
growth of Massachusetts were not wholly due to general conditions is indicated also by the fact that, while her population,
in the next two decades, was considerably less than doubled,
that of New Hampshire was nearly tripled, Rhode Island increased five-fold, and Connecticut four-fold.[2] The actual
numbers are even more striking than the percentages. Massachusetts, starting the period with fourteen thousand, added
less than ten thousand, while the other three, beginning with
but three thousand, added nearly nine thousand. Connecticut's growth, moreover, was made in spite of the fact that
apparently Massachusetts made even greater efforts to divert
emigrants from that colony than were being made in England
to divert them from herself; so that Hooker, in complaining
of the methods employed by her citizens, was forced to write
to Winthrop, that "such impudent forgery is scant found in
hell."[3]

In the absence of any attempt by England to unify these
scattered settlements, the only tendency toward unification,
as against the centrifugal forces at work, had been the process
of annexation and attempted domination by Massachusetts.
The growth of the frontier, however, with the resultant Pequot
war, had fostered a sense of unity in the face of a common
danger among those exposed to it. As Professor Turner points
out, in speaking of the colonies in general, particularism was
always strongest in those not so exposed, and the Indian
frontier "stretched along the western border like a cord of
union."[4] The extension, northward and westward, had also
brought the English into immediate and hostile contact with
both French and Dutch. Apparently as a result of the somewhat inefficient joint action in the Pequot war, a confederation between the colonies was informally discussed at Boston
in 1637, and a draft prepared by Massachusetts the following

---

[1] J. Winthrop, *History*, vol. II, pp. 103 *ff.*, 113, 156.
[2] *Century of Population*, p. 9.
[3] Letter in *Connecticut Historical Society Collections*, vol. I, pp. 4 *ff.*
[4] Turner, *Significance of the Frontier*, p. 92.

year.[1] Connecticut objected to one of the terms, the ground of her dislike, Winthrop wrote, being her "shyness of coming under our government." [2] The smaller colony, however, had, within a few years, so far got over her shyness as to be ready to "entertain a firm combination for a defensive and offensive war, and all other mutual offices of love," as the records somewhat quaintly word it.[3] The decrease in immigration, and the business panic throughout the colonies, may have helped to bring them to a more realizing sense of their isolation from England, and of the need of mutual dependence, which was greatly increased by a threatened renewal of Indian hostilities in 1642. The latter is the sole reason given by Bradford for the remarkable effort now made to combine the colonies into a confederation, in regard to which all our contemporary authorities are singularly silent.[4]

The settlements, however, were well fitted to be thus joined in closer bonds, in spite of minor differences. The country in which they were planted formed a geographical unit, the natural boundaries of which were emphasized by the human elements of hostile French, Indians, and Dutch. The economic and social life, based upon the geographical, religious, and political factors, was, in the main, remarkably homogeneous. Their attitude toward English policy, and their trade-relations with the rest of the empire, were very similar. There was not only no such clashing of interests as divided them from the staple colonies of the West Indies, but not even the minor differences that would have made impossible such a combination between Pennsylvania and Virginia. United action in the Indian war, and the religious Synod of the same year, had been the first steps taken in the formation of the political machinery for consideration of joint affairs. The way was smoothly paved, therefore, for the establishment of a genuine union

There was, however, one stumbling-block, which was the

---

[1] J. Winthrop, *History*, vol. 1, pp. 283 f.
[2] *Ibid.*, p. 342; *Connecticut Historical Society Collections*, vol. 1, p. 9.
[3] *Conn. Col. Records*, vol. 1, p. 31.　　[4] Bradford, *Plymouth*, pp. 416 f.

intense local feeling and exaggerated sense of importance of the separate settlements. The leaders in each of them must often have dreamed of what the future might have in store for the little colonies in which they had cast their lots, but it is impossible to say what those dreams may have been. They could not have included the actual development of the present British Empire or of the United States, the creation of each of which has been largely dependent upon economic forces and scientific inventions beyond the vision of any seventeenth-century mind. Whatever their dreams may have been, in practice the leaders adopted an opportunist policy, which, in general, may be described as the endeavor to keep from being entangled with England without losing the value of her protection. That any of them could seriously have thought that their individual colonies, as such, could ever become powerful nations, is unlikely. Added, therefore, to their policy regarding England was probably an opportunist policy regarding their neighbors. The extent and nature of the New England country had, by this time, become fairly well known, and the rate of growth could be more or less accurately forecast. With extending frontiers and but ill-defined territorial limits, disputes, already occurring, could also be foreseen as bound to become more frequent and more serious.

All of the colonies had shown the tendency toward expansion. Plymouth had started her trading posts on the rivers of Maine and Connecticut; settlements multiplied in Rhode Island; New Haven, from the meadows of Quinnipiack, was soon planting on Long Island, and nearing the Dutch boundaries on the Sound; while Connecticut, through her purchase of Saybrook from the disappointed patentees in 1644,[1] and her planting of towns westward even of New Haven's expansion, was rapidly stretching east and west. Massachusetts had long adopted the definite policy of extending her claims and control as fast and as far as possible. In the race for land and power, her numbers, resources, and central position, all gave her immense advantages, to which was added the no mean

[1] *Conn. Col. Records*, vol. I, pp. 266 ff.

one of an unscrupulous disregard for the prior rights of others. On the one hand, then, the weaker colonies might hope to gain from union some protection, not only from the Indian and the foreigner, but from the growing aggressiveness of Massachusetts. On the other, that colony might anticipate dominating the councils of the Confederacy, while free scope was still left for her own aggrandizement.

Although they were far inferior to her as military powers, the acknowledgment of Plymouth, Connecticut, and New Haven as of equal political weight in the Union served largely to protect them against the Bay Colony; but there was no such protection for Maine or for the towns in Rhode Island, which were refused admission to the league. The inhabitants of the former were not received, Winthrop wrote, because the people of Agamenticus had recently "made a taylor their mayor, and had entertained one Hull, an excommunicated person, and very contentious, for their minister." [1] These somewhat surprising reasons for refusing representation to the few inhabitants of a territory equal in size to all the rest of New England combined may be dismissed as not the true ones. We are more likely to find the latter in that new interpretation of her charter by which Massachusetts laid claim to all this vast tract, which she formally annexed ten years later. To have allowed its inhabitants representation in the proposed confederacy would have been to acknowledge their right to be considered an independent colony, and so would have placed awkward moral obstacles in the way of the manifest destiny of God's elect. In regard to the Rhode Island plantations, in spite of Winthrop's affection for Williams, the Bay Colony had always exhibited a vindictive spite, the extreme virulence of which it is somewhat difficult to understand, even after making all allowances for the known facts. In 1640, under the administration of Dudley, the Massachusetts General Court had received a letter from the magistrates of Connecticut, New Haven, and Aquidneck, "wherein they declared their dislike of such as would have the Indians rooted out," and their desire of "seeking to gain them by justice and kindness," although carefully watching them for any hostile intent. While the Massachusetts Court voted its assent, it also insisted that the answer should be addressed only to the magistrates of Connecticut and New Haven, formally exclud- ing any communication with those of Aquidneck "as men not to bee capitulated withall by us, either for themselves or the people of the iland where they inhabit." [1]   Silly bigotry, as well as intercolonial discourtesy, could hardly go further than in this childish refusal even to discuss a humanitarian project of importance and of common interest.   The real motive, how- ever, may have been, as in the case of Maine, to leave the way open to annexation by refusing to acknowledge any separate government; and when, a year after the confederacy was formed, the Rhode Island towns applied for admission, the answer, un- doubtedly dictated by Massachusetts, was an "utter refusall" unless they would "absolutely and without reservacon sub- mitt" to either Plymouth or herself.[2]

At the time of the formation of the Confederacy, Massa- chusetts had just driven the entering wedge at Providence and absorbed New Hampshire, and was engaged in encroaching upon the northern bounds of Plymouth and Connecticut.   The three smaller colonies, therefore, had everything to gain by having their existence recognized by being admitted as political equals in the league; while they were further protected by the third clause in the Articles, which guaranteed the independ- ence of each of them, and even forbade the voluntary union of any colony with another without consent of the Confedera- tion.   On the other hand, Massachusetts, with the rich ter- ritories to the north and south — which she was already ab- sorbing — left open to her, had also much to gain by having a body that could give some sort of legal approval to her illegal poachings; and her own power, in extreme circumstances, could be counted upon to nullify any adverse vote.   These were prob- ably the reasons which induced her to enter a Confederation in

---

[1] J. Winthrop, *History*, vol. II, p. 24; *Massachusetts Records*, vol. I, p. 305.
[2] *Acts United Colonies*, vol. I, p. 23.

which her two commissioners had only an equal voting power with those of each of the three smaller colonies in the governing board of eight.

Although the Articles of Confederation agreed that the four colonies should thereafter be known as the United Colonies of New England, the machinery set up was not that of a genuine federal state, but simply that of "a firme and perpetual league of friendship and amity for offence and defence, mutual advice and succor."[1]   Even the very moderate powers granted the board of commissioners, which constituted the only organ of the league, tended to decline, and it can hardly be considered as other than a joint committee to consider matters of mutual interest and to proffer advice to the general courts of the several colonies.   According to the Articles, however, the commissioners, when they met at the regular annual meetings, were to be possessed of full authority from their home courts to determine all military matters, it being provided that no colony should engage in either offensive or defensive war without the consent of at least six of the eight commissioners.   This was the majority required to decide all other questions, and in case six could not agree, the matter in dispute was to be referred back to the general courts.

The Confederation, which no more recognized the existence of England than the "constitutions" of Connecticut and New Haven had done, possessed no means of operating directly upon the people as individuals, or of enforcing its will upon a recalcitrant colony.   It was a useful piece of machinery, but not a new government, and it failed to call forth affection or loyalty from its members.   It is impossible to say what it might have developed into had the colonies remained permanently as independent of England as they were until the restoration of the Stuarts in 1660.   The various results of that event did away, in time, with the possibility, or the necessity, of such an organization.   But, during the Union's existence, it performed valuable service, not merely in accustoming

[1] The articles have been many times reprinted.   The citations above are from *Acts United Colonies*, vol. 1, pp. 3 ff.

the colonies to act together, but also in concentrating their resources in military emergencies, and, negatively, in saving the smaller members from the encroachments of Massachusetts. As was inevitable, that colony largely dominated its councils, and the attitude that the commissioners adopted upon questions of civil and religious polity was, in the main, that of Massachusetts rather than that of Plymouth or Connecticut. In all that concerned the liberty of the individual, the weight of their authority was, as a rule, thrown upon the side of reaction, rather than of progress. The small extent of their real powers, however, is indicated by the fact that the history of New England under the Confederacy continued to be the history of Massachusetts and her neighbors, and not that of the "United Colonies of New England."

CHAPTER X

CROSS-CURRENTS IN THE CONFEDERACY

From the formation of the Confederacy in 1643, until the restoration of the English monarchy in 1660, the colonies were practically free to make what use they could of an entire liberty of action, unhampered by any serious attempt on the part of the British government to interfere with them. The whole situation was favorable. The settlements had passed the experimental stage, and were well rooted. If the decline in immigration entailed certain disadvantages, on the other hand it relieved the existing order from the necessity of absorbing new elements. The more powerful colonies had signed articles of union, and no Indian war of any magnitude was to interrupt their peaceful development. The economic position slowly improved, and reached a sounder basis than before. Yet the pages which record the story of those seventeen years are among the least attractive in New England history. There is hardly an incident to stir the imagination or to fire a noble pride. Freed from all restraint, the best use that the colonies could make of their liberty was to quarrel among themselves over boundaries, annexations, and taxes; to contend, without honor, with the Dutch and French; to carry on inglorious controversies with the savages; and to indulge in the only example of bloody religious persecution that the United States has known. Looking at the history of those years, however, from the standpoint of the development of personal liberty, there were two movements that redeem its otherwise disheartening aspects. One was the bringing of order out of chaos in Rhode Island, where the settlers proved that democracy and a broad toleration could, after all, be combined with political stability. The other was the success of the people of Massachusetts in securing the fundamental body of laws already noted, and the unmistakable rejection of their theocratical leaders, lay and clerical.

On the return of Acadia to France by the treaty of St. Germain, one Claude de Razilly had been commissioned to rule the territory; and after his death, three years later, d'Aulnay and de la Tour, both of whom had possessed grants and trading posts within his jurisdiction, aspired to replace him in the supreme command.[1] After various encounters, in one of which d'Aulnay captured de la Tour, the latter, in 1643, arrived at Boston with one hundred and forty men, and asked for help against his rival. Winthrop, who was then governor, called together a few of the magistrates and deputies, who assured de la Tour that, although they could not grant him aid officially, he might have permission to hire ships and engage volunteers for his expedition.[2] "The rumour of these things soon spreading," however, they encountered so much adverse criticism that Winthrop consulted with additional members of the Court, and, of course, the clergy. The question was long debated, whether it was lawful for Christians to aid idolaters, and, somewhat more pertinently, whether it was expedient in this particular case. The debate is given at length by Winthrop, and affords an instructive example of Puritan casuistry. A matter of so much importance should, of course, have been referred to the General Court, and, also, under the terms of the new Confederacy, to the Commissioners of that body. The Boston merchants, however, seem to have brought powerful influences to bear, and the little job in dollar-diplomacy was rushed through, regardless of obligations or consequences. The question was not referred to the Court, Winthrop wrote, because if it "had been assembled, we knew they would not have given him aid without consent of the commissioners of the other colonies, and for a bare permission, we might do it without the court." [3] Saltonstall and others afterwards wrote,

---

[1] Cf. Parkman, The old Régime in Canada (Boston, 1911), pp. 1 ff.

[2] J. Winthrop, History, vol. II, pp. 128, 130.

[3] Ibid., vol. II, pp. 135, 138. The agreement is in Hazard, Historical Collections, vol. I, pp. 499 ff. Robert Keaynes, of the "sow case," was apparently interested in the venture.

strongly condemning the action, urging that the real rights of the case had not been known, that wars involving the subjects of another nation ought not to be undertaken without the knowledge of the home government; and brushed away the sophistical distinctions made by the Boston clique between private permission by the colony's rulers and their official sanction. "D'Aulnay, nor France," they wrote, "are not so feeble in their intellectuals as to deeme it no act of state." [1]

The expedition, however, had been allowed to sail, carrying a somewhat fatuous letter from Winthrop to d'Aulnay, stating that the Massachusetts volunteers were, if possible, to effect a reconciliation, that they possessed no commission, and that, if they did anything "against the rules of justice and good-neighborhood," they should be held accountable. [2] In spite of this, some of the men attacked d'Aulnay's plantation, burned his mill, killed his cattle, and plundered one of his vessels of beaver skins. The latter were brought back to Boston and sold at auction, and the proceeds were divided among the soldiers. [3] The enterprise had been neither successful, glorious, nor profitable; and when de la Tour again applied for help, in July of the following year, Endicott, who had opposed the original participation of the colony, had succeeded Winthrop as governor. The only result of de la Tour's suit, therefore, was a proclamation of neutrality "till the next general court," and the dispatch of a letter to d'Aulnay offering satisfaction, and likewise requesting it for his own earlier depredations on the Penobscot. [4] In September, the Commissioners of the United Colonies met and passed a resolution forbidding, in future, such acts of volunteers as Massachusetts had connived at. [5]

The struggle between the two rivals had not been limited to fighting in America, but had been carried on at the French Court, where each had striven for recognition. In this d'Aulnay had been successful, and the ignominious end of the whole

---

[1] Hutchinson, *Papers*, vol. I, p. 131.   [2] J. Winthrop, *History*, vol. II, p. 151.

[3] Paper signed by Saltonstall and Hathorne. *Ibid.*, vol. II, Appendix O, pp. 464 ff.

[4] *Ibid.*, p. 220.   [5] *Acts United Colonies*, vol. I, p. 22.

matter for the English was that Massachusetts finally had to abandon her claims against him, and to make him a gift as an acknowledgment of her own wrong in joining de la Tour's expedition.[1] The affair, however, helped to strengthen the deputies against the body of ministers and magistrates, whose unwarranted action, as well as lack of statesmanship and even of common prudence, had been mainly instrumental in bringing unnecessary humiliation upon the colony without the consent of its representatives.

Nor did the Bay and other colonies derive much greater honor from their diplomacy with the Dutch, one of the main results of which, indeed, was to develop such a conflict of interests among themselves as threatened to break up the Confederation. As we have already seen, it was an open question whether England or Holland had the better title to the central portion at least, of the territory claimed by the latter. As to the title of the individual settlers, English and Dutch, on the Connecticut and the Delaware, it would appear that the Dutch, who were there by the authority of their home government, were in a much better legal position than the English, who were mere squatters in the wilderness, without any patent or charter rights. The New Englanders, however, outnumbered their neighbors twenty to one, and the land in dispute was good. The advice of the British Ambassador in the States General was, therefore, acted upon with the consciousness of overwhelming force. "Crowd on," he wrote, "crowding the Dutch out of those places they have, but without hostility or any act of violence."[2] Steadily the advancing flood of the English overwhelmed Dutch claims. It poured westward on Long Island and along the Sound, up the Connecticut,— encircling the little fort of Good Hope,— up the Housatonic, and stopped only a few miles from New Amsterdam itself. A trading company formed in New Haven, but including capitalists from Massachusetts, tried also to

---

[1] J. Winthrop, *History*, vol. II, pp. 318, 334 *ff.*; *Massachusetts Records*, vol. III, pp. 44, 74 *ff.*; *Acts United Colonies*, vol. I, pp. 56 *ff.*

[2] Letter from Sir William Boswell to Dr. Wright, 1642; *Conn. Col. Records*, vol. I, pp. 565 *f.*

plant on the Delaware in despite of both Dutch and Swedes.[1] The situation was bound to result in constant causes for disputes, grave or trifling. At the bottom of all was the desire of the English for the land, and the sense of injury and inferior numbers on the part of the Dutch. Governor Kieft touched the point, when, in reply to a letter of complaint from the United Colonies, concerning some alleged misdemeanors by the garrison of the little Dutch post at Good Hope, he wrote that "when we heare the inhabitants of Hartford complayninge of us, we seem to heare Esops wolfe complayninge of the lambe." [2]

The several attempts to plant forcibly on the Delaware were successfully repulsed by the two nations already in possession there; and in 1646, Kieft sent a protest to the New Haven magistrates against their settling on the Housatonic. To this they replied that they could not imagine what river the Dutch could mean, and unfairly offered to leave any dispute to the English Parliament as arbitrators; while at the New Haven court, "it was fully and satisfyeingly voted" that they would make good their titles "at the trading house, and leave the issue of things to God." [3]

Contentions, new and old, dragged along, embittering relations, and filling a very large portion of the United Colonies' time and records. Finally, after Stuyvesant had been governor for three years, he went to Hartford to try to arrange an amicable settlement of all outstanding grievances between the colonies of the two nations. The negotiations were carried on in writing; and both then and in subsequent correspondence, it must be confessed that, in dignity and courtesy, the Dutch Governor shone by comparison with the English Commissioners. His tone throughout was statesmanlike and dignified,

[1] For relations with the latter, *cf.* A. Johnson, *The Swedish Settlements on the Delaware* (Univ. of Pa., 1911), vols. I, pp. 380 *ff.*, and II, p. 755; *New Haven Records*, vol I, pp. 56 *f.*, 106 *f.*

[2] *Acts United Colonies*, vol. I, p. 77.

[3] *New Haven Records*, vol. I, pp. 265 *f.* The Dutch spoke of the river as the Mauritius. In their reply, the New Haven people stated that they had built on the Paugusset "within our owne lymitts."

while that of the Puritans was frequently low, and, at times, insulting.

It was finally decided that each side should appoint two deputies to negotiate a treaty, and Stuyvesant nominated, as his, two Englishmen, then resident in the Dutch colony.[1] As a result of their deliberations, a treaty was signed, in September, 1650, which should have set the disputed matters finally at rest.[2] Most of the smaller questions were passed over, while that of the Delaware was referred to Europe. The explanation of the Dutch Governor as to a ship seized at New Haven, some years earlier, was accepted as final,[3] and a definite boundary line agreed upon, which gave to the English all territory, except Fort Good Hope, lying eastward of Oyster Bay on Long Island and of a line beginning four miles west of Greenwich on the mainland, and running north, provided it came nowhere within ten miles of the Hudson. Greenwich, also, was to remain to the Dutch, who were otherwise not to build within six miles of the new boundary, which was to be referred to England and Holland for ratification. Holland subsequently accepted it,[4] but England never acted, as to have done so would have been to recognize Dutch claims as valid, which she persistently refused to do.

Nor, from their later correspondence, can we conclude that all the English colonies themselves intended to accept the settlement as final, or that they really desired a friendly end to the controversies. Within a year after the signing of the treaty, New Haven attempted further encroachments upon the Delaware, and, when stopped by Stuyvesant, complained to the United Colonies, whose Commissioners wrote a bullying letter to the Dutch Governor.[5] The following year, in Europe, Cromwell forced war upon Holland, and New Haven and Connecticut felt that their chance had come to make an end of their neighbor, whose chief offense seems to have been the prior possession of lands the English coveted. They claimed,

---

[1] *Acts United Colonies*, vol. I, pp. 186 f.   [2] *Ibid.*, pp. 188 ff.

[3] *New Haven Records*, vol. I, pp. 333, 508; *Acts United Colonies*, vol. I, pp. 112, 146.

[4] *N. Y. Col. Docts.*, vol. II, pp. 258 f.

[5] *Acts United Colonies*, vol. I, pp. 214 f.; New Haven s complaint is on pp. 210 ff.

indeed, to have information that Stuyvesant was stirring up the Indians to attack them, and were, or pretended to be, in mortal terror; but there is no substantial evidence that any such plot existed, and when questioned about it, the sachems Mixim, Pesacus, and Ninigret denied it in the most positive terms.[1]

Three commissioners, whom the United Colonies sent to New Amsterdam to investigate the rumor, were met with fairness by Stuyvesant, who placed no obstacle in their way for taking any testimony they wished, asking only, which was reasonable enough, that the inquiries should be conducted jointly. This the English refused, but set down all the gossip they could gather, treated the Governor with great rudeness, and then left, refusing at the last moment to wait even a few hours to receive an answer Stuyvesant had prepared.[2] The fact may well have been that, in view of the overwhelming odds against them, the Dutch were counting upon using the Indians as auxiliaries in case they should have been attacked; but there was nothing to indicate, what would have been exceedingly unlikely, that they had been planning to assume the offensive, even by savage proxy.

War, however, was ardently desired by both Connecticut and New Haven, and Rhode Island, somewhat liberally interpreting orders from England, started privateering on her own account against Dutch ships.[3] Connecticut, on the strength of similar orders, hastily sequestrated the Dutch fort at Good Hope, which she never again relinquished.[4]

Massachusetts, however, had no interest in the quarrel. The lands she coveted did not lie in that direction, and she professed to be unable to go to war save in a just cause.[5] Her moral stand might be considered more sincere, were it not

---

[1] *Acts United Colonies*, vol. II, pp. 6 ff. [2] *Ibid.*, vol. II, pp. 59, 65.

[3] *Ibid.*, vol. II, pp. 54, 90, 92; *R. I. Records*, vol. I, pp. 261, 266, 271. During the course of the war, Cromwell sent Major Sedgwick and Captain Leverett to the "United Collonyes" to see what aid he could count upon in an attack upon New Amsterdam. *Mass. Hist. Soc. Coll.*, Series IV, vol. II, pp. 230 ff.; *New Haven Records*, vol. II, pp. 100, 107, 112; *Conn. Col. Records*, vol. I, p. 259; *Cal. State Pap., Col., 1574–1660*, p. 390.

[4] *Conn. Col. Records*, vol. I, pp. 254, 275.

[5] *Acts United Colonies*, vol. II, pp. 56, 75, 80, 86.

for the quite contrary position she consistently assumed when her own interests were at stake. Her refusal, however, undoubtedly prevented an act of great injustice, although her action permanently weakened the Confederacy; for she claimed, in spite of the obvious intention of the Articles, that the Commissioners had no power to declare an offensive, but only a defensive, war. This unwarranted construction was bitterly opposed by the other three members, who properly claimed that, if any of the colonies had the right, on occasion, to alter the Articles to suit herself, then the league must necessarily "breake and bee dissolved." "Whether this violation proceed from some unwarrantable Scruple of Conscience or from some other engagement of sperit," they wrote, "the Massachusetts neither expresse, nor will the Commissioners determine." [1]   In the wilderness, men come to know one another well; and her neighbors' faith in the Bay Colony's purity of motive had been too often sorely tried to permit them, perhaps, to do her entire justice. War was declared in September, seven of the eight Commissioners voting in favor of it, although Massachusetts refused to be bound. [2] Her interpretation of the Articles having been vehemently denied by the western colonies, she turned to Plymouth, but failed to overawe her little neighbor, who bluntly answered that the Articles "are so full and plaine that they occasion not any such queries." [3]

Peace having been declared in Europe, however, the war was not prosecuted, and in the following year Massachusetts completely reversed her position, and agreed to be bound by the Articles of Union in their "literall sence and true meaning." [4]   The real motive for her refusal to attack the Dutch may, perhaps, be found in that fear, on the part of the East, of any rapid extension of the western frontier, which we have already noted. Had the western colonies acquired the Hudson River and the sources of the rich fur-trade possessed by the Dutch, the supremacy of Massachusetts might readily

---

[1] *Acts United Colonies*, vol. II, p. 82.   [2] *Ibid.*, pp. 102, 108 *f.*
[3] *Ibid.*, pp. 111 *f.*   [4] *Ibid.*, p. 114.

have been lost to the younger colonies, which, on the other hand, could be counted upon to remain subordinate to herself in power and numbers if westward expansion were denied them. So long as the balance remained undisturbed, or was altered only in her favor, she could count upon the Confederacy to aid her own plans, nullifying any decision adverse to her interests by her greater strength, as she had just done. Having gained her point, it was, therefore, to her advantage to restore the fullest authority to the league; and the suggestion by her three colleagues, quoted above, that her action might have been dictated by "some other engagement of sperit" than conscientious scruples, would indicate that they perfectly recognized the situation.

During the decade and a half that we are now considering, there was continual uneasiness among the savages, but no serious outbreak. Their relations with the whites, however, were the subject of constant negotiations, which, with the entries concerning the Dutch, absorb almost the whole of the records of the Confederacy. The most striking incident was one which, unfortunately, redounded but little to the credit of the colonists.

In 1643, a quarrel broke out between Uncas and a sachem named Sequasson, and after the English had ineffectually attempted to preserve peace between them, Uncas attacked Sequasson, killing seven or eight of his men, and securing considerable booty.[1] The defeated sachem was an ally of the Narragansett chief Miantanomo, who requested permission from the English for liberty to revenge himself upon the Mohegan. This was granted, and Miantanomo, followed by a thousand warriors, fell upon Uncas, who was supported by less than one half that number.[2] The Mohegans, nevertheless were successful, and Miantanomo was taken prisoner, through treachery. It will be recalled that Samuel Gorton had bought his lands through the Narragansett chief from two of his sachems, who had subsequently repudiated the trans-

---

[1] J. Winthrop, *History*, vol. II, p. 155.   [2] *Acts United Colonies*, vol. I, p. 11.

action, and placed themselves under the jurisdiction of Massachusetts. It will be remembered also that Miantanomo, in spite of recent suspicions, had consistently been a friend of the English, that he had sheltered Williams, when banished from Massachusetts, and that, through the influence of the latter, the Narragansetts had sided with the colonists in the Pequot war. Gorton now unwisely tried to save the savage's life by writing a letter to Uncas, threatening him should he harm his prisoner.[1] Uncas, upon its receipt, hurried the captive to Hartford, to advise with the authorities as to what course he should take. At Miantanomo's own request, he was placed in custody of the English.

There had been rumors of a general rising of the natives in the preceding year, and the Commissioners of the United Colonies, meeting at Boston, after serious consideration decided that it would not be safe to set the unexpected captive free; but they had no grounds upon which to kill him. As usual, they turned to the church for advice, and, as usual, that advice was for blood, "the most judicious elders," who had been consulted, unanimously agreeing "that he ought to be put to death." Of the four reasons for their decision as given by Winthrop, not one justified the sentence. One of them, that he was "of a turbulent and proud spirit," was hardly a capital offense even in Massachusetts, nor could the beating of one of his own subjects be thus construed. His alleged heading of an Indian conspiracy had not been proved, and if the authorities had really believed it, it is not likely that they would have granted him formal permission to take the war-path with a thousand warriors against another of their own allies. Opposed to the charges were to be set the facts that, in the past, he had performed inestimable service as a friend of the English, and that he was now in their hands at his own suggestion, trusting in the white man's justice. He had not, however, reckoned on the church, and it is impossible not to agree with the often expressed surmise that the leaders of that institution condemned him, not as the enemy of the English, but as the friend of the heretic Gorton and the tolerant Williams.[1]

There had been no pretense of trial, and neither the accused nor any witnesses had been summoned. Nor did the English execute the sentence, which duty they entrusted to Uncas, who was promised protection against the Narragansetts if he would perform it.[2] Uncas readily undertook the work, and Miantanomo, probably cursing his folly for having ever trusted a white man, was put to death. "That the Indians might know that the English did approve of it, they sent 12 or 14 musketeers home with Uncas to abide a time with him for his defence, if need should be"; which shows how little real credence was placed in the story of a general rising.[3] The savages could have made no complaint, had the English from the beginning preserved a strict neutrality; but they had not done so. They had given Miantanomo leave to take the war-path, and, when he was captured, they had assumed the responsibility of seeing that justice should be done. They had, nevertheless, observed none of its forms, and had merely handed the prisoner back to his savage captor with what amounted to orders for his death, without trial and without a hearing. Aside from the injustice of the course pursued, it is difficult to think of one more certain to turn the "proud and turbulent" spirits of the slain man's thousand followers permanently against the English settlers.[4] Nevertheless, for the present, in spite of a threatened outbreak upon their part two years after the slaying of their chief, the Indian relations of the colonists for long consisted mainly in efforts to preserve the peace among rival native tribes and to collect tribute.[5]

The disputes of the colonies, however, were by no means limited to those with foreigners and savages. The union, which had been so seriously threatened by the Dutch war, had

---

[1] Cf., e.g., editor's note in J. Winthrop, *History*, vol. ii, pp. 158 f.
[2] *Acts United Colonies*, vol. i, p. 11; J. Winthrop, *History*, vol. ii, p. 158.
[3] *Ibid.*, p. 162.
[4] Cf. letter from the sachems to Massachusetts, 1644, in *R. I. Records*, vol. i, pp. 136 ff.
[5] For the causes of the Narragansett "war" of 1645, cf. *Acts United Colonies*, vol. i, pp. 50 ff. For the war with Ninigret, *Ibid.*, vol. ii, pp. 101 ff.

earlier suffered another severe strain in a controversy between
Connecticut and Massachusetts over questions of taxation.
When the fort at Saybrook was bought from Fenwick by the
former colony, for the purpose of protecting and controlling
the mouth of the river, the contract provided that he should
receive, in part payment, certain tolls to be levied upon mer-
chandise exported by all the River Towns.[1]   A few months
later, the General Court passed a law regulating the amounts
of these duties and providing for their collection.[2]   The
boundary line between Connecticut and Massachusetts was
still undetermined; but as the latter colony claimed Springfield, which was under its jurisdiction, that town objected to
being taxed by Connecticut, and refused to pay the duties demanded.[3]   The question was referred to the Commissioners of
the United Colonies by Connecticut in 1647, though the fort
had then been destroyed by fire. The objections of Massachusetts, presented in writing, were not well taken, and one
was an absolutely false statement, Connecticut having no
difficulty in showing that the Bay Colony's contention that
the question of a river-toll had delayed the formation of the
Confederacy by ten years was palpably absurd and impossible.[4]
Another contention, that the toll was not levied upon the
Dutch at Good Hope, was also of no import, for the commerce
of that tiny post was slight, and by taxing it, international
questions would have been raised, to no advantage. Moreover, as the main value of the fort at Saybrook was to protect
the river from the Dutch, its upkeep could hardly be considered as a charge of which that nation shared the advantages.
The duties required were not discriminatory, and Connecticut
was merely asking that the other permanent settlers up the
river should share the same burden which she imposed upon
herself.

Although the justice of her claim was upheld by the Commissioners of New Haven and Plymouth, Massachusetts refused to accept the decision as binding, and threatened retalia-

---

[1] *Conn. Col. Records*, vol. I, pp. 119 *ff.*, 266 *ff.*   [2] *Ibid.*, pp., 189 *ff.*
[3] *Acts United Colonies*, vol. I, p. 80; *Mass. Hist. Soc. Coll.*, Series IV, vol. VI, p. 380.
[4] *Acts United Colonies*, vol. I, pp. 89 *ff.*

tion, which, in 1649, took the form of an import duty on all
goods from the three colonies entering at Boston Harbor,
which was then the main channel through which all business
was conducted with Europe.[1] The wording of the act made
it obvious that it was to punish the three smaller colonies for
not having agreed with herself; and the Confederacy's delegates resolved that "how fare the premisses agree with the lawe
of love and with the tenure and import of the articles of Confederation, the Commissioners tender and recomend to the
serius Concideration of the Generall Court of the Massachu-
sits." Wearied with her continuous rejection of their valid
rulings for five years, they also added that they "desire to bee
spared in all further agitations Concerning sprinkfield."[2] Apparently, however, the pertinacity of Massachusetts won the
struggle, to which bitterness was added by her persistent refusal, for seventy years, to acknowledge the real location of
her southern boundary line, which she had extended slightly
into Connecticut territory.[3] That "line" she had had surveyed, in 1642, by the somewhat odd method of having two
"skillful artists," as she called them, locate a point three miles
south of the Charles River, and then, in order to avoid the
long walk across country, sail around by the Sound, and ascend the Connecticut River to a point which they agreed was
in the same latitude as that from which they had started. A
map, a pen, and a ruler completed this arduous bit of surveying work in the wilderness.[4] Unfortunately, it did not satisfy
Connecticut.

There was always a certain latitude, not astronomical, in
the Bay Colony's treatment of boundaries, however; and, in
spite of the reasonably strict definition of her own by her charter, the colony slowly expanded, like a balloon filling with gas.
We have already seen how she had annexed New Hampshire,
and, by her new interpretation of the charter, laid claim to
Maine. The state of affairs in England, during the Civil War

---

[1] *Massachusetts Records*, vol. II, p. 269. This had been anticipated by Connecticut;
Mass. Hist. Soc. Coll., Series IV, vol. VI, p. 383.
[2] *Acts United Colonies*, vol. I, p. 158. [3] *Ibid.*, vol. I, pp. 151 *f.*
[4] C. W. Bowen, *The Boundary Disputes of Connecticut* (Boston, 1882), pp. 19, 53 *ff.*

and Commonwealth, offered her the opportunity to make that claim a reality; and by 1658, the entire province had been annexed, bit by bit. In the midst of the civil commotions in the home country, the royalist Gorges had died, and his heirs had had no chance to answer their colonists' letters or to look after their affairs in America. Godfrey was elected governor of the settlements about York, the inhabitants there, "with one free and universanimous consent," binding themselves into a body politic,[1] while farther east, the feud between Cleeve and Winter, the latter representing Trelawney's interests, had been continued. Trelawney, a royalist like Gorges, was imprisoned in England by the Parliament, and soon after died. Cleeve went to England, procured the assistance of Alexander Rigby, who had bought the questionable Lygonia patent, and secured from him a confirmation and extension of his own holdings. This was three years before the election of Godfrey at York in 1649, and Josselyn, who was then representing the Gorges interests, disputed Cleeve's claims, and both parties agreed to arbitration by Massachusetts. The jury failed to find a verdict, and the dispute continued.[2] The following year, the Commissioners of Plantations confirmed Rigby's patent, even enlarging its interpretation, and so confined the Gorges territory to that south of Saco.[3] Cleeve established a government within the now legal, if not equitable, Lygonia grant, and the quarrel between him and Godfrey seems to have been settled. Affairs promised to assume a more ordered aspect, and in 1651 Godfrey sent a petition to Parliament, asking that the inhabitants of Maine be declared "Members of the Common Wealth of England," and confirmed in their rights.[4]

Massachusetts saw her opportunity slipping, and decided to act. In May of the following year, the General Court voted that the northern boundary of the colony was a line running from sea to sea and passing through a point three

---

[1] *Farnham Papers*, vol. I, p. 266.   [2] J. Winthrop, *History*, vol. II, pp. 314 f.
[3] *Ibid.*, p. 391.
[4] *Farnham Papers*, vol. I, pp. 267 f. Williamson says it was carried to England by Cleeve; *History of Maine*, vol. I, p. 336.

miles north of the most northerly section of the Merrimack, sending out more "skilfull artists" to find the exact latitude.[1] Godfrey vigorously objected, recalling to Massachusetts the services he had rendered her in England when her charter had been questioned, and denying the validity of her new claim.[2] His protest, of course, was of no avail, and in May, 1653, Massachusetts sent a commission, headed by Bradstreet, forcibly to require the submission of the inhabitants at Kittery. After much debate among the settlers, they agreed to submit, provided their conditions were accepted. This, however, was "wholy denied by the comissioners, who told them they must first submitt to the government, and then they should be ready to affoord such liberties and imunities as they should think meete to graunt."[3] To this demand, as illegal as it was arrogant, the settlers were forced to yield an unconditional assent; and Godfrey returned to England, to add another, in the day of reckoning, to the enemies of Massachusetts. The country was organized as the County of York, and the towns incorporated with the same privileges as Dover.[4] Later in the same year, the commission continued its journey, and Wells, Cape Porpus, and Saco were likewise forced to submit.[5] Five years later, in spite of repeated protests from Cleeve, the whole of Maine and Lygonia were absorbed as far as Casco Bay, and the process of annexation was complete.[6] Of the principalities that Mason and Gorges had spent their fortunes to acquire, not a foot was left to their heirs.

By her policy of annexation, Massachusetts had added over forty thousand square miles to her territory; while by that of nullification, she had patently shown that the bonds uniting the New England Confederacy were but ropes of sand. Confederation was a failure and imperial control as yet impossible. The unification of New England was progressing rapidly, but

[1] *Massachusetts Records*, vol. III, pp. 274, 288.
[2] The answer of Massachusetts and Godfrey's second letter are in Hazard, *Historical Collections*, vol. I, pp. 564 ff. Godfrey's protest, stating that £35,000 had been spent in settling, and that Massachusetts had recognized the lawful jurisdiction of the settlers for the past 20 years, is in Baxter MSS., *Doct. Hist. Maine*, vol. IV, pp. 15 f.
[3] *Massachusetts Records*, vol. IV, pt. i, p. 123.   [4] *Ibid.*, pp. 123–26.
[5] *Ibid.*, pp. 158 ff.   [6] *Ibid.*, pp. 175, 250, 312, 357, 360.

it was a mere process of absorption by Massachusetts. Had there been no hindrance offered by England to the movement, the fate of the other colonies was amply foreshadowed. A single state, with its capital at Boston, guided by the reactionary ideas of its leaders, would probably have arisen, and much of the work already accomplished for the enfranchisement of the individual by Connecticut and Rhode Island, as well as the progress so far made by Massachusetts herself, might have been lost.

Although her policy had met with so little real resistance in the north, it received an unexpected check in the south, from the despised Rhode Islanders, while the restoration of the monarchy in England was permanently to save the independence of that colony and of Connecticut. In view of the circumstances, that event, and the assertion of imperial control which followed it, cannot be considered as so inimical to the interests of liberty and the colonies as writers whose attention and sympathy have been wholly devoted to Massachusetts have usually pictured it. In spite of the many fine qualities of the Bay Colony, and the services which she rendered in the settlement of New England, it was fortunate that her career of aggrandizement was halted, for the United States could ill afford to have lost the independent contributions made to her intellectual and political life by the smaller colonies. Indeed, it may even be questioned, if a single powerful, unscrupulous, and aggressive state had come to occupy the whole of New England, and possibly the Hudson Valley, whether the United States, as a federal nation in its present form, would have come into existence at all. When one considers the possibilities involved in a wholly different balance of power among the colonies in the following century, the early career of Massachusetts and the checks it encountered take on a larger interest.

The four settlements about Narragansett Bay, whose extreme individualism and disinclination to submit to any superior government have already been noted, would probably have been exceedingly slow to form a combination, had it not been for the danger to their existence, threatened by their neighbors. Massachusetts had already set up claims to a portion of the territory, and assumed jurisdiction over some of the natives at the time of the Gorton affair in 1643; and contemplated more aggressive action by attempting to secure a charter from the Commissioners of Plantations, in the same year. While never legally granted, this pretended patent was at first used by the colony to bolster its claims.[1] At the same time at which Massachusetts was trying to obtain that document, Williams, then in England for the purpose, was also endeavoring to secure a patent which would enable the settlements legally to resist encroachment. In this he was successful, and, after that, "the country about us was more friendly," he wrote, "and treated us as an authorized colony, only the difference of our consciences much obstructed." [2] The charter named the towns of Providence, Newport, and Portsmouth, and incorporated a vague territory bounded in part by Plymouth, Massachusetts, and the Pequot River, as "the Providence Plantations in the Narragansett Bay in New England." [3] The settlers were given the right to erect any form of government which they might choose.

The Narragansett Indians, after the death of Miantanomo, had agreed to place themselves directly under the protection of the English crown; and Gorton, who, after his release from Massachusetts, had gone back to Warwick, was chosen by them to go to England and carry their submission to the King.[4] In 1644, Plymouth had renewed her claim to Warwick; but in the following year, twenty families from Braintree having petitioned the Massachusetts General Court for permission to settle on Gorton's lands, the Court had granted them ten thousand acres there, and arranged for the organization of a town.[5] A Plymouth settler objected, however, when the party

[1] *Mass. Hist. Soc. Proceedings*, Series I, vol. v, pp. 398 *ff.*; Arnold, *History of Rhode Island*, vol. I, pp. 118 *f.*; Osgood, *American Colonies*, vol. I, p. 354.
[2] *R. I. Records*, vol. I, p. 458.   [3] *Ibid.*, pp. 143 *ff.*
[4] *Cal. State Pap., Col., 1574–1660*, p. 326; *R. I. Records*, vol. I, pp. 134 *ff.*
[5] Cited by Arnold, *Rhode Island*, vol. I, p. 159; *Massachusetts Records*, vol. III, p. 49; J. Winthrop, *History*, vol. II, p. 308.

arrived, and the new planters dispersed to other places. At the same meeting of the court at which the Braintree men were granted their land, a letter was ordered sent to Williams, stating that Massachusetts had received a charter for Narragansett Bay, and ordering him to desist from exercising any authority.[1]

Nothing had been done by the Narragansett towns to combine under their patent, until May, 1647, when a meeting attended by freemen from all four, was held at Portsmouth, at which it was voted to give Warwick the same privileges as Providence.[2] The new government derived directly from the people, and not from the towns. those present also agreeing that it should be "democraticall, that is to say, a Government held by the free and voluntarie consent of all, or the greater parte of the free Inhabitants." [3] Legislation was, in the main, to be initiated by the people in town meeting, and not by the Assembly, which latter was to be a representative body, consisting of six delegates from each township. Such bills as might be initiated in the Assembly, or General Court, were required to be submitted to the four towns at their meetings, the whole legislative system thus being "a crude combination of initiative and referendum." [4]

Meanwhile, Gorton had obtained a letter from the Commissioners for Plantations, granting him safe conduct through Massachusetts, and allowing him to resettle upon his lands without molestation, until the disputed title should be decided.[5] To this, Massachusetts returned an answer defending her actions in the case and her refusal to allow of appeals to England; but Gorton was permitted to pass through her territory on his way to Warwick.[6] The settlers there, however, were much troubled by the Indians, whom Massachusetts claimed as under her jurisdiction; and after receiving two complaints from the Warwick people, the Commissioners of the United Colonies finally returned answer that they were

[1] *Massachusetts Records*, vol. III, p. 49; *R. I. Records*, vol. I, p. 133.
[2] *Ibid.*, pp. 147 ff.   [3] *Ibid.*, p. 156.
[4] Osgood, *American Colonies*, vol. I, p. 358.
[5] *R. I. Records*, vol. I, pp. 367 ff.; J. Winthrop, *History*, vol. II, p. 333.
[6] *Massachusetts Records*, vol. III, pp. 95 ff.; J. Winthrop, *History*, vol. II, pp. 360 ff.

ready to undertake the settlement of the question as to "under what Colonie youer Plantation doth fall." [1] The following year, 1650, Massachusetts, by agreement with Plymouth, acquired all rights which that colony might possess about Warwick, but the Commissioners of the United Colonies refused to sanction the transfer. [2]

As before, however, there was a party at Patuxet working in the interests of the Bay Colony, and in 1651, certain settlers there appealed to her for protection against taxes levied upon them. Massachusetts, still claiming jurisdiction, wrote to Williams, requiring that the government refrain from taxing the residents of Warwick, and stating that in case it refused to comply, Massachusetts would seek satisfaction "in such manner as God shall put into theire hands." [3] There was no doubt what this meant.

There was, moreover, additional trouble in store for the distracted settlements. William Coddington, one of the original settlers at Aquidneck, had treacherously gone to England, and there procured a commission appointing him Governor of Rhode Island, his territory thus including the two towns of Portsmouth and Newport. [4] This would have disrupted the union, and have left the mainland towns a prey to Massachusetts. The four towns, being now at last closely united in aim by the common danger, sent Williams and Clarke to England, to protest against Coddington's action; and, largely through the influence of Williams's friendship with Vane, they were entirely successful. Coddington's commission was withdrawn; Williams obtained a safe conduct through Massachusetts, and brought a letter from Vane urging the colonists to unite peaceably and to avoid tumult and disorder. [5] In

[1] *Acts United Colonies*, vol. I, p. 150. The previous complaint, and the Commissioners' mild rebuke to the Indians, are on p. 111.

[2] *Massachusetts Records*, vol. III, pp. 198 f.; *Acts United Colonies*, vol. I, pp. 170 f.; *Massachusetts Records*, vol. III, p. 216.

[3] *Ibid.*, p. 228, and vol. IV, pt. i, p. 47.

[4] *Cal. State Pap., Col., 1574–1660*, p. 354.

[5] I. Backus, *History of New England with particular Reference to the Denomination of Christians called Baptists* (1871), vol. I, pp. 223, 232; Hazard, *Historical Collection*, vol. I, p. 495.

1654, the towns reunited by formal action, and two years later, Coddington submitted to the authorities.[1] In 1658, Massachusetts at last resigned her pretensions,[2] while, to guard against any such troubles in future as had been brought about by that colony's faction in Patuxet, Rhode Island passed a law, somewhat later, that, if any citizen should attempt to place his lands under the jurisdiction of another colony, they should be forfeited.[3]

The government, however, was by no means through with Massachusetts, nor with its other neighbor, Connecticut, both of whom were soon to lay claim to the soil in another direction. The Pawcatuck River, which is the present western boundary of the state, had also been the dividing line between the Narragansetts on the east and the Pequots on the west; and after the destruction of the latter, both Connecticut and Massachusetts had claimed the Pequot country by right of conquest. In spite of attempts to divide the spoil between them, the dispute dragged along, with clashings of interests and of jurisdiction.[4] Massachusetts, however, not content with claiming a large part of the country west of the Pawcatuck as a reward for her share in the war, was also constantly endeavoring to establish her claims to the rich tract lying between the east bank of that river and Narragansett Bay, known as the Narragansett country. In spite of her defeat in the Gorton episode, she continued her efforts, and in 1659, a year after Southertown, the present Stonington, had been declared by the Massachusetts Court to be a part of Suffolk County in that colony,[5] the Atherton Company was formed, mainly by Massachusetts land-speculators, to secure title to the Narragansett lands.[6] A grant was obtained by the

[1] *R. I. Records*, vol. 1, pp. 278 *ff.*, 327.

[2] *Massachusetts Records*, vol. IV, pt. i, p. 333.

[3] *R. I. Records*, vol. 1, p. 401.

[4] *Acts United Colonies*, vols. I, pp. 19, 79, 97, and II, pp. 209, 228; *R. I. Records*, vol. I, pp. 451 *ff.*, 457; *Conn. Col. Records*, vol. I, pp. 570 *ff.*; Bowen, *Boundary Disputes of Connecticut*, pp. 31 *ff.*; *Massachusetts Records*, vols. II, p. 160, and IV, pt. i, p. 315.

[5] *Ibid.*, vol. IV, pt. i, p. 353.

[6] The members included Gov. Winthrop of Connecticut, and Richard Smith; *R. I. Records*, vol. I., p. 464.

company from one of the sachems, and, in the following year, four others, in order to meet a fine which had been imposed upon them by the United Colonies, executed a mortgage deed of the entire Narragansett country to the Atherton Company, except such parts as might have already been granted, the Indians having six months in which to redeem the pledged lands, which, of course, they failed to do.[1]

Massachusetts herself had no valid claim to any of the territory, to which, on the other hand, Rhode Island was justly entitled under her charter, which had named the "Pequot River and Country" as the western boundary.[2] In October, 1661, a clash occurred between Rhode Island citizens claiming lands at Stonington and the Massachusetts authorities, three Rhode Islanders being carried off to Boston, and imprisoned.[3] The Rhode Island government protested, and denied the pretensions of Massachusetts to the disputed territories, and herself claimed jurisdiction over the lands owned by the Atherton Company. Massachusetts, some months later, renewed the old fiction of her Narragansett patent, and asserted, what she must have known to be false, that under it she had a valid title to "all that tract of land, from Pequot River to Plymouth line," and ordered the Rhode Island authorities to desist from exercising any government within their limits.[4]

The troubles between Rhode Island and Massachusetts, between Massachusetts and Connecticut, and between Connecticut and Rhode Island, were thus rapidly approaching the point at which a general intercolonial war might easily have resulted in the annihilation of the smallest colony, and a possible quarrel over the spoils by the two victors, already bitterly quarreling over the spoils of a war of twenty years earlier. The disgraceful spectacle of two colonies, planted in the wilderness ostensibly for the glory of God, and still pretending to be guided by his laws, annihilating a weaker

[1] *Acts United Colonies*, vol. II, p. 248; *R. I. Records*, vol. I, pp. 465 f.

[2] As we have already noted, the bounds were vaguely stated, but this western one was clear enough; *Ibid.*, p. 144.

[3] *Ibid.*, pp. 455 f.   [4] *Ibid.*, pp. 469 ff., 461.

neighbor in order to annex her harbors and rich lands, was fortunately prevented by the reassertion of imperial control by England.

Meanwhile, the little Rhode Island commonwealth had established its internal affairs upon a firm and orderly basis, and in spite of the dire forebodings, and every possible impediment thrown in his way by Massachusetts, Williams had finally succeeded in his effort to prove that civil and religious liberty was not incompatible with a well-ordered state. Against all her enemies, without and within, the colony had won her way to intellectual freedom, and had advanced along the path in which it has been the glory of the nation to follow, while the restoration of the monarchy in England intervened to save her from further molestation from her powerful Puritan neighbors, and enabled her to pursue her chosen ways in peace.

CHAPTER XI

THE DEFEAT OF THE THEOCRACY

THE same decade and a half, the political events of which
we traced in the last chapter, was to witness also religious
movements of utmost importance. The firm establishment
of the government of Rhode Island, based upon religious
liberty, and the preservation of the independence of that
colony and of its democratic neighbor, Connecticut, were
matters of profound import in the political and intellectual
life of America. Not less so was the struggle between the
leaders of the theocracy and the growing liberalism of the
people of Massachusetts. As usual, the political and religious
movements were inextricably intertwined, and the same conditions that brought forth the political disturbance over the
petition of Dr. Child and his associates, in 1645, were responsible for the most important step taken in the ecclesiastical
organization of the theocracy some months later.

That petition had called attention to undoubted evils and
injustices in the political and religious régime in Massachusetts; and however effectually the government might silence
the protesting leaders, the underlying causes were so widespread as to necessitate some action in regard to them. Owing
to the church-membership test for the franchise, the unenfranchised class was so large, and the disadvantage under
which it labored was so palpably unjust, that the demand for
reform was growing steadily louder. Not only had there been
from the very beginning a considerable element in the population which, under no circumstances, cared to join the New
England churches, but there was also a large one which would
have been glad to do so, had the process not been made so
difficult for them. It was not enough that a person should
believe in the doctrines of the Church, that he should desire

to live a godly life and be in communion with it, but he was also required to have experienced some special motion of God in his heart, by which he had been convicted of his sin, and become regenerate. Of that conversion, he was further obliged to make a public declaration before the congregation, describing the particular manner in which he had thus felt the workings of the spirit within him. Many blameless Christian men and women did not feel that they could discover any such extraordinary change in their lives as their rulers demanded; and modesty and a natural reticence prevented many more from attempting the trying ordeal of publicly detailing such an intimate spiritual experience.[1] Failing that, however, they were debarred from Christian communion and from all voice in the civil government, and their children were also denied baptism and participation in the life of the Church. As in Massachusetts no churches were allowed except such as partook of the "New England way," it followed that those who could not join them were politically disfranchised, and that they and their children were cut off from the advantages of Christian fellowship and discipline.

In so far as the resultant political disabilities were concerned, there were two ways in which the situation might have been remedied. The first and, according to modern ideas, the natural one would have been to do away with the religious qualification for the franchise. This was, theoretically at least, the method of Plymouth and Connecticut and Rhode Island, and of the Bay Colony in so far as its possessions in Maine were concerned. Nevertheless, it did not commend itself to the Massachusetts leaders, and for that reason, and also to meet the religious features of the case, a second method was favored by many, of making less rigid the requirements for admission to the church. Of the two methods, the latter would, of course, be more acceptable to the clergy, not as a step forward, but as the lesser of two evils. They were, in fact, at that very time planning a more formal organization of all the churches, and the establishment of a uniform practice

[1] Lechford, *Plain Dealing*, pp. 66 ff.

among them.[1] The creation of such a standard can hardly be considered as consistent with the principles in which Congregationalism had originated; but the Church in Massachusetts had become as completely a state church as the Anglican had ever been in England.[2]

In 1646, soon after the presentation of the Child petition, some of the Elders presented a bill to the General Court, asking that body to call a synod at the end of the summer, to consider these various problems. The bill was promptly passed by the magistrates; but the deputies demurred, denying that the civil authorities had power over the ecclesiastical. It was conceded, however, that the call might go out as a request and not as a command.[3] According to the notice, the synod was to agree "upon one forme of government and discipline," and to consider whether "more liberty and latitude" might be yielded in the matters of church membership and baptism.[4] When their labors should be finished, the result was to be submitted to the General Court, to receive "such approbation as is meete." [5] When the synod met, the churches of Boston and Salem refused to join, partly because they believed that it was intended to bind the liberty of churches by the passage of ecclesiastical laws by the General Court, "whereby men should be forced under penalty to submit to them." In view of a point to be discussed later in the chapter, Winthrop's account of the origin of the objections is interesting. The principal men who raised them, he wrote, were some "who came lately from England, where such a vast liberty was allowed, and sought for by all that went under the name of Independents, not only the anabaptists, antinomians, familists, seekers, etc., but even the most godly and orthodox, as Mr. Goodwin, Mr. Nye, Mr. Burrows, etc., who in the assembly there had stood in opposition to the presbytery, and also the greater part of the house of commons, who by their commissioners had sent order to all English plantations in the West Indies and Summers Islands, that all men should enjoy their liberty

---

[1] J. Winthrop, *History*, vol. II, p. 323.   [2] *Cf.* Walker, *Creeds*, pp. 166 f.
[3] J. Winthrop, *History*, vol. II, pp. 323 f.
[4] *Massachusetts Records*, vol. III, pp. 71 f.   [5] *Ibid.*, p. 72.

of conscience, and had by letters intimated the same to us." [1]
Some weeks were consumed in endeavors to change the opinions of the two churches, and when, after much difficulty, that
was finally accomplished, there was little time left for the work
of the synod, which adjourned in September, to meet the following June. It was not until midsummer, 1648, however,
that, after another adjournment, it finally completed its labors.

During the two years which it had been in session, Cromwell and the Independents in England had removed all fear for
Massachusetts of Presbyterian or other interference from that
country, and the temporary alarm of the leaders had subsided.
The question of a more liberal policy, therefore, fell into the
background, and the synod occupied itself with the formulation
of a strict polity by which innovation might be resisted. Agreement with the recent declaration of Parliament in matters of
doctrine was voted by adopting, with certain reservations, the
Westminster Confession of Faith; but the suggested religious
toleration was, of course, denied. [2] Quite on the contrary, in
fact, the Cambridge Platform, as the order of discipline adopted
has always been called, provided that the full power of the state
should be used to enforce obedience and conformity to the
rule and decisions of the priesthood. "Idolatry, Blasphemy,
Heresy, Venting corrupt and pernicious opinions," the Platform
read, "are to be restrayned and punished by civil authority.
If any church one or more shall grow schismaticall, rending
it self from the communion of other churches, or shall walke
incorrigibly or obstinately in any corrupt way of their own, contrary to the rule of the word; in such case, the Magistrate is
to put forth his coercive power, as the matter shall require." [3]
What these early American persecutors, drunk with their own
conceit, were to think the "matter shall require," when other
men refused to accept their personal interpretation of the mind
and ways of Almighty God as infallible, will be only too clearly
shown in the course of this chapter.

[1] J. Winthrop, *History*, vol. II, p. 329.
[2] "Cambridge Platform," in Walker, *Creeds*, p. 195.
[3] Sections 8 and 9 of chap. xvii, of "Cambridge Platform"; *Ibid.*, p. 237.

When the Platform was presented for ratification by the General Court, through the towns, it seems to have met with considerable opposition on the part of the deputies. The magistrates, owing to their customary close working agreement with the ministers, approved of it unanimously; but the deputies, representing public opinion rather than the oligarchy, repeated their opposition of several years earlier. When, in 1645, new laws had been proposed for the punishment of heretics, a brief entry in the records tells of the struggle at that time. "The Howse of Deputies," so it reads, "cannot concur with our honored magistrates in their bill to punish excommunicate persons." [1] They were defeated, however, and the next year a long act was passed for the purpose. [2] Although the Cambridge Platform had been adopted by the synod in 1648, and had been considered several times by the General Court, the deputies of many of the towns, even three years later, still professed themselves unable to "see light to impose any forms as necessary to be observed by the churches as a bindinge rule." [3] When it was finally passed by the Court, in October, 1651, fourteen of the deputies still refused to concur, and their names, an honored roll, are inscribed in the margin of the records. [4] The towns they represented were Boston, Salem, Braintree, Watertown, Roxbury, Wenham, Reading, Sudbury, Weymouth, and Hingham, in Massachusetts, and Hampton in New Hampshire. [5]

The Platform represented no mere abstract doctrine. The whole history of the oligarchy, thus far, indicated that the clauses regarding heresy and schism were not intended to remain dead letters. The new relations of the churches to one another, and the strengthened combination of the civil and ecclesiastical authorities, mark the high point attained by the theocracy in its organized opposition to liberty of thought. It had been growing steadily narrower and more intolerant, more insistent upon the extirpation of every idea, religious or political, that disturbed its own control over the minds and

---

[1] *Massachusetts Records*, vol. III, p. 16. [2] *Ibid.*, p. 99.
[3] *Ibid.*, p. 236. [4] *Ibid.*, p. 240.
[5] Walker, *Creeds*, p. 188 *n.*

lives of men. Unfortunately, at the very time when new power for evil was thus being placed in its hands by the action of the synod and the General Court, the more conservative leaders, both of Massachusetts and Connecticut, were lost to their communities by death, and the dangerous weapons were to be wielded by two of the most bigoted and blood-thirsty fanatics whom either Old or New England had produced.

Thomas Hooker died in 1647, as the work of the synod was beginning, and John Winthrop in 1649, as it was ending. There is no comparison in the debt that the political thought of America owes to the two men, whose ideas have already been contrasted on an earlier page. Hooker led the way along which the people of the United States were to follow, while Winthrop was engaged in the attempt to found a state in a politically impossible form. In spite of his inestimable services in the beginnings of the colony, there was no originality in his contribution to thought, and his subservience to the demands of the theocracy had been foreshadowed by his statement in early manhood that he so honored a faithful minister that he "could have kissed his feet." [1] Of high nobility of character, gentle, forgiving, frequently kindest to those from whom he differed most, there was little in his nature of the born persecutor. Led into acts of intolerant zeal by the ministers whom he so devoutly followed, there is considerable probability in the story related by Hutchinson, that when on his death-bed, being pressed by Dudley to sign a warrant for the banishment of a heretic, he refused, saying that "he had done too much of that work already." [2] His portrait depicts a face of gentleness rather than of strength. His unquestioned integrity, his modesty, and his self-sacrificing devotion to the interests of the colony as he saw them, amply fulfilled the high opinion which the original undertakers of the enterprise had formed of him, although, as in the case of most of the leaders, the effect upon mind and character of the transplanting to America was not wholly a happy one. "He was of a more

[1] R. C. Winthrop, *J. Winthrop*, vol. 1, p. 61.
[2] Hutchinson, *History*, vol. 1, p. 142.

catholic spirit than some of his brethren before he left England," wrote Hutchinson; "but afterward he grew more contracted, and was disposed to lay too great stress upon indifferent matters." [1]

The same effect had been felt in the case of John Cotton. The most tolerant, as he was one of the ablest, of the Massachusetts divines, we have already seen how he had started upon the true path when, dismayed by the universal ecclesiastical clamor raised by the Antinomian controversy, he drew back, like Winthrop, and ever after submitted to smaller men. Nevertheless, his death, some months after the final adoption of the Cambridge Platform, removed the last of the three men who by inclination and influence might have done something to stay the theocracy from the course into which it was soon to throw itself headlong. In place of Winthrop and Cotton, its leaders became Endicott and Norton. Able, stern, fiercely bigoted, absolutely convinced of their own infallibility in interpreting the word of God, undeterred by doubt, and unrestrained by pity, they were unwittingly to water the seeds of liberty with the blood of their victims.

In the midsummer of the year in which the Platform was finally adopted by the Court, John Clark, one of the ablest citizens of Rhode Island, Obadiah Holmes, and John Crandall, as representatives of the Baptist church of Newport, arrived at Lynn to visit an aged member of that church, who was too infirm to make a journey himself.[2] In 1644, a law had been passed punishing with banishment anyone who should openly or secretly speak against the orthodox Massachusetts doctrine regarding baptism; and the three Baptists were at once arrested.[3] Clark was fined £20, Holmes £30, and Crandall £5, in default of which they were to be whipped. The spirit of the court that tried them is vividly shown by two incidents as told by the prisoners themselves. Clark, having asked by what law he was punished, the penalty not being that pre-

---

[1] Hutchinson, *History*, vol. 1, p. 142.
[2] Newport Church Papers, cited by Backus, *Baptists*, vol. 1, p. 178.
[3] Backus, *Baptists*, vol. 1, p. 198 *n*.

scribed by the ordinance of 1644, relates that Endicott "stept up to us, and told us we had denied Infants Baptism, and being somewhat transported broke forth, and told me I had deserved death, and said he would not have such trash brought into this jurisdiction." [1]   Holmes, describing his own trial, wrote that, when receiving sentence, "I exprest myself in these words; I blesse God I am counted worthy to suffer for the name of Jesus; whereupon John Wilson (their pastor as they call him) strook me before the Judgment Seat, and cursed me, saying, the Curse of God, or Jesus goe with thee." [2]

Crandall, who had figured but little in the proceedings, was released on bail; while, without his knowledge, some unknown well-wisher paid Clark's fine. Holmes, however, refused to pay his fine or allow others to pay it for him, and insisted upon the sentence being executed in its full barbarity. Thirty strokes, with a three-corded whip, were laid upon his bare back. Two bystanders who, moved by pity, had the temerity to take the prisoner by the hand as he left the whipping-post, were themselves arrested and sentenced to pay forty shillings or be whipped.[3]   To one of them, who affirmed to Endicott that he believed Holmes was a godly man and "carried himself as did become a Christian," the Governor threatened that "we will deal with you as we have dealt with him." "I am in the hands of God," the prisoner replied.

The following year, Clark went to England with Williams in regard to the Coddington matter in Rhode Island, and, while there, published his account of the treatment the Baptists had met with in Massachusetts.[4]   As so often before, the

[1] John Clark, "Ill Newes from New England" (London, 1652), in *Mass. Hist. Soc. Coll.*, Series IV, vol. II, p. 33.

[2] *Ibid.*, p. 47.

[3] The Court that passed the sentences was composed of the magistrates only.

[4] Palfrey's far-fetched theory, that the whole affair was engineered by Clark in order to acquire a grievance to be used in England later, has no foundation whatever in any contemporary conjecture, and in any case would not alter in the slightest the facts so far as Massachusetts is concerned. It is of interest only as showing to what lengths that colony's clerical historians have gone in their efforts to defend in New England everything which they condemn in old England, and to treat the Massachusetts settlers as saints instead of very human Englishmen of the seventeenth century. Palfrey, *History*, vol. II, pp. 350, 354.

intolerance of the new country was severely criticized by its friends in the old. [1] "It doth not a little grieve my spirit," wrote Saltonstall to Cotton and Wilson, "what sadd things are reported dayly of your tyranny and persecution in New England. . . . These rigid wayse have layd you very lowe in the hearts of the saynts. I doe assure I have heard them pray in the publique assemblies that the Lord would give you meeke and humble spirits, not to stryve soe much for uniformity as to keepe the unity of the Spirit in the bond of peace." He warns them "not to practice those courses in a wilderness, which you went so farre to prevent"; and adds, "I hope you doe not assume to yourselves infallibillities of judgment, when the most learned of the Apostles confesseth he knew but in parte." [2]

In Cotton's reply, the ministers defended the acts of the Court, and, speaking of the victims' imprisonment, Cotton even descended so low as to write, "I believe they neither of them fared better at home, and I am sure Holmes had not been so well clad of many years before." More interesting, however, is his plain enunciation of the doctrine that they alone knew the will of God and should lay it down for the community, which we noted in an earlier chapter as one of the outstanding characteristics of Puritanism in every age. "There is a vast difference," he wrote, "between men's inventions and God's institutions; we fled from men's inventions, to which we else should have been compelled; we compel none to men's inventions." The inference was, of course, that, whatever the rest of mankind might think, any institution decreed by the Massachusetts ministers was, *ipso facto*, God's. Therefore, "if the worship be lawful in itself, the magistrate compelling him to come to it, compelleth him not to sin, but the sin is in his own will that needs to be compelled to a Christian duty." [3] Four fifths of their fellow citizens might refuse to join their churches; the noblest spirits among

---

[1] *Cf.* Chap. VII, *supra.*
[2] Hutchinson, *Papers*, vol. II, pp. 127 *ff.*; Backus, *Baptists*, vol. I, pp. 198 *f.*
[3] Hutchinson, *Papers*, vol. II, pp. 131 *f.*

the Puritan element in England might plead with them; but in vain. The theocracy had now reached such a height of intellectual pride, of intolerable belief in themselves as the sole possessors of the knowledge of God, and as the only legitimate interpreters of his will to the world, that either all freedom of thought in Massachusetts must die, or their power must be destroyed. In that struggle, the ministers and the magistrates were willing to shed unlimited blood. Fortunately, noble men and women were not lacking to offer themselves as victims that the liberty of God might be made manifest.

The two who had dared to take Obadiah Holmes by the hand, as, streaming with blood, he left the stake, were the silent witnesses of a great body of liberal opinion. While the ministers and magistrates were, of course, supported everywhere by very considerable numbers among the narrower and more zealous members of the churches, many causes were at work to reduce their proportion in relation to the community at large. Not only had the body of non-church members always constituted the great majority of the population, but even among the members themselves a new generation was growing up, which had known nothing of the spiritual experiences in England, and the struggle there against the established Church. Such a struggle, as the Massachusetts authorities were soon to find in the case of the Quakers, serves to intensify the zeal of the innovators. But in Massachusetts, the former innovators had become transformed into thoroughly orthodox members of a state church, supported by the arm of the civil power, enjoying all the comfortable, safe, and deadening results of an "establishment." Their faith being no longer tried by opposition, the inevitable consequence was a decline in interest and in zeal. This was recognized by the ministers, and the rather curious situation resulted, in which we find them adopting an apparently more liberal attitude than the lay members themselves toward the question of admission to membership. If, however, in the ministerial convention of 1657 and the synod of 1662, the clergy were rather the more anxious of the two to effect a compromise on that point,[1] the cause is not far to seek. Their power and influence — and it must always be remembered that they thought they were using both for the work of the Lord — were dependent upon the maintenance of the numbers of the Church, quite as much as upon that of strict conformity and discipline. The theocracy was, in fact, in very unstable equilibrium, and was equally in danger from an increase in toleration or from a decrease in church-membership. It was the preservation of their influence, from high motives as well as from low, which was leading the clergy on the path to the "Half-Way Covenant"; and the fact that they felt the need of lowering the requirements for admission to the church is the strongest sort of evidence as to the extent to which liberal opinion had developed among the mass of laymen.

If, however, the clergy were to make the attempt, on the one hand, to prevent the numbers of their followers from declining, by no longer requiring them to have passed through the experience of conversion, on the other, they were about to engage in the most determined effort yet made to enforce conformity in matters of doctrine.

Of all the sects that had arisen during the religious ferment following the Reformation, none seems to have been more misunderstood or to have encountered greater opposition than the Quakers. In the middle of the seventeenth century, both the beliefs and the practices of the sect were in an inchoate state, and the vagaries of many of its adherents from the lower walks of life seem not only to have called forth unparalleled torrents of abuse from all quarters, but to have made men fear that these inoffensive people were to repeat the excesses of some of the frenzied sects of a century earlier. These fears and prejudices were largely increased by the writings of various ministers, many of whom were closely connected with New England.[2]

Both the ideas and the carriage of the Quakers were such

---

[1] Walker, *Creeds*, pp. 244 *ff.*

[2] For example, Francis Higginson, Thomas Welde, Samuel Eaton, Christopher Marshall. Jones, *Quakers*, p. 29.

as to be especially repugnant to the leaders of the theocracy in Massachusetts. Their democratic tendency and peculiarities of social usage were extremely offensive to persons who regarded themselves as an aristocracy of the Saints of God, and who looked upon any lack of respect offered to magistrates or ministers as little short of blasphemy. Moreover, religion as professed by the Quakers was at the opposite pole of thought and experience from that professed by the Puritans. The latter looked upon the Bible as the only complete and final revelation of God to man, of which the minister was the official expounder. To them, the covenant between man and God, the preaching of the word, the scrupulous observance of the Sabbath and of the letter of the Judaic laws, the hard-won privilege of receiving the Sacrament, were all of the essence of religion. On the other hand, the Quakers laid special stress upon the divine illumination in the individual heart, and upon a continuing revelation of Himself by God to man. They denied to the Bible the position assigned to it by the Puritans, and were bitter in their denunciations of "a hireling ministry." To them the sacraments were shadows, while their lives were saturated with the spirit of the New Testament, not the Old. It was in this antithesis that lay the real answer to George Bishop's question to the Massachusetts magistrates, when he asked: "Why was it that the coming of two women so shook ye, as if a formidable army had invaded your borders?" [1]

Mary Fisher and Ann Austin, the two women in question, arrived at Boston, from Barbadoes, in July, 1656, a few weeks after Ann Hibbens had been hung as a witch.[2] Governor Endicott was away at the time, but the Deputy Governor, Bellingham, took charge of the proceedings which were immediately begun against them. Their baggage was searched, and a hundred volumes, considered heretical, were confiscated and burned, without compensation. Although there was nothing about their case to suggest witchcraft, the authorities had

[1] George Bishop, *New England Judged by the Spirit of the Lord* (London, 1703), p. 2.
[2] *Massachusetts Records*, vol. IV, pt. i, p. 269.

them stripped stark naked and examined for evidences, with unnecessary indignities.[1] They were imprisoned, deprived of light in their cell, and refused communication with anyone. Finally, after five weeks of this illegal punishment, they were shipped back to Barbadoes, fortunate in having escaped before Endicott's return.

Within a few days of their leaving, eight more Quakers arrived on a ship from London, and were promptly accorded similar treatment, except that witchcraft was not charged.[2] Endicott's attitude was shown at once. "Take heed you break not our Ecclesiastical Laws," he said to them, "for then ye are sure to stretch by a Halter." At the trial, when they asked for a copy of the laws against them, he refused to allow them to see one — "to the grieving of the People then present," wrote our contemporary authority, "who said openly in the Court — How shall they know then when they Transgress?"[3] After some weeks' confinement, they were shipped back to England, and the Massachusetts authorities addressed a letter to the United Colonies, asking for the passage of a general regulation against allowing "such pests" as Quakers to be admitted to any of the colonies.[4] In October, the Massachusetts General Court passed the first law specifically directed against the sect, which provided that any master of a ship bringing a known Quaker to Massachusetts should be fined £100, and be required to give bonds for taking such out of the colony again, in default of which he was to be imprisoned. The Quaker was to be committed to the "house of correction," to be severely whipped, "kept constantly to worke," and not permitted to speak with anyone. If any resident of the colony defended any Quaker opinion, he was to be fined or, on

---

[1] Bishop, *New England Judged*, pp. 4 *f.*, 12; *Swarthmore Collection*, vol. 1, p. 66, cited in Jones, *Quakers*, p. 28 *n.* One of the curious elements in the psychology of the Puritans was their morbid interest in the most indecent sexual matters. One may find the details of a similar physical examination set forth by Winthrop, and the pages of his journal, as those of Bradford, the records of colonies and towns, the letters of clergymen, etc., all contain minute accounts of matters which to-day would find their place only in a limited class of medical textbooks.

[2] Richard Smith also arrived from Long Island, being deported thither again.

[3] Bishop, *New England Judged*, p. 10.   [4] *Acts United Colonies*, vol. II, p. 156.

the third offense, banished; while any person "reviling" a magistrate or minister, which meant criticizing them, was to be fined or whipped.[1] Few bits of legislation can be more complete than this, which thus provided punishment for an offender, denied anyone the right to speak in his behalf, and made it a crime to criticize the men who had passed the law. One voice, nevertheless, was publicly raised on behalf of liberty. Nicholas Upshall, "a weakly old man," who, when the two Quakeresses were being starved in prison, had bribed the jailer to give them food, heard the new law being proclaimed in the streets. He protested against it, and for his temerity in daring to criticize the magistrates, he was fined £20, and banished at the beginning of winter.[2] On his way to free Rhode Island, he was offered a home by an Indian who took pity upon him, and who, after hearing of his misfortune, exclaimed, "What a God have the English who deal so with one another about the worship of their God!"[3] Upshall, however, continued his journey to Gorton's settlement, where he was welcomed and cared for.

The following year, a band of Quaker missionaries from England landed at Newport, and were kindly received by the Rhode Islanders.[4] This at once aroused the other colonies, whose Commissioners wrote to the Rhode Island government of the "prudent care" that Massachusetts had taken when Quakers had sought her hospitality, and requested that government to banish such Quakers as were already on the Island, and to prohibit any more from coming, so that the "contagion" might not spread. The letter ended with the threat that, if the little colony did not take such action, "wee apprehend that it will be our duty seriously to consider what further provision God may call us to make to prevent the aforesaid mischiefe."[5]

To this bullying letter, Rhode Island sent an answer as wise as it was dignified. After stating their desire to live in loving correspondence with all the colonies, they wrote: —

---

[1] *Massachusetts Records*, vol. IV, pt. i, pp. 277 f.   [2] *Ibid.*, pp. 279 f.
[3] Bishop, *New England Judged*, p. 40.
[4] Jones, *Quakers*, pp. 45 ff.   [5] *Acts United Colonies*, vol. II, pp. 180 f.

"As concerning these quakers (so called), which are now among us, we have no law among us, whereby to punish any for only declaring by words, &c., theire mindes and understandings concerning the things and ways of God, as to salvation and an eternal condition. And we, moreover, finde, that in those places where these people aforesaid, in this colony, are most of all suffered to declare themselves freely, and are only opposed by arguments in discourse, there they least of all desire to come, and we are informed that they begin to loath this place for that they are not opposed by the civill authority, but with all patience and meekness are suffered to say over their pretended revelations and admonitions, nor are they like or able to gain many here to their way; surely we find that they delight to be persecuted by civill powers, and when they are soe, they are like to gain more adherents by the conseyte of their patient sufferings, than by consent to their pernicious sayings: And yet we conceive, that theire doctrines tend to very absolute cuttinge downe and overturninge relations and civill government among men, if generally received." [1]

The General Assembly sent a similar reply, some months later, in which they stated that freedom of conscience was the principal ground of their charter, "which freedom we still prize as the greatest hapiness that men can possess in this world"; and added that Quakers were "suffered to live in England; yea even in the heart of the nation." [2] Apparently the only answer the United Colonies could make to the worldly wisdom and nobility of their little neighbor, was to threaten to cut off her trade and to deprive her of the necessities of life.[3] Nor has the letter, which is one of the landmarks in the struggle for religious liberty in America, fared better at the hands of New England's clerical historians. Palfrey, who devotes thirty-five pages to an extenuating account of the Massachusetts persecution, conceals Rhode Island's stand in a footnote; and Dr. Ellis speaks of that colony's protest as "a quaint letter," in which, incredibly, he finds only "naïveté and humor." [4]

---

[1] *R. I. Records*, vol. I, pp. 376 *f.*   [2] *Ibid.*, I, pp. 378 *ff.*
[3] *Ibid.*, pp. 396 *ff.*
[4] Palfrey, *History*, vol. II, p. 472 *n.*; Ellis, *Puritan Age*, pp. xvii, 457.

Meanwhile, the other four colonies proceeded to pass more stringent laws themselves, though those of Plymouth and Connecticut were less severe than those of New Haven, where the penalties rose to branding the letter H on the hands of male Quakers, and boring the tongues of Quakeresses with a red-hot iron.[1] This latter punishment, as well as the cutting off of ears, was likewise added to the Massachusetts laws.[2] In 1658, the Commissioners of the United Colonies "seriously comended" to the several colonies that they pass legislation declaring that, if any Quaker, once banished, returned, the offender should suffer death.[3] Massachusetts, however, which was clearly behind the suggestion, was the only colony that did so. Connecticut, which was lenient in its treatment, had but little trouble, and Governor Winthrop of that colony told the Massachusetts magistrates that he would go down on his bare knees to beg that they would not execute the death-penalty. Plymouth was more influenced by its powerful neighbor, and one of the magistrates, deposed for his toleration of the sect, wrote of the persecution in Massachusetts, "we expect that we must do the like, we must dance after their Pipe; now Plymouth-Saddle is upon the Bay-Horse." [4]

In spite of a petition signed by twenty-five names, which was presented to the General Court in Boston, asking for severer laws against the Quakers,[5] and which was probably inspired by the Reverend John Norton, there was a strong sentiment in the colony against such action. The cruel sufferings that the authorities by this time had inflicted upon Mary Dyer, Mary Clark, Christopher Holden, the Southwicks, Richard Dowdney, and many others, and their patience under affliction, were telling heavily in favor of the Quakers and

[1] *Plymouth Col. Records*, vol. xi, pp. 100, 101, 125, and *passim; Conn. Col. Records*, vol. i, pp. 283 *f*, 303, 308; *New Haven Records*, vol. ii, pp. 217, 238 *ff.*; Bishop, *New England Judged*, pp. 160 *ff.*, 203 *ff.*, 226 *ff.*

[2] *Massachusetts Records*, vol. iv, pt. i, pp. 308 *f*.

[3] *Acts United Colonies*, vol. ii, p. 212. John Winthrop, of Connecticut, signed with the notation: "looking att the last as a query and not as an Act; I subscribe."

[4] Letter from Cudworth, in *New England a degenerate Plant* (London, 1659), p. 16.

[5] *Massachusetts Archives*, cited by R. P. Hallowell, *The Quaker Invasion of Massachusetts* (Boston, 1887), pp. 153 *ff*.

against the clergy.[1] In the case of William Brend, the people became so aroused as temporarily to frighten the authorities in their mad course. He had been put "into Irons, Neck and Heels, lockt so close together, as there was no more room between each, than for the Horse-Lock that fastened them on"; and was kept in that way for sixteen hours, without food, after having been whipped. The next day he was whipped again with a tarred rope, so severely that the rope untwisted; but a new one was procured, and he was given ninety-seven more blows. "His Flesh was beaten Black, and as into a Gelly; and under his Arms the bruised Flesh and Blood hung down, clodded as it were in Baggs." The next morning, after threatening to give him more, the Puritan jailer went to church. Brend, who had then been some days without food, finally became unconscious. The people, learning the facts, protested loudly, and a tumult was raised. Endicott sent "his Chyrurgion, to see what might be done (such Fear was fallen upon you," writes our authority, "lest ye should suffer for his Blood) who thought it impossible according unto Men that he should live, but that his Flesh would Rot from off his Bones, ere that bruised Flesh could be brought to digest (this was the Judgment of your Governors Chirurgion), and such a cry was made by the People that came in to see him, that ye were constrained, for the satisfaction of them, to set up a Paper at your Meeting-House-Door, and up and down the Streets, That the Jaylor should be dealt withal the next Court; but it was soon taken down again, upon the instigation of John Norton (your High-Priest unto whom, as the Fountain or Principal, most of the Cruelty and Bloodshed herein rehearsed, is to be imputed) and the Jaylor let alone: For, said John Norton (but how Cruelly let the Sober judge) — W. Brend endeavored to beat our Gospel-Ordinances black and blue; and if he was beaten black and blue, it was Just upon him; and said he would appear in the Jaylor's behalf."[2]

It is not intended to go into all the details of the many other and, happily, somewhat less terrible cases of the persecution;

---

[1] Bishop, *New England Judged*, pp. 47–62. [2] *Ibid.*, p. 67.

and the above extract from a contemporary has been given because the grim realities of the past are apt to be blurred by our easy modern phrases.

The Reverend John Norton, the Reverend Charles Chauncey, and other divines, as well as the Governor and other leading laymen, continued to press for a law allowing them to execute the death-penalty legally. The struggle, as usual, ranged the people against the theocratical leaders, and the deputies refused to pass the law prepared by the clergy and voted by the magistrates, which not only imposed death upon any Quaker who should return after banishment, but denied the right of trial by jury, and relegated the cases to a court composed of three magistrates, a majority of whom could impose the penalty.[1] The House of Deputies, which contained twenty-six members, finally consented to the passage of the law, somewhat amended, by a majority of one, owing to the absence, on account of illness, of one of those who had opposed the bill.[2] In view of the severe penalties imposed upon all who might speak in defense of Quaker doctrines, the thirteen who stood out to the end deserve all praise.

Immediate steps were taken to influence public opinion in favor of the new law, and Norton was appointed by the Court to write a treatise in support of it, which was published the following year.[3] Meanwhile, the persecution continued unabated. At the same court at which the law was passed, six Quakers were banished on pain of death, and four months later, the children of two of them, Daniel and Provided South-

---

[1] Bishop, *New England Judged*, p. 101.

[2] *Ibid.*, p. 102. The law is in *Massachusetts Records*, vol. iv, pt. i, pp. 345 *ff*.

[3] *Massachusetts Records*, vol. iv, pt. i, p. 348; also, *The Heart of New England rent at the Blasphemies of the present Generation*; Cambridge, 1659. The liberty of conscience which the more liberal part of the community was striving for he denounced as liberty "to answer the dictates of the errors of Conscience in walking contrary to Rule. It is a liberty to blaspheme, a liberty to seduce others from the true God. A liberty to tell lies in the name of the Lord" (p. 51). We may note here that several New England historians, as one of the defenses of Massachusetts, lay stress upon the vituperative language employed by the Quakers. As a matter of fact, none found in the contemporary records at all equals that of the Puritans, the violence of whose language is open for any to read in their legislative enactments and state documents. Many remarks addressed by officers of the Puritan courts, from Endicott down, to their helpless prisoners, could be expressed in modern books only by a series of dashes.

wick, were ordered sold into bondage in Virginia or the West
Indies, by the County Treasurer, to pay the accumulated fines
imposed upon them for not attending a Puritan church.   No
ship's captain, however, sufficiently hardened in the religion
of New England could be found to share in the guilt of this
transaction.[1]   There is no need of going into the details of
the other cases, which were soon overshadowed by those of the
martyrs who voluntarily suffered the extreme penalty, in order
to testify to the truth as they saw it, and to die for liberty of
opinion.

There is no doubt that Mary Dyer, William Robinson, and
Marmaduke Stevenson had counted the full cost when they
returned from banishment to face certain death, in the autumn
of 1659.   Sentence was pronounced on the eighteenth of October, and the execution took place a few days later.[2]   On
the petition of her son, Mary Dyer had been reprieved, and
was once more banished; but with a fiendish ingenuity of
cruelty, she was not to know of it, and was to be led to the
gallows with a rope about her neck, and to wait while the two
men were being hung.   As they were led to execution, the
three walked hand in hand.   "Are you not ashamed to walk
between two young men?" asked the Puritan marshal, with
characteristic coarseness.   "It is an hour of the greatest joy
I can enjoy in this world," answered the pure-hearted woman.
"No eye can see, no ear can hear, no tongue can speak, no
heart can understand, the sweet incomes and refreshing of the
spirit of the Lord which I now enjoy." [3]   After the others had
died, her hands and legs were bound, her face covered, and
the rope adjusted around her neck.   At that moment her
reprieve was announced to her.   She refused to accept her life,
but was taken to Rhode Island by her family.   The following
spring, however, she returned and told the General Court that
she was to bear witness against the unjust law, which this
time was allowed to take its course.[4]   A few months later,

[1] *Massachusetts Records*, vol. IV, pt. i, pp. 349, 367, 366; Bishop, *New England
Judged*, p. 107.
[2] *Massachusetts Records*, vol. IV, pt. i, pp. 383 *f.*
[3] Bishop, *New England Judged*, p. 134.
[4] *Massachusetts Records*, vol. IV, pt. i, p. 419.

another Quaker, William Leddra, suffered the same penalty.

So far, in the Puritan colonies, mainly in Massachusetts, over forty had been whipped, sixty-four imprisoned, over forty banished, one branded, three had had their ears cut off, five had had the right of appeal to England denied them, four had been put to death, while many others had suffered in diverse ways.[1]

There are many contemporary evidences, however, to show that the sympathy of the people went out more and more to the victims. At the time of the execution of Robinson and Stevenson, a heavy guard had been necessary to allow the sentence to be carried out, and the Court had found it needful to prepare a long defense of their action against such as might feel "pitty and comiseration," and others who might look upon the magistrates as "bloody persecutors." Apologetic broadsides were printed to the same effect.[2]

While the trial of Leddra was in progress, a banished Quaker, Wenlock Christison, suddenly appeared in court, and after declaring his identity, looked into the stern face of Endicott, and solemnly said to him, "I am come here to warn you that you should shed no more innocent blood, for the blood that you have shed already, cries to the Lord for vengeance to come upon you."[3]   He was immediately arrested, and at his trial protested that the colony had no authority to make laws repugnant to the laws of England, and that there was no law there providing for capital punishment against Quakers. But by this time even the magistrates had begun to hesitate in their course, and several refused to vote for his death. Endicott, in a fury, pounded the table, and ordered another vote, thundering out, "You that will not consent, record it: I thank God I am not afraid to give judgment."   It is said that the result was uncertain, and that the Governor himself precipitately passed the sentence of death.[4]

[1] Besse, *Abstract of the Sufferings, etc.*, cited by Jones, *Quakers*, pp. 91 *ff*.

[2] *Massachusetts Records*, vol. IV, pt. i, pp. 384 *ff*; *Mass. Hist. Soc. Proceedings*, Series III, vol. II, p. 203.

[3] W. Sewel, *History of the Quakers* (New York, 1844), vol. I, p. 338.

[4] *Ibid.*, p. 344; *Massachusetts Records*, vol. IV, pt. ii, p. 20.

The sentence, however, was never executed. Not only had the people of Massachusetts now risen in revolt against the persecuting tyranny of the ministers and magistrates, but the colony was to be stayed in its course by a stronger power. The English monarchy had been restored a year before, and the relations of Massachusetts to the mother-country were about to undergo a marked change.

Complaints had been made to King Charles of the persecutions in New England, and word of this had been received privately in Massachusetts. Partly from fear of his possible action, and partly in deference to the evident opposition of the people, a new law was passed, which, while still preserving the death-penalty, evidently intended to make it less necessary of enforcement.[1] Under this new act, Christison and twenty-seven others were released from prison, though two were stripped to the waist, and whipped through the town.[2]

On receiving news of Leddra's death, Edward Burrough, an English Quaker, had secured an audience with the King, and told him that "there was a vein of innocent blood opened in his dominions, which if it were not stopped would overrun all"; to which the monarch answered, "but I will stop that vein." His secretary was called, and an order at once prepared to be sent to the Massachusetts government. As no royal ship was then sailing, the Quakers hired one and dispatched the "king's missive," by Samuel Shattuck, a banished Massachusetts Quaker. In six weeks, the condemned man, now a King's messenger, confronted Endicott, and delivered the letter, ordering that no further proceedings be taken against Quakers, and that such as were under charges be sent to England. Endicott read it, and with what must have been the most painful emotion of his life, he looked at the hated heretic and said, "We shall obey his Majesty's commands." [3] Orders were issued for the release of all Quakers, and Shattuck,

---

[1] *Acts Privy Council, Colonial, 1613–1680*, p. 312; *Massachusetts Records*, vol. IV, pt. ii, p. 20.

[2] Sewel, *Quakers*, vol. I, p. 345; *Massachusetts Records*, vol. IV, pt. ii, p. 24.

[3] The account is from Sewel, *Quakers*, vol. I, pp. 345 *ff*. The letter has often been reprinted. *Cf*. Jones, *Quakers*, p. 98; *Cal. State Pap., Col., 1661–68*, pp. 55 *f*.

speaking of the colonists, said that "many mouths are now opened, which were before shutt, and some of them now say, Its the welcomest ship that ever came into the land."[1]

Though no more of the sect were put to death, their persecution was by no means ended. The new law had provided that every Quaker should be apprehended, stripped from the waist up, tied to a cart's tail, and whipped through every town to the boundary of the colony. This was to be repeated if they returned, and on the fourth offense they were to be branded, and, on the fifth, banished on pain of death.[2] This law was modified by limiting the whippings to three towns only, in 1662, although an answer to the address of Massachusetts to the King had been received some months earlier, withdrawing much of the royal protection formerly offered to the Quakers.[3] The change was evidently due, therefore, to public sentiment in the colony. Of the barbarous treatment accorded the victims under the act, it is unnecessary to speak in detail. To mention one of the worst cases, we may note that three women were stripped to the waist, tied to the cart's tail, and, in the end of December, forced to tramp through deep snow, receiving ten lashes on their bare backs in eleven successive towns.[4] The end, however, was not far off. In 1665, Endicott

[1] The laws were temporarily suspended. *Massachusetts Records*, vol. IV, pt. ii, p. 34. A popular ballad, supposed to have been written about 1676, is interesting, not only for its confirmation of other contemporary sources as to where the blame rested, but as showing the popular feeling.

> But may we know the Counsellors
>   that brought our Rulers in,
> To be so guilty as they are,
>   of the aforesaid sin?
> They were the tribe of Ministers,
>   as they are said to be,
> Who always to our Magistrates,
>   must be the eyes to see.
>
>   .   .   .
>
> And I am not alone herein,
>   there's many hundreds more
> That have for many Years ago
>   spoke much upon that Score.

Peter Folger, "A Looking Glass for the Times"; S. S. Rider, *R. I. Tracts*, Series V, vol. XVI, pp. 6, 12.

[2] *Massachusetts Records*, vol. IV, pt. ii, pp. 2 ff.

[3] *Ibid.*, pp. 59, 164 ff; *Cal. State Pap., Col., 1661–1668*, p. 94.

[4] The modern reader may find cases and references in Jones, *Quakers*, pp. 101 ff.

died, and the Royal Commissioners also commanded the Massachusetts General Court not to molest Quakers in their secular business.[1]

Although a considerable body of opinion had, undoubtedly, been throughout in favor of the course taken by the ministers and magistrates,[2] all the evidence points to a large and increasing body against it. The facts that the deputies were opposed to it, that the Court, usually somewhat arrogant in the assertion of its authority, had to stoop to public explanations and propaganda, that even the magistrates finally revolted, and that in the last case, the death-penalty could not be enforced even when passed, all indicate clearly enough the refusal of the people to follow their ministers in their frantic efforts to maintain orthodoxy at any cost.

It is needless to say that the seventeenth century cannot be judged by the standards of the nineteenth, but the second half of the earlier one was by no means as intolerant as many would have us believe. Opinion in England and in all of the colonies, although naturally bigoted as yet, on the part of many, was, beyond question, becoming far more liberal. We have already noted the frequent remonstrances addressed to Massachusetts by her friends at home. We have seen the consistent stand of Rhode Island from the start, and noted the tolerant tendencies in Plymouth and Connecticut. In England, Vane was raising his voice in Parliament for religious liberty in its most extreme form.[3] In the same body, Cromwell was asking, "Is it ingenuous to ask liberty and not to give it? What greater hypocrisy than for those who were opposed by the Bishops to become the greatest oppressors themselves, as soon as their yoke was removed." [4] Maryland had possessed religious freedom for all professing Christ, since 1649, and in 1665 the New Jersey Concession provided for complete liberty of conscience, as did the charter of South Carolina four years

[1] *Massachusetts Records*, vol. IV, pt. ii, p. 212.
[2] *Cf.*, *e.g.*, the petition of the inhabitants of Dover in 1662 against the increase of Quakers. *Massachusetts Records*, vol. IV, pt. ii, p. 69.
[3] Burton's Diary, cited by Hosmer, *Young Sir Harry Vane*, p. 501.
[4] Carlyle, *Letters and Speeches of Oliver Cromwell* (London, n.d.), p. 94.

later.[1]   In Jamaica, toleration, with full civil liberties to all Christians, including Quakers, was proclaimed in 1662.[2]   Public opinion notoriously outruns legislation, yet in addition to the above examples and others, Pennsylvania, in 1682, provided in its laws for equal liberty for all who believed in God; while the Toleration Act, a landmark in the struggle in England, was passed seven years later.[3]

The progress made in the generation since Bradford and his little band had tried to flee secretly from England had been great.   A large section of the people, however, both at home and in the colonies, was undoubtedly as bigoted and intolerant as ever;   and, unfortunately, the leaders in charge of the destinies of the largest of the New England colonies at the critical period we have been describing were numbered among them.   They had made a desperate stand, and hesitated at nothing,— not even inflicting torture and taking human life,— in order to maintain their position;   and, happily for America, they had been defeated, though not until they had set an indelible stain on the pages of American history.

The struggle we have been describing has not been related at length because of its antiquarian or dramatic interest.   In toleration of opinions lies the one hope for the advancement of the human race.   If the earthly end of man "is the highest and most harmonious development of his powers to a complete and consistent whole," [4] free scope must be provided for differing opinion, and varieties in the experiment of living.   The contest in Massachusetts happened to be fought out on religious lines, because it was an age of religious interests.   It happened to be fought against the ministers and magistrates because, in that time and place, they represented the forces opposed to freedom and to change.   But there are other elements in man's nature than religion; and tyranny and opposition to all innovation may be as securely enthroned in the public opinion of a

---

[1] Macdonald, *Select Charters* (New York, 1906), pp. 142, 165.
[2] *Cal. State Pap., Col., 1661–1668*, p. 111.
[3] H. F. Russell Smith, *Theory of Religious Liberty in the Reigns of Charles II and James II* (Cambridge University Press, 1911), pp. 53, 1 ff.
[4] Humboldt; cited by J. S. Mill, *On Liberty* (Oxford), p. 71.

democracy as in the leaders of a theocracy. So far as experience has shown, they are certain to be, in a socialistic or communistic state; and the battle for toleration of opinion, for the liberty of the individual personality to expand along its own unique lines, for the chance of any further development in the possibilities for the advancement of the race, may have to be fought out again upon a grander scale than any the world has yet seen.

That the course which the Massachusetts authorities took was wholly unnecessary was proved by the events in the other colonies. What happened was largely the consequence of their own acts. Rhode Island had shown the just, and, at the same time, the wise course to pursue. As she pointed out, wherever Quakers were not persecuted, they gave no trouble. One of the glories of the present nation is its complete toleration, in so far, at least, as religion is concerned; and its hard-won liberty is in no small measure due to the people of its smallest state, and to the noble men and women who suffered and gave their lives that the power of the Massachusetts theocracy might be broken, and the human mind unshackled. The debt which, in other ways, America owes to the largest of the Puritan colonies is too great to require that aught but the truth be told. It is not necessary to exalt erring and fallible men to the rank of saints in order to show our gratitude to them or our loyalty to our country. But the leaders and citizens of Rhode Island, the martyred Quakers, and the men and women of Massachusetts and the other colonies, who so lived and wrought and died that the glory of an heritage of intellectual freedom might be ours, are the Americans whom, in the struggle we have been reciting, it should be our duty to honor.

CHAPTER XII

THE THEORY OF EMPIRE

In the last chapter we mentioned the change that was to take place in the relations between New England and the mother-country in the years following the Restoration. That change was one of practical politics rather than of theory, which latter had been but little altered from the beginning of the colonial settlement, although the exigencies of events in England had largely prevented its being translated into a consistent course of action. In order to understand the imperial theory of the day, and to appraise the wisdom and justice of the positions taken both by England and by her colonies, it is necessary to shift our standpoint temporarily, and to study the empire from its centre, and not from one of its less important outposts. Business men in contact with large affairs are familiar with the relations that exist between the central administrative office of a great corporation — whose sources of raw materials, producing plants, and selling agencies may be scattered over half a continent — and the local manager of one of its units. If we consult the latter, we may learn of local conditions as they affect him, and, perhaps, of his grievances against the policy of the corporation; but if we would properly understand the whole situation, we must study it at the centre of the entire complicated system.

The New England colonies were but parts, and, at this period, unimportant parts, of such a system. Not only can their history not be understood, if we attempt to trace it without reference to England, but neither can their relations with that country, unless we take the entire colonial organization into account. The colonies were not independent states.[1]

[1] *Cf.* W. MacDonald, "A neglected Point of View in American Colonial History," *American Historical Association Report*, 1902, vol. I, pp. 171 *ff.*

They were not even, primarily, independent states in the making. The fact that a few of them, which happened to have a continent at their back and unlimited room for expansion, revolted after a century and a half, has tended to obscure their real contemporary relation to England, much as the refraction of water alters the apparent position of objects under it when seen from an angle. The angle from which we Americans always look at the original colonies is that of our present independent nation; but by doing so we unwittingly shift their position from integral parts of a complicated imperial system to incipient independent commonwealths, assumed to have been unjustly held in thraldom. Needless to say, such a viewpoint vitiates our appraisal of every contemporary act and opinion. It is possible that after some hundreds of years the present United States may be divided into two or more nations; but to-day they form one system, and no one would think of interpreting the present relations between North and South, or East and West, in the light of a possible separation centuries hence. In the same way, the relations between England and her colonies in the seventeenth century should be interpreted in the light of their then actual and prospective union and the political theories current, and not in that of a subsequent, and more or less accidental, separation, and of the wholly different theories of a later age.[1]

When James I ascended the throne of England, the British Empire was not in existence. The map of the world would have been searched in vain for any settlement of English men on English soil outside of the British Isles. When, less than half a dozen decades later, the third Stuart returned from "his travels," amidst the acclaims of the nation, it was to become the head of an empire which already encircled the

---

[1] I speak of the separation as accidental, not because the forces then at work did not make it almost inevitable, but because altered economic theories and scientific discoveries, the latter largely eliminating the extremely important elements, in the original problem, of time and distance, occurred a half-century after the separation took place. Had they occurred sooner, they might have prevented it, as they have been largely instrumental in holding the remainder of the empire together and greatly adding to it. The influence of free-trade, steam, and electricity has been of vast importance in imperial politics.

globe. From Newfoundland to the Caribbean, English colonies stretched in a great arc upon islands and mainland, while the Bermudas, equidistant, roughly speaking, from all its parts, formed a strategic centre far out in the Atlantic. Across that ocean, Fort Comantine on the coast of Guinea protected the African slave-trade, and the fortified island of St. Helena was a half-way station for the Indian fleets. Passing around the Cape, the next English possession was Gombroon, on the Persian Gulf; while, still farther east, in India, lay the factories on the Madras and Bombay shores and the Bay of Bengal. Beyond those, again, English traders were permanently established on Sumatra, Java, and the Celebes. Such an imperial structure could not have been raised in less than the allotted three-score years and ten of individual life by a practice wholly tyrannical, or a colonial theory wholly false.

The great trans-oceanic empires which were attempted in the seventeenth century by the leading European powers were political phenomena of an absolutely new type. Neither the colonies of the city-states of Greece, nor the slow continental expansion of Rome offered any adequate parallel to the political results of the age of discovery, or any solutions of the problems created.[1] Of those new empires, the English not only has proved the most lasting and the greatest, but has secured, from its very beginning, the largest comparative amount of freedom to the colonists. Assertions have often been made that its development has been unintentional and unconscious; that the English race, as the phrase goes, has peopled half the world in a fit of absence of mind. This is true only in the sense that the Empire's growth has been slow, normal, and unhurried, and that its strength has lain in the character of the people rather than in any consistent policy of aggression upon the part of their rulers. That it has been unconscious in the sense that it has been unobserved is, of course, disproved by the contemporary literature relating to imperial problems in almost every decade from the sixteenth

[1] Cf. E. A. Freeman, *Greater Greece and Greater Britain* (London, 1886); C. P. Lucas, *Greater Rome and Greater Britain* (Oxford, 1912).

century to the present day; while the wars of the entire seventeenth and eighteenth centuries were largely caused by trade and colonial questions.[1]

Englishmen could not emigrate to distant parts of the world, and found settlements, without, in many and serious ways, involving the English nation — and that apart from the fact that the soil on which the most populous of the colonies grew up was the unquestioned property of the English Crown. From the very beginning of colonization, therefore, even before any permanent success had been achieved, we find the question being discussed as to what use, if any, to the English people were these distant settlements, with their possible disadvantages and certain responsibilities.[2]

If the establishment of the British Empire was not the result of absent-mindedness, neither was it prompted by motives of philanthropy toward generations yet unborn in countries overseas. Exploration, settlement, far-distant foreign trade, ensuing wars with competing powers, and the policing of trade-routes, were costly and hazardous matters, and not to be undertaken without the prospect of very tangible rewards of one sort or another. As we endeavored to show in an earlier chapter, the main underlying motive that led to the great discoveries of the fifteenth and sixteenth centuries, and, in the main, to the colonizing movements of the seventeenth, was economic. It was, therefore, entirely natural that the speculation as to the advantages and disadvantages of empire, and as to the relations of England to her dependencies, should be based upon the economic theories of the day. The question, moreover, as to what advantages, if any, would accrue from founding, or allowing to be founded, colonies not yet in existence, was almost necessarily, what those advantages would be for England herself. After the Empire had come into existence, the point of view shifted somewhat, and, theoretically, the question became one of what advantage a policy might prove to the Empire

[1] J. R. Seeley, *Expansion of England* (London, 1884), pp. 110 *ff*.

[2] The beginnings of the discussion were noted in an earlier chapter. For the view at the end of the 19th century, *cf.* C. P. Lucas's Introduction, in Lewis, *Government of Dependencies* (Oxford, 1891), pp. xlv *ff*.

as a whole, although, as its greatest aggregation of wealth and population, the source of protection, the seat of power, the centre of all exchanges, in a word, the heart of empire, the local interests of England would still outweigh those of any of the dependencies. In no case would those at the head of the imperial government, aside from selfish motives, of which there were plenty, have thought it the part of either wisdom or justice to uphold the citizens of any one colony in a course that seemed to run counter to the interests of the Empire as a whole.

We have already noted how the breaking up of the unity of Christendom by the development of state churches was but a phase of the operation of new forces at work, at the beginning of the modern era, which were moulding men's thoughts and emotions along national lines. In their religious aspect, these gave rise to the post-Reformation churches, and in their political aspect, to the growth of the modern state. They were equally powerful in the economic field; and the so-called Mercantile Theory, which was the ground of the imperial theories of the time, was but the reasoned expression of this nationalizing of the economic life of the peoples. In the Middle Ages, the life of the individual, in its various relations, had been decentralized. In his political allegiance he had looked one way, in his religious another, and in his economic still another. The growing strength of the feeling of nationality was gradually drawing all toward a common centre.

The balance of trade, which forms one of the essential features of the Mercantile Theory, was not a new conception. It was, however, of great practical influence upon economic doctrine and state policies when applied to the nations. After speaking of how a merchant balances his private books, and how the head of a family looks after his estate, an early writer goes on to say that "the Royall Merchant, the Regall Father of that great family of a Kingdom, if He will know the Estate of his Kingdome, Hee will compare the Gaine thereof with the Expense; that is, the Native Commodities issued and sent out, with the Forraine Commodities received in; and if it appeare that the Forraine Commodities doe exceed the Native, either he must increase the Native, or lessen the Forraine, or else looke for nothing else, but the Decay of Trade and therein the losse of his Revenue, and Impoverishing of his People." [1]

This theory was developed into a system by Mun, who affirmed that the best method to "increase our wealth and treasure is by Forraign Trade, wherein wee must ever observe this rule; to sell more to strangers yearly than wee consume of theirs in value." [2] The effects of this doctrine were vastly increased and modified by the current belief that the precious metals constituted the real wealth of a kingdom, and that its whole trade, therefore, should be considered mainly in reference to the resultant balance with foreigners in gold and silver. For example, Mun states that if pepper be worth twenty pence in Amsterdam, and threepence in the East Indies, it is a gain to the nation to buy it in the latter, even though the freight and other charges make it cost more in England than if it were imported from Holland, because those charges are paid by Englishmen to Englishmen, so that only threepence in actual coin leaves the country, as compared with twenty. In this particular, he points out, his countrymen "must ever distinguish between the gain of the kingdom, and the profit of the Merchant." [3]

The effect of this theory upon the questions of colonization and colonial policy was profound. "I conceive, no forein Plantation should be undertaken or prosecuted," wrote Samuel Fortrey, "but in such countreys that may increase the wealth and trade of this nation, either in furnishing us, with what

---

[1] E. M[isselden], *The Circle of Commerce or the Ballance of Trade* (London, 1623), p. 131.

[2] Thomas Mun, *England's Treasure by Forraign Trade*, 1664 (ed. New York, 1910), p. 7. *Cf.* J. R. McCulloch, *A Short Collection of Early English Tracts on Commerce* (London, 1856), p. vi.

[3] Mun, *England's Treasure*, p. 14. In his defense of the East India Company, he advanced upon his predecessors in advocating the export of bullion, if, as a direct result, a larger amount could be shown to be imported. *Cf.* chaps. v and vi of his *Considerations on the East India Trade* (London, 1701); reprinted in *Early English Tracts*, pp. 1-49.

we are otherwise forced to purchase from strangers, or else by
increasing such commodities, as are vendible abroad; which
may both increase our shipping, and profitably employ our
people; but otherwise, it is always carefully to be avoided,
especially where the charge is greater than the profit, for we
want not already a countrey sufficient for double our people,
were they rightly employed; and a Prince is more powerfull
that hath his strength and force united, then he that is weakly
scattered in many places." [1] Granted the assumptions that
real wealth consists only of the precious metals, and that,
in a country without mines, these can be acquired only as a
result of a favorable trade with strangers, the colonial theory
of the European nations in the seventeenth and eighteenth
centuries was as logical as it was patriotic. The assumptions
may have been wrong, but in this, as in so many other cases,
we must remember that delusions are "as effective in social
evolution as are unassailable facts." [2]

The *pacte coloniale*, therefore, was, in some of its aspects,
similar to the ideal of the modern "trust," which would combine in one enormous organization the sources of its raw
materials, its means of transportation, manufacturing plants,
and selling agencies. The ideal empire, according to the
Mercantile Theory, would embrace the home country, which,
aside from the production of certain raw materials, was, in
the main, the source of credit, the seat of manufactures, the
selling agency to the world for the whole empire, the centre of
administration, and the protective power to guard the system.
The colonies in the temperate zone were to supply the typical
products of their regions, the East and West Indies materials
found in the tropics, and the African stations the supply of
negro labor.

It must be distinctly remembered that this was not merely
an English ideal. It was the end toward which the most
advanced European nations were striving in building up their

    [1] *England's Interest and Improvement*, 1663; reprint, Johns Hopkins University,
1907, p. 35.
    [2] G. L. Beer, *The Old Colonial System* (New York, 1912), vol. I, p. 37.

empires according to what was then considered as unquestionably the soundest economic doctrine. France, under Colbert, was endeavoring, with a logical rigor that was not equaled by the English, to erect just such a completely balanced system. She, too, had her North American temperate-zone colony in Canada, her fishing fleets off Newfoundland, her West Indian possessions, her African supply in Senegal, and her factories in the East Indies.[1]

Such a system, closed against the world, presupposed that every part would be willing to subordinate itself to the theoretical needs of the whole, and that the production of every unit could be so nicely adjusted in nature and amount as to maintain the internal balances, and allow the home country, as the selling agency, to establish a favorable balance with the world external to the empire. Although some of the nations, notably England and France, were able to block out empires so located, as to their parts, as apparently to fulfil the requirements, no such perfect adjustment of colonial production could ever be reached as to fit the needs of the theory; while its logic, seemingly so perfect, left out of account the fact that the colonists were human beings, who would surely develop their own local interests, troubles, and aspirations, and not insensible parts of a great machine.

The English Empire was the most complete embodiment of the ideal. The factories in the Spice Islands and on the coasts of India supplied the products of the Orient, not to be obtained elsewhere. Africa provided the negroes, upon whose labor was based the production of sugar in the West Indies, which formed one of the mainstays of the Empire's commerce. St. Helena and Bermuda were strategic points on the Indian and American trade-routes. Virginia and Maryland were wholly devoted to the staple crop of tobacco, which was another of the important elements in British trade. The fisheries of Newfoundland provided England with an article to exchange with the Catholic countries of southern Europe for the wine, salt, and other products imported from them; and they fitted in perfectly with

[1] Mims, *Colbert's West Indian Policy*, pp. 8, 315, 319, 335.

the imperial scheme [1] All these distant possessions, by employing an increasing amount of shipping, under the laws to be mentioned later, built up the merchant fleet upon which rested England's naval power and her ability to defend the Empire ; while all of them consumed English manufactured goods.

New England, however, did not fit into this elaborate and delicately adjusted trade-machine. In spite of her enormous forest-resources, which had been counted upon to provide the Empire with naval stores and timber, she failed utterly in competition with the countries on the Baltic. [2] Her agricultural products were practically identical with those of the old country, and so competed with them. There was no staple crop, like sugar or tobacco, to form an element of imperial commerce. Her fisheries, which had loomed so large at the time of the first settlement, served, for various reasons, only to compete with those of Newfoundland, and at once to reduce England's profits and to retard the increase of her fishing fleet. The purely colonial shipping, which the New England colonies early produced, drew away English seamen, competed with English vessels, and reduced the naval strength of the mother-country. Following the economic crisis of 1640, Massachusetts and her sister colonies made strenuous and partly successful efforts to establish home manufactures, which curtailed the market for English goods. [3] As, even then, those colonies imported much more from England than they exported to her, they had to seek an outlet for such products as were not adapted for the English trade, in order to obtain the money to settle their English bills. The West Indian colonies, on the other hand, exported to England far more than they imported. Consequently New England sold her timber and provisions to the island settlements, and used their bills of exchange to

---

[1] Beer, *Old Colonial System*, vol. I, pp. 319 *ff.*; *Origins of the British Colonial System*, p. 294: Osgood, *American Colonies*, pp. 111, 139 *ff.*

[2] Efforts were continually made, however, to secure naval stores from her. *Cf.*, under the Commonwealth, *Cal. State Pap., Col., 1574–1660*, pp. 392, 399.

[3] *Cf.* J. Winthrop, *History*, vol. II, pp. 29 *f.*; V. S. Clark, *Manufacturing in the U. S.*, pp. 31, 34, 40, 50.

pay her English debts. In this, however, she seemed to be in part merely drawing away the trade-balance of the West Indies by increasing her competition with the home-country.[1] Nor, as the shrewd and thrifty New England merchants grew in numbers and in wealth, did the English West Indian islands afford them sufficient outlet for their commercial energies; and there gradually developed that system of trade with the French island-group which was to be one of the causes of the Revolution.[2]

When we add to this economic maladjustment, according to the current theory, the unique position of the New England colonies as chartered or practically independent governments, it is obvious how anomalous their relations were to the imperial scheme. From the standpoint of contemporary opinion, it was not unnatural that they should be regarded by many as "the unfortunate results of misdirected efforts." Nor was it merely that they failed to fit in with the rest of the Empire. As they grew in population, and in their avowed independence of all external control of any sort, many an Englishman must have felt the fear expressed by one of the ablest economic writers of the latter part of the Empire's first century. Of all the American plantations, D'Avenant wrote in 1698, New England "is the most proper for building ships and breeding seamen, and their soil affords plenty of cattle; besides which, they have good fisheries, so that, if we should go to cultivate among them the art of navigation, and teach them to have a naval force, they may set up for themselves, and make the greatest part of our West-Indian Trade precarious," as well as absorbing the colonial carrying trade and merchandizing.[3] It has, indeed, been conjectured that Cromwell's attempt, in 1665, to induce a large number of the New Englanders to emigrate to the newly conquered island of Jamaica derived directly from the failure of their colonies to fit into the mercan-

[1] Beer, *Origins*, pp. 268, 285 *f.*; *Old Colonial System*, vol. ii, pp. 210, 221, 230 *ff.*

[2] Mims, *Colbert's West Indian Policy*, pp. 224 *f.*

[3] C. D'Avenant, "On the Plantation Trade, 1698," in his *Discourses on the Public Revenue, etc.* (London, 1771), vol. ii, p. 9; *Cal. State Pap., Col., 1574–1660*, p. 430.

tile empire,[1] although, to the present writer, other economic and military motives seem quite as likely.[2]

From this theory of empire sprang certain practical corollaries. In part to avoid allowing foreigners to benefit from the imperial trade, and to retain the carrying profits within the Empire, but mainly to build up the merchant fleet, it was decreed that all goods must be transported in vessels belonging to the mother-country or her colonies. Foreign goods, according to the theory, would have to be excluded as far as possible from the colonial markets, the products of the latter limited to the English market, and colonial manufacturing restrained so as not to compete with home-made goods, although the theory was never fully translated into practice. On the other hand, as a partial offset to such laws as were passed, which mainly redounded to the benefit of England so far as their direct results were concerned, colonial produce was, to some extent, given preferential treatment in that country, and, in some important particulars, Englishmen were forbidden to compete with the colonists. The colonies were also afforded protection against the aggression of foreign nations. No colony could possibly have remained independent. The choice was not between the English Empire and independence, but between being subject to Protestant and, as the world went then, liberal England, or to Catholic France or Spain.

As we have already said, in the second half of the seventeenth century, Colbert, the great minister of Louis XIV, was applying the Mercantile doctrine to the upbuilding of the French overseas empire with a rigor that the English never attained. When he excluded all foreign vessels from the French colonial carrying-trade, there was, as yet, no sufficient French merchant fleet to serve colonial needs, and the West India

[1] *New Haven Colonial Records*, vol. I, p. 180; G. L. Beer, "Cromwell's Policy in its Economic Aspects," *Political Science Quarterly*, vol. XVI, p. 611.

[2] The main idea seems to have been the peopling of the island with English — "from Nevis, St. Christopher's, New England, or any of the other plantations in America." *Cal. State Pap., Col., 1574–1660*, pp. 450, 453. *Cf.* also F. Strong, "The Causes of Cromwell's West Indian Expedition," *American Historical Review*, vol. IV, pp. 229 *ff.*; I. S., *A brief and perfect Journal of the late proceedings and success*, etc. (London, 1655), pp. 2 *ff.*; *The Clarke Papers* (Camden Society, 1899), pp. 203 *ff.*

planters were brought to the verge of starvation and ruin.   If
they "were hungry, barefooted and in rags," writes the historian of Colbert's policy, "they must count these things as a
bit of temporary suffering, to be endured for the upbuilding of
French commerce.   They must wait for the law of supply and
demand to operate and bring them, sooner or later, an abundance from France. . . . But he was demanding too much.
What meant the noble idea of restoring French commerce and
the upbuilding of a mighty colonial empire to the planters in
the West Indies, whose empty bellies were crying for food,
whose nakedness demanded to be clothed?" [1]   Nor were the
colonial measures of the other nations less repressive.[2]   Both
religious and economic interests, therefore, made it desirable
that the English colonies should remain within the English
Empire; and it was the power of England alone which enabled
them to do so.   For it was not a question, for example, of the
sturdy New England settlers warding off attacks from the far
fewer French inhabitants of Canada.   No colony was self-sup-
porting or economically self-contained.   Cut off from access to
the mother-country, deprived of her protection on the ocean
trade-routes, they would inevitably wither and die, or be absorbed into one of the rival and less liberal empires.[3]   The allegiance of the colonists of various nations was in only slight
measure determined by their own comparative strengths, and
almost wholly by the naval powers of the home countries.

Such, in brief outline, was the European theory of empire
held during our colonial period, some of the main features in
the practical application of which can be traced back for sev-

[1] Mims, *Colbert's West Indian Policy*, p. 194.

[2] *Cf.* Dutch prohibition of colonial manufactures, in Egerton, *Origin and Growth of British Dominions*, p. 118 n.; Beer, *Old Colonial System*, vol. I, p. 150, for Portuguese policy.

[3] For an example of the work England did in policing the trade routes, *cf.* the case of the King David.   Sailing from Newfoundland to Tangier, she met with Algerine pirates off Cape St. Vincent, whom she fought off in a three-days running fight.   Later, meeting with "Five Pirats more," she was forced to surrender.   A few days later, she is rescued by a ship of the English navy; but the two vessels meeting with "Six Pirats more," the King David was a second time captured, to be rescued once again some days later by another English ship, and safely escorted into Malaga.   *Acts Privy Council, Colonial, 1613–1680*, pp. xxxvi, 541.

eral centuries before ever the question of empire arose, as we have indicated in our earlier chapters.[1] The old life of the Middle Ages, which had been largely municipal, had become national. The extraordinary energy of the new period, facing an entire globe to be appropriated and exploited, rapidly developed national spirit into imperial ambition, and the old ideas and practices of a small and legally restricted commerce had to be suddenly adapted and enlarged to meet a situation unprecedented in history. The surprising fact is not that, in so many ways, the theory and practice of empire-making should have contained errors and worked injustices, but that one which, after all, proved highly successful, should have been developed so immediately and so surely.

Until comparatively recently, the Mercantile Theory was regarded as a sinister device to give play to the selfish profiteering of the English merchant-class. It is, however, coming more and more to be recognized as a necessary step in the evolution of the modern state. "What was at stake," writes Schmoller, who was the leader in these newer views, "was the creation of real *political* economies as unified organisms, the centre of which should be, not merely a state policy reaching out in all directions, but rather the living heart-beat of a united sentiment. Only he who thus conceives of mercantilism will understand it; in its innermost kernel it is nothing but state-making, not state-making in a narrow sense, but state-making and national-economy-making at the same time; state-making in the modern sense, which creates out of the political community an economic community, and so gives it a heightened meaning. The essence of the system," he adds, "lies not in some doctrine of money, or of the balance of trade; not in tariff barriers, protective duties, or navigation laws; but in something far greater, namely, in the total transformation of society and its organization, as well as of the state and its institutions; in the replacing of a local and territorial economic policy by that of the national state." [2]

Modern critics of the theory have been prone to lay stress

[1] *Cf.* also Osgood, *American Colonies*, vol. III, pp. 195 *ff.*

[2] G. Schmoller, *The Mercantile System and its Historical Significance* (New York, 1896), pp. 49 *ff.*

upon the obvious defects and shortcomings which appear in the workings of the enactments designed to translate it into practice. As a matter of fact, the policy proved successful, in spite of the eventual loss to England, a century later, of a portion of her colonies; while in a different and higher form, that of an imperial federated *Zollverein*, it is still regarded by many as the solution of the possibly insoluble problem of imperial government.

In a speech at the Savoy, in London, in 1917, the Premier of Newfoundland, England's oldest colony, gave notable expression to such a return to the policy of an earlier day. "This Empire," he said, "cannot live as a political empire unless it is developed as an economic empire. All the raw material produced in the Empire should be manufactured in the Empire before it leaves the Empire, and nothing should be admitted into the Empire that could be produced in the Empire." [1] Let us not condemn too hastily the economic theories of the seventeenth century until we are quite sure whither those of the twentieth are to lead us.

The strength of an ocean empire lies wholly in sea-power, and the roots of sea-power in the merchant marine. By her application of the Mercantile Theory, England forced the Dutch, who had "run hackney all the world over," from the carrying-trade of her colonies; and for all the centuries since, she has been the great commercial nation of the world. France, who abandoned Colbert's policy, and turned her back on the sea in 1672, embarking upon a career of Continental conquest, was, during the next century, to be beaten by England singlehanded for the first time since the Middle Ages, to have her merchant shipping swept away, and to lose Martinique, Guadaloupe, Canada, and India to her rival. [2]

It has too frequently been assumed to be an obvious conclusion that the Navigation Acts of the seventeenth century were a colossal blunder, because, in part, the commercial policy

---

[1] Sir Edward Morris, Speech at the Savoy, March 14, 1917. Given in London *Times*, March 15, p. 6, col. 3.

[2] *Cf.* A. T. Mahan, *Influence of Sea Power upon History* (Boston, 1898), pp. 88, 540, 73, 75 *f*.

of England lost her the continental colonies in the eighteenth. Those who would commit themselves to such a view might well determine whether, had England not made use of the weapons of the earlier century, and thus developed that naval power which alone enabled her to protect her American possessions, she would have had any colonies left, continental or other, to be kept or lost by any policies which she might adopt in the later period.

Having glanced at the theory of empire as it was understood by those at home, we must turn to consider the measures adopted to reduce it to practice, and also the views of imperial relations held by the colonists.

We may again emphasize the fact that the colonies were dependencies of England, and not independent nations. It was as much the right and duty of England to assert and maintain some sort of imperial control over them as it has been of the United States to do the same over her own territorial possessions. The colonists were Englishmen, settled upon English lands, subject to English laws, entitled to the rights of Englishmen at home, protected by English power. The control exercised over them was not that of a foreign nation, or imposed by conquest; and the mere fact that some control should be exercised could not in itself be construed as an act of oppression or tyranny. Had the waste lands on which these emigrating Englishmen settled been contiguous to the borders of any English county, none of the questions that arose as to their relations to English sovereignty would have arisen. They were all due to the distance, translated into time, that separated these English subjects from the seat of authority, and to the new conditions of their strange environment. From those two elements, "arose all that was peculiar and exceptional in their relations with the British government." [1]

---

[1] Osgood, *American Colonies*, vol. III, pp. 4 f.; "The English colonies, however, were not sister communities of England, but dependent local jurisdictions for whose welfare and safety the mother-country had assumed the responsibility." Beer, *Origins*, p. 301. For discussion of the element of distance, cf. Lucas, *Greater Rome and Greater Britain*, pp. 32 ff.

At the time when the New England colonies were planted, the doctrine of Parliamentary sovereignty, of the supreme authority in the state of that body which had hitherto been regarded rather as a judicial than a legislative one, was beginning to take hold of men's minds. It required, however, the ordeal by battle of a civil war to decide the question; and it was not until the Restoration that Parliament took its permanent place among English institutions.[1] The close connection of the colonies with the Crown arose from the fact that, during the period of their founding, their relations to the government of England were mainly with the Executive and as occupiers of the soil, the executive power being then lodged in the King in Council, and the title to the land being vested in the Crown.[2] As the constitutional situation gradually altered, the colonies remained, of course, subject to the sovereign power, wherever located, as did Englishmen at home, although so complex, and difficult of both legal and equitable settlement, were the questions of sovereignty in the Empire raised by the phenomena of overseas dominions, that it is highly questionable whether their solution has ever been found. Only a few years ago, a brilliant Englishman could speak of the bonds then uniting England and her colonies as "a confusion of legal formulas and brittle sympathies"; and although, as tested in the world-crisis of the Great War, those sympathies have proved anything but brittle, his conclusion that imperial sovereignty is, in reality, non-existent, seems irrefutable. [3] The ship of state to-day, compared to that of the seventeenth century, is as a dreadnought to the Mayflower; but if, after three centuries, the problem of imperial organization is yet awaiting solution, with the best of will on the part of both England and the dominions, there need be little surprise, and certainly no bitterness, over the slow and blundering beginnings. Unfortunately, owing to the uncer-

[1] C. H. McIlwain, *The High Court of Parliament and its Supremacy* (Yale University Press, New Haven, 1910), pp. 109, 158, 352 *ff.*, 137, 145.

[2] Osgood, *American Colonies*, vol. III, p. 15; C. M. Andrews, *British Committees*, p. 10.

[3] F. S. Oliver, *Alexander Hamilton* (London, n.d.), pp. 450, 447.

tainty, in the course of England's political evolution, as to where sovereignty really lay, and also to the inherent difficulties involved in the question of the realm and the dominions, alluded to in an earlier chapter, the way was all too open for controversial misunderstandings on purely technical grounds between the colonies and the mother-country. And this quite apart from the difficulties raised by distance, and the attempted course of Stuart usurpation, against which latter, it must be remembered, the forces of freedom were to struggle in old England as well as in her colonies.

During the period covered by this volume, control over the colonies was asserted in various ways and at various times by both Parliament and the Crown. Patentees of the royal charters not infrequently asked Parliament to confirm their privileges; while that body often inquired into the use which was being made of those monopolistic documents; for it is sometimes forgotten that such a charter as that obtained by Massachusetts, for example, while regarded by the company as the basis of its liberties, could also, quite as legitimately, be regarded by the nation as creating a monopoly in one of its worst forms — that of the exclusive use of the Crown, or public, lands. For the most part, however, Parliament confined itself to passing legislation regarding trade only, its control over the customs being continuous from 1641. [1]

Those who intended to found plantations necessarily had to apply to the king for a charter, in order to obtain possession of the soil and exemption from certain laws covering emigration and export. Technically, the charters of the corporate colonies ranked merely with those of English municipal corporations. According to a strict interpretation of the law, therefore, so long as the private rights of individuals were not infringed, the English government would be technically justified in altering colonial institutions, or in dividing and combining colonies, without the consent of the inhabitants. [2] As

[1] Osgood, *American Colonies*, vol. III, p. 14; Beer, *Origins*, p. 341; *Acts and Ordinances of the Interregnum* (London, 1911), vol. II, p. 425.

[2] Osgood, *American Colonies*, vol. III, pp. 7 *ff*. The provinces were the equivalents of English counties.

is always the case, old laws and institutions were slightly altered by the use of legal fictions and by modifications in practice, to meet the needs of a new situation. It is unthinkable that an entirely new body of law, and a wholly new set of institutions, should have been created, to serve political contingencies that could by no means have been foreseen.

The element of distance again came into play, to alter profoundly the practical effect of legal technicalities. In England the sovereign power, in exercising its jurisdiction over municipalities, had local knowledge of conditions, and could take immediate and effective action. Moreover, even when the citizens of the municipality were not represented in Parliament, they were yet largely protected from acts of oppression by the fact that such acts were prevented by the self-defensive foresight of other municipalities, which were represented. The situation in regard to the colonies was entirely different. Owing to the distance which separated them from home, it was impossible that either the king or Parliament could have accurate knowledge of local conditions, or take prompt measures. The difficulties as to both these points, in the unsettled state of England in the earlier part of the seventeenth century, were responsible for the extraordinary freedom which the colonists enjoyed from interference in their domestic political affairs. In addition, as their local conditions were little understood, and of but slight moment to the bulk of Englishmen at home, and as the interests of one colony frequently conflicted with those of another differently situated, their rights, in the absence of parliamentary representation, did not possess even that vicarious protection enjoyed by their legal equivalents, the unrepresented municipal corporations in England. Of necessity, therefore, colonial interests, from the standpoint of the colonists, were bound to be in part neglected by England, and in part misunderstood, while they served, to a far greater extent than was possible with those of any class or body at home, as the hunting-ground of rival cliques of self-interested individuals or groups.

Down to 1643, when Parliament, as a result of the Civil

War, assumed the position of executive head of the government, colonial affairs had been in the hands of the King in
Council, and had been managed by a succession of committees, sub-committees, and commissions, one of which we have
already encountered on the other side of the water at the time
of the troubles over the Massachusetts charter.[1] During the
period of the Interregnum, these were replaced by a tangle of
committees of Parliament and the Protector's Council, none
of which were continuous, or able to formulate and carry
through a consistent policy. We have already seen the results of the administrative confusion, in the opportunity which
it gave the New England colonies, and of which they made
full use, to develop their local institutions and policy in almost
entire disregard of their position in the Empire.

This almost complete absence of any steady policy or consistent control over the component parts of the imperial
structure not only was unacceptable to the merchants at home,
but would probably have been destructive of the Empire had
it continued without change. Certain measures of far-reaching importance, however, had already been enacted under
Cromwell; and the Restoration, which strengthened the government and united the people, enabled England to undertake a more comprehensive scheme for imperial organization,
although in New England, owing to the incorrigible tendencies
of the Stuarts, it blundered into criminal folly.

At first, two councils were created, one for Trade, and the
other for Plantations, their instructions largely following
drafts prepared by the London merchants Povey and Noell,
who had for some years been actively engaged in the study of
colonial questions, and the formulation of a colonial policy.[2]
However these instructions might strike colonists who refused
to acknowledge any right of control whatever by the mother-
country, they could not but appear wise and just to the statesmen and citizens at home. The councillors were ordered, in

---

[1] Cf. Andrews, British Committees, pp. 12 ff.; P. L. Kaye, The Colonial Executive
prior to the Restoration (J. H. U. S.), pp. 55 ff.
[2] Andrews, British Committees, pp. 38, 56, 67 ff.

the first place, to make a complete survey — by means of correspondence with the colonial governors — of the laws and institutions, population and means of defense of each colony. They were to study "means for the rendering those dominions usefull to England, and England helpful to them, and for the bringing the several Colonies and Plantations, within themselves, into a more certain civill and uniforme waie of government and for the better ordering and distributing of publique justice among them." They were, further, to maintain a correspondence with the local authorities in the several colonies, so that they might have constant knowledge of "their complaints, their wants, their abundance," and their shipping, the latter for revision of the Navigation Laws. Finally, they were to study the methods employed by other states in their colonial government, and to call experts to their assistance in any particular when needed.[1] The Council was made up of able men, almost all of them authorities on colonial questions, and in close touch with the colonies, while the business, in the first instance, was frequently entrusted to experts.[2] Of the work of the Council, Professor Andrews writes, that "there was not an important phase of colonial life and government, not a colonial claim or dispute, that was not considered carefully, thoroughly, and in the main, impartially."[3] In fact, an unbiased study of the actions taken by the Privy Council and its committees during nearly the whole of the seventeenth century leads one to agree with the editor of the Acts, that, as a governing body, it was "anxious to help, willing to take advice, free from preconception."[4]

The only individual connecting link between New England and the government in England was the unofficial "agent" whom one or another of the colonies appointed at times of

[1] Andrews, *British Committees*, where the texts of the Instructions and of Povey's Overtures are both given.

[2] The membership included Sir Anthony Ashley Cooper, who had served on Plantation Committees during the Interregnum; Robert Boyle, President of the Corporation for the Propagation of the Gospel in New England; Sir Peter Leere and Sir James Draxe, old Barbadian planters; Povey, Noell, Digges, and Colleton, all merchants and experts on colonial trade. *Ibid.*, pp. 76 f.

[3] *Ibid.*, p. 76.   [4] *Acts Privy Council, Colonial, 1613–1680*, p. xi.

crisis, such as the Hocking murder or the Dr. Child petition, to present their case to the authorities. Although unofficial, the office was recognized by the English government, and such agents were employed by most of the colonies, island as well as continental, the office becoming an integral part of the administrative machinery of the following century.[1]

Such, in bare outline, were the organs employed by England in the administration of the colonies. Of the legislative enactments designed to build up the Empire, the most important were precursors of the more famous Navigation Acts of the following century. In 1650, 1651, 1660, and 1663, ordinances were passed for the control of trade and shipping, which, in the period now under review, were more important in their political than in their economic influence upon New England. Holland had been the first of the European nations to understand the effect upon economic prosperity at home of the building up of colonial trade, and in the middle of the seventeenth century threatened to absorb the entire carrying trade of the world, the value of goods shipped annually in Dutch bottoms having been estimated at a billion francs.[2] The English Navigation Acts of Cromwell and Charles II, like the policy initiated by Colbert in France, were aimed mainly at breaking the monopoly of Holland, and building up the national merchant-marines of England and France. Even the fisheries off the coasts of England and Scotland had passed into Dutch hands, and Englishmen had long been clamoring for some means of fighting commercially the growing menace of Dutch sea power.[3]

As the effects upon New England, until the following century, were mainly indirect, it is not necessary to give the details of the various acts in the order in which they were passed. Their aim was twofold — destructive and constructive.

---

[1] Cf. L. P. Kellogg, "The American Colonial Charter," *Annual Report, American Historical Association*, 1903, vol. I, p. 228; E. P. Tanner, "Colonial Agencies in England during the 18th Century," *Political Science Quarterly*, vol. XVI, pp. 24 ff.

[2] Mahan, *Sea Power*, p. 96. Cf. Leroy-Beaulieu, *De la Colonisation chez les peuples modernes*, vol. I, pp. 113 ff.

[3] G. Edmundson, *Anglo-Dutch Rivalry* (Oxford, 1912), pp. 36 ff., 79, 154.

In the former aspect, they aimed at diminishing, if not wholly destroying, the shipping, and so both the commerce and the naval power of competing states. On their constructive side, their design was to build up the shipping of the English Empire, and, in reference to certain articles, to make England the sole market for their trade. As to the first point, the colonies were put upon the same basis as England herself; and, in exchange for the advantages derived by her from the second, she offered the colonists certain privileges in the home markets. It was, therefore, enacted that no trade could be carried on between England and her dominions except in ships owned by her or them, and manned by English or colonial crews, the same restriction applying to all goods imported into either from any foreign country or colony in America, Asia, and Africa.[1] This was merely an extension of acts already frequently passed, or provisions in the early charters, such as we have already noted.

The other main point, that of limiting the markets in certain goods to England, was also merely an extension of another long-familiar idea. When the economic organization, in the later Middle Ages, was still largely municipal, it had been found advantageous to designate certain towns as the sole markets, or "staple," for certain goods. For some centuries, the belief in the economic soundness of this practice continued to be held; and, as we noted in the very first charter relating to America,— that of Cabot, in 1496,— it was required that all goods should pass through the port of Bristol. The Navigation Act of Charles II required that certain "enumerated" commodities produced in the colonies should be sold only in England, and not directly to foreigners, thus making England the "staple" for the Empire in the same way in which certain municipalities had formerly been the staples for the kingdom. Theoretically, the colonists were in the same relative position to England in the matter as were Englishmen at home to the staple municipalities, although, of course, the practical disadvantages and injustice to the colonists were much greater when the scheme was made imperial.

[1] Macdonald, *Select Charters*, pp. 106 *ff.*, 110 *ff.*, 133 *ff.*

The list of enumerated commodities in the seventeenth century, however, was very limited, and no such restrictions were placed upon purely intercolonial commerce. A number of the most important colonial exports, such as wheat and fish, were not included; while of the more important ones named, none were produced in New England, and but one— tobacco — by any of the American continental colonies. As an offset to the advantages accruing to England by thus controlling the sale of the enumerated commodities, that country placed prohibitive duties on many of them when imported from other countries, thus giving the colonies the monopoly of the market to which they were limited. In the case of tobacco, which was successfully grown in England, she incurred the resentment of a considerable element in her own agricultural classes by forbidding its culture. So great, indeed, was the opposition to giving the American planters the monopoly of the English market, that the government had for many years to use armed forces against its own citizens to keep faith with the colonies.[1]

The only other point of importance in these early acts was the provision in that of 1663, that no European manufactured goods could be shipped to the colonies unless first landed in England, Wales, or Berwick. Owing, however, to a system of drawbacks on the duties paid in these cases, such goods frequently sold in the colonies at lower prices than they could be sold for in England itself; and certain exceptions, such as Portuguese wines, and salt for the fisheries, were of especial benefit to New England. Indeed, it is noteworthy that the New England colonies, although the least desirable part of the Empire from the English standpoint, and constantly giving trouble politically, were nevertheless accorded particularly considerate treatment from time to time, within the limits of the imperial system. Under the Commonwealth, in 1644, they had been exempted from the payment of all English

[1] Tobacco was raised in eighteen English counties, to be trampled down annually by royal troops of horse, so strongly had both the plant and the colonial theory, respectively, taken root in English soil and English minds. *Cf.* Beer, *Origins*, pp. 117 *ff.* *Acts Privy Council, Colonial, 1613–1680*, pp. xxii *ff.*

import and export duties, which naturally gave them a great advantage over the other colonies, and made them the envy of the Empire.[1] A dozen years later, by an act of Parliament, foreign ships were allowed to carry fish from both the New-foundland and New England fisheries, nullifying to that extent the Act of 1650; and, after the Restoration, their trade was specifically exempted from certain onerous clauses in the Navigation Acts, as then interpreted, although that of the other colonies was not.[2]

As to the success of the above acts, there can now be little question, and their former condemnation on economic grounds has given place to the recognition of the fact that they did indeed secure the objects intended, and that the welfare of the Empire as a whole, as well as that of England herself, was promoted by them. The merchant marine was doubled in eighteen years, the Dutch and other competitors beaten off, and the Empire, and notably New England, greatly increased in power and wealth.

As we have already indicated, however, European imperial theory in the seventeenth century had one serious defect. It failed to take account of human nature in the colonist. Like so many modern theories which consider the state as all, and the individual as nothing, it made the blunder of treating the abstraction as human, and the human as an abstraction. It asked too much of the individual, and, entirely apart from selfish motives, which were found in the colonies quite as much as in the mother-country, it almost of necessity subor-dinated the interests of the former to those of the latter. The success of the Empire as a whole was doubtless far more de-pendent upon the strength and prosperity of England than upon the fortunes of any individual colony; but that was a point of view more likely to be appreciated by the contem-porary citizens at home, and the historians of a later day, than by the contemporary colonist, who saw his particular interests made to suffer for those of the Empire, and his local pride constantly wounded by a sense of subordination to a power

[1] *Interregnum, Acts and Ordinances*, vol. I, p. 571.   [2] Beer, *Origins*, pp. 397, 114.

three thousand miles away. For in all the difficulties between England and her colonies, we continually have to come back to the element of distance. What made the acts of the government seem autocratic was not the fact that the colonists were not directly represented in Parliament,— for neither were a large number of Englishmen at home,— but that, by virtue of the effects of distance, the central government was external to the colonists, in a sense in which it never was to the unrepresented Englishmen in England itself. It is difficult to see how any system of representation could have been devised which would have improved the position of the colonies, although representation in the English Parliament was proposed by Barbadoes as early as 1652.[1] There was, in fact, no original thought contributed by any of the colonies, which was of practical use in devising any better scheme of imperial control than that which England was gradually evolving. During the formative period, the colonies offered nothing of a constructive character to the solution of the problem, and contented themselves with a purely obstructionist attitude of attempting to ignore or oppose any measure which they deemed in conflict with their local interests.

At more than one period, English colonists have been accused of believing that "it is the undoubted right of every Englishman to settle where he likes, to behave as he sees fit, and to call upon the Mother-Country to foot the bill."[2] This, however, is not merely a colonial characteristic: it is the spirit developed upon every frontier, as the later history of American westward expansion may be called upon to illustrate; and, as we have pointed out, the whole chain of colonies formed the long encircling frontier of England. The spirit of stubborn resistance to any interference with their legal rights, or even with their mere freedom of action, was quite as often found in the island-colonies of both France and England as it was in the continental ones now included in the United

---

[1] *Cal. State Pap., Col., 1574-1660*, p. 373. *Cf. The Groans of the Plantations* (London, 1689), pp. 15 *f.*, 23 *f.*
[2] *Acts Privy Council, Colonial, 1613-1680*, p. xxix.

States.   The residents of Barbadoes, for example, in a memorial condemning the Navigation Act of 1651, used language which has a ring that has often been considered peculiarly American. After denying that Parliament had any jurisdiction over them, because they were unrepresented, the settlers went on to say that, if they could not obtain a peaceful settlement of the dispute, yet "wee will not alienate ourselves from those old heroick virtues of true Englishmen to prostitute our freedom and privileges to which we are borne to the will and opinion of any one; neither do wee think our number so contemptible, nor our resolution so weake as to be forced or perswaded to so ignoble a submission, and we cannot think that there are any amongst us who are soe simple and soe unworthily minded, that they would not rather chuse a noble death than forsake their ould liberties and privileges." [1]

In spite of the nobility of the sentiment, however, the position assumed, as was frequently the case in Massachusetts, was in fact unwarranted from a strictly legal point of view. Had the stand taken by England on important points in the long colonial controversy been indeed illegal, the problem would have been enormously simplified.   As a matter of fact, it was rather the contentions of the colonists which were, from the strict technical standpoint, the illegal ones. [2]   But the real questions were not questions of law, although, with the instincts of their race, the Englishmen on both sides of the water fought them out as if they were.   One might as well have passed laws to forbid a boy outgrowing his clothes, as to forbid rapidly developing and far-separated colonies from outgrowing the doctrine of a centralized imperial sovereignty. This fact, which is now wholly admitted by the most patriotic Englishmen, both at home and in the dominions, was unfortunately beyond the ken of seventeenth-century thought.

The attitude of the most powerful colony in New England had been foreshadowed from the very beginning.   The transfer

---

[1] R. H. Schomburgk, *History of Barbadoes* (London, 1848), pp. 706 *ff*.   *Cf*., for a similar spirit in Bermuda, Beer, *Old Colonial System*, vol. ii, p. 99.

[2] *Cf*. McIlwain, *High Court of Parliament*, pp. 364 *ff*.

of the Massachusetts charter to the colony itself had obviously been for the purpose of escaping as far as possible from the jurisdiction of the English courts, and establishing a virtually independent government, under a strained construction of that document. We have already seen how the colony had arrogated to itself sovereign powers, how it had over and over refused appeals to the home courts and Crown, how it had erected fortifications, and taken other military measures to resist by force the assertion of her authority by England, and how it had made treaties of both war and peace with foreign powers. In 1652, it established a mint, the coins having the famous device of the pine tree and the word "Massachusetts" on one side, and "New England" and the date on the other, but with no recognition of the king.[1] Even the mere oath of allegiance was refused whenever possible, although required by the charter itself.[2] All of these acts represented a consistent policy, openly avowed among themselves by the leaders, of disputing any claims of the home country to any authority whatsoever over the colony.

From time to time, crises in its affairs brought out official declarations of its attitude. Owing to the exigencies of the Civil War in England, Parliament had issued commissions to certain officers of the merchant marine, authorizing them to make prizes of any vessels which they might find in the royal service. In the summer of 1644, one of these officers, a Captain Stagg, appeared in an armed ship in Boston harbor, and there made prize of a Bristol ship, according to his orders. A tumult was raised, and many of the magistrates and clergy, asserting that "the people's liberties" had been violated, were in favor of forcing the release of the seized vessel. A majority, however, decided that the Parliament's commission must be recognized; for, if its authority were denied in this, then the

[1] *Massachusetts Records*, vol. IV, pt. i, pp. 84, 104. The right to coin money was occasionally granted in the early charters, but not in that of Massachusetts.

[2] *Cf.* the form of oath in *Massachusetts Records*, vol. IV, pt. ii, p. 201. In 1665, under pressure from the Royal Commission, the General Court agreed that it would "order the taking of the oath of allegeance, according as the charter comands." *Ibid.*, p. 206.

foundation of the colony's patent also would be denied, and if they relied solely upon their Indian purchases to give them title to the country, they would have to renounce "England's protection, which were a great weakness in us, seing their care hath been to strengthen our liberties and not overthrow them"; and, also, if they should by opposing the Parliament "cause them to forsake us, we could have no protection or countenance from any, but should lie open as a prey to all men." The way for resistance at any time, however, was left open by declaring that, by the course of affairs in England, the Parliament had taught that "*salus populi* is *suprema lex*," and that, in case that body should ever prove of a "malignant spirit," "we may make use of *salus populi* to withstand any authority from thence to our hurt." During the discussion, some had maintained that by their patent the colony was subject "to no other power but among ourselves"; but that was denied.[1]

Two years later, however, in connection with the Dr. Child petition, and the order of the English Commissioners concerning Samuel Gorton, the local aspects of which have been discussed in a previous chapter, the General Court undertook to define the colony's relations to England more definitely. While there was some difference of opinion, the majority of the magistrates and of the clergy consulted took the stand that by the charter they had "absolute power of government," with authority to "make laws, to erect all sorts of magistracy, to correct, punish, pardon, govern, and rule the people absolutely," without the interposition of any superior power. They denied that any appeal lay against any of their proceedings, or that they were bound, "further than in a way of justification," to make answer to any complaints against them in England. They drew a distinction between corporations within England and those without, asserted that plantations were above the rank of ordinary corporations, and added that "our allegiance binds us not to the laws of England any longer than while we live in England, for the laws of the parliament of England reach no further, nor do the King's writs under the

[1] J. Winthrop, *History*, vol. ii, p. 223 *f*.

great seal." They did, indeed, acknowledge some sort of shadowy and undefined allegiance, and claimed protection by the mother-country as a right.[1]

This theory of virtual independence was reasserted by the Court in the year following the Restoration, with the addition that they conceived that "any imposition prejudicial to the country, contrary to any just law" not repugnant to the laws of England, was an infringement of their rights, and that the colony was privileged to defend itself, even by force of arms, against any who should attempt its "destruction, invasion, detriment or annoyance."[2]   The duties of allegiance were defined somewhat more exactly than they had been fifteen years earlier, and somewhat differently; but any sovereign rights of the English government over its dependencies in the Empire were denied.[3]   More and more, not merely in theory, but in the form that the colony's negotiations took with the home authorities through its agents, it was endeavoring to assume the position, not of an integral part of an empire, but of an allied sovereign power.

The attitude of Massachusetts has been noted because her position was far more pronouncedly anti-English than was that of her sister colonies in the group. Not only were the governments of Plymouth, Rhode Island, and Connecticut more democratic than that of Massachusetts, but the individual citizens of those plantations were quite as tenacious of their individual rights. Nevertheless, there was a much less aggressive tone in their relations with the mother-country, and a greater readiness to acknowledge imperial obligations in return for imperial benefits. As we have seen, however, the frontier-spirit was at work throughout the entire range of empire; and, while probably, neither at that time, nor at any period down to the formation of the union, was the anti-English element in Massachusetts as large as used to be thought, nevertheless it was the radical, and not the loyal and conservative ele-

---

[1] J. Winthrop, *History*, vol. ii, pp. 341, 345, 354 *f*., 352.
[2] *Massachusetts Records*, vol. iv, pt. ii, p. 25.
[3] Kaye, *English Colonial Administration under Clarendon*, p. 142.

ment, which mainly determined her policy, and, gradually, that of New England.

If we wish to apportion fairly the praise and blame due to individuals and peoples in history,— if indeed it is ever possible to do so,— we must endeavor to look at their actions from a purely contemporary point of view, and to ignore long-subsequent results. The modern historian has come to realize that the qualities of a people, the characteristics of an epoch, the motives of a great struggle or movement, are by no means the clear-cut, sharply defined matters sketched by the patriotic writers of a simpler day. In the enormously complicated development of modern society from the struggle of class with class, the conflict of interest with interest, the clash of one element against another, it is recognized that the contest was at no time between clearly aligned forces of the powers of darkness and the powers of light. "It is beginning to be seen," writes Professor McIlwain, speaking of the early constitutional struggle at the time of de Montfort, "that men in the past have really advanced the cause of liberty, though often entirely unconscious of any such intention, or even when their aims were entirely selfish." [1]

The resistance to England by her colonies in the past, on many occasions and from many quarters, has undoubtedly advanced the cause of liberty throughout the entire Anglo-Saxon race. The statesmen of England in the seventeenth century, however, were confronted, as statesmen usually are, by a practical problem, to be solved in the light of contemporary knowledge, practices, and beliefs. As we have already noted, neither Massachusetts, Barbadoes, Bermuda, nor any other of the colonies engaged in defying and obstructing the attempts of England to unify and govern the Empire, had any practicable suggestion to offer. They could not be allowed by England to become independent without running the risk of their being absorbed by her rivals, France or Spain. Nor did the colonies themselves wish to lose her protection. Much as they might talk of armed resistance, the wisest men in them

[1] McIlwain, *High Court of Parliament*, pp. 12 ff.

knew that they could not subsist alone, and preferred the rule
of England to that of any of the other empires. The letter
from Pynchon, quoted in an earlier chapter, the words of
Winthrop cited above, as well as other contemporary evidence,
show that the colonists realized and counted upon the power
of England to shield them, so that they should not, as Winthrop
said, "lie open as a prey to all men."

If England is to be condemned for interpreting the law,
which was indubitably on her side, in too narrow a spirit, and
of caring too much for her own interests in building up those
of the Empire, on the other hand it is difficult to acquit the
colonies of a selfishness almost as great, in their attempts to
secure all the advantages of empire, without being hampered
by its restrictions. They insisted, for example, upon protection as a right, at the very time that they were flouting the
Navigation laws designed to foster that naval strength upon
which alone such protection could be based.

Although the thought of England was constructive in reference to the Empire, and that of the colonies was destructive,
nevertheless contemporary imperialism was destined to be influenced quite as much by colonial fact as by English theory.
There was much in the imperial scheme that the colonist, from
his isolated position and limited outlook, failed to see, just as
there was much which, because of its conflict with his individual
interest, he refused to accept. But the facts that failed to
fit into the theory were far more obvious to him than to the
Englishman at home. The slower movement of the historical
process in the old world made it more difficult for the Englishman at the centre of empire to foresee its future; while, owing
to the swifter course of evolution on the periphery of the system, and the simplifications of the frontier, the colonist was
to a great extent already living in that future without thinking about it at all.

His interests, however, soon became wholly colonial and
extremely provincial, and his political thought became entirely
centred upon his local government, the development of which
grew more and more absorbing in proportion as its political de-

pendence was diminished. But the real problem of the day was not a domestic one for the several colonies, profound as were the results to ensue from the development of the local New England political institutions. The real problem was, how to bring these local institutions into working relations with the still necessary sovereign power at the centre of the system. The colonists might offer legal objections or armed resistance, in the way of criticism, but so long as they offered no help in devising a workable solution of the problem, the obligation to do so devolved upon England alone. The rapid material success of the colonists, their new surroundings, their isolation, their necessary self-reliance, and their new local pride, were all developing, not, indeed, new thought, but new feeling. Although the empire evolved from the Mercantile Theory was a necessary step in the evolution of the empire of to-day, the Englishman's thought and the colonists' feelings were bound to clash over it, for the differences went far deeper than mere economic interests. The problem of composing those differences, great as it may have seemed to the contemporary rulers in Europe, or to the protesting settler on every frontier, were in reality far greater, even, than either of them dreamed. Moreover, difficult as the question would have been in any case, it had been rendered far more so by the disorganization of authority at home in the constitutional struggle. With the return of settled conditions at the Restoration of the monarchy in England, it seemed as if a serious attempt were at last to be made to bring order out of the increasing chaos of the imperial situation. Unfortunately, the combined weakness and tyranny of the restored Stuarts served to postpone, until after that dynasty's second dethronement, the success of any efforts to evolve and apply a considered and consistent colonial policy.

CHAPTER XIII

THE REASSERTION OF IMPERIAL CONTROL

THE Puritan Revolution in England had failed to establish a permanent government, which should provide for the liberty of the individual, and be consonant with the genius of the English race. The ensuing restoration of the monarchy was not the return of a king crushing rebellion by force of arms. It was the peaceful reëstablishment of an institution demanded by large and important elements among the people, who considered it as essential to the welfare of the state, and who believed that the individuals who might occupy the throne had been taught sufficiently by the events of the preceding two decades not to attempt to overstep the position that had come to be assigned to them in the popular view of the constitution. But if, in the sphere of practical politics, the Revolution had merely shattered the political edifice without having been able to build another, in the domain of political thought it had left a rich legacy of ideas, which were to mould into modern form the institutions now reëstablished by the will of the people. We have already seen how quickly the anti-English party in Massachusetts had seized upon one of the most revolutionary of the Commonwealth doctrines, and proclaimed for themselves, as taught by Parliament, that "*salus populi* is *suprema lex.*" These ideas, however, were not to bear their full fruit until detached from their theological origin and divested of their religious associations. This secularization of politics, by the substitution of parties for churches as political forces, was necessary before further advances could be made either in religious toleration or in civil liberty; and it was in the years following the Restoration that the transition occurred both in old England and in New.[1]

[1] *Cf.* Lord Acton, *Modern History*, pp. 205 *f.*

In the latter, and more particularly in Massachusetts, theology and politics had been more closely intertwined than anywhere else in the Empire, and the earlier course of the struggle to break them asunder has been indicated in the preceding chapters. As we have there pointed out, the fundamental idea of theocracy was such as to preclude the possibility of either civil or religious freedom. The latter was too evidently fatal to the maintenance of that peculiar form of government to be allowed, if it could possibly be suppressed; and the former could not exist in a state in which the entire political power was to be permanently wielded by a small minority, whose essential qualification was its assent to an unique form of ecclesiastical organization. To what lengths the theocratical party in Massachusetts were willing to go in their efforts to remain in power had been shown by their contest with the Quakers. Although they were defeated in that struggle, amid many evidences that religion and politics were becoming more and more distinct in the minds of the people, the struggle was by no means ended, nor the transition complete. The political contest with the mother-country, which was now to begin in earnest, and which has often been made to seem a struggle for liberty against tyranny, was in large part, in this early stage, merely a continuance, under another guise, of the attempt of the theocracy to maintain its position and to defy all efforts, either from within or without, to interfere with its unrestricted exercise of power.

The early years of the Restoration mark, in many respects, the beginning of the modern period of English history; and this is as true of the Empire as a whole as of the constitutional developments at home. The far-seeing colonial policy of Clarendon sought to take advantage of the new outburst of energy which marked the people at that time, in order to round out and consolidate the nation's colonial possessions; and the main aspects of imperial policy became military and commercial. The Act of Uniformity, passed in 1662, and aimed at the Puritans, did not include the colonies in its operation; and the course of events proved that the influence of the home authorities was thenceforth to be on the side of toleration in so far as America was concerned.

When Clarendon entered office, the colonial dependencies of England in the New World consisted in general of two isolated groups of settlements on the continent, with island outposts at the extreme north and south. A study of a map of the period reveals the essential weakness of the English position from the standpoint both of trade and of imperial defence. The two most important colonial events in Clarendon's ministry — the great extension of English continental territory to the south by the settlement of the Carolinas, and the acquisition of New Netherland — added enormously to the strength and unity of the Empire. By the elimination of the Dutch, Clarendon argued that not only would the northern and southern colonies be relieved of the presence of a hostile state lying between them, but the menace of a flank or rear attack by the French would be largely removed from New England by securing the important military advantages of the Hudson-Mohawk route, the Lake Champlain gateway, and the friendship of the Iroquois. Moreover, so long as Holland, which was England's most serious rival in the world's carrying trade, should remain in possession of New York, New Jersey, Pennsylvania, and Delaware, it would obviously be almost impossible to enforce the Navigation Acts, upon the observance of which, it was rightly believed at that stage, that the Empire's commercial success and power of defense almost wholly depended.

In this last respect, however, New England, although settled ostensibly by loyal Englishmen, was almost as much of a danger as was New Netherland, settled by the Empire's rivals. New England's foreign commerce, which had amounted to very little before the English Civil War, had grown rapidly with the prosperity of the West-Indian sugar colonies, and by the time of the Restoration had assumed considerable proportions, both with the other colonies and with foreign countries. But New England merchants paid almost no attention to the laws of trade.[1] In 1665, Captain Leverett, who had seized a

<hr>

[1] Hutchinson, *History*, vol. 1, pp. 174, 179.

Dutch vessel from Amsterdam trading at Boston, was strongly censured by the Massachusetts General Court, which announced that such seizures under the Navigation Acts would not be permitted "without the consent or allowance of authoritie heere established"; and the officer escaped severer punishment only by apologies and by solemnly protesting his fidelity to the local administration.[1] Two years later, and again in 1658, Rhode Island officially proclaimed free trade with the Dutch; and in 1660, Connecticut, through her governor, denied that she had any laws not permitting it.[2]

New England's flouting of imperial authority, and more particularly, the pretensions of Massachusetts to what was virtually an independent sovereignty, were becoming notorious throughout the Empire and in foreign countries. If England should suffer herself to be defied with impunity by her own subjects, the decline in her prestige could hardly fail to result in the disintegration of the Empire, both from internal revolts and from external aggression. It may be pointed out that such a result, although serious for England, would have been fatal to the colonies, which would have played the part of Red Riding Hood to the French wolf.

The colonial policy of Clarendon was probably influenced, in the main, by the above considerations in respect to North America. But, when the new government came into power at the Restoration, there were other reasons why its attention should immediately be turned to New England. We have already noted how the trampling upon private rights by Massachusetts in her aggressive policy of annexation, the dissatisfaction with her government on the part of many of her own citizens, the persecution endured by the Quakers, and the various disputes between the colonies over boundaries and other matters, had occasioned complaints, increasing in number and seriousness. Owing mainly to the extraordinary

[1] *Massachusetts Records*, vol. IV, pt. i, p. 229.

[2] *R. I. Records*, vol. I, pp. 356, 389; *New York Colonial Documents*, vol. XIV, p. 459. In the same year, the directors of the Dutch West India Company wrote to Stuyvesant that he should treat the English frigate, "which lies at New Haven and has already threatened the communication between the Manhattans and New England," as a pirate. *Ibid.*, p. 458. *Cf. Ibid.*, p. 453.

ability and persistence which the Bay Colony had shown in the "gentle art of making enemies" for the past thirty years, all of the above matters, and others, in their worst possible light, were promptly brought to the attention of the restored King and Council. Throughout the years 1660 and 1661, the ghosts of old wrongs done by Massachusetts seem constantly to have haunted the meetings of the Council, to plead their cause against that colony. The appeals of the Quakers, and the effective but temporary succor afforded them, have already been noted in an earlier chapter. Edward Godfrey, who had been forced out of his government in Maine by the Massachusetts Commissioners, filed long reports of his grievances and of "the usurpations of the Bostoners." [1] Robert Mason protested against the annexation of New Hampshire, and disregard of his rights there, as did Ferdinando Gorges, grandson of old Sir Ferdinando, in reference to his Province of Maine.[2] Captain Breedon gave a description of the political conditions in Massachusetts, emphasizing the distinction between freemen and non-freemen, the pretensions of sovereignty, and the refusal to use the oath of allegiance, and called attention to the shelter then being given to Whalley and Goffe, two of the regicide judges, who had been received with open friendliness by the colonial authorities.[3] A group of English merchants, who had invested £15,000 — the equivalent of, perhaps, $300,000 to-day — in iron-works at Lynn, claimed that, for alleged debts, their agents had been arrested, their property seized, and that they were unable to gain satisfaction in the colonial courts.[4]

A number of other petitions were, with one exception, directed against Massachusetts, and complained mainly of the illegality or disloyalty of that colony's actions. Giles Sylvester, of Shelter Island, in the exception noted, asserted that New Haven had wrongfully confiscated three thousand acres of his

---

[1] *Cal. State Pap., Col., 1661–68*, pp. 12, 18, 26.   [2] *Ibid.*, pp. 26, 22.
[3] *Ibid.*, pp. 15 f.
[4] *Ibid.*, p. 17. The *Massachusetts Records* say £13,000. The suit was brought by Josiah Winslow and Robert Keaynes, the latter being the one who was involved in the "sow case" and the La Tour episode. *Massachusetts Records*, vol. IV, pt. i, p. 219.

land, because he would not acknowledge himself to be under its government.[1]

Of more interest, however, than these petitions for the righting of individual wrongs, were the information and advice given by Samuel Maverick, who happened to be in England at the return of Charles. Maverick, as we have seen, had been living in Massachusetts some years before John Endicott or John Winthrop had thought of going there. For nearly forty years, since 1624, he had watched its development, and, as he possessed considerable ability and a fairly sound judgment, in addition to his almost unique personal knowledge of the colony's history, his opinion would naturally carry weight with the English authorities. He had steadily opposed the political and religious policy of the Massachusetts leaders, and had been one of the signers of the Child petition in 1646. In the letters which, for some years following 1660, he frequently wrote to Lord Clarendon, his complaints of the past occupy a minor position, and his plans for the reorganization of the colonies evidently either coincided with those of the minister or largely helped to form them.

His suggestions embraced the elimination of the Dutch danger by the taking of New Netherland, for which he rightly thought that a small force would suffice. In view of the religious intolerance, the political disabilities, the pronounced disloyalty, the encroachments and boundary disputes, in evidence in New England, he also advised the strengthening of the royal control. He suggested that the oath of allegiance be insisted upon; that the colonial laws be revised so as to agree as nearly as possible with those of England; that writs be issued

[1] *Cal. State Pap., Col., 1661–68*, p. 18. The *New Haven Records* are silent as to the case; but the Sylvesters were disliked by New Haven, in part because they sheltered Quakers from persecution. For that reason, and because he was said to have written a "blasphemous" letter against the New England magistrates, New Haven seized £100 belonging to Giles Sylvester until he should give satisfaction, if the charges, which were noted as hearsay, should be proved. Considering that the New Haven settlers were mere squatters without any legal rights, that Sylvester properly denied their jurisdiction over him, and that the amount, equivalent to about $2000 to-day, was illegally seized on merely hearsay evidence that Sylvester had criticized them, the case may be taken as showing the possibilities for strangers of Puritan colonial justice. *New Haven Records*, vol. II, p. 364.

in the king's name; that liberty of conscience be allowed; that the franchise be given to all freeholders, and the bounds of every patent accurately determined.[1]   As he estimated that three fourths of the people were loyal, and that the greater part of the Massachusetts non-freemen would favor the plan, he looked for no resistance; and although he suggested sending out a commission, he thought that no force would be necessary except for the capture of New Netherland.   He certainly knew the colonies well, and, in part at least, may have been right in his assumptions.   Outside of the government clique in Massachusetts there was undoubtedly a party of substantial men who would have welcomed such a settlement of matters, and the local authorities there were apparently doubtful as to how far their course of opposition to England would be acquiesced in by the country at large, should all the facts become known.

On the other hand, if the years following the Restoration marked the beginning of modern England, no less did they embrace the actual beginning of American history.   The first settlers were in no real sense Americans.   They were Englishmen, with English associations, connections, and habits of thought.   Their natures were not altered fundamentally by sailing to a land where the sun rose five hours later.   The remoteness of that land from the mother-country, and the frontier conditions which prevailed in it did, indeed, change, gradually but profoundly, the attitude of the settlers toward many matters.   But that took time, and it was only with the rise of the second generation, which knew nothing of England by personal experience; which had no close ties with the home-land; whose minds and characters, for the worse as well as for the better, were wholly the products of the frontier, and whose interests and outlook were entirely provincial, that an American, as distinct from an English, strain may be said to appear in the history of our common race. New England had been settled for approximately a generation when the Restoration occurred, and there must have been, by then, a considerable element of native-born colonials from

[1] *Clarendon Papers* (New York Historical Society), pp. 21, 27, 35 f., 43.

twenty to thirty years old. If, however, the ties which bound these younger citizens to England were looser, their education was poorer, their religious feelings weaker, and their opposition to the old theocratic policy stronger.

It is impossible, from these conflicting factors, and with only the evidence at hand, to say how nearly right was Maverick's estimate of the people's loyalty; but he was certainly wrong in believing that it would stand the test of taxes imposed from above, or of blundering and tactless officials. He was right, however, in urging that comprehensive reforms be undertaken in colonial management, and that the case was urgent in that it would become more difficult year by year. Something, indeed, required to be done, for the good of the colonies as well as of the Empire; and could it have been done wisely and tactfully, this was undoubtedly the moment to have accomplished it.

All those interested in New England could not fail to recognize, with varying emotions, that the situation had altered. The possibility that England might at last be able to exercise authority over her dependencies could bode nothing but evil to the rulers of Massachusetts, in view of their record, theological beliefs, and political aspirations. To the proprietors of Maine and New Hampshire, on the other hand, it meant the possibility of recovering their properties, which, in turn, portended unsettlement and trouble for the inhabitants of those provinces. For, although the course of Massachusetts in annexing the eastern settlements had been overbearing, illegal, and unscrupulous, the inhabitants were undoubtedly better off than they would have been under absentee proprietors, whose main interest would be in land-titles and taxes. Connecticut and New Haven, which were not possessed of any charters, and were exercising the powers of government without any warrant, could not but be anxious for the future; and Rhode Island, hoping, perhaps, for aid against her selfish and aggressive neighbors, hastened to proclaim the King within her borders.[1]

[1] *R. I. Records*, vol. i, p. 432 (October 18, 1660).

In 1661, John Winthrop the younger, then, and for fifteen years following, Governor of Connecticut,[1] was appointed as agent to go to England, in order to present his colony's address to the King and, if possible, to procure a charter.[2] He was instructed to try to secure one as nearly like that of Massachusetts as might be, though this seems to have been considered improbable of attainment. He was also to have the bounds extended southward to Delaware Bay, and eastward to Plymouth, thus cynically ignoring the rights, legal or not, of New Netherland, New Haven, and Rhode Island. This conscienceless imperialism, which the colonists would have denounced as tyranny and usurpation if indulged in by England, was oddly balanced by New England conservatism in money matters; for Connecticut's agent was instructed, in case he should be unable to acquire all of the coast to Virginia, to content himself with reaching the Hudson River, as the colony did "not judge it requisite to expend money upon a Pattent."[3]

As a matter of fact, however, an expenditure was made of about £500; and, possibly as a result of the judicious disposal of this sum among the needy courtiers about the throne, Winthrop secured a charter so liberal in its terms as to serve as the constitution of colony and state until 1818.[4] It created a corporation upon the place, provided for exactly the form of government which the colonists already enjoyed, permitted them to erect courts and make laws, and defined their bounds as extending from "Narragansett river, commonly called Narragansett Bay," to the Pacific Ocean.[5] These new limits not only included a large strip of Dutch territory and almost the whole of Rhode Island, but wiped out New Haven entirely.

The latter colony had made no effort to secure a patent since 1645, when the agent dispatched for that purpose had been drowned in the ill-fated and mysterious ship that had carried down with it, not only the political hopes, but the

[1] The law against serving two successive terms was repealed May 17, 1660. *Conn. Col. Records*, vol. 1, p. 347.

[2] *Ibid.*, pp. 367 ff., 582.   [3] *Ibid.*, pp. 580 f., 581 n.

[4] *Ibid.*, p. 369. *Cf.* A. Johnston, *Connecticut* (Boston, 1887), pp. 17 ff.

[5] *Cal. State Pap., Col., 1661–68*, pp. 87 f. (April 23, 1662).

financial fortunes, of the colonists.[1]   There had been a growing element in the colony, as in Massachusetts, which was
opposed to its theocratical government, and about the time
of the Restoration, this opposition was giving Davenport and
his followers much trouble.   To the demand of sundry non-
freemen that the franchise be extended, the New Haven
Court had replied that they could not commit "weighty civill or military trusts into the hands of either a crafty Achito-
phell or a bloody Joab," and that any one who should make
such suggestions would be considered "troublers of our peace
and disturbers of our Israell."   They asserted that to grant
a voice in the government to any but church members would
be to defeat the main end of the plantation, from "which we
cannot be perswaded to divert." [2]   This was exactly the stand
and reasoning persisted in by the Massachusetts leaders at
the same time.   Both groups stood stubbornly with their
backs toward the future, and their eyes on Judea, attempting
to block the path to individual liberty with the whole strength
of civil power and religious prejudice.   They as little understood the new day which was dawning as did the restored
Stuarts in England; and the New England theocrats and the
English monarchs were at one in their resistance to the forces
of freedom.

The disaffected element in New Haven, however, was
large and important; and when Connecticut's imperialistic
ambitions were gratified, and she obtained a charter which
gave her all her neighbor's territory, a very large proportion
of New Haven's inhabitants indicated that they preferred the
"Christless rule" of Connecticut, with its property qualification for the franchise, to that of the New Haven churches.
Throughout the whole process of absorption of the smaller
colony by its now aggrandized neighbor, both the action and
the manner of Connecticut are difficult to defend.   New
Haven, however, could not have stood alone much longer.

---

[1] *New Haven Records*, vols. I, pp. 149, 211, and II, p. 519.   The early references to
the real and phantom ships are gathered in Atwater, *New Haven*, pp. 537 *ff.*

[2] *New Haven Records*, vol. II, p. 404; *cf.* pp. 429 *ff.*

Her commercial hopes had been proved without foundation; she had unnecessarily, but seriously, offended the English Crown; her theocratic government was inflexible; and her annexation by the more democratic and progressive commonwealth was wholly an advantage, then and later.[1]

In the ill-defined bounds of the Connecticut charter lay the seeds of many a future contest; but the effect upon Rhode Island was as immediate as upon New Haven. As we have already seen, the Narragansett country had for some time been a matter of controversy between the three adjoining colonies. As Connecticut now extended to the Bay, by royal grant, Massachusetts was seemingly excluded, and the contest lay between Rhode Island's patent rights and those conferred in her neighbor's new charter. John Clarke, in England at the same time as Winthrop, immediately petitioned the King for a new charter for Rhode Island.[2] This was granted, its governmental provisions being virtually the same as those of the Connecticut patent, except for the notable clause that, as the Rhode Islanders were then holding forth the "livelie experiment that a most flourishing civell state may stand and best bee maintained . . . with a full libertie in religious concernments," therefore no person in the colony should ever be "molested, punished, disquieted, or called in question, for any differences in opinione in matters of religion," any law enacted in England notwithstanding.[3] This patent, like the Connecticut one, was so liberal, and so well drawn, that it remained the constitution of colony and state for one hundred and eighty years.[4]

While the issue of the charter was pending, Clarke and Winthrop had submitted the matter of the boundary between

[1] For the events connected with the transfer, vide New Haven Records, vol. II, pp. 513 ff.; Acts United Colonies, vol. II, pp. 308 ff., 318, 324 f.; Conn. Col. Records, vol. II, pp. 407, 415, 437, 586 ff.

[2] R. I. Records, vol. I, pp. 485 ff., 489 ff.

[3] Ibid., vol. II, pp. 4 ff.; Cal. State Pap., Col., 1661–68, pp. 148 ff.

[4] For the theory that these exceptionally liberal charters were granted as part of a policy to alienate the southern colonies from Massachusetts, vide Kaye, Colonial Administration under Clarendon, pp. 75 ff. His arguments for placing the important paper, 706, in Cal. State Pap., Col., 1661–68 under date 1666–67, instead of 1664, seem conclusive.

their two colonies to arbitration; and as a result, it had been agreed between them that the dividing line should be the Pawcatuck River, henceforth to be called the Narragansett.[1] In the Rhode Island charter, therefore, that colony's western boundary was made as agreed upon, the "clause in a late grant" to Connecticut notwithstanding.[2] Connecticut, however, which had now become even more reckless in its career of land-grabbing than Massachusetts, repudiated its agent's act, and undertook to enforce its claims to Rhode Island's richest territory.[3] Not only was Connecticut's attitude selfish and unjust, but the dispute could not fail to add another legitimate reason for the exercise of imperial control by England. As Sir Thomas Holdich points out, "It was the man with the spade,— the agriculturist,— who first found the necessity for definite boundaries"; [4] and while the fur trade or other activities of rival colonizing nations, or of separate colonies of the same nation, might give rise to disputes over frontiers, the extreme frequency and bitterness of such quarrels in New England were largely due to the type of political and economic life developed there. Without question, their adjustment demanded the intervention of the higher power of the home country.

At the time of Charles's return, Massachusetts was represented in England by John Leverett, as her agent, who immediately sent word of the complaints beginning to pour in against the colony. As a result, the General Court dispatched addresses both to the King and to Parliament, and appointed Richard Saltonstall and Henry Ashurst to assist Leverett in the controversy now imminent.[5] In the letter to Charles, the Court prayed that monarch, now "King over your British Israel, to cast a favorable eye upon your poore Mephibbosheth"; and defended themselves against sundry charges, par-

---

[1] Agreement in *R. I. Records*, vol. I, p. 518; *Cal. State Pap., Col., 1661–68*, pp. 148 ff.

[2] *R. I. Records*, vol. II, pp. 18 ff.

[3] *Conn. Col. Records*, vol. I, pp. 407, 435; Bowen, *Boundary Disputes*, 33 ff.

[4] *Political Frontiers and Boundary Making* (London, 1916), p. 10.

[5] *Massachusetts Records*, vol. IV, pt. i, pp. 449 ff.

ticularly those concerning the killing of the Quakers. "Such was theire daingerous, impetuous and desperat turbulency," the writers affirmed, that the magistrates had perforce had "to keepe the passage with the point of the sword held towards them"; and the Court unblushingly added that, had the Quakers not been restrained, "there was too much cause to feare that wee ourselves must quickly have died." [1]

In the private instructions to the colony's agents, they were ordered to gain the interest of as many in Parliament and near the King as possible, to secure the renewal of the charter, to see that no superior power should be imposed, or appeals admitted, and even, if possible, to have the colony free from the English customs duties. If called upon to answer any charges embarrassing to the colony, they were instructed to plead lack of authority. [2] The agents seem, however, to have done nothing in England to aid the colony; and Leverett's remark that, if forced to admit appeals to the home country, the colonists would deliver New England to the Spaniards, although stupid enough, could hardly add to the government's idea of the colonists' loyalty or discretion. [3]

Although the King's answer to the address was conciliatory, the Massachusetts Court, upon its receipt, appointed a committee to determine what, in its opinion, were the legal relations between the colony and England. Their report, which we have already discussed in the preceding chapter, considered Massachusetts to be virtually an independent sovereign state, with the right to defend itself by force of arms against any "annoyance." [4] The following spring, a thousand acres of land were granted to the Artillery Company of Middlesex, orders were issued for the better accommodation of the troopers of Essex, and work was ordered rushed in order to complete the fortifications on Castle Island. [5]

Meanwhile, "considering the weight of theire occasions in

---

[1] *Massachusetts Records*, vol. IV, pt. i, p. 451.   [2] *Ibid.*, pp. 455 f.

[3] Maverick, in *Clarendon Papers*, p. 30.

[4] *Massachusetts Records*, vol. IV, pt. i, p. 25; *cf.* Hutchinson, *History*, vol. I, pp. 230 f.

[5] *Massachusetts Records*, vol. IV, pt. i, pp. 45, 44, 42 f.

England," the Court appointed Simon Bradstreet and the Reverend John Norton to present a second address to the King, and to "indeavor to take off all scandal and objections" against the colony.[1] Although their work in England was bitterly denounced as a failure, by some of the oligarchy, they seem, in reality, to have done fairly well, and the letter which the King next dispatched to the General Court was mild in tone and required nothing that did not make for the greater liberty of the individual colonist. After expressing himself as well pleased with the colony's agents, the monarch confirmed the charter, and granted pardon to all who had infringed its terms in the past, as well as to any in the colony who had committed offenses against him in the late Civil War. Although he partially withdrew his protection from the Quakers, he required that any person wishing to worship according to the Book of Common Prayer be allowed to do so, and that persons of good and honest lives be admitted to the Communion, and their children to baptism. The franchise was to be granted to all those of competent estate, orthodox in religion, and not vicious in their lives. He also required that the oath of allegiance be taken, and that justice be administered in his name.[2]

The results of an increase in religious liberty were as much dreaded by the leaders and their followers in the theocracy as was any limitation placed by England upon those powers which they had endeavored to make absolute. At a meeting of the General Court in October, at which the letter was read, the atrociously brutal law against the Quakers was immediately put in force again, and the only compliances with the King's requirements were the order that legal processes should run in his name, and the issuing of directions that his letter be published. Other action toward complying with its terms was postponed until the next meeting of the Court. At that meeting, seven months later, the letter was merely referred to

<hr>

[1] *Massachusetts Records*, vol. iv, pt. i, p. 37.
[2] *Cal. State Pap., Col., 1661–68*, pp. 93 *f*.

a committee, which was to report again at the next meeting, five months later still; at which, again, nothing was done. It was the old policy, advised by the clergy nearly thirty years earlier, of "avoid or protract," of ignoring and obstructing. However such a policy might fit an emergency under peculiar conditions, it obviously could not form the basis of permanent relations between organic parts of an empire.[1]

Trouble also arose for the colony from another direction. It was impossible, in ordinary justice, that England should ignore the complaints of the heirs of the original Gorges and Mason regarding the illegal encroachments of Massachusetts upon the lands claimed by them. Mason's petition was referred to a committee of seven. Of these Mason was one, although obviously the English government should not have permitted him to be at once plaintiff and judge. But, aside from irrelevant strictures upon the policy of Massachusetts, the committee made a reasonable report, finding that Mason had inherited a good title from his grandfather, and that for many years Massachusetts had publicly recognized the line three miles north of the Merrimac as her true boundary.[2]

Meanwhile, Gorges, who had petitioned the King in April, 1661, for possession of his province, did not wait for the process of law, but appointed commissioners to go to Maine, proclaim the King, collect the quit-rents, and establish a government, notifying Massachusetts of their actions.[3] That colony promptly ordered that all the inhabitants should yield obedience only to herself and sent commissioners into the province with instructions to suppress any disobedience by the use of force, as they should see fit.[4] Under this conflict of authorities,

[1] *Massachusetts Records*, vol. IV, pt. i, pp. 58 f., 74.

[2] The report is in Belknap (*History of New Hampshire*, vol. I, pp. 300 f.), who reprinted it from a copy in the Recorder's office of Rockingham County. Doyle states that there is no copy among the State Papers. *Puritan Colonies*, vol. II, p. 139 n. That given in *Cal. State Pap., Col., 1661-68*, p. 75, however, while differing in a few minor particulars from that given by Belknap, is evidently the same document. For references to the "bound-house," *cf. Massachusetts Records*, vol. I, p. 167; *New Hampshire Provincial Papers*, vol. I, pp. 146, 249, 330; *Clarendon Papers*, p. 71; J. Dow, *History of Town of Hampton*, vol. I, pp. 7 f.

[3] *Cal. State Pap., Col., 1661-68*, pp. 22, 63 f.

[4] *Massachusetts Records*, vol. IV, pt. i, pp. 70, 76 f.

the affairs of Maine, the inhabitants of which province were scattered and somewhat unruly, were bound to drift into anarchy. Daniel Gookin, of Boston, wrote a conciliatory letter to Gorges, explaining the conditions from the standpoint of the good of the people; but, a year later, the King, upon a report of the technical legal aspects of the case, and apparently taking into consideration the losses of Gorges's royalist grandfather, ordered the inhabitants to submit to Gorges, or to give reasons to the contrary without delay.[1]

The conditions in New England, in 1663, thus clearly necessitated the sending out of a Royal Commission. The legal disputes between Massachusetts and the English heirs of Gorges and Mason could not fairly be left to the decision of Massachusetts courts. Nor was the question one of technical legal title alone; for, as the committee reporting on the Mason claims had themselves pointed out, "publique interest and goverment" were "much intermixt and concerned with the private interest of the peticioners."[2] Moreover, for nearly thirty years, not only had boundary disputes between all the New England colonies been growing steadily more complicated and serious, but the colonies had proved themselves incapable, in practically every case, of settling them permanently and amicably. The contests could evidently be determined, in the absence of any superior power, only by the use of force by the claimants; and with the consistent attitude of Massachusetts and the now rapidly increasing aggressiveness of Connecticut, peace was seriously imperiled, and the fate of the smaller colonies practically sealed. Rhode Island, at once the most loyal and the most devoted to liberty of thought and action, was already in imminent danger of annihilation. In the disputed Narragansett country, the Atherton Company claimed rights which could not be justly adjudicated by any of the three colonies pretending jurisdiction, and prayed the King for intervention.[3]

---

[1] *Cal. State Pap., Col., 1661–68*, pp. 145, 214.
[2] Belknap, *New Hampshire*, vol. I, p. 301.
[3] *Cal. State Pap., Col., 1661–68*, pp. 143 f.

The accounts of practically every observer agreed as to the disloyalty of Massachusetts and her assumption of sovereignty, which were obviously confirmed by her official acts. In addition, the attitude of all the colonies to the English leaders during the Revolution, the neglect of all, except Rhode Island, promptly to proclaim the King, their protection of the regicide judges, and the refusal to observe the Navigation Acts, raised suspicions against them all. There was, besides, the religious discrimination by Massachusetts, depriving her citizens of rights which they would otherwise have enjoyed as Englishmen, and the cases of alleged injustice in colonial courts affecting English citizens with property rights in the colonies. In the absence of a royal governor, or any other means by which the home government could secure first-hand information, there was no course to follow except to appoint a Commission to go out and secure it, if the exceedingly complicated situation was to be handled intelligently. The government had shown itself more than willing to treat with the colonies through their agents; but Massachusetts purposely denied to them any authority, so as to obstruct and delay any action — an outworn policy which had now become transparently clear to the home government.

The attitude of Massachusetts was, in fact, the crux of the whole problem. The theocratical party there had developed a theory,— based apparently upon an extension of the church-covenant idea through the plantation covenant,— that the charter itself was a covenant which reserved no rights to the king and imperial government save those specifically mentioned. From this she deduced that her obligation to the Empire was so tenuous as to be virtually non-existent.[1] However satisfactorily to themselves the leaders and their followers might spin such theories, they did not agree with either the economic, political, or legal facts. At this stage, the economic welfare of the New England colonies was, of necessity, bound up with that of the Empire, from the trade of which they would be excluded if they ceased to be parts of it. Politically, they

[1] Cf. Hutchinson, *History*, vol. 1, pp. 230 ff.

had to be considered as either in it or out of it, and, obviously, from the standpoint of abstract justice as well as of practical administration, they could not consider themselves as now one and now the other, according to their local interests at a given moment.

Nor could it be conceded that, by the granting of the charters, England had relinquished all rights of control, or the power to determine whether or not their terms were being complied with. That would have opened the way to the grossest misuse of power by any of the local administrations thus created, and would have been against public policy. Moreover, in practically every charter, including that of Massachusetts, the clause had appeared that no laws should be passed repugnant to those of England. Massachusetts had already passed many such, carrying with them, in some cases, the penalty of capital punishment. The clause obviously implied that there must be an authority somewhere, which could decide whether the colonial laws were repugnant or not; and it could hardly be claimed that the colonial courts which passed them were intended to be the sole judges of their conformity.[1] This would have meant that not only the inhabitants of any chartered colony, but the citizens of all the rest of the Empire having relations with it, directly or as potential emigrants, would be absolutely at the mercy of the local government, no matter what that government might do, or however criminally it might disregard the rights that the charters had specifically safeguarded. It must not be lost to sight that the contemporary merchant in England or the West Indies had as legitimate a right to require that England should protect his legal interests in Massachusetts or Connecticut as any citizen of the United States to-day has to expect that his rights will be assured to him in New Mexico or Alaska. It must also be recalled that America was the heritage of the English people, much as our West was the heritage of our citizens; and the Englishman, both for himself and for his

[1] *Cf.* E. B. Russell, *Review of American Colonial Legislation by the King in Council* (Columbia University, 1915), pp. 17 *ff.*

children, had as legitimate an interest in the nature of the government erected in any part of the Empire as we have in that set up in any part of our territorial domains. There was little more reason why a group of settlers should preëmpt Massachusetts, pass laws repugnant to those of England, and hang any Englishman whose political or religious views were obnoxious to them, than there would be for the stockholders and officers of a business corporation in Alaska, who might have been granted land and some minor police powers, to do the same thing to-day.

If the contentions of Massachusetts were to be allowed,— that she might pass any laws she chose and be sole judge of them; that she might trample upon the colonial rights of Englishmen at home, quarrel with her neighbors, determine her own bounds, be the sole interpreter of the terms of her charter, and sole judge of whether they had been complied with; deny that the king's writ passed beyond England, or that the home country had any right to pass laws affecting the colonies even in their intercolonial and imperial relations,— then, it must be confessed, there was no empire. There was merely an imperial anarchy of conflicting local interests and warring elements, whose only common bond was their claim that England should protect them against the aggression of foreign and land-hungry powers.

If the rule of England in the seventeenth century had become tyrannical and oppressive to the extent that revolution had become justifiable, and if the colonies had become strong enough, in the state of the world as it then was, to stand alone, nothing could be said against their openly throwing off the imperial yoke. The full development of the forces already at work was, a century later, to bring about that very consummation, the discussion of which belongs to a later period. That, however, was not the case as yet, and the position which Massachusetts assumed was untenable and could eventually lead only to the loss of her charter, and not to independence. Nor could she profess loyalty in the most obsequious terms, claim all the military and commercial advantages of being a part of the Empire, and, at the same time, act as an independent state. It was a policy which, however unjustifiable, might be successful, perhaps, when essayed by her as the most powerful member in a New England confederacy. It could be neither, when the part was attempted to be played by that same colony in its rôle of an unimportant dependency in a great empire.

Nor had individual liberty anything to gain in the contest. The only possible outcome would be the loss of the charter, with all the possibilities involved in the then immediate dependence upon a Stuart monarch. At this stage, the real struggle for freedom, intellectual and political, was against the theocracy. If its leaders lost the game they were playing, as was practically inevitable, then the liberties of the colony, as embodied in the charter and related to England, would also be lost. If, on the other hand, they should by any chance win against the Crown, then their own power would be greatly strengthened and the struggle against them increased in difficulty. In either event, therefore, the liberal element in the colony had everything to fear from the policy pursued by the leaders. That policy, however, from the standpoint of the latter, found its justification in the fact that the suggested alterations in the franchise, and other religious matters, would end the power of the theocracy, which would surely go down before liberty of opinion. As the leaders had already hesitated at nothing, not even the blood of their victims, to maintain their theory of the church-state, so now they preferred to risk the practically certain loss of the charter and all its civil privileges, rather than yield to the claim of individual freedom. Fortunately, in spite of an apparent temporary success, they were to lose, and England win; and, owing to the people of England itself, the real cause of liberty was eventually to gain.

The chaotic state of New England had engaged the attention of the Council for Plantations and the Privy Council almost from the moment of the Restoration; while the sending of Commissioners to adjust differences, and to report on

conditions, had been under consideration since early in 1662.[1]
Two years later, action regarding the matters which had
been considered as of prime importance was taken at last,
and a commission was actually sent to New England; and
New Netherland, with little trouble, was wrested from the
Dutch. The two objects — of which the latter was considered the more important—were closely connected, and the
most influential member of the Commission, Colonel Richard Nicolls, was appointed Governor of the new province of
New York. Of the other three Commissioners, Samuel Maverick was undoubtedly useful, from his great knowledge of
Massachusetts affairs, although otherwise unfitted, from his
strong partisanship; but neither Sir Robert Carr nor George
Cartwright possessed the qualifications to ensure successful results, although the latter was able and conscientious in his
work.[2]

Two series of instructions were issued to the Commissioners
for their guidance, the one public and the other confidential,
as was also the custom of Massachusetts in sending agents
to England. In the first, it was ordered that the Commission
should consider the best means for reducing the Dutch, investigate the condition of the Indians and of public education,
and see that the Navigation Acts were observed, and that,
according to the laws of England, no one was debarred from
the free exercise of his religion. In the confidential instructions, these points were repeated with additional details, the
Commissioners being further required to examine the various
charters and the laws passed; to have, if possible, a General
Assembly elected in Massachusetts, in which the members
would be favorably inclined toward the King, and to have an
acceptable governor and commander of the militia appointed

---

[1] *Cal. State Pap., Col., 1661–68*, pp. 22, 24 *f.*, 30, 32, 110, 128; *Acts Privy Council, Colonial, 1613–80*, pp. 308, 338; *Clarendon Papers*, p. 43. *Cf.* Kaye, *English Colonial Administration under Clarendon*, pp. 75 *ff.*

[2] Professor Osgood considered that, "taken as a whole, the appointments were as wise as under the circumstances could reasonably be expected." *American Colonies*, vol. III, p. 172. For the opposition to Maverick's appointment, *vide Clarendon Papers*, pp. 48 *ff.*

or elected. They were to try to secure the coöperation of the other four colonies, and, in both sets of orders, were instructed to avoid giving offense.[1] The King also wrote a conciliatory letter to each of the colonies, in which he spoke of the calumnies against them, the difficulty of settling boundary disputes among themselves, and other matters requiring investigation and settlement.[2] In the commissions issued to Nicolls and the others, they were empowered to hear complaints and appeals, and to take measures for settling the peace of the country.[3]

In Massachusetts the news of the sending of the Commissioners created considerable alarm, and the General Court passed orders that none of their force of under-officers or soldiers should be allowed to land, except unarmed and in small numbers. The fort on Castle Island was ordered to be manned and prepared, sentries posted, and the charter hidden.[4]

In July, the Commissioners arrived at Boston, and presented their commissions and the King's letter to the Court, together with that part of their instructions which related to raising a force against the Dutch. The request was complied with, and the Court also hastily passed a new election law, which ostensibly made the franchise independent of a religious test, but which in practice could have no such effect. According to the new law, all church members, regardless of property qualifications, were given the franchise, as before, but non-church members were required to be freeholders and householders, to present certificates signed by ministers that they were orthodox in belief and not vicious in their lives, to be elected as freemen by the General Court, and to possess an estate which paid a tax of ten shillings in a single levy. There were other requirements, also; but the fact that not one man in a hundred was said to have the property qualification required only from non-church members showed the farcical nature of the law. The enactment has sometimes been called

[1] *Cal. State Pap., Col., 1661–68*, pp. 200 ff.; *N. Y. Col. Docts.*, vol. III, pp. 51 f.
[2] *Ibid.*, pp. 61 ff. [3] *Ibid.*, pp. 64 f.
[4] *Massachusetts Records*, vol. IV, pt. ii, pp. 101, 102, 110.

"shrewd"; but, in reality, it deceived no one, least of all the Commissioners, and its obvious disingenuousness served only to prejudice the case of the colony still further. Yet, in writing to the King, the colonial government stated that, in passing this law, they had applied themselves "to the utmost to sattisfy" him in "so farr as doth consist with conscience of our duty towards God, and the just liberties and priviledges" of their patent.[1]

Nor was the character of the rest of the petition, or of the letters which they wrote, asking aid, to Boyle, the head of the Society for Propagating the Gospel, and to Lord Clarendon, of a sort likely to improve the opinion held regarding the colony. It was obviously impossible to comply with their request to withdraw the Commission. In a just and temperate reply, the King pointed out that investigation by such a body had been the only method left to the English government to inform itself as to conditions in the colonies. Nor did Boyle take any different view of the matter; and Clarendon wrote of the petition: "I am so much a friend to your colony, that if it had been communicated to nobody but myself, I should have disswaded the presenting the same to his Majesty"; and pointed out the impossible character of the complaints and demands.[2]

The double nature of the Commissioners' duties now served to interrupt their work in Massachusetts; and until the beginning of the following year, they were occupied at New Amsterdam, and on the Delaware, in settling matters in the conquered Dutch colony — among others, the adjustment of its boundary with Connecticut. The case of the boundary between that colony and Rhode Island also came up; and although the final disposition was left for the home government, it was settled, in so far as the colonies were concerned, by erecting the disputed territory into a separate province, to be known as the King's Province. The jurisdiction was given to

[1] *Massachusetts Records*, vol. IV, pt. ii, pp. 118, 205, 130. *Cf.* McKinley, *Suffrage Franchise*, pp. 324 ff.; *Clarendon Papers*, pp. 83 ff.
[2] *Cal. State Pap., Col., 1661–68*, p. 282; Hutchinson, *History*, vol. I, pp. 464 f.

Rhode Island, while the claims of Massachusetts and the Atherton Land Company were properly declared invalid.[1]

Throughout their dealings with Connecticut, Rhode Island, and Plymouth, the Commissioners had met with little or no opposition; and it was only upon their reassembling at Boston, about the first of May, 1665, that the real struggle began.[2] Endicott had recently died, and Bellingham had been elected governor. The negotiations between the new government and the Commissioners, however, were entered upon with some bad feeling upon both sides. The Commissioners had previously asked that all the inhabitants be summoned to attend the Court, in order that the King's views might be made known to them directly; but this somewhat impossible plan had been discouraged, if not secretly hindered, by the colonial government, and many false statements regarding the Commission had also been circulated, tending to throw discredit upon them — all of which they naturally resented.[3]

The Commissioners now made known all of their public instructions, and the Court made answer to their various requests and accusations. In regard to some of the minor matters, such as public education, there was no difficulty; but in regard to the more important ones, except issuing writs in the King's name, the colony virtually had no case. The new oath of allegiance, which the Court had had drawn up, had been purposely vitiated by the insertion of a clause referring to the charter, and can be considered only as an attempt to deceive the Commissioners and the home government, which it failed to do. As to ecclesiastical matters, the Court stated merely that they followed "the word of the Lord," which, as they denied any interpretation of that word except their own, meant that they followed their own opinions, and refused to allow any one else to have any. Their statement, in a later paper, that "the authority here have not imposed upon church or people any one particular forme or order, for the restreijning

---

[1] *Massachusetts Records*, vol. IV, pt. ii, pp. 175 ff.; *Clarendon Papers*, pp. 90 ff.; *Cal. State Pap., Col. 1661–68*, pp. 202, 286.

[2] *Massachusetts Records*, vol. IV, pt. ii, pp. 177.   [3] *Ibid.*, pp. 173, 179–184.

or limiting them in the exercise of their devotions towards God," and their reference to "the great freedome" in religious matters, is startling in its distortion of the truth, in view of the laws then on their statute-books, and of their consistent course of persecution, from the Brownes in 1628 to the last Quaker hung in 1660. In response to another request of the English government, at this very time, they flatly denied permission to any law-abiding citizen to use his prayer-book, on the ground that "it will disturbe our peace in our present enjoyments." Referring to the Navigation Acts, they could make no better defense than to say that they were not conscious that they had "greatly violated the same," and that any laws apparently against them had been repealed.[1]

It is needless to follow the details of the controversy, which culminated in the struggle over the question of appeals. These had already been heard in Rhode Island by the Commissioners, under the authority of somewhat conflicting clauses in their instructions and commissions; and it was now undertaken to hear two in Boston. One of them concerned an individual, who seems to have been of a worthless sort, and the other, a violation of the Navigation Act. The General Court refused to allow the proceedings, claimed a breach of the charter, and officially warned all citizens not to attend the hearings, which were never held, as the Commissioners had no force to uphold their authority, even had they cared to employ it.[2] Soon after this, the Commission left Boston, both the colony and the King's officers making long reports to the government in England.[3]

The whole contest had now obviously reached the fundamental point of sovereignty, which was clearly stated in a letter to Massachusetts, a few weeks later, from Carr, Cartwright, and Maverick, who were then in New Hampshire. "The King did not grant away his Soveraigntie over you,"

---

[1] *Massachusetts Records*, vol. IV, pt. ii, pp. 177 *ff.*, 200 *f.*, 202 *ff.*, 220 *f.*

[2] *Ibid.*, pp. 209 *ff.*, 216 *ff.*

[3] *Cal. State Pap., Col., 1661–68*, pp. 341 *ff.*; *Massachusetts Records*, vol. IV, pt. ii, pp. 274 *ff.*

they wrote, "when he made you a Corporation. When His Majesty gave you power to make wholesome laws and to administer Justice by them, he parted not with his right of judging whether those laws were wholesom or whether justice was administered accordingly or no. When His Majesty gave you authority over such of his subjects as lived within the limits of your jurisdiction, he made them not your subjects nor you their supream authority." Unpalatable as these words may have been to the Massachusetts Court, there can be no doubt that they expressed the truth, as did also the Commissioners' warning that "striveing to grasp too much, may make you hold but a little." The future was clearly fore-shadowed. "'T is possible that the Charter which you so much idolize may be forfeited," the Commissioners added, "until you have cleared yourselves of those many injustices, oppressions, violences, and bloud for which you are complained against, to which complaints you have refused to answer." [1] There was, indeed, to be no other course. If Massachusetts under her charter should persist in considering herself superior to the power which had granted it, that power would have no option but to recognize her complete independence or to annul the charter.

In New Hampshire, the acts of the three Commissioners were ill-judged and but little likely to reflect credit upon the King, or to secure the adherence of the people, while Massachusetts by prompt and forceful measures asserted her claims in the face of the royal agents. [2] In Maine, the latter attempted to organize a temporary government, pending the settlement of the dispute between Massachusetts and Gorges, and they likewise endeavored, even more unsuccessfully, to set up administrative machinery in the territory east of Pemaquid, which had been granted to the Duke of York. Within less than three years, Massachusetts, assisted by the desire of the

---

[1] *N. Y. Col. Docts.*, vol. III, p. 99.

[2] *Massachusetts Records*, vol. IV, pt. ii, pp. 265 *ff.*; *New Hampshire Provincial Papers*, vol. I, pp. 270 *ff.*; *N. Y. Col. Docts.*, vol. III, pp. 99 *ff.*; *Clarendon Papers*, pp. 72 *ff.*; *Cal. State Pap., Col., 1661–68*, pp. 310 *f.*, 314.

inhabitants for a settled government, had once more taken the province under her jurisdiction, although not without local opposition.[1]

In what had been considered their most important work, the reduction of the Dutch and the establishment of the English authority at New York, the Commissioners had been entirely successful, as they had been also in their relations with the three southern colonies in New England; and the settlement of the dispute between Massachusetts, Connecticut, Rhode Island, and the Atherton Company was of great benefit to the colonies. In the matter of Massachusetts, however, they had completely failed. Three of them advised taking away the charter, while Maverick made several suggestions, including the prohibiting of trade with the recalcitrant colony, as did Nicolls also.[2]

In 1666, the King sent a circular letter to the various colonies, expressing satisfaction with all except Massachusetts, whose claim of independent sovereignty, he noted, was "a matter of such high consequence as every man discerns where it must end"; and he commanded the colony to send four or five agents to England, including Bellingham and Hathorne, to answer the charges against her.[3] This the Court flatly refused to do, and so notified the King, though they sent him their prayers for his eternal happiness.[4] Their refusal, however, by no means met with unanimous approval among the influential elements in the colony. A petition was presented to the Court, signed by a hundred and seventy-one individuals, including such names as Winslow, Brattle, Gerrish, Hale, Coffin, Perkins, Hubbard, and others of note in Boston, Salem, Newbury, and Ipswich, while most of the people of Hingham were said to have signed also, although their deputy refused to deliver their

---

[1] *N. Y. Col. Docts.*, vol. III, p. 101; *Cal. State Pap., Col., 1661–68*, pp. 191 *f.*, 348, 569; *Massachusetts Records*, vol. IV, pt. ii, pp. 370 *f.*, 400 *f.*

[2] *N. Y. Col. Docts.*, vol. III, p. 102; *Clarendon Papers*, p. 70; *Cal. State Pap., Col., 1661–68*, p. 416.

[3] *Cal. State Pap., Col., 1661–68*, pp. 372 *f.*

[4] *Massachusetts Records*, vol. IV, pt. ii, p. 317.

petition.[1] The signers pleaded that nothing further be done justly to offend the home government, and that the agents asked for be sent. They pointed out that "the doubtful interpretation of the words of a patent, which there can be no reason should ever be construed to the divesting of a sovereign prince of his royall power over his naturall subjects and liege people, is too frail a foundation to build such a transcendent immunity and privilege upon." [2]

But those attempting to maintain the power of the theocracy would not be turned from their course, though by it they made the eventual loss of the charter both necessary and certain. Owing to the fact that England was now at war with both Holland and France, neither time nor thought could be given to a rebellious colony, and Massachusetts was to be allowed to go her way for another decade. Her own rulers, however, had definitely determined what her fate should be when the authorities in England should once more be free to act. In a little more than that period, she was to find herself, without a charter and without a friend, defenseless before the last of the Stuarts; and it was only the final revolt of the people of England against that dynasty which was to save her from the full effects of the policy of her theocracy, and to secure to all her citizens the same measure of political equality that was enjoyed by their neighbors.

[1] *Clarendon Papers*, pp. 127, 132 *ff.*; *Massachusetts Records*, vol. IV, pt. ii, pp. 317 *f.*; *Mass. Hist. Soc. Proceedings*, Series II, vol. VI, pp. 469 *ff.*

[2] *Clarendon Papers*, p. 133.

CHAPTER XIV

THE INEVITABLE CONFLICT

DURING the quarter of a century preceding 1675, the growth of the New England colonies, both in numbers and resources, had been marked. Their refusal, on the one hand, to observe such of the imperial laws as might in any way hamper their commerce, and, on the other, the opportunities offered by the growth of the Empire, under those laws, had resulted in an enormous expansion, comparatively, in the colonies' inter-colonial and foreign trade. With no Indian war of any magnitude for a generation, and with ample areas of free land upon which to expand, the frontier extended rapidly, and the population doubled. At the opening of the inter-racial conflict which is the subject of this chapter, the settlers probably numbered about fifty-two thousand, of whom approximately thirty-seven thousand were located in the seaboard colonies from Maine to Plymouth, three thousand in Rhode Island, and twelve thousand in Connecticut.[1] The numbers of the Indians can be estimated with even less certainty than those of the whites; but it is probable that the colonists outnumbered them by at least four to one.[2] The Narragansetts, who were

[1] There are no exact figures. The estimate in *Century of Population Growth*, pp. 4 ff., is about 54,000. Dexter, *Estimates of Population in American Colonies*, gives about the same (pp. 26 ff.). Palfrey estimates from 40,000 to 45,000 in 1665 (*History*, vol. III, pp. 35 ff.). If we accept the usual military ratio of one military effective to five persons, a contemporary estimate in 1675 by [William?] Harris gives 44,000, which would be increased by the fact that Massachusetts insisted upon carrying a smaller proportion of the military burden than the other colonies. *Cal. State Pap., Col., 1675-76*, p. 220. L. K. Mathews's estimate of 120,000, in her generally accurate *Expansion of New England* (p. 56), may be taken from *Cal. State Pap., Col., 1675-76*, p. 362, where that greatly exaggerated figure is given, but as a query, and is disproved by the additional statistics of 13,000 families and 16,000 effectives given in the same statement. Osgood adopts the figure of 80,000 (*American Colonies*, vol. I, p. 543).

[2] Palfrey's suggestion of about equal numbers for the two races seems to have little foundation. *History*, vol. III, p. 167. On the other hand, Osgood's estimate of only 10,500 (*American Colonies*, vol. I, p. 543) seems a little low.

by far the most numerous, as well as the most powerful, may have counted five thousand individuals in all.[1]

The geographical relations of the two races had been almost as greatly altered, in a generation, as had their numerical proportions. At the time of the Pequot war, in 1637, at least four fifths of the entire white population formed a compact mass along the eastern shore of the present state of Massachusetts. The scattered settlements of Maine and New Hampshire, the handful of people about Narragansett Bay, and the beginnings of the River Towns in Connecticut, were but isolated outposts in what was otherwise an unbroken wilderness, peopled only by the savages. The whites were thus hemmed in on every side except the ocean.[2] By 1675, the situation in southern New England had been completely reversed. The settled area, which by that year extended westward from the sea one third of the way across Massachusetts, was continued from Cape Cod along the Sound and up the Connecticut River, and the western Massachusetts towns were scattered up the valley of the latter as far as Northfield. It was now the Indian who found himself, not simply far outnumbered, but entirely surrounded, by his white neighbors. It was only in the northeastern settlements, where the English population was much sparser, and where the short rivers and broken uplands offered no attractions to tempt the settlers from the coast, that the earlier conditions still prevailed, and the savages as yet had free range.

In the Puritan colonies, the practical identity of church and town, and the whole social, religious, and political life of the people precluded any wide dispersal of individual settlers in the wilderness. Even when individuals wished to go off by themselves, they were, as a rule, not allowed to do so, and Plymouth was not the only colony to take drastic measures to discipline such as preferred "liveing lonely and in a heathenish way from good societie."[3] The unit of the southern New

---

[1] Hodge, *Handbook*, vol. II, p. 29.

[2] The maps in Mathews' *Expansion of New England* are of great value in studying the movement of the frontier.

[3] *Plymouth Records*, vol. v, p. 169.

England frontier was not the solitary hunter or trapper, not even the family of the pioneer farmer, but the town. When a bit of the wilderness was cleared, it was to plant therein, not an isolated cabin, but the homes of an organized community, fully equipped with a church and town government, destined, almost at once, to be a new centre of civilization alien to the savage, permanent, irremovable, expanding. When a French trader or trapper plunged into the forest, and the green leaves closed behind him, it was to mingle with the life of the natives, which, in its main aspects, flowed on unaltered by his presence. When, on the other hand, Englishmen cleared their fields, built a town and a church, and by virtue of their title-deeds claimed undivided ownership of their newly acquired square miles of land, it was as if they had planted a great rock in the stream of savage life, which must thereafter flow around this new obstruction. As the English frontier crept ever farther and farther inland, from the shores of ocean and Sound, and up the valleys of such streams as the Merrimac, Thames, or Connecticut, and town succeeded town, it was as if, adding stone to stone, great dykes were being built, which more and more dammed up the waters of native life. It was almost inevitable that a point would be reached when these imprisoned waters would burst forth, and possibly carry away all New England in their flood.

The land-hunger of the whites, however, was insatiable. Almost any trouble with the natives became a sufficient excuse for an extorted cession of territory, either immediate or deferred. From the very beginning, the English had recognized an Indian title to the country, as distinct from the rights conveyed by the king in his patents. Indeed, in view of the use to which the settlers wished to put the lands, and the basis upon which they necessarily lived in relation to the native occupants, they could not well do otherwise, and peaceful possession was cheaply secured at the expense of a few coats or hoes. But, as we saw in an earlier chapter, the Indian theory of ownership was entirely different from that of the whites; and although the English, for the most part, observed the legal forms of their own race, the parchments which the savage signed with his mark were as ethically invalid as a child's sale of his inheritance for a stick of candy. Not only, in the beginning, had the natives failed to understand the nature of the transaction itself, but in their utter ignorance of Europe, and of what was bound to ensue from the steady stream of emigration thence, they could not foresee — what was reasonably clear to the colonists — that the result of their having welcomed the stranger would eventually be their own annihilation or completely altered status.

Whatever may be thought of the abstract justice of the earlier purchases, as the whites increased in numbers and comparative power, and as their first fears of the savages, and the desire to convert them, gave place to dislike, contempt, spiritual indifference, and self-confidence, their dealings with them sank to a lower ethical plane. It took but a few years for the methods of land-acquisition to become greatly modified. It was no longer considered necessary to treat with the Indian as an equal, whose just title could be acquired only for a valuable consideration. The theory was formulated that the native could be punished for a breach of the Englishman's laws, and that the fine or damage imposed might take the form of a cession of land. Troubles with the savages, on a larger scale, resulted in making use of the title by conquest, by which the larger part of Connecticut was acquired. Later, in the case of the Narragansetts, as we have already seen, overdue tribute, of questionable validity, was used by a speculative land company as a basis for advancing money on mortgage, by means of which it was hoped to obtain the rich territorial possessions of that entire tribe. All the colonies, indeed, in order to protect the Indians from the commoner forms of fraud, and themselves from the dangerous results of disputes, had made it illegal for individuals to bargain for land; and the laws requiring the general courts to pass upon all land-dealings were wise and just, and, undoubtedly, prevented much petty trickery and mischief. It is needless to point out, however, the subtle temptation for the colonies to pick a quarrel with the natives, to interfere with their internal affairs, or to conduct some little military expedition, when the result was likely to be the acquisition of desirable lands by a mere show of force.

As the whites encroached more and more upon the Indians, the lands of the latter gradually came to be looked upon as reservations, upon which their native owners were allowed to live until a convenient opportunity, or the growing needs of the settlers, might bring about a farther advance.   Moreover, as the Indian lands dwindled in extent, and the whites rapidly increased numerically, in proportion to the natives, the settlers adopted an attitude of superiority and authority over the native tribes.   This really amounted to establishing a protectorate over them, and relegated them to the rank of dependent peoples shorn of all sovereign power.   It was a natural evolution in the relations between the two races, but was no more acceptable to the Indians for that reason.   Nor were the Puritans, who were by nature harsh and overbearing, and who failed to display even the ordinary good manners of the time in their dealings with the Dutch, likely to exhibit any great amount of tact or courtesy in those which they had with the despised heathen and "children of the devil."   Personal pride and a strict observance of etiquette were marked characteristics of the savages, and chiefs and sachems could not fail to be stung to the quick when they were summoned, with more and more frequency, and less and less courtesy, to travel long distances and answer to complaints before the courts of Plymouth or Massachusetts, with but little regard for their dignity or standing among their own people.

Not seldom, moreover, they knew that such a demand was but the prelude to extending English authority, and sending them home shorn of possessions and respect.   To cite, as an example, a case somewhat closely connected with the events of this chapter, in 1671, as a sequel to a rumored rising of the Indians in Plymouth Colony, the Squaw Sachem Awashunks was summoned to appear; and having done so voluntarily, she was required to submit "the disposall of her lands to the authoritie" of the colony, and was forced to engage herself to pay £50, to recompense the English for their trouble in the matter. As it was impossible that she could pay any such sum, the eventual "disposall" of her lands would not be difficult to foresee.[1] Land, as Roger Williams wrote, was becoming "one of the gods of New England," and judicial punishments were coming curiously often to involve forced concessions regarding coveted bits of territory. Subtly, and perhaps unconsciously, but no less surely, the land-hunger of the whites was poisoning the wells of justice.

As a result of the relations, territorial and political, which were developing between the races, and as a natural corollary of the protectorate theory, the English were also gradually enacting, on the one hand, a body of law applicable among themselves to the Indian only, and, on the other, forcing the "protected" Indians to observe English law, even when living apart from the settlers. Such regulations as Connecticut passed for the Pequots on their reservation in the spring of 1675 were evidence of what all the protected Indians might expect in time. Any native, for example, heathen or Christian, who profaned the Sabbath day by hunting, fishing, carrying firewood, or other misdemeanors, was to be fined or whipped; while all were ordered to "heare the word of God preached by Mr. Fitch, or any other minister sent amongst them," subject to four shillings fine or corporal punishment.[2] A most unjust law, in view of the well-understood inability of the Indian to withstand the temptation of strong waters, and the willingness of the colonists, in spite of legal prohibition, to sell them to him, was that which provided that any native found drunk should have to labor twelve days for whoever accused him and proved the case, one half of the proceeds of his labor to go to the accuser, and one half to the county treasury. It was only necessary, therefore, secretly to induce a savage to take one or two drinks, in order to secure six days' forced labor from him *gratis*.[3] We need not credit the pre-

---

[1] *Plymouth Records*, vol. v, p. 75.   [2] *Conn. Col. Records*, vol. ii, pp. 575 *f.*
[3] *Ibid.*, p. 257.

posterous contemporary accusation that the Massachusetts government, under a similar law, connived at making Indians drunk, so as to hasten the work on Castle Island, in order to realize the ample possibilities for evil in such a statute.[1]

The close proximity in which the whites and natives dwelt in many places was the source of endless friction and petty annoyance, particularly to the Indians. The live-stock of the settlers was forever being allowed to stray into the cultivated lands of the savages; and at the time of the troubles in 1671, the colony of Plymouth had to appoint committees in no less than eleven different towns, "to view the Damage done to the Indians by the Horses and Hoggs of the English."[2] The question of firearms was the subject of frequent legislation by the colonial courts, and of friction with the natives, in the altered condition of whose life they had become practically essential as a means of procuring food.[3] Notwithstanding this fact, and the obvious one that the guns, having been paid for by the Indians with their own money, were their property, the English, frequently, when alarmed by rumors of hostility, required that the savages deliver all their arms into the hands of the authorities, considering as enemies those who refused.[4] Not only was this a hardship and a humiliation, but, on a number of occasions, the English refused to return the weapons, simply confiscating them. In 1671, for example, in Plymouth, after Philip had been required to deposit the guns of his people with the Court, that body determined that they were "justly forfeit," and coolly divided them among the towns of the colony.[5] At one stroke, not only were the natives deprived of their means of livelihood and defense, but the weapons, which they had honestly bought, were thus, by legalized robbery, turned against themselves. No individual with the instinct of self-respect and self-pres-

---

[1] *Cal. State Pap., Col., 1675-76*, p. 307. This document, apparently by Capt. Wyborne, was used in the Mason-Gorges case against Massachusetts.

[2] *Plymouth Records*, vol. v, p. 62.

[3] *Cf. Conn. Col. Records*, vol. I, pp. 74, 79, 163, 263; *Massachusetts Records*, vols. IV, pt. ii, p. 564, and v, pp. 44, 304; *Plymouth Records*, vol. v, p. 64.

[4] *E.g., Conn. Col. Records*, vol. I, p. 240.   [5] *Plymouth Records*, vol. v, p. 63.

ervation could fail to see that his eventual choice would lie between resistance and virtual slavery.

The missionary efforts of the English differed from those of the French precisely as did their exploitation of the land. In French America, the religious counterpart of the lonely trapper or trader was the Jesuit priest, who, cross in hand, and frequently without a companion, penetrated to the far depths of the forest, to carry his message to the heathen wherever found. In New England, however, as it was the town and not the trader that pushed the frontier forward, so the lonely missionary was replaced by the organizer of communities, and the savages on the fringe of civilization were gathered into villages within the bounds of white settlement, there to have the gospel preached to them, and to be joined in a covenanted church. Such work was practically negligible in Rhode Island and Connecticut, but, by the outbreak of Philip's War, had made considerable progress in Massachusetts and Plymouth. In the latter two colonies, the labors of the Reverend John Eliot, who had translated the Bible into the Indian tongue, of Thomas Mayhew, Richard Bourne, and others,— paid for almost wholly with funds raised in England, — had resulted in the gathering of perhaps four thousand converts.[1] A considerable number of these "Praying Indians," as they were called, were scattered in villages on Martha's Vineyard and Nantucket, and in some twenty localities in Plymouth, and about eleven hundred were located in Massachusetts. Of the latter, the earlier and most dependable ones dwelt in the seven towns of Chelmsford, Littleton, Natick, Marlborough, Hopkinton, Grafton, and Stoughton, which were located at intervals of a dozen miles or so along the frontier of the eastern settlements, and which might have been used as a possible line of defense against any hostile movement from the unoccupied central portion of the colony, which lay between them and the towns of the Connecticut River.[2] In

---

[1] D. Gookin, "Historical Collections of the Indians of New England," *Mass. Hist. Soc. Coll.*, Series I, vol. I, pp. 195 *ff.* For the work of these men, which deserves all praise, *vide* the tracts reprinted in *Ibid.*, Series III, vol. IV.

[2] D. Gookin, "Christian Indians," in *Archeologia Americana*, vol. II, p. 435.

a large proportion of cases, the conversion seems to have been genuine, and the Indians, more particularly in the seven towns named, to have become sincere friends of the English, although the more recent converts in the Nipmuck country soon went over to the enemy.

To the bulk of the savages, however, the humdrum existence led by their praying brethren in the little reservations allotted to them by the English, and their position of humble dependence upon the white lords of the soil, could hardly make a serious appeal. The past was too recent, and its contrast with the present was too vivid. It was becoming clear to the dullest witted that the future could hold little else, however, unless the power of the whites could be broken once and for all.

Massasoit, the aged Sachem of the Wampanoags, who had been a consistent friend to the settlers since 1620, died in the winter of 1660–61, and his son Alexander, who succeeded him, also died a few months later. In fact, his death is said to have been due, in part, to his anger and chagrin at having been forcibly seized by the authorities of Plymouth when called upon to make his appearance before them.[1] The change of relations between the whites and Indians was well exemplified by the difference between the formal and dignified embassy sent from Plymouth in 1620, to visit Massasoit and to negotiate a treaty with him, and the "eight or ten stout men," under Major Winslow, who surprised Alexander in his hunting-lodge, seized his arms, and commanded him to travel to that same Plymouth, to appear before the governor.

Philip had not long succeeded his brother Alexander as sachem, when he, in turn, was curtly summoned to appear before the Court, to clear himself of rumored disloyalty. Although nothing whatever was proved, and Philip offered to leave another of his brothers as hostage, he was forced to sign a treaty ratifying all former ones, acknowledge himself an English subject, and agree not to alienate any of his lands

[1] W. Hubbard, *History of the Indian Wars in New England* (ed. S. G. Drake, 1865), vol. I, p. 50. A more favorable account of the Alexander incident is given in a letter from John Cotton to Increase Mather, in 1677. *Mass. Hist. Soc. Coll.*, Series IV, vol. VIII, pp. 233 *f*.

without the consent of the Court.[1] Five years later, on renewed rumors of his disloyalty, his arms were taken away,
and he was again forced to appear before the magistrates.
Although once more no evidence was produced against him,
and his arms were returned, he was nevertheless required to
give his note for £40 as part of the charge for the expedition
which had been sent after him.[2] In 1671, for wholly inadequate causes, he was forced, not to make a new treaty, but,
without option, to sign "several propositions," by one of
which he had to agree to pay a fine of "one hundred pounds
in such things as I have," although, as he had no such sum,
he asked for three years in which to pay it. He was also
required to acknowledge himself in subjection, not merely
to the English Crown, but to the little colony of Plymouth;
to pay an annual tribute; to sell land only subject to the
colony's approval; and, with exceeding unfairness, to agree
in advance to submit, in case of any dispute between the
colony and himself, to the verdict of the governor as arbi-
trator.[3] It was on this occasion, as already noted, that all
the guns that his people had delivered to the English were
confiscated.

This treatment, accorded to the son of that sachem to whom
the now grasping colony had, in its infancy, owed its very life,
and who had been its friend for over forty years, could not
fail to goad him into rebellion, if, indeed, he had not already
considered it. Within four years from the time when the son
of Massasoit affixed his scrawling mark to the humiliating and
confiscatory document, the storm broke which was to drench
New England in a sea of blood.

In the absence of any written records of the Indians, from
which the story of those four years or so of preparation upon
their part might be ascertained, the nature and scope of Philip's
plans must remain wholly a matter of inference from the

[1] *Plymouth Records*, vol. IV, pp. 25 f.　　　　　[2] *Ibid.*, pp. 165 f.
[3] *Ibid.*, vol. v, p. 79. The accusations against him are on p. 78. These were only
that he had refused to deliver some of his guns; that, on occasion, he had refused to
journey to Plymouth when sent for; that he harbored enemy Indians; that he had
misrepresented Plymouth to Massachusetts; and that he had been uncivil.

subsequent events. That he nursed his revenge, and carried on negotiations with other tribes for a simultaneous rising against the whites over a considerable territory, would seem to be well established. On the other hand, the time was more or less ripe for the inevitable conflict to occur throughout all the colonies. Once started, the example of a native rising would prove contagious; and there is little evidence to prove that the widespread movements along the seaboard were connected by threads that centred in the hut of the Wampanoag. His tribe itself was weak and inconspicuous, and in Philip's apparent lack of personal bravery and some of the other qualities most admired in a savage leader, there is nothing to indicate — what, indeed, events tend to disprove — that he was personally popular among the natives. Nor, even if we grant that he was surprised into hostilities in that spring of 1675, before all his plans had matured, is there any evidence, in his later conduct of the campaign, of that great ability for organization which has sometimes been attributed to him. There seems to be no doubt, however, that at that time he was engaged in preparing for a general rising, and that he had the sympathy of some of the other New England tribes.

Meanwhile, the English seem to have been singularly oblivious to the realities of the situation. They claimed, and undoubtedly felt, that they had treated the natives with justice. In the beginning, they had naturally failed to understand the Indian character, government, and theory of property. As, on the one hand, they came to know these better, on the other, the contempt they developed for the heathen and the savage, who, incidentally, was in possession of lands coveted by the Saints of God, tended to lessen their belief in his abstract rights. Economically, they had outgrown their early dependence upon the native; and their increasing sense of safety, due to the rapidly developing disparity in numbers, tended to make them callous to the feelings of the "great naked dirty beast," as Colonel Church described Philip, and they ceased to fear the power of the savage without coming to respect the rights of the man.[1] They failed to realize the broader aspects of the struggle, and even the practical fact that they were driving a still powerful race of savages into a corner, where they were not likely to stand at bay without making, at some time, a supreme effort to escape.

When the Indians finally did strike back, the English not only were wholly unprepared but do not seem to have understood the results of their own acts. Instead of regarding the approaching conflict as an inevitable consequence of the relations between the two races, and as having been, more immediately, brought about by themselves, they looked upon it as sent from God; and in a hasty self-examination as to why the Deity should have so afflicted them, the Massachusetts General Court decided that He was then engaged in burning towns and murdering women and children along the frontier, because Massachusetts had become somewhat lax in persecuting the Quakers, and because her men had begun to wear periwigs and their women to indulge in "cutting, curling and immodest laying out theire haire."[2]

The genius of New England has never been military. Her people, in a cause in which they believe, can fight doggedly and well, but she has never given to the nation a great soldier, either as leader or organizer, and King Philip's War presented no exception. From its nature, it was less a war than a series of raids by the savages and retaliatory expeditions by the English; but it was the only sort of war which the colonies could have expected, or for which they ought to have been prepared. There was, however, practically no intercolonial organization. The United Colonies, the efficiency of which as a war-machine had early been damaged by Massachusetts, had received another blow by the loss of a member when New Haven was absorbed by Connecticut. Although Plymouth's suggestion, at that time, to dissolve the Confederacy entirely, had not been approved, the bond had become looser than ever, and under

---

[1] *Cf.* Winslow's letter of justification in Hubbard, *Indian Wars*, vol. I, pp. 56 *f.*, and "Narrative of the Beginning of the War," in *Acts United Colonies*, vol. II, pp. 362 *f.*
[2] *Massachusetts Records*, vol. v, pp. 59 *ff.*

the altered articles, the representatives of the three remaining members were to meet only triennially.[1]

In spite of the invaluable material that the colonies possessed in the friendly Indians, none of them had been employed as spies among the enemy, of whose plans preceding the war the colonists seem to have had no information other than vague rumors. In spite of their experience, moreover, the settlers appear, in part, to have been curiously ignorant of Indian warfare. Even in the matter of weapons, they made the mistake, at first, of equipping men with the wholly useless pike; and in the earliest expeditions, the English carried the cumbrous old matchlock guns, which were much inferior to the newer flintlocks used by the savages.[2] The commissariat frequently broke down, and in a number of cases important expeditions had to be abandoned because of failure of supplies. The regulation, necessary on account of the jealousy of the several colonies, that, in joint operations, the ranking officer of the colony in which the operations happened to be conducted at the moment should be the commander-in-chief of the whole, naturally made friction and tended to confusion.[3] From the same spirit of jealousy, there also arose disputes, sometimes almost amounting to mutiny, between the troops of one colony and those of another, which were further fostered by the lack of unity in plans, and inadequate communication.[4] Insubordination was not always limited to the rank and file, and in the case of Colonel Moseley,— who had married a niece of Governor Leverett of Massachusetts,— rose to such a point, against both his superior officers and the state, as should have brought him to a court-martial.[5] As the war progressed, the difficulty of raising troops became great, both from lack of men in some places and from their disinclination to serve. In

[1] *Acts United Colonies*, vol. II, pp. 324, 319, 340 *ff.*

[2] *Cf. Massachusetts Records*, vol. v, p. 47; S. G. Drake, *Old Indian Chronicle* (Boston, 1836), p. 8; G. M. Bodge, *Soldiers in King Philip's War* (Leominster, 1896), pp. 45 *ff.*

[3] *Acts United Colonies*, vol. II, p. 359.

[4] *Cf.* Bodge, *Soldiers*, pp. 150 *f.*

[5] Mather, *Philip's War*, p. 240 *n.;* Gookin, *Praying Indians*, pp. 495 *f;* Bodge, *Soldiers*, p. 76. For the mutiny of a Plymouth officer and his men, *cf. Plymouth Records*, vol. v, pp. 189 *f.* There were other cases.

Plymouth, it was ordered that boys under the military age of sixteen should be used for guard-duty; while any man pressed for service who refused to obey should be fined five pounds, or made to run the gauntlet, or both.[1] Connecticut had to offer her troops, officers as well as men, the plunder of the Indians, as to both their goods and their persons, in addition to the regular pay, and to forbid any male resident between the ages of fourteen and seventy to emigrate from the colony.[2] Massachusetts, "taking into consideration the great disappointment" that soldiers pressed for duty refused to serve, provided that those who continued refractory should be punished with death.[3] On the other hand, the drab coloring of the war, uninspiring as the conflict was in many of its aspects, was relieved over and over by exhibitions of a fine courage on the part of individual soldiers, and of a cool daring in the face of unspeakable horrors, shown by women as well as men.

The character of the war would, in any case, probably have been mainly a series of raids; but the fact that Philip had apparently to enter upon hostilities before his preparations were complete, and the lack of unity and organized effective action among the colonies, made the course of the contest even more desultory than it might otherwise have been. We cannot here give more than an outline of the chief events of the struggle, which was more important in its results than in its conduct.[4]

In the latter part of 1674, John Sassamon, a Christian Indian, discovered a plot among the natives of Namasket, and immediately informed the authorities of Plymouth, stating that he would be in danger of his life if Philip should learn of his disclosures.[5] His fears were fulfilled, and in January, 1675, he was murdered, apparently by Philip's orders, the three Indians implicated in his death being seized, tried,

---

[1] *Plymouth Records*, vol. v, pp. 193, 198.   [2] *Conn. Col. Records*, vol. ii, pp. 418, 272.
[3] *Massachusetts Records*, vol. v, p. 78.
[4] The general reader may consult Ellis and Morris, *King Philip's War*; New York, 1906. The volume is more trustworthy than the unfortunate slip in its opening sentence might seem to indicate.
[5] Hubbard, *Indian Wars*, vol. i, p. 61.

and executed by the English in the following spring.[1]   The
Squaw-Sachem Weetamoo, who seems to have been opposed
to the rising, although she was the sister-in-law of Philip,
also warned the English of what was planned; but they do not
seem to have taken any measures for defense, or to have done
anything at all beyond remonstrating with Philip.[2]   He had
already committed himself too far, however, to have drawn
back, even if he would; and, in spite of the premature discovery of the design, the younger warriors from neighboring
tribes began to come in and urge the immediate beginning of
hostilities.

On June 24, at Swansea, after having provoked a settler
to draw the first blood, the savages fell upon the whites, and
killed eight or nine.   Two more, who had been dispatched to
get a surgeon, were waylaid and slain, and their bodies found
by an embassy then on its way from the government of Plymouth to Philip.   In the six months since the English had
been told of the plot, they had been strangely inactive.   Two
days after the murders at Swansea, however, five companies
were mustered, partly in Plymouth and partly in Boston, and
were on the march.[3]   A raid on the Indians by these united
forces, on the 30th, so frightened the savages, that Philip and
his followers fled from Mount Hope and took refuge in a swamp
at Pocasset, although the intelligence service of the English,
through their failure to use native scouts, was so imperfect
that they were unaware of the move of the enemy, and did not
follow up the pursuit.   Pocasset was in the territory of Weetamoo, and the English, by driving Philip into her jurisdiction,
and failing to follow him, practically forced her to join with
him and his warriors.

Although, as yet, in spite of their ancient wrongs, the Narragansetts had shown no hostility, nevertheless, at the instant
when the attack on Philip should have been followed up, the
Massachusetts troops received orders to pass into the Narragansett country, and to "make peace with a sword in their

[1] *Plymouth Records*, vol. v, p. 167.   [2] *Acts United Colonies*, vol. ii, p. 363.
[3] Hubbard, *Indian Wars*, vol. i, pp. 66 *ff.*

hand." [1] Canonicus, the sachem, could not be found; but the Massachusetts agents, joined by those from Connecticut, negotiated a treaty with a few unimportant individuals, who were forced to obligate the tribe to join the English in making aggressive war on Philip, and to confirm all former land-grants.[2] The English must have realized, not only that such a treaty was not binding, but that, so far from gaining the most powerful of the New England tribes as allies, it would have just the opposite effect. On the other hand, had the Massachusetts troops remained with those of Plymouth, and pursued and captured Philip, the war might possibly have been ended at once, and the Narragansetts not have entered it at all.

Unless we assume the military incapacity of the Massachusetts Court, we can hardly avoid the suggestion that that colony, and perhaps Connecticut also, saw an opportunity to strengthen their claims to the rich lands possessed by the natives whom they were forcing into opposition, and desired, by being first on the spot and negotiating the farcical treaty, to establish a basis for future title. That the mind of Boston was not bent solely upon the defense of the frontier, or the devilish effects of periwigs, is suggested by a letter from that godly town on July 6, which announced that "the land already gained is worth £10,000." [3] And this in the first fortnight! The good dames — and their spouses — may be pardoned if they were tempted toward heresy regarding the fatal results of curling-tongs and switches.

The treaty negotiated, most of the Massachusetts troops were immediately ordered back to Boston, only about one hundred, under command of Captain Henchman, being left with those of Plymouth to guard the swamp in which Philip had taken refuge. After a skirmish on the 18th, these decided that it was "ill fighting with a wild beast in his own den," and resolved to starve Philip out. That wily savage, however, gave his cautious watchers the slip, and escaped to central

[1] Hubbard, *Indian Wars*, vol. 1, p. 75.
[2] The text of the treaty is in Hubbard, vol. 1, pp. 76 *ff.*
[3] *Cal. State Pap., Col., 1675-76*, p. 253.

Massachusetts, with his followers.   Again owing to inadequate
scouting, it was only after some days that the English found
that they were guarding an empty trap, and then their pursuit
had been too long delayed to be successful.[1]

Philip's presence decided the Massachusetts Indians, with
whom the colonial authorities were then negotiating. Captains Wheeler and Hutchinson, with a small party of whites
and three Christian Indians, who were sent to treat with the
Nipmucks, were treacherously attacked near the place the
savages had appointed for a parley, and about one third of
the colonists were slain.   The survivors fled to Brookfield,
gaining that place in safety only with the help of the Christian
Indians, who had warned them of the treachery in advance,
without avail.[2]   The town was attacked by the natives almost
before the whites could reach it, all the buildings being burned
except the one in which the inhabitants had taken refuge.
After the inmates, for three days, had warded off the efforts
of several hundred savages to set fire to the house which was
their only protection, they were rescued by Major Willard
and a troop from Lancaster, although the town had to be
abandoned.[3]

The Springfield Indians now joined the enemy, and Connecticut and Massachusetts troops were concentrated at Hadley,
under command of Major Pynchon.   On the first of September,
Deerfield was attacked for the first time, and most of the
houses burned.[4]   The following day the savages fell upon
Northfield, killed eight persons, and destroyed the buildings.[5]
A relief party, under Captain Beers, which, unaware of the

[1] Hubbard, *Indian Wars*, vol. I, pp. 88 *ff.*; B. Church, *History of King Philip's War*
(ed. H. M. Dexter, Boston, 1865), pp. 25 *ff.*

[2] Bodge, *Soldiers*, pp. 107 *ff.*; Gookin, *Christian Indians*, pp. 447 *f.*; Hubbard,
Indian Wars, vol. I, p. 99.   The latter fails to state that the rescuers were natives.
Wheeler, in his report, also ignored it, although he subsequently certified to the Indians'
good conduct.

[3] Mather, *Philip's War*, p. 68; Hubbard, *Indian Wars*, vol. I, pp. 100 *ff.*

[4] Mather, *Philip's War*, pp. 72 *ff.*; Hubbard, *Indian Wars*, vol. I, p. 110.   For the
traditional attack on Hadley, and the story of the regicide Judge Goffe, *vide* S. Judd,
History of Hadley (1905), pp. 138 *ff.*, and G. Sheldon, *History of Deerfield* (1895),
vol. I, pp. 93 *f.*

[5] Bodge, *Soldiers*, p. 130; Hubbard, *Indian Wars*, vol. II, p. 44.

disaster, was bringing up supplies, was ambushed, and twenty men out of the thirty were killed after a desperate fight, the remainder taking refuge at Hadley, as did also the inhabitants of Northfield, who now abandoned their town.[1]

Heretofore, in the Massachusetts operations, Major Treat had been in command of the Connecticut forces, and Major Pynchon of those from the Bay Colony, Treat's instructions having been to advise with Pynchon but to act with him only when convinced of the wisdom of a move.[2] Massachusetts now decided to abandon the field, and merely to garrison the towns; but this supine policy, which could not have been permanent, and was a virtual admission of defeat, did not satisfy Connecticut. As a result of negotiations, the United Colonies decided to raise the total number of troops to one thousand, and to put Pynchon in supreme command in the upper Connecticut Valley. The Commissioners confessed that they did not know how many troops were already in the field, or anything of the strength of the enemy.[3] This lack of information was characteristic both in the major conduct of the war and in minor operations.

Only a few days after these arrangements were made, Deerfield had been attacked again, and Captain Lathrop, with about sixty men, "the very flower of the county of Essex," was detailed to convoy some provisions accumulated there into Hadley. Although these troops were operating in a country filled with hostile savages, and the line of march lay in part through a dense forest, where they might easily be ambushed, the company had no scouts ahead, and many of the soldiers had stowed their arms in the carts, while they themselves gathered grapes by the roadside. Lathrop was familiar with the road and its dangerous places; but it was at one

---

[1] Hubbard, *Indian Wars*, vol. I, p. 110; Mather, *Philip's War*, p. 79; Bodge, *Soldiers*, p. 131.

[2] *Conn. Col. Records*, vol. II, p. 358.

[3] *Ibid.*, pp. 364, 367. Massachusetts was to supply 527, Plymouth, 158, Connecticut, 315. The figures were based upon the new Articles of Confederation, which were unduly favorable to Massachusetts. Based upon population, they would probably have been about 640, 100, and 260, respectively.

of these, the spot where the trail crossed the little stream ever since known as Bloody Brook, that the troop encountered the fatal result of their criminal folly. As they were crossing the ford, with their heavy wagons lumbering in the mud, the Indian war-whoop rang out on all sides, and the soldiers fell under the bullets of their unseen foe. The massacre was virtually complete. Hardly a man escaped, and not one would have done so, had not Colonel Moseley with another small troop, heard the shooting and hurried to the rescue. He, in turn, was being forced back, and was facing annihilation, when Major Treat, having likewise heard firing, hastened up with some Connecticut troops and friendly Indians, and saved the day.[1] The survivors, however, who fell back upon Deerfield, were obliged to evacuate the town a few days later, it thus being the third surrendered to the enemy.

On September 26, a slight attack was made upon Springfield, followed by demonstrations against Hadley. Some troops having been hurried thither from Springfield, the Indians, successful in their ruse, if that had been their plan, returned and attacked that town in force, destroying it on October 5.[2] Major Appleton now replaced Pynchon as commander; but Treat having retired with part of his troops to Connecticut, in view of the danger threatening Hartford, his lieutenant refused to obey Appleton, as he considered Treat to be his immediate superior. The matter became a subject of dispute between the colonies, but, the danger to Connecticut having passed, Treat returned, and Connecticut troops continued to garrison the Massachusetts towns throughout the winter.[3]

Connecticut from the start had adopted the policy of utilizing to the full the services of the friendly Indians, which Massachusetts, for the most part had refused, with disastrous consequences. Not only had she failed to make use of them as scouts and troops, but by removing the Praying Indians

[1] Mather, *Philip's War*, pp. 85 f.; Bodge, *Soldiers*, pp. 67, 135 f.; Sheldon, *Deerfield*, vol. I, pp. 100 ff.; Hubbard, *Indian Wars*, vol. I, pp. 113 ff.

[2] Hubbard, *Indian Wars*, vol. I, p. 122; Mather, *Philip's War*, p. 97.

[3] *Conn. Col. Records*, vol. II, pp. 370, 372 ff., 380 ff.

from the line of towns in which they had been settled, and placing them in a concentration camp on Deer Island, she had weakened her whole line of defense.[1] But, unfortunately, it was not a question of merely failing to utilize valuable resources. Her treatment of her civilized natives, individually and collectively, must be considered as cruel and inhumane, although the ministers and the magistrates seem, on the whole, to have endeavored to restrain the lawless persecution of the mob, and the savagery of their more brutal leaders, such as Moseley. Innocent Indians were insulted, and plundered of their possessions, and, in some cases, their women and children were murdered in cold blood. Yet juries refused to convict the offenders, and the General Court frequently yielded to the clamor, until letters from England, and the discovery of a hideous plot by the whites to massacre all the converts gathered on Deer Island, awoke them to some sense of their duty. The blind fury against the Praying Indians was by no means confined to the rabble. Moseley, whose refusal to use their services in the war had cost many English lives, treated them at Marlborough and Nashobeh with the most wanton brutality, although the execution of a squaw, taken prisoner on his expedition near Hatfield, is, we hope, unique in American military history. The laconic note of her fate merely reads that she was "ordered to be torn in peeces by Doggs, and she was soe dealt withal." [2] It recalls, however, the earlier advice of Massachusetts, that the Indians be hunted down with mastiffs.[3] Although he was censured for his various acts of inhumanity and insubordination, no action was taken against Moseley by the authorities, who thus share his guilt; and so high did the feeling run that it became dangerous, even in Boston, for such men as Eliot and Gookin to speak a word in defense of the persecuted Christian natives.

In the early winter, it seemed as if the enemy had been successful everywhere. Philip, who apparently had not been

---

[1] *Massachusetts Records*, vol. v, pp. 46, 55, 57, 64, 84.

[2] Mather, *Philip's War*, p. 101 *n.*; Bodge, *Soldiers*, p. 69; Gookin, *Christian Indians*, pp. 455 *ff.*, 500 *ff.*

[3] *Acts United Colonies*, vol. ii, p. 168.

present in any of the fights, had gone into winter quarters near Albany,[1] but it is probable that the war had long since passed out of his control; and there is nothing to indicate any concerted plan governing the actions of the various tribes now, or soon to be, on the war-path. By far the most powerful of those surviving were the Narragansetts; and their Sachem Canonchet, the son of Miantonomo, both from his position and his ability, was probably a more important factor than Philip; although, as yet, in spite of the ancient wrong done him in the judicial murder of his father, and the recent act of the English in forcing the treaty of July 15 upon some of his people, the sachem had committed no overt act against the settlers. A number of hostile Indians, however, had fled to his country for refuge; and in October, either from a deliberate purpose to provoke him into active hostility, or in the vain hope that he would be forced into an alliance with them by threats, the Massachusetts authorities required him to sign a treaty ratifying the one of July 15, and agreeing to give up all refugees to the English.[2] It is doubtful whether the sentiment of his people would have permitted this surrender; but, in any case, little opportunity was given to test it, and on November 2, only two weeks after having forced Canonchet to sign a humiliating peace, the English abruptly declared war.[3] Old Uncas, who had hated the Narragansetts for a lifetime, had long been scheming to bring about the conflict, and the land possessed by Canonchet and the refugee Awashonks was a most potent argument. A journal-letter from a citizen of Boston, dated only a few days after the treaty with the Narragansett, complains of his not having delivered up the squaw-sachem, but that there was prospect of force being used, and that, if she could be captured, "her Lands will more than pay all the charge we have been at in this unhappy War." [4] About a week after the date of this letter, the Commissioners of the United Colonies, at the same meeting at which war was de-

---

[1] *Conn. Col. Records*, vol. ii, pp. 397, 407.   [2] *Acts United Colonies*, vol. ii, p. 360.
[3] *Ibid.*, p. 357.
[4] *Conn. Col. Records*, vol. ii, p. 236; *Old Indian Chronicle*, p. 36.

clared, arranged for a levy of a thousand more troops, and an immediate expedition was planned against the Narragansetts, under command of Governor Winslow of Plymouth.[1] The Massachusetts Council, with an eye to the long-coveted country, proclaimed that, if her soldiers "played the man," and drove the Narragansetts out of it, the army should receive allotments of the land in addition to their pay.[2]

The various units of the new force, after sundry isolated skirmishes with the enemy, finally united at Pettisquamscott, late in the afternoon of December 18, and lay in the open that night in a severe snowstorm. The Indians, between three and four thousand in number, had taken refuge in a fortified position, on an island of four or five acres, in the middle of a large swamp, about sixteen miles from the English camp. Before daybreak, on the morning of the 19th, the army began its march, reaching the swamp about one in the afternoon. Some of the enemy were encountered upon its edge, but immediately fled, pursued, without order, by the English, straight to the entrance of the native fort. For three hours the fighting was desperate, and it was only after darkness began to fall that the colonists succeeded in capturing the Indians' blockhouse and other works. Then came the same order which had been issued in the Pequot swamp fight thirty years earlier, and the torch was applied to the four hundred wigwams and accumulated stores of the savages. It is impossible to tell how many of the warriors fell in the fight, or how many of the old people, women, and children were roasted alive in the flames; but the contemporary estimates run from four hundred to a thousand or more. The English loss was about seventy killed and a hundred and fifty wounded.[3]

Although the Narragansetts had received a terrible blow, they had not been so nearly annihilated as had the Pequots

---

[1] *Acts United Colonies*, vol. II, p. 357; *Conn. Col. Records*, vol. II, p. 384; *Massachusetts Records*, vol. v, p. 69; *Plymouth Records*, vol. v, pp. 182 *f.*

[2] Bodge, *Soldiers*, p. 180.

[3] *Ibid.*, pp. 190 *f. Cf. Conn. Col. Records*, vol. II, p. 398. Hubbard, *Indian Wars*, vol. I, pp. 144 *ff.*; Mather, *Philip's War*, p. 108; Church, *King Philip's War*, pp. 53 *ff.* *A Continuation of the State of New England* (London, 1676), estimates the English losses as, killed and wounded, 207, and 600 Indians killed.

in the preceding generation; and the English, in view of their own actions, could now look for nothing less than a war to the death, waged with a ferocity equal at least to their own. An immediate levy of a thousand additional men was arranged for, divided among the colonies, and a new expedition was sent into the Nipmuck country, where the Narragansetts had joined some of Philip's forces.[1] The commissariat broke down, and the short campaign, known as "the hungry march," accomplished nothing. On February 10, the savages fell upon Lancaster and nearly destroyed the town. Within the next few weeks, attacks were made upon such widely separated points as Medfield, Northampton, Hatfield, Providence, Groton, Longmeadow, and Marlborough.

The Indians, however, had suffered severely during the winter from want of food, and, as spring came on, Canonchet realized that crops must be raised during the summer if the war were to be maintained. He proposed that the conquered lands in the Connecticut Valley be planted, and he himself, with a small party, volunteered to go back to Seakonk, near Mount Hope, to procure seed-corn. The venture cost him his life, for he was taken captive by a party of Connecticut men and Indians operating in the Narragansett country, and was immediately condemned to death. When told of the sentence, the savage, who possessed to the full the courage lacked by Philip, replied that "he liked it well that he should die before his heart was soft, or had spoken anything unworthy of himself." [2]

In spite of further attacks by the Indians, one as near Boston as Sudbury, the tide now turned in favor of the English throughout southern New England. A heavy blow was struck at the Upper Falls of the Connecticut, where a great company of natives had gathered to fish, and where Captain Turner inflicted a severe defeat upon them, in spite of his own heavy losses. The privations of the winter, the prospect of semi-starvation to come, the loss of Canonchet, and the breakdown

[1] *Plymouth Records*, vol. v, p. 184; *Conn. Col. Records*, vol. ii, p. 391.
[2] Hubbard, *Indian Wars*, vol. ii, p. 60.

of Philip as a leader, rapidly sapped the morale of the natives, who became disorganized and demoralized. Detachments of English hunted down and slaughtered or captured the scattered bands of savages. Philip, who had returned to his old home near Mount Hope, narrowly escaped being taken early in August, his wife and son falling into the hands of the English. A few weeks later, he himself was slain in a swamp, by one of Captain Church's Indians, and the main phase of the war, which, by bearing his name, has unduly exalted his part in it, was over.[1]

Hostilities, however, continued in the eastern settlements of Maine and New Hampshire for two years longer. Owing to their scattered character, and the difficulty of inflicting any telling blow upon the savages, who could disappear into the limitless forests, and were supplied by the French with arms and other necessities, Maine suffered proportionately even more severely than its more populous neighbors to the south. The story of the war there is the record of tragedy after tragedy enacted in lonely farmhouse or isolated village. One episode only, and that because of its later effect upon the Indian relations of the settlers, need be alluded to. In the autumn of 1676, following the signing of a treaty in July and a proclamation by the Massachusetts Court, several hundred natives congregated at Major Waldron's house at Dover, with the intention, apparently, of accepting terms of amnesty, and of testifying to their friendly relations with the whites, although there were some who had borne arms against them. Unexpectedly, they were all taken into custody by Massachusetts agents and carried off to Boston, and a large proportion of them was sold into slavery in the West Indies. There are various versions of the affair, and it is impossible to unravel the truth, but, whether rightly or not, the eastern Indians felt that they had been treacherously dealt with, and never forgot or forgave the transaction.[2] Massachusetts, moreover,

[1] Hubbard, *Indian Wars*, vol. I, p. 265; Church, *King Philip's War*, pp. 145 *ff*.

[2] *Cf*. Bodge, *Soldiers*, pp. 304 *ff*.; *N. H. Prov. Papers*, vol. I, pp. 354 *ff*.; *Massachusetts Records*, vol. v, p. 72.

was unable to protect the eastern settlements; and the treaty finally made with the Indians, in the spring of 1678, carried the humiliating condition that the whites were to pay an annual tribute to the natives.[1] The unfortunate result of the war in that section was that the Indians felt themselves superior to the whites in power, and they had come to believe that the word of the latter could not be trusted.

The captives taken in Philip's War were variously treated. Some, who were considered especially guilty, were killed, and great numbers were distributed among the whites as servants for a limited period.   Many were sold into slavery in the West Indies.[2]   Among these unfortunates were the wife and son of Philip, the latter a little lad of nine.[3]   Even the life of this grandson of Massasoit hung in the balance, and the clergy, to whom the problem of his disposal was referred, advised that he should be slain; but, as usual, the people were more merciful than the ministers. Although even the Old Testament offered difficulties in the way of precedents, John Cotton and Increase Mather thought that they might be found, and called for the lad's blood,[4] Mather pointing out that, although David indeed spared the life of little Hadad, it might have been better had he not.   The saintly Eliot, who throughout the war had pleaded with the people of Massachusetts for justice and mercy for the Christian Indians, as Williams had pleaded for the Pequots a generation before, protested against the whole system of selling off the natives, and in a letter to the Governor and Council uttered the prophetic saying that "to sell soules for mony seemeth to me a dangerous merchandize."[5] But his voice, like Williams's, found no echo.

The losses that the colonies had suffered were enormous. Maine did not recover for half a century, and there was not

---

[1] Belknap, *History*, vol. I, p. 129.   He does not give the text, nor is it in the *N. H. Prov. Papers*, though there is a letter relative to it in the latter, vol. I, p. 365.

[2] *Conn. Col. Records*, vol. II, pp. 297 *f*.   The Assembly in Barbadoes drew a bill to prevent the importation of these Indian slaves from New England. *Cal. State Pap., Col., 1674-75*, p. 378.

[3] Church, *King Philip's War*, p. 127.

[4] Their letters are in *Mass. Hist. Soc. Coll.*, Series IV, vol. VIII, p. 689.

[5] *Acts United Colonies*, vol. II, p. 452.

a white man left in Kennebec County. In Massachusetts sixteen towns were wholly destroyed or abandoned, and four in Rhode Island.[1] Along the entire New England frontier burned buildings and abandoned farms bore mute witness to the fury of the struggle. Plymouth reported her war expenses as £11,743, Connecticut hers as £22,173, and Massachusetts hers as £46,292, a total equivalent to-day of over $2,000,000.[2] One man out of every sixteen of military age had been killed. The struggle, however, had been inevitable, and it is fortunate that it occurred when it did; for it is improbable that the colonies could have sustained a double attack from south and north had the domestic contest coincided with the French war fifteen years later. Although they had been weakened in some respects, their losses were only temporary, while the removal of the Indian menace within their borders was a permanent gain. The ruined towns were rebuilt, new lands were opened up, and the fact that, entirely by their own efforts and without aid from England, the colonists had won possession of their territory with the unlimited expenditure of their own blood and treasure was of no little effect, then and later.

[1] *Cf.* Mathews, *Expansion of New England*, pp. 57 *ff.*; Hubbard, *Indian Wars*, vol. II, pp. 39 *ff.*; *Old Indian Chronicle*, pp. 101 *f.*
[2] *Acts United Colonies*, vol. II, pp. 402, 392, 393.

CHAPTER XV

LOSS OF THE MASSACHUSETTS CHARTER

The year 1676 was doubly noteworthy in the history of New England. As we have seen in the preceding chapter, it marked the definite end of the internal menace of the Indians in the colonies, which henceforth, except for border wars, could develop their life without that lurking fear of the savage that had always haunted the dwellers in such little towns as were planted beyond the area of compact settlement. If, on the one hand, the year thus seemed to open an era of an even more unrestricted development for the peculiar polity of New England, on the other, it also marked the beginning of a more determined effort on the part of the mother-country to exert her power over the colonies, and to bring them within the administrative scope of a better organized empire. The resultant contest, the earlier phases of which have already been described, was, in the main, carried on between Massachusetts and the Crown, and continued intermittently during the quarter of a century from the Restoration of the Stuarts to the inevitable loss of the colony's charter in 1684. In a less critical day, it was wont to be described as an unmitigated struggle between liberty-loving colonists fighting for freedom, and a king bent solely upon wreaking his tyrannical will. But the door of the past is not to be unlocked with so crude a key, and historians have learned to distrust simple formulas.

In the domestic affairs of England, the question that was more and more urgently pressing for solution was that of the location of sovereignty, and the source of power. Following the Reformation, with the development of the modern nationalities, the establishment of state-churches, and the growth of dissent, the sixteenth century had witnessed the transfer of allegiance from ecclesiastical to civil authority. The idea of law, however, as non-moral and as derived from sanctions other than divine, was but slowly coming into being. The theory of the divine right of a king to rule, although it might be used to further the purposes of a self-seeking monarch, had not been originated to serve that end. It was a natural and necessary stage in the transfer of authoritative sanction from the Papacy to the civil rulers. It was, in a word, "the assertion that civil society has an inherent right to exist apart from its ecclesiastical utility," and that it has a sanctity of its own, which may be set off against the claims of the theocrats.[1]

If we would understand the expression of a political idea, it is as essential to study it in relation to the previous one which it was brought forth to contradict, as it is to analyze it philosophically. From the first standpoint, the doctrine of the divine right of kings performed a useful bit of service, while, philosophically, it is neither more nor less legitimate than that of the divine right of a majority. Liberty is not, as our forefathers were too often told, a natural fact. The only natural liberty is that granted to the individual, human or brute, to sustain his life and propagate his species if he can, in the face of a universe almost overwhelmingly bent upon their destruction. Civil liberty, on the other hand, is purely social, and is a very delicate and varying adjustment of rights and duties in the succeeding stages of man's institutional development, which has risen and fallen in the past as that equilibrium has been disturbed. The divine right of kings was a protest against the divine right of the Pope. The divine right of a majority is a protest against the divine right of kings; but democracy has yet to prove whether it is any more capable than theocracy or monarchy of the sustained moral effort necessary to maintain the balance between rights and duties, so as to preserve and enlarge the liberty of the individual.

Aside from this question of divine right, there was a good deal to be said for the theory of sovereignty held by the later Stuarts, who possessed not only the legal, but the recognized, right to summon and dissolve Parliament, to create enough

[1] J. N. Figgis, "Political Thought in the 16th Century," in *Cambridge Modern History*, vol. III, pp. 751, 763. *Cf.* the same author's *Divine Right of Kings* (Cambridge University Press, 1914), pp. 44 *f.*, 54, 100.

peers, lay and spiritual, and to charter enough boroughs, to alter completely the composition of both the Houses. With such a relationship, they may well have considered their Parliaments as but emanations of their own power. There is, however, even more to be admitted as to their later colonial policy. For while, in their domestic struggle with Parliament, they were setting themselves in opposition to almost all the progressive influences of the times, in their colonial plans, they were furthering some of the most important. The reign of Charles II may be taken to mark the end of religion and the beginning of commerce as the prime influence in national politics and international relations. From 1672, when Protestant England joined with Catholic France to crush Protestant Holland, until 1815, the wars of England were wars for trade; and the long duel for empire between that country and France was to make the imperial question essentially one of trade and defense. It was becoming more and more evident, indeed, that the seventeenth-century empire rested, fundamentally, upon trade; and it is probable that the pressure exerted by the merchant class was quite as large an element in shaping policy as was any personal design of the King.

The beginnings of settlement, scattered and unimportant, had in no way presaged the empire which was to develop within a half-century, and not only had territory been granted away recklessly, but the monarchs had been equally heedless of the future in the forms of government which they had permitted to grow up. By the time our story has now reached, the colonial problem, aside from any question of tyranny, undoubtedly called for new treatment. If the Empire were not to be a source of great military weakness, and if the Navigation Acts, upon which its commercial power rested, were to be properly enforced, it was obvious that a much greater degree of administrative unity and control would have to be realized. In particular, the granting of the charters, in which no provision had been made for a royal governor or for any definite channel of communication between the imperial government and the colony, had undoubtedly been a serious administrative blunder, which the attitude of Massachusetts had made at once worse and more obvious.

Indeed, just at a time when a strong administrative control was most necessary, it may well have appeared as if the Empire were drifting toward disruption. However different the material for colonization may have been in the various colonies, — and, in the main, it is now considered as more uniform than was formerly thought to have been the case,— the frontier influence was at work in them all; and the main characteristic which they possessed in common was their insistence upon the right of self-government. Not only among the continental colonies, but among the island ones as well, we find the same spirit from the start, and the same reiterated demand for assemblies and self-taxation. The story varies only in detail, whether we study Tobago, Trinidad, Antigua, Nevis, Jamaica, Barbadoes, Bermuda, or New England.[1] These two points were wholly compatible with a well-organized empire, however, and England, for the most part, made no effort to interfere with either.

It was a different matter when the colonies declined to admit that the imperial government possessed any authority over them, or refused to observe those laws made for the regulation of the Empire as a whole. The case of Massachusetts had become notorious, not only throughout the Empire, but even among foreigners; and Colbert's agent in the French West Indies could write that "the English who dwell near Boston will not worry themselves about the prohibitions which the King of England may issue, because they hardly recognize his authority."[2] Although, with reference to Virginia, it was reported that this "New England disease is very catching,"[3] it seems to have been indigenous in the soil of most of the colonies. It had long since been reported that many in Barbadoes wished to become independent "and not run any fortune with

[1] H. E. Egerton, in *Cambridge Modern History*, vol. iv, p. 758; V. L. Oliver, *History of the Island of Antigua* (London, 1894–99), vol. i, p. xxxix; *Cal. State Pap., Col., 1661–68*, pp. 545, 169 ff., 96.

[2] Cited by Mims, *Colbert's West Indian Policy*, p. 222.

[3] *Cal. State Pap., Col., 1675–76*, p. 153.

England either in peace or war," but to erect their "little limb of the Commonwealth into a free state." [1]   In the very year in which Massachusetts lost her charter, the inhabitants of Bermuda were proclaiming that "we are free-born people, our Lands are our own, and wee will doe with our own what wee please, and if wee doe not like of the King's Government wee can desert the Country." [2]

Aside from the influence of the frontier, however, the element of time was also beginning to make itself felt.   In New England, practically the entire first generation of settlers had died by the end of Philip's War.   The "freemen" who were now guiding her destinies had, for the most part, been born in the settlements, and were colonials, in the strict sense of the word. They possessed no fond memories of the mother-country, or close personal ties with individuals there.   Their interests and outlook were provincial and local to a degree that we can hardly realize.   They were caught in a little back-water, and the great current of English life was sweeping on with but slight influence upon them.   The first planters had been drawn to a large extent from a very sound element in the England of their day, but, with few exceptions, they were men of narrow outlook, which had naturally become still narrower in their laborious, isolated life in America.   Among the religious elements in the new communities, the intensity of their faith in the divine nature of their mission, combined with their extraordinary self-consciousness, tended to breed a belief in their own superiority, which infected not only the whole of New England, but much subsequent historical writing. Stoughton's preaching that "God sifted a whole nation that he might send choice grain over into this wilderness" was but a mild expression of what the New Englanders thoroughly believed and loved to be told.[3]

We have already expressed our high appreciation of the character of much of the early immigration to that section of

---

[1] *Cal. State Pap., Col., 1574–1660*, pp. 384, 408.   [2] *Ibid., 1685–88*, p. 49.
[3] *New England's true Interest not to Lie;* cited by Tyler, *History of American Litera-ture* (New York, 1879), vol. II, p. 163.

the country; but it cannot be claimed that it included any of the real leaders in England in any line of thought or action; and figures which loom large against the background of the wilderness change their proportions materially when measured by the national life in the old country. It has been claimed that Cromwell, at one time, thought seriously of emigrating to New England; and it is illuminating to consider, had he done so, the resultant comparative stature, in view of the new standard of measure thus introduced, of such men as Bradstreet and Stoughton. The New England leaders were, indeed, of a more intellectual type generally than came to the other colonies, and there was, perhaps, more play of mind among the people than in either the southern continental or the island settlements. Common-school education was fostered to a degree unknown elsewhere at the time, and the village school, with the town-meeting and the Congregational church, soon took its place in New England's typical community life. In 1647, Massachusetts passed a law requiring every town of fifty families to maintain a teacher of reading and writing, and each town of one hundred families to establish a grammar school.[1] Every town in Connecticut had its provision for elementary education, and each county its Latin school. Even Plymouth, in spite of its poverty, was also fairly well provided.[2] In Harvard, which was founded as early as 1636, the colonies long possessed the only English institution of higher learning in the new world, although there was a French college in Quebec, founded at virtually the same time as Harvard.[3] The early Virginia settlers were, at first, indeed, as solicitous as the New Englanders about education, but the results of the geographic environment were felt as strongly in this as in the other matters on which we have already touched. With the bad roads and the scattered life

[1] *Massachusetts Records*, vol. II, p. 203.

[2] *Conn. Col. Records*, vols. II, p. 307, and III, p. 9; *Plymouth Records*, vol. II, pp. 81, 102. Rhode Island seems to have been backward, but had at least one school as early as 1640. *Vide* Arnold, *Rhode Island*, vol. I, p. 145.

[3] *Massachusetts Records*, vol. I, p. 183; G. M. Wrong, *Conquest of New France* (Yale University Press, 1918), p. 42.

of the plantations, it was impossible for the common school to take root as it did in the compact little villages of New England. But if the common schooling was somewhat less diffused, the culture of the educated class was wider, and the private libraries of the Virginians offer to the booklover a refreshing contrast to the dead weight of theology on the New England shelves. Nor were these southern libraries confined, as used to be thought, to a few families, research tending constantly to minimize the supposed difference between New England and the rest of the colonies in this regard.[1]

Moreover, although her devotion to education was to bear noble fruit in the years to come, and is one of the chief contributions of New England to our national life, its original object, and almost the sole use to which it was put, was religious, and it may be questioned whether its earlier influence upon the people at large was not narrowing rather than broadening. For, in the absence, for the average citizen in New England, of almost any books other than theological, and of any intellectual stimulus other than the sermon, the earlier result of such education as the people received seems to have been mainly an intensified preoccupation with the problems of Calvinism, and a remarkable extension of the influence of the priesthood. The attitude of Massachusetts, in extirpating so far as possible all ideas opposed to her official theology, in banishing those who persisted in giving expression to them, and in exercising a strict censorship over the only printing-press in New England, nullified, to a great extent, the benefits that might otherwise have been derived from her "educational" system in the sense of schools.[2] In the writings of the men who settled Massachusetts or visited it in the earliest period, there is a freshness and charm of outlook and phrase which allures the reader even of to-day. In Smith or Brad-

---

[1] Cf. *Virginia Magazine*, vols. III, pp. 388 ff., VII, pp. 299 ff., X, pp. 399 ff., and XVII, pp. 147 f.; *William and Mary Quarterly*, vols. II, pp. 169 ff., III, pp. 43 f., 132 f., 180 f., 246 f., and IV, pp. 15 f., 94, 156. Cf. J. H. Tuttle "The Libraries of the Mathers," in *American Antiquarian Society Proceedings*, N. S., vol. XX, pp. 269 ff.

[2] C. A. Duniway, *Development of Freedom of the Press in Massachusetts* (Harvard University Press, 1906), pp. 22 ff.

ford, Higginson or Wood, one feels in the presence of a healthy mind, actively interested in this world or the next; but when these men have passed, the balance of the century leaves us hardly a work which, for a modern reader, possesses any interest other than antiquarian or historical.

In England, men's minds had been profoundly stirred by the great parliamentary struggle, the Civil War, and all the influences of the new period. In science, Ray was founding systematic zoölogy, Harvey had discovered the circulation of the blood, Newton the law of gravitation, Boyle the law of gases which bears his name, and Halley was working in his observatory at Greenwich. Among the numerous contemporary writers whom our educated colonists might have been reading had they been in England, we may mention, at hazard, Locke, Hobbes, Butler, Marvell, Sir Thomas Browne, Milton, Taylor, Izaak Walton, Bunyan, Fuller, Clarendon, Herbert, Dryden, and Herrick. But of all this varied intellectual life, it may be said that practically nothing reached the vast majority of New Englanders, whose science was still made up of the superstitious observances of "special providences," and whose political life was centred in the meeting of church or town. If they felt the need of verse, they read Uriah Oakes or Michael Wigglesworth, and the need must have been as great as its reward was inadequate. Of other printed literature indigenous to the soil, there was practically none except theological, and the few historical accounts brought out by the Indian wars.[1]

Such impoverishment of the intellectual life was a necessary consequence of living in the wilderness in the seventeenth century; but it was none the less a misfortune because inevitable. In New England, however, a peculiar result ensued from the combination of the extreme rarity of the intellectual atmosphere and the partial education of her people. In the other colonies, men may have been more ignorant of books,

---

[1] *Vide* the appallingly theological and dreary catalogue of the Boston bookseller, Michael Perry, in John Dunton's *Letters from New England* (Prince Society, 1867), pp. 314 *ff*. The whole intellectual life of the period in England noted above is unrepresented by a single volume except *Pilgrim's Progress*.

but they were healthy-minded. In New England, the concentration of an awakened mental life almost wholly upon the problems of election or damnation created a condition of ethical morbidity, and bequeathed to us the legacy of what may almost be called that section's fourth contribution to American life — the New England conscience, with its pathological questionings and elaborate system of taboos. It is an interesting psychological study, not without its immediate historical bearings, to contrast the diaries of such English officials as Pepys or Evelyn with that kept by the active Massachusetts official, Sewall, who could amuse himself all Christmas Day arranging the coffins in the family vault, and pronounce the occupation to have been "an awfull yet pleasing Treat."[1] Toward the end of the seventeenth century, public opinion in New England, economic, religious, political, and social, had grown largely out of touch with that in the old country; but the nature of the case demanded that, in the last analysis, the government of the Empire must be mainly determined by the latter and not by the former.

As in England, however, parties based on civil differences were replacing the old religious ones, so in New England, parties were forming due to the rise of altered economic conditions, and the passing of the early religious spirit. We have already noted the presence in Massachusetts, from the start, of a considerable body of dissent from the doctrine and polity of the colonial state church, and the decline in fervor even within the group of the Saints themselves. Men who, according to the official church theory, were not of the elect, and yet who were conscious of trying to live helpful, honest, God-fearing lives, refused to acknowledge the truth of the denunciations which, under penalty of fine, they were forced to listen to, Sunday after Sunday, hurled at themselves by the leading divines. Hooker might thunder that "no carrion in a ditch smells more loathsomely in the nostrils of man, than a natural man's works do in the nostrils of the Almighty"; or Shepard declare that the mind of the natural man "is a nest of all the foul opinions, heresies, that ever were vented," and his heart "a foul sink all of atheism, sodomy, blasphemy, murder, whoredom, adultery, witchcraft, buggery." [1] The bow had been bent too long, and had lost its spring. Bradstreet might still demand that "the old stand firm" against "that cursed Bratt Toleration," but Bishop reported more truly "that many are gospel-glutted and growing weary." [2]

At the time when religion was thus gradually passing as the leading cause of division in New England, other forces were at work to align the citizens into new parties. In a former chapter, we called attention to the early beginning, on a small scale, of the divergence between the life of the frontiers and that of the older and more established settlements. With the growth of a few of the larger centres, notably Boston, there also developed the conflict of economic interests and political outlook between town and country. [3] The prosperity of the Empire under the Navigation Acts had increased enormously, and New England, although refusing to obey the laws, had shared to the full in the resultant growth of trade and wealth. From all these causes, there had developed fairly distinct opposing groups — a large element of liberals in theology, as against the maintainers of rigid orthodoxy; a conservative "east" against a radical "west," a progressive urban population, contrasted with the more narrow-minded, unchanging rural laborers and farmers; and a trading, moneyed class, with views and interests differing from the agricultural. [4] The distinctions are real and marked, though the numbers of those in the various parties, and their exact groupings on special questions, can only be approximated. The magistrates, consisting, for the most part, of men of wealth and position chosen

[1] Extracts, in Tyler, *American Literature*, vol. I, pp. 201, 208.

[2] Letters to Increase Mather, in *Mass. Hist. Soc. Coll.*, Series IV, vol. VIII, pp. 478, 314.

[3] Cf. *Queries upon the present state of the New English affairs*, by S. E. (London, circa 1689); Sabin reprint, New York, 1865, p. 17.

[4] Randolph wrote in Feb., 1686: "There are no small endeavors betwixt the Landed men and the Merct how to ease the publick Charges: The Mercts are for land Taxes, but Mr. Dudley, Stoughton and others who have gott very larg tracts of Land are for Laying all upon the trading party," etc. *Randolph Papers*, vol. VI, p. 211.

from the larger centres, and the deputies, resident in each of
the towns from which they were elected, represented, in their
differing attitudes, the moderate and radical opinion of the
colonies as a whole.   In the relations with England, those who
were liberal in theology, in closer personal or commercial
contact with the old country, and more conservative in their
outlook, would naturally favor a conciliatory attitude.   Those,
on the other hand, who believed that the supreme object at
stake was the maintaining of the peculiar ecclesiastical organization of their church-state, with its religious franchise tests,
and those who had no direct business relations with England
or other countries, would as naturally tend to adopt an un-
yielding attitude of opposition.   There is a direct line of descent from the moderate party of 1676 to the Loyalist party of
1776; and, as the wholesale condemnation of the latter is now
considered uncritical, so, also, we cannot off-hand divide the
parties of the earlier struggle into traitors and patriots.

As in old England the main question of the day was the
location of sovereignty, so it was in the New, and in the relations between the two.   The theory of the state as based upon
original contract, which, although implicit in feudalism, was,
as we have seen, probably derived in New England from the
church covenant, had even less historical or philosophical basis
than that of divine right.   However, the advances made by
mankind are not less real because they have nearly always been
contemporaneously justified by false assumptions.   In such
cases "conclusions are more permanent than premises," as Mr.
Balfour points out in speaking of "the incongruity between the
causes by which beliefs are sustained, and the official reasons
by which they are from time to time justified." [1]   It is in this
very failure of man to reason rightly as to the grounds of his
own efforts that we perceive most clearly the operations of
forces in human history independent of man's own will and
thought, precisely where, for himself, the illusion of a reasoned
freedom is strongest.   Although the theories of divine right
and of original compact have now both been discarded among

[1] A. J. Balfour, *Foundations of Belief* (New York, 1918), p. 227.

the philosophical lumber of the past, the latter theory was of enormous influence in shaping American political thought. Before, however, that thought could legitimately give expression to the dictum, "No taxation without representation," it was necessary that the community as a whole, and not a religious sect, should be considered to be the "people"; and before Massachusetts could join in declaring that "All men are created equal," she had to abandon her earlier politico-religious distinction between a minority born to be everlasting saints and a majority doomed to eternal damnation. We must now turn to consider, more in detail, the story of how that result was achieved.

The heirs of Mason and Gorges had never abandoned their claims to the territory in New Hampshire and Maine which had been illegally absorbed by Massachusetts, and, of late, they had been pressing their respective cases with more and more insistence. In May, 1675, the law officers of the Crown reported to the Committee for Foreign Plantations that, in their opinion, both claims were based upon valid titles.[1] It was not mainly, however, the complaints of these individual claimants, or Mason's detailed recommendations to send commissioners to New England,[2] which decided the government to take a more active part in the administration of the colonies. Peace had been signed with the Dutch in the preceding year, and the ending of the war provided leisure for undertaking more seriously the reorganization of colonial administration. The reform began at home with the abolition of the old Council Committee, and the placing of colonial affairs in the hands of a new committee known as the Lords of Trade and Plantations. Its members were able men, well qualified for their work, and displayed considerable energy, holding eighty-nine meetings in the first year after their organization.[3]

The New England question promptly came in for a share of their attention. We have already noted the many and

---

[1] Cal. State Pap., Col., 1675-76, pp. 232 f.   [2] Ibid. pp. 222 ff.
[3] Cf. W. T. Root, "Lords of Trade and Plantations, 1675-1696," in American Historical Review, vol. XXIII, pp. 21 ff. Also, Andrews, British Committees, pp. 111 ff.

constant complaints in regard to Massachusetts, and the attitude of that colony toward the Royal Commissioners in 1664. While all these old matters, as well as the newly delivered legal opinions regarding the Mason and Gorges claims, were before the Lords of Trade, they probably found their chief ground for dissatisfaction with Massachusetts in her disregard of the Navigation Acts, and the assumption of virtual independence. Captain Wyborne of H. M. S. Garland, after a visit to Boston, reported that New England's trade to Europe and the West Indies had become very great, and that the magistrates refused to act regarding violations of the law, the people looking upon themselves as "a free state." [1] About six weeks later, twenty-eight English merchants complained that New England was illegally trading on a great scale between Europe and the various parts of the British Empire, and so underselling the English in both markets, and ruining business. [2] New England herself produced none of the "enumerated commodities," and, had she confined herself to legitimate trade, would not have been placed at any appreciable disadvantage by the Navigation Acts of this period. By evading the law, however, she gained not only the advantage of an unrestricted commerce, when such was not allowed in any of the over-seas empires of the time, but also an extra, illegitimate profit, over and above her law-abiding competitors, exactly as a smuggler of dutiable articles makes a larger profit than the legitimate merchant, solely by virtue of the existence of the very laws that the former evades. The amount lost by England on New England's domestic illegal trade was not great; but, if the rapidly increasing business of those colonies between Europe and the rest of the Empire were allowed to go on unchecked, the integrity of the whole imperial structure would be seriously threatened. [3]

[1] *Cal. State Pap., Col., 1675-76*, pp. 306 ff.; Beer, *Old Colonial System*, vol. II, pp. 257 f.

[2] *Cal. State Pap., Col., 1675-76*, p. 337. The complaint is given in full in *Randolph Papers*, vol. I, pp. 49 n. The latter gives 25 signers, while the Calendar gives 28.

[3] *Cf.* Beer, *Old Colonial System*, vol. II, pp. 256 f., 308 f.

Mason had advised that a new commissioner, or a governor general, be sent to New England; but the English government refused, on the ground that it would give needless affront, and "would look like awarding execution on those people before they were heard."[1] It was, therefore, decided that Massachusetts should be asked to send over agents; and, probably in view of the colony's now well-known policy of delay, it was determined to transmit the demand by a special messenger, who should bring back personally the answer of the General Court. The individual selected for this task was Edward Randolph, who was instructed, not only to deliver the King's letter, and receive the reply, but also to make a report on trade and other conditions in the colony, in order that the government might have a better basis for intelligent action.[2]

Randolph was of the narrow-minded, official type, a stickler for technicalities, a thorough believer in centralized imperial control, and easily influenced by prejudice, but possessed of enormous energy, and of very considerable ability. He had the not uncommon fault of forcing facts to fit his theories rather than building theories from the facts; but in his long connection with the colonies, in offices in which it would have been peculiarly easy to live by bribes, he was incorruptibly honest, a rare quality in that day. Moreover, although always poor, and in his later life embittered, he could yet be generous toward the distress of others; and when Mason's motherless children were suffering from poverty in England, he allowed them £20 a year from his own scanty income.[3] While he was violently opposed to the decentralization of authority involved in the charter governments, he was not anxious to play the tyrant, and seems to have believed that the changes he had at heart would benefit not only the Empire, but the colonists as well. On more than one occasion, indeed, this "blasted wretch," as Mather called him, defended their interests against the Crown. No English official in our colonial history, however, was more thoroughly hated, and he returned the feeling

[1] *Cal. State Pap., Col., 1675-76*, p. 308.   [2] *Ibid.*, pp. 322, 358, 362.
[3] *Randolph Papers*, vol. IV, p. 69.

in so far as the ruling powers of Massachusetts were concerned. In this he was hardly to be blamed, for their attitude and policy toward him, from the first, consisted in covert obstruction and open insult.

He arrived in Boston early in June, and at once showed his credentials, and stated his errand, to Governor Leverett. At the meeting of the Council, at which the King's letter was presented, the Governor and all but three magistrates kept their hats on while the missive was being read, refusing to uncover according to the usual custom. When the reading was concluded, Leverett curtly stated that "the matters therein contained were very inconsiderable things and easily answered," although, in reality, it was the most important communication that the local government had ever received. When Randolph called their attention to the demand of the King that an answer be returned, he was simply told that the matter would be considered.[1]

Although his instructions were that he should remain a month, in order to gather the data required before returning, the Council announced, within two days, that they had an answer prepared to the royal letter, which they were going to send immediately, but which they would not entrust to Randolph, offering him only a copy, despite the King's express command. When Randolph asked if they could have well considered so weighty a matter in forty-eight hours, he was curtly requested to withdraw, unless he had further orders from the King, as the Councillors looked upon him as Mason's agent.

Meanwhile, several ships had arrived direct from various European ports, contrary to the Navigation Acts, of which Randolph spoke to the Governor in the course of an interview on the following day. Leverett thereupon declared that the laws made by King and Parliament did not apply to Massachusetts, and that any dispute between England and the colony was to be decided by the colony and not by England.[2]

[1] *Randolph Papers*, vol. ii, pp. 216 f.

[2] *Ibid.*, pp. 218 f. While our account is derived from Randolph, there is no reason to doubt its accuracy, for the statement contained nothing contrary to the frequently avowed policy of the colony, as we have already found.

Randolph next proceeded into New Hampshire, where he showed letters from Mason, and naturally received many complaints from disaffected inhabitants in regard to Massachusetts. For his actions there, he was sharply rebuked by Leverett, who accused him of trying to "make a mutiny and disturbance." Randolph had also suggested, just before going to New Hampshire, that the General Court be summoned, in order to consider the King's dispatch; but this was not done, and he finally sailed for England with only a copy of the letter written by the Council.[1] In that letter, Leverett wrote, with considerable effrontery, that the complaints of Mason and Gorges were "impertinencies, mistakes and falsehoods," but said nothing about complying with the demand to send agents, except that the General Court, which, he claimed, could not then be summoned on account of sickness and the Indian War, would be convened later.[2]

Owing to the unwise course of the rulers, Randolph could hardly fail to have been biased by the information received from their opponents; and the result is evident in the long report which he submitted to the Lords of Trade on his return. Although, owing to his preconceived ideas, and the circumstances of his stay, he misjudged the strength of the opposing parties in the colony, and although certain of his statistics were greatly exaggerated, the report, on the whole, gave a detailed and truthful presentation of the general situation, and confirmed other information possessed in England.[3] For, while Randolph was on his way west, the Lords of Trade had pursued their investigations, and summoned before them merchants trading with New England. Of these, "some were shy to unfold the mystery, others pretended ignorance, but most declared plainly" that New England traders were regularly breaking the law, and that, by their direct trade in European goods

---

[1] *Randolph Papers*, vol. ii, pp. 220, 224 f., 203 ff.
[2] *Cal. State Pap., Col., 1675-76*, pp. 402 f.
[3] Osgood's estimate of the report, as well as Beer's, seems to me more just than Doyle's. Osgood, *American Colonies*, vol. iii, pp. 316 f.; Beer, *Old Colonial System*, vol. ii, p. 265; Doyle, *Puritan Colonies*, vol. ii, pp. 196 f. The report is given in full in *Randolph Papers*, vol. ii, pp. 225 ff.

with the other colonies they were able to undersell, by twenty
per cent, those doing a legitimate business.[1] This was confirmed, a few weeks later, by an official returned from a trip
to the West Indies, who reported seventeen New England
ships engaged there in a clandestine trade with Europe in log-
wood for dyeing, which not only threatened to involve the
whole Empire in a war with Spain, but provided England's
rivals with cheaper dyes than she herself obtained.[2] It was
becoming more and more evident, the deeper the matter was
probed, that the question was not a domestic one for Massachusetts, whatever she might choose to assume, but one that
involved the interests of England and the Empire.

The meeting of the General Court in Massachusetts, to
consider the King's letter, was not held until August, when the
question of complying with the order to send agents to England
was referred for advice to the clergy, as usual. Their opinion
being in favor of obedience, the people's representatives, in the
following month, adopted an address to the King, and appointed Stoughton and Bulkley as agents.[3] The address was
accompanied by a long statement of the claims of Massachusetts to the disputed eastern territory, which presented her
interpretation of her boundaries, and the benefits to the inhabitants of her government there, in as favorable a light as
possible, dismissing the claims of Mason and Gorges, adjudged
valid by the Crown lawyers, as "frivolous and insignificant
allegations."[4] The colony still delayed, however, and her
agents did not reach England until January of the following
year. Their position was evidently realized to be an unenviable one, for the Reverend John Eliot wrote in his diary,
"Mr. Stoughton & mr. Bulkly were sent to England to agent
for the Country. Lord p'ty ym."[5] They were furnished with
two sets of instructions, according to which they were given
authority to act in regard to the Mason-Gorges matters only,
and to plead lack of power as to all others. They were also,

[1] *Cal. State Pap., Col., 1675-76*, pp. 377, 379 f.
[2] *Ibid.*, p. 398; Beer, *Old Colonial System*, vol. II, p. 256.
[3] *Massachusetts Records*, vol. v, pp. 99 f., 113.   [4] *Ibid.* pp 108 ff.
[5] *Boston Record Commissioners' Report*, vol. vi, p. 195.

on the one hand, to represent to the King that the eastern provinces were of little value, and, on the other, to endeavor to purchase them from Mason and Gorges, if possible.[1]

In limiting her agents to the one matter of the eastern provinces, Massachusetts was technically complying with the King's request; but the New England question was much wider in scope than that, and the unhappy agents soon found themselves in deep waters. The colony's policy had been such that the English government could not expect more from other agents than from those who were then actually present, who were, after all, primarily English subjects and not colonial representatives, and who could, therefore, well be called upon to explain their colony's acts, though they could not bind her by agreements. Randolph was now busily engaged in pressing his views on the government, listing the crimes and misdemeanors of the colony, and outlining a course of action. While some of his accusations were so exaggerated as to be palpably false, others were unquestionably true, such as denying appeals to England, violating the Navigation Acts, imposing an oath of fidelity to the local government while refusing the oath of allegiance to England, and putting English citizens to death for religious opinions.[2] He proposed that the King issue a general pardon for all past offenses, confirm real-estate titles on payment of a moderate quit-rent, grant liberty of conscience, and organize the colony as a royal province.[3] Detailed evidence, in reference to the illegal trading, derived from such widely separated points as London, Jamaica, and Amsterdam, was also laid before the Committee.[4] All these various allegations, together with the question of the validity of the charter, and the laws made by the General Court, were divided into "matters of law" and "matters of state," and submitted to the Judges and Privy Council respectively.[5] While the decisions were pending, the

---

[1] *Massachusetts Records*, vol. v, pp. 113–117.
[2] *Randolph Papers*, vol. II., pp. 265 *ff.*   [3] *Ibid.*, pp. 265 *ff.*
[4] *Ibid.*, pp. 268 *ff.*; *Cal. State Pap., Col., 1677–80*, p. 102.
[5] *Randolph Papers*, pp. 270 *ff.*

agents were questioned in reference to the complaints against the colony, and answered as "private men," admitting some of the statements, as to coining money and violating the Navigation Acts, but denying that the Quakers had been put to death on account of their religion only.[1]

The decisions of the judges in regard to the matters submitted to them were eminently fair. The validity of the Massachusetts charter was upheld as originally granted, and it was further stated that the document had created the patentees a corporation upon the place. The latter opinion, which was of very doubtful legality, not only decided, in so far as it went, that the transfer of the charter to New England had been legal, but also settled in favor of the colony the question whether or not the *Quo Warranto* proceedings of 1635 had in reality dissolved the corporation. In regard to the geographical limits of the colony, however, the interpretation that Massachusetts had developed, in order to cover her encroachments, was declared to be without foundation. But at the last moment either the agents or the colony's counsel had themselves retracted the absurd claims, in spite of their recent statement that those of Gorges and Mason were "frivolous," and the earlier characterization of them as impertinent falsehoods. Those of the former were now sustained in full, both as to ownership and power of government. Mason was declared not to have received any legal rights to govern, although his title to the land north of the Merrimac was pronounced a valid one. As to the smaller territory in dispute, lying between that river and Salem, the Attorney-General was of the opinion that Mason had never taken legal possession, and that his claim, therefore, was probably not good against the actual possession by Massachusetts settlers for fifty years; but that the question would have to be tried in courts upon the place.[2]

In regard to the Massachusetts laws, the Attorney-General

---

[1] *Randolph Papers*, vol. II, pp. 276 f.

[2] *Cal. State Pap., Col., 1677-80*, pp. 118 ff.; Hutchinson, *History*, vol. I, pp. 284 ff.; *Acts Privy Council, Colonial, 1613-80*, pp. 722 ff.

properly objected to making capital such offenses "which are
so by the word of God," it being "suspicious what are so."
He pointed in particular, also, to such statutes as provided for
the putting to death of stubborn and rebellious children, for
civil marriage, for levying fines for observing Christmas Day,
and laying penalties upon children for playing on Sunday, as
well as those against heresy, and to the lack of provision for
the oath of allegiance.[1]

All these matters were then discussed with the agents, who
were told that Massachusetts must confine herself to her legal
boundaries, that she must ask pardon for having coined money,
prepare to accept a supplementary charter, observe the Navigation Acts, receive a royal revenue officer, and repeal such
laws as were repugnant to the laws of England. The question of the colony's assumed right to tax non-freemen and
strangers was also raised. The agents were further told that
they could not return home as yet, as their presence would be
useful; and as for their not having full powers, "his Majesty
did not think of treating with his own subjects as with foreigners." The whole course of Massachusetts in reference
to the Royal Commissioners and her own agents, and her assuming to deal with the home government or not as she
pleased, as if she were in reality independent and sovereign,
had made some such step necessary, unless England was willing to allow the Empire to disintegrate. The agents were also
sharply reminded that although, twelve years previously, the
colony had been told that it could not retain the exclusive
religious test for the franchise, and a law had been passed
ostensibly granting it to non-church members, yet in reality
the law was disregarded, and virtually only church members
were allowed to vote.

To this the agents made a reply so disingenuous as to be
false. They stated that they knew of no such practice, and
that religious opinion was no bar to being elected a freeman,
although the records indicate that only one man who was not
a church member had been given the franchise in the pre-

[1] *Cal. State Pap., Col., 1677-80*, pp. 139 ff.

ceding eleven years, as compared with eight hundred and seventy-five who were church members.[1] Moreover, only five years previously, in the legal code of 1672, the law disfranchising all persons who did not attend the Congregational church had been reënacted, and, in fact, remained in force until the forfeiture of the charter.

The agents having sent home an account of their mission, the General Court passed a law requiring obedience to the Navigation Acts, and, without foundation, stated in a preamble that the King's desire that the laws be enforced had not "binn before now signified unto us," although the colony's failure to observe them had been one of the main complaints of the Royal Commissioners in 1665, and in that year, the Court had promised to obey them and had repealed laws inconsistent with them.[2] The government immediately called this false statement to the attention of the colony's agents, who attempted to apologize for it as an "act of precipitation," made just as the Court was rising,[3] which could hardly improve the government's opinion of the honesty of the colonial authorities, or of the attention they were giving to a very serious situation. As a matter of fact, it is difficult to find excuse for the statement; for not only were all the earlier proceedings a matter of record, but of the eleven magistrates who now declared that the colony had never had any knowledge of the matter before, nine had been members of the earlier Court, which had received the complaints, and passed the legislation. The Court's own communication thus seemed to prove Randolph's contention, and the evidence from other sources, that Massachusetts was, in reality, paying no attention to the laws of trade.

No effort was made by the Court to meet the other charges or requirements, and, so far from enforcing the oath of alle-

---

[1] The nature of the law has already been discussed. McKinley states that from 1664 to 1680 inclusive, 20 non-church members were admitted on certificates. Of these six were in 1664 and four in 1680. Of the remaining ten, however, reference to the Records seems to show that nine were church members, leaving only the one mentioned in my text. McKinley, *Suffrage*, pp. 328 *f.*; *Massachusetts Records*, vol. IV, pt. ii, pp. 145 *f.*, 408.

[2] *Ibid.*, pp. 193, 202, and vol. v, p. 155.   [3] *Randolph Papers*, vol. II, p. 295.

giance, they passed a new ordinance that any one in the colony, stranger or resident, who refused to take the local oath of fidelity, should be deprived of all legal rights and protection.[1] In spite of the failure of the Court to attempt to meet any of the other points raised by the English government, they petitioned for an extension of the colony's northern boundary so as to include the land lying between the Merrimac and the Piscataqua, and again instructed their agents to buy Maine from Gorges.[2]

Randolph had no difficulty in exposing the misstatements as to the franchise and the Navigation Acts, and made further representations to the Lords of Trade. That body was now thoroughly tired of the attitude and tactics of Massachusetts, and decided that, so far from granting that colony an extension of territory, the "whole matter ought to bee considered from the Very Root."[3] They decided that the colonists both ignored "fair persuasions" and took no notice of orders, and that it was evidently impossible, judging presumably from the statements that were made by both the colonial government and its agents, to determine whether the laws were being enforced or not. In view of the facts, some of the Lords were of the opinion that nothing would solve the problem except the sending out of a royal governor, who could look after imperial interests and serve as a real channel of communication between the colony and the home government. As this could not be done under the charter, the question was referred to the Attorney-General whether, if the charter were, indeed, valid, the violations of its provisions had been sufficient to warrant its forfeiture.[4] His opinion being that the violations were great enough to justify action, the Lords advised that *Quo Warranto* proceedings be instituted, and that Randolph be appointed Collector of Customs in New England. Shortly

---

[1] *Massachusetts Records*, vol. v, pp. 154 f.

[2] *Ibid.*, 158, 164; *Cal. State Pap., Col., 1677–80*, pp. 147 ff., 198.

[3] *Randolph Papers*, vols. II, p. 297, and VI, pp. 73 f.

[4] *Ibid.*, vol. II, p. 297. In spite of the former decision, serious doubts had been cast upon its validity, which cannot be dismissed lightly. *Cf.* Osgood, *American Colonies*, vol. III, p. 322.

after, he received the appointment, in spite of the protests
of the agents.[1]   For the first time there was now to be resident
in the colony an official directly responsible to the imperial,
and not to the local, government. The choice of both office
and person for the introduction of a new system of control
was unfortunate, but the change in the system itself had been
forced by the colony's own rulers.

Meanwhile, Massachusetts was doing nothing to render her
position more favorable, and the purchase of Maine, which
the agents had effected privately with Gorges for £1250,
further irritated the government.[2]   Moreover, although Gorges
could not alienate his rights of government, Massachusetts
proceeded to exercise them in defiance of the royal order, of
her own legal powers, and gradually, it would seem, of the
desires of the inhabitants.[3] The disaffection of the Maine
people, who had been fairly contented before, may have been
caused in part by the levying of quit-rents by Massachusetts,
who, on becoming proprietor in place of Gorges, may have
taken this means of reimbursing herself for the £1250 expended; for the records show that she did exercise such rights,
and considered herself as in receipt of a regular income from
quit-rents in her new province.[4]

To add to the bad odor of New England affairs, the Atherton
Land Company chose this particular juncture to reassert its
claim to the Narragansett country, and that question rose to
the surface again, Holden and Greene, of Rhode Island, making
serious complaints before the Crown of the encroachments of
Massachusetts. Although, so far as Connecticut and the
Bay Colony were concerned, the whole question of the King's
Province had been settled a dozen years previously, they had
both continued to plague their smaller neighbor with their

---

[1] *Randolph Papers*, vols. III, pp. 3 ff., and VI, pp. 75 ff.
[2] *Cal. State Pap., Col., 1677–80*, p. 224; *Massachusetts Records*, vol. v, pp. 195, 203.
[3] It is difficult to judge public sentiment by petitions, but in 1680 a petition signed
by 136 inhabitants of York, Kittery, and Wells prayed for release from Massachusetts.
Later, what was evidently intended as a counter-petition from the General Assembly,
was signed by 16 burgesses. *Cal. State Pap., Col., 1677–80*, pp. 608, 622. *Cf.* Hutchinson, *History*, vol. I, p. 296.
[4] *Massachusetts Records*, vol. v, pp. 451, 326 f.

claims, and Rhode Island now asked that the King appoint a "Supreme Court of Judicature" over all the New England colonies, to settle boundary disputes.[1] Although this was not done, Massachusetts was told to let the province alone,[2] and the whole episode could not fail to impress the English government more forcibly than ever with the necessity of establishing a greater degree of local royal control. Soon after, the same suggestion of a Supreme Court was made in the curious case of a Connecticut Indian, who had made his way to England to complain both of fraud against himself and of the general treatment of his race by the colonists, against whom, he claimed, it was impossible to secure justice in the colonial courts.[3]

In the fall of 1678, the Massachusetts Court finally agreed to administer the oath of allegiance, and to pass a law against treason; but beyond that they refused to go.[4] In fact, in their answer to the Attorney-General regarding their laws, they announced that the laws of England did "not reach Amererica," and that, as the colonies were not represented in Parliament, they were not subject to the Navigation Acts. These, however, the Court reënacted, in order, according to their theory, to give them validity within Massachusetts.[5]

The doctrine of no taxation without representation is a natural deduction from the contract theory, and has as little historical or philosophical justification as has that of the theoretical contract itself. It is mere commonplace to dwell on the philosophical weakness of the doctrine, the brief expression of which was to become the rallying cry of a continent a century later. From a practical standpoint, however, it may be pointed out, that what may be called the historical

---

[1] *Cal. State Pap., Col., 1677–80*, p. 279. *Cf.* the land company's advertisement for settlers and claims of title, in *R. I. Records*, vol. III, p. 18.

[2] *Cal. State Pap., Col., 1677–80*, p. 309.

[3] *Ibid.*, p. 340. There is additional reference to this case in *Conn. Col. Records*, vol. III, pp. 281 *ff*. *Cf.* also the unjust action of Connecticut toward the Indians the same year, when, in order to recover £30 damage done by some drunken individual, the colony confiscated 600 acres of Mohegan lands. *Ibid.*, pp. 43 *n.*, 56.

[4] *Massachusetts Records*, vol. V, pp. 192, 194.

[5] *Ibid.*, pp. 200 *f.*; *Randolph Papers*, vol. III, p. 60.

basis of representation in England in the seventeenth century was quite different from the numerical basis in the United States to-day, and that, in the former sense, the inhabitants of Massachusets were as fully represented for purposes of taxation as were the vast majority of the citizens then resident in England, except for the unavoidable effects of distance alluded to in an earlier chapter.[1] If, on the other hand, it be claimed that the colony's government had in mind representation in the modern American sense, then they were acting even more tyrannically than was England, for they were themselves, without any legal right to do so under the charter, taxing the four fifths of the residents of Massachusets who had no voice in the local government, save in exactly the same vicarious way in which all the colonists were represented in Parliament. It may also be noted that we, to-day, deny such representation, as Massachusets was now claiming, to our own citizens resident in our territories and colonies. The theory of direct representation in Parliament of England's overseas possessions was not a new one, however, nor was it evolved in America. In the sixteenth century, Calais had been represented for a short time,[2] while Barbadoes had declared how "impracticable" it was that they should be taxed when unrepresented in Parliament, five years before the cry was raised in New England.[3] Nor was that cry raised solely in the cause of freedom. The demand, in reality, was, not that there should be no taxation without representation, but that the members of the Congregational church should be confirmed in their claim to tax the entire community without interference from England.

---

[1] The difference in the two methods was then beginning to be understood and was clearly brought out in a discussion in Carolina in 1685. *Cal. State Pap., Col., 1685–88*, pp. 12 *f.*

[2] Maitland, *Constitutional History*, p. 239.

[3] *Cal. State Pap., Col., 1669–74*, p. 475. *Cf.*, also, *The Groans of the Plantations* (London, 1689), p. 23. "Our Masters the Projectors think they have a great advantage over us, in regard we have none to represent *us* in Parliament. 'T is true, we have not: but we hope we may have them. It is no disparagement to the Kingdom of Portugall, rather it is the only thing that looks great; that in that assembly of their Estates the Deputies of the City of Goa have their place among their other cities."

In the letter which the King sent to the colony by its agents, who, on account of the attention of the government being entirely absorbed with the Popish Plot, were at last permitted to leave in June, 1679, he again returned to the question of religion and the suffrage. He insisted upon toleration for all except Papists, and a property qualification as the only one necessary for the franchise.[1] He also expressed his displeasure at the colony's secret purchase of Maine, and directed the surrender of the title-deeds upon repayment of the price paid. The colony was also instructed to withdraw all commissions granted for governing New Hampshire, as the legal right of administration was vested in the Crown, which was then considering a new establishment there. Other agents, in place of those now returning, were ordered to be sent within six months, duly instructed to act in the necessary regulating of the colony's affairs.[2]

Massachusetts persisted in her old tactics, and it was over three years before she sent the required agents to England. Meanwhile, Randolph, during his first year as customs officer, had met with no assistance, and every possible obstruction, in the performance of his duties, so that not a single ship had been seized for irregular trading.[3] In the court of February, 1680, the royal instructions were considered, and during the early part of the year a committee was appointed to revise the laws, while the New Hampshire commissions were canceled. The colony, however, proceeded to establish its own government in Maine, under the presidency of Danforth, despite the King's commands and a local disturbance at Casco.[4] In two letters to the English Secretary of State, Bradstreet, who had succeeded Leverett as governor, defended the purchase of the province, and virtually refused to alter the colony's practice in the matter of the franchise, except by nominally conceding that members of the Church of England would not be

---

[1] *Randolph Papers*, vol. III, pp. 50, 68.   [2] *Ibid.*, pp. 48 *ff*.

[3] *Ibid.*, vols. III, pp. 60, 70 *ff*., 86, and VI, pp. 99 *ff*.; *Cal. State Pap., Col., 1677–80*, pp. 372 *f*.; *Records of the Court of Assistants of Massachusetts Bay* (Boston, 1901), vol. I, pp. 149 *f*., 160, 168, 171, 176 *f*., *et passim*.

[4] *Massachusetts Records*, vol. v, pp. 268, 263.

considered heterodox. He held out no prospect of agents being sent, alleging the poverty of the colony and the danger of the "Turkish" pirates, who had captured several vessels.[1] In reply, the King wrote, in September, insisting that agents be sent within three months, with sufficient powers to settle all outstanding questions, and with such evidences of title as the colony might claim, to the strip of land in dispute with Mason.[2]

In January, 1681, this letter was read at a special meeting of the General Court, and Stoughton and Samuel Nowell were appointed agents. Stoughton evidently had no desire to repeat his former experiences, and, two months later, John Richards, a wealthy Boston merchant, was appointed in his place.[3] The months went by, however, and the end of the year found the agents still in America.

The patience of the English government had now become exhausted. For twenty years, since the Restoration, that government had been endeavoring, by every means in its power, to settle the New England question in a way that would be satisfactory to all the colonists, regardless of creed, and would, at the same time, permit the maintenance of the trade-system upon which the Empire was based. Had Massachusetts at any time been willing to give up her illicit profits, she could very possibly have saved her charter. The violations of that instrument upon which final action was taken were as palpable and actual in 1660 as in 1684. Had the English government merely wished to overthrow that of Massachusetts, it could legally have done so at any time it desired; and the prompt dispatch of a thousand English troops, at the time of Bacon's rebellion in Virginia, showed that it was capable of vigorous and effective action, when it was felt to be necessary. But every evidence points to the fact that it did not wish to be bothered with the problem in Massachusetts, or to proceed to

[1] *Massachusetts Records*, vol. v, pp. 268, 286, 278, 287 *ff.*
[2] *Randolph Papers*, vol. iii, pp. 81 *ff.*
[3] *Massachusetts Records*, vol. v, pp. 304, 307.

strong measures until absolutely forced to do so by the persistent attitude of the colony, which was virtually seceding
from the Empire.[1] The "New England disease" of avowed independence and nullification was infecting the rest of the Empire, and undermining England's prestige both within and without. The colony's increasing illegal trade was threatening the
destruction of the legitimate business of colonial and home merchants alike, as well as the Empire's international relations.
Although New England's domestic trade was of slight value
to the mother-country, she occupied a strategic position of
first importance in relation to the valuable staple colonies of
the south and the West Indies, and, in case of war with France,
it was essential that England should have some means of
official communication with, and control over, her strongest
colony on the enemy's frontier in America.

Over two years had now elapsed since Massachusetts had received orders to send agents, but she had sent none. She
was, nevertheless, given one last chance. At the end of 1681,
Randolph, who had been in England strongly urging *Quo
Warranto* proceedings against the charter, arrived in Boston
bearing a letter from the King. It required that more assistance be given to Randolph as collector, that the Navigation
Acts be enforced, and that agents be sent within three months,
or "wee shall take such further resolutions as are necessary to
preserve our authority from being neglected."[2] The letter
was much milder than the situation really warranted, and
than the wording of a suggested draft by the Lords of Trade.[3]

In February, 1682, the letter was read at a General Court,
and, a month later, Stoughton and Joseph Dudley were elected

---

[1] *Cf.* Beer, *Old Colonial System*, vol. II, pp. 305 *f.*
[2] *Randolph Papers*, vol. III, pp. 110 *ff.*
[3] *Cal. State Pap., Col., 1681–85*, pp. 129 *f.* Osgood (*American Colonies*, vol. III,
p. 328) states that this draft accompanied the King's letter, as does Doyle (*Puritan
Colonies*, vol. II, p. 216). Hutchinson does not mention it in his account, however
(*History*, vol. I, pp. 300 *f.*), and it seems to me that this document, which is undated,
is merely the preliminary draft, as its heading indicates, of the final letter, which is
in *Cal. State Pap., Col., 1681–85*, pp. 128 *ff.* The final drafts were often milder in
expression than the preliminary ones.

agents against considerable opposition. Stoughton again refused to serve, and Richards was chosen in his place.[1] Although comparatively little is known of him, it appears that he was strongly opposed to any concessions, whereas Dudley's more pliant nature and moderate views, influenced perhaps by ambition to take a leading place under the altered conditions which he evidently considered inevitable, led him to an early and willing coöperation with the English government after the blow had fallen.[2] Over three months more elapsed before the agents sailed, and it was midsummer when they reached England.[3] Although they carried with them confidential instructions, and a public defense of the colony, they were given no powers to treat of anything that might tend to infringe "the liberties and priviledges" granted by the charter as interpreted by Massachusetts.[4] It was obvious, therefore, that nothing could come of the negotiations, and that there was no recourse left to the English government except to acknowledge the virtual independence of the colony, or to void its charter.

In the answer that the agents made on their arrival, there was little that was new.[5] When it was pointed out to them that the requirement for the franchise had been that no religious distinction should be made, and no qualification be necessary, except that the applicant be a freeholder, of the Protestant religion, taxable at ten shillings, they stated that there was no other distinction, and that all contrary laws had been repealed. As was shown by both the law and the practice of the colony, this statement was false both in fact and in implication. In reference to the three-years' delay in complying with the request for agents, they alleged the danger of the

---

[1] *Massachusetts Records*, vol. v, pp. 333, 346; Hutchinson, *History*, vol. i, p. 301; *Mass. Hist. Soc. Coll.*, Series IV, vol. VIII, p. 494.

[2] Randolph's description of Dudley as an opposer of the "faction," and a man who "hath his fortune to make," is well known. *Randolph Papers*, vol. III, pp. 145, 171, 172. *Cf.* E. Kimball, *Public Life of Joseph Dudley* (Harvard Historical Studies, 1911), pp. 1–21.

[3] Hutchinson gives the date of sailing as May 31, N. S.; *History*, vol. i, p. 301.

[4] *Massachusetts Records*, vol. v, pp. 346 *ff.*

[5] *Cal. State Pap., Col., 1681–85*, pp. 288 *ff.*

seas, and lack of money, which latter was soon disproved by their clumsy and unsuccessful attempt to bribe the Lord Treasurer with £2000, which made them the laughing-stock of the Court.[1] Their answers in other respects were almost equally unsatisfactory, and their lack of power having been acknowledged, they were told that they must secure sufficient authority from the colony or that the *Quo Warranto* proceedings would begin.[2]

At the end of March, 1683, the General Court sent them additional instructions, but did not enlarge their powers, except that they were authorized to "tender" Maine or anything else which "our charter will not warrant our keeping." They were to reiterate their statements as to the franchise, and to consent to nothing which would alter their "liberties and privileges in matters of religion."[3] In the last analysis, it became evident that the one thing the controlling element in Massachusetts would not yield was its ecclesiastical power.

The King hesitated no longer. Randolph, however, who carried the notice of the beginning of *Quo Warranto* proceedings to Boston, was authorized, at his own suggestion, to offer to Massachusetts the promise of a full protection of private interests and property rights, and a liberal regulation of the charter, if she would voluntarily submit, in which case the proceedings would be abandoned.[4] The wholesale "regulation" of charters, as then being conducted by the Stuarts in England, held out little hope of the colony's securing any such liberties in a new charter as she possessed in the old; but, on the other hand, not to yield was to lose all, and, in view of her past record, she could expect little sympathy from any quarter.

The magistrates were in favor of accepting the offer, but the deputies refused, and the Court continued deadlocked.[5] It is impossible to determine what the public opinion was as to the situation. In the annual election, in spite of a determined effort to defeat him, Bradstreet, who was a moderate, secured

---

[1] Hutchinson, *History*, vol. I, p. 303; *Cal. State Pap., Col., 1681–85*, p. 373.
[2] *Ibid.*, p. 296. [3] *Massachusetts Records*, vol. v, pp. 390 *f.*
[4] *Randolph Papers*, vol. III, pp. 242, 246 *f.* [5] *Ibid.*, pp. 271 *ff.*

690 votes, against 631 for Danforth, who belonged to the radicals.[1] Dudley, indeed, failed of reëlection, but so, also, did Richards; and the general result seems to represent only a slight preponderance for the party of no compromise. It must be remembered also that, owing to the fact that only one fifth of the men of the colony possessed the franchise, and that they were all church members, the vote cannot be taken to represent the sentiment of the colony as a whole, much of the discontented element necessarily not showing in the returns. Under the circumstances, it is significant that over one half of the church members seem to have voted for Bradstreet and compromise, for it is fair to presume that they would include a much larger proportion of irreconcilables than the unenfranchised body of non-church members, who would have nothing to gain by fighting England to a finish, in order to preserve a church of which they were not members, and a theocratical government which excluded them from power. Their very legitimate grievance may well have been, indeed, that that same government, in its effort to preserve privileges for itself which meant nothing, or worse than nothing, to four fifths of the inhabitants of the colony, had sacrificed those other privileges which did mean something to them.

We need not enter into the legal details of the course by which the charter was canceled. The *Quo Warranto* proceedings having proved abortive, a writ of *Scire Facias* was entered, and, on October 13, 1684, Massachusetts ceased to be a chartered colony, and found herself without a single one of the rights to which she had clung so tenaciously.[2]

There seems to be no question of the technical legality of the proceedings; but, passing beyond those, there is nothing to regret in the course pursued by the Crown. The interpretation of the charter by the church party not only was inconsistent

---

[1] Hutchinson, *History*, vol. I, p. 306. Doyle (*Puritan Colonies*, vol. II, p. 222) makes a slip in this connection. He states that only one freeman in ten cast his vote. As a matter of fact there were not over 1500 freemen (McKinley, *Suffrage*, pp. 334 f.), so that the 1321 votes cast would seem to indicate great interest in the election, instead of the lack of it which Doyle suggests.

[2] For the legal proceedings, *vide* Winsor, *Memorial History*, vol. I, pp. 378 f.

with the terms of that instrument itself, so that any government built upon it was illegal and constantly open to attack, but was inconsistent, also, with the development of liberty itself in its widest sense. If it were, indeed, true that the charter formed an unalterable constitution, under which company members alone were able to become enfranchised citizens, then the power to govern the state could legally have been confined forever to the two or three dozen "freemen" who alone were called for by the charter. The pressure had been so great that the number of freemen had been greatly enlarged, it is true; but, according to the leaders' interpretation, this had been merely a boon granted out of good-will, and no additional freemen need ever be admitted. Their number might again be allowed to shrink, by death or disfranchisement, to the few required to fill the offices, who would, according to this theory, have the sole power of all government, including life and death, over the rest of the thirty-five thousand inhabitants. Although this, of course, was unlikely, nevertheless, those in control had shown definitely, when in order to maintain the theocracy they had sacrificed the whole political structure, rather than abandon their position with reference to extending the franchise, that nothing but a power so overwhelming as to be unopposable would have forced them peaceably to do so.

When we speak of liberty in connection with this early struggle with the home country, we should realize clearly that the party opposed to England fought to the end to perpetuate religious intolerance, and the intrenched privilege of a minority to tax an unenfranchised majority four times as numerous, and for the right to concentrate all political power in the hands of one religious sect. The clergy, who had wielded an extraordinary influence in the counsels of this governing minority, had, in many instances, been men of marked ability and fanatically devoted to the truth as they saw it. But as leaders, in the highest sense, they had very largely failed. From the beginning, they had striven to banish from the colony all ideas not in harmony with their own, and had thus lowered and impoverished the intellectual life of the community. On nearly every occasion, they had led in fanning the flames of intolerance and persecution. Over and over, they had helped to brutalize the natures of the citizens by calling for the blood of victims to whom the community would otherwise have shown mercy. One such example was yet to come, before the colony, disillusioned, was to reject their leadership finally in civil affairs.

But the present situation must have been of marked effect, when the people as a whole, non-church members as well as church members, found that, in the effort to perpetuate the theocracy, every civil right and safeguard, which they had considered they possessed under the charter, had been allowed to be taken from them. It is impossible, as we have said, accurately to gauge the public sentiment of the time from any data now available.[1] The people, unquestionably, could be trusted to resist any real efforts from across the water to restrict such liberties as they were prepared to enjoy. We seem too often to take it for granted, not only that liberty is something which all men are entitled to, but that they are at all times ready for it. The story of their gradually being moulded, so that they are, in an ever-increasing degree, fit for it, would seem quite as important as that of their struggle to obtain it.

It would have been a great misfortune had the Massachusetts of 1684 been allowed to go her own way, and to strengthen and perpetuate the combined ecclesiastical and political system for which her leaders had fought. As it is, the influence remains too strong of her fundamental doctrine that, in matters in any degree tinged with an ethical value, a minority has the "divine right" to force its will upon the majority, and to use the arm of the civil power to enforce its moral views upon the nation. In the town-meeting and the public school, the founders of Massachusetts, lay and clerical,

[1] The report of a meeting in Boston, from which non-freemen were excluded, a vote being then taken after an exhortation from Mather, cannot be considered as evidence of the sentiment of the community at large. The very fact that the non-freemen were not allowed to be present is in itself significant.

had made two contributions of untold influence to American political life; but it was well for personal liberty and intellectual freedom, when the real struggle came and independence was achieved, that it was for a people who had had some training in religious toleration and political equality, regardless of class or creed. And, curiously enough, so tangled is the skein of history, the laws which voiced and fostered those beliefs were due to one of the most shameless of English kings, and not to the fathers of the New England commonwealth.

CHAPTER XVI

AN EXPERIMENT IN ADMINISTRATION

In the preceding chapters, we have tried to show the comprehensive nature of that expansion of Europe which, with ever-accelerating swiftness, has been in operation since the age of discovery, and to indicate that, however great an importance any single colony, English or other, might attribute to itself, its contemporary significance could be measured relatively only to the interests of that empire of which it formed a part. For more or less obvious reasons, this great movement of expansion has usually been treated from the geographical standpoint. We think, for example, of England acquiring a foothold in the Far East or a post in Africa, the island of Jamaica or that section of America known as Virginia, rather than of her adding to her empire spices, slaves, sugar, or tobacco. Columbus, however, did not sail in search of a new land, but only of a new way to a market; and throughout the whole of the earlier expansion of Europe, we shall miss much of its significance, fail to understand its motives and methods, and misjudge its political ethics and standards, if we allow ourselves to fall into the way of thinking in geographical units, with their localized governments, instead of imperially and in terms of commodities and trade.

In the struggle of nations, not for land, but for materials and markets, on a world-scale, it has been necessary that each contending empire should be as economically self-contained, as closely united politically, and as militarily formidable as possible. Toward the close of the seventeenth century, the conditions of successful competition were beginning to stand out in somewhat clearer relief, as a result of the blind gropings and fortuitous groupings of a century of experiment, in a world whose economic possibilities had been but little known. In view of these requirements, and of the way in which the local New England policy ran counter to them, there is no need to invoke any malignant spirit, or even any very deeply selfish aim, on the part of the later Stuarts, to account for their attempt to unify and consolidate the Empire. Their policy may have been shaped only gradually in their own minds, and, in any case, could assume tangible form only by overcoming the obstacles of existing conditions and institutions, and by the use of such instruments as the times, fate, and their own natures allowed to them. The remainder of this volume will be occupied with the efforts of themselves and their successors to bring back the New England colonies into the general life of the Empire, and to establish those political relations which were to subsist for another century.

The first opportunity for putting into practice the new policy of consolidated administration and royal control was offered by New Hampshire when Massachusetts canceled the commissions of her officials there, in accordance with the King's orders, in February, 1680. Unfortunately for the colonists, and for any possible chance of success for the new order, the question was complicated by the entirely extraneous one of Mason's title to the land.[1] Technically legal as that may have been, and not wholly without its points even on the ground of abstract justice, it was not likely that squatters, who had enjoyed all the rights of possession for two generations, and who had put their labor into their property, would be willing to yield, even on nominal terms, unless forced to do so. Juries would certainly have to be packed if decisions so inimical to the pocket-books of the colonists were to be obtained in courts upon the spot; and nothing but ill-feeling and a travesty of justice could be anticipated, whichever way the verdicts went; and the King had no intention of spending his hard-won income to establish Mason's claims by force.

Indeed, the royal policy at first was wholly conciliatory. The

[1] The story of the Masonian Proprietors is given by O. G. Hammond, *The Mason Title and its relations to New Hampshire and Massachusetts;* American Antiquarian Society, 1916.

government provided consisted of a President and council, appointed by the King, and a popularly elected assembly, which latter was to make the laws and levy the taxes, legislation being subject to veto by the president and council in the colony, and by the King in Council in England.[1] John Cutt, the first President, and Martyn, Vaughan, Daniel, Gilman, and Waldron, of the Council, were all prominent men in the colony; some of them had been officials under Massachusetts. In fact, under this first royal government in New England, there was but little change; and the code of laws enacted by the Assembly was virtually a reënactment of the Massachusetts code, including some of the characteristic Puritanical criminal legislation already objected to by the English judges.[2] The laws which were passed confirming the land-titles of towns and individuals, and providing that, in controversies over lands, the juries should be "chosen by the freemen of each town," were, of course, aimed at the Mason menace, while the method of selecting juries was inconsistent with English law in the matter.

Having foreseen trouble over the land-question, the King had required Mason to agree not to demand any compensation for his property prior to June 12, 1680, and to confirm any individual in possession of his title forever, subject to a quit-rent of not over sixpence in the pound, reserving for his own disposition only the lands not already taken up.[3] In December, Mason and his friend Richard Chamberlain, an English lawyer, who had been appointed Secretary to the province, arrived in New Hampshire, and, in compliance with royal orders, Mason was given a seat in the Council.[4] In view, both of the difficulties which had been experienced, for fifty years, with the

---

[1] The commission is given in *N. H. Prov. Papers*, vol. I, pp. 373 *ff.*, and *Laws of New Hampshire Provincial Period* (ed. A. S. Batchellor, 1904), vol. I, pp. 72 *ff.* The government is described in Osgood, *American Colonies*, vol. III, pp. 337 *f.*, and Fry, *New Hampshire*, pp. 66 *ff.*

[2] The so-called "Cutt Code" is in *Laws of N. H.*, vol. I, pp. 11 *ff.*, and *N. H. Prov. Papers*, vol. I, pp. 382 *ff.*

[3] These conditions are given in Cutt's commission.

[4] *Cal. State Pap., Col., 1677–80*, pp. 592, 608; *Ibid., 1681–85*, p. 44; *N. H. Prov. Papers*, vol. I, pp. 420 *f.*

colony's neighbor on the south, and of the fact that the King had appointed local men to all the government offices, the necessity of having at least one official who could be relied upon for information was obvious, and Chamberlain was instructed to transmit regularly reports of matters transacted in his office.[1]

The Council, however, not only made trouble about accepting him as Secretary, but endeavored to bind him by an oath of secrecy, which would have prevented the English government from obtaining information as to events in that part of the Empire, and have brought about the same absurd and impossible state of affairs, from an administrative standpoint, which Massachusetts was trying to perpetuate. Indeed, the attempt to govern the province by local officials broke down all along the line. Perhaps the least serious of the difficulties was that Mason was said to have "no more right to land in New Hampshire than Robin Hood," and that he was thwarted at every turn. So far as that was concerned, he had already had but scant encouragement in England, where, although his claims had to be acknowledged as having possible legal validity, they seem to have been recognized, by a government anxious to avoid trouble, as being likely to create a great deal more of it than it cared to find on its hands. Had the local government shown any inclination to meet the imperial one half-way in its endeavor to bring about some sort of administrative connection between the two, and observance of the Navigation Acts, it is probable that otherwise it would have been left fairly free, and that the home officials would have been glad enough to rid themselves of Mason by abandoning him and his trouble-breeding claims to the local courts.[2] This, however, the colonists refused to do. Complaints, some of them well-founded, began to pour in to the authorities in England, not merely in regard to the treatment of Mason, but as to the loyalty of the province, the recognition of the King's authority, the character of the laws, the refusal to observe the Navigation Acts, and other matters, which indi-

[1] *Cal. State Pap., Col., 1677–80*, p. 608.   [2] *Ibid., 1681–85*, pp. 27, 49 ff., 62 ff.

cated that the local government as organized could not cope with the situation.[1] The Lords of Trade, therefore, reported that it would be better to reorganize the government and appoint a governor from home, both as a military and as an administrative measure. Aside from other questions, there was evident danger in having a disloyal and disorganized province on the French frontier in America.

Amply justified as the English government might have been in its appointment of a home official to the post of governor, its choice of the individual selected was most unfortunate. It might be said, indeed, to have been inexcusable, did not the memory of our own happenings during the reconstruction of the South, for example, after the Civil War, preclude too free a use of vivid but satisfying adjectives. Edward Cranfield, however, whose commission was dated May 9, 1682,[2] was, perhaps, the most sordid and reckless character who ever served the Crown as a provincial governor, and might have sat as a model to any "carpet-bagger" of our post-bellum period; and his three years in New Hampshire are but mildly characterized as "an unbroken record of vulgar oppression and extortion." [3]

He had been but a short time in his new office when he began to have dazzling visions of the wealth to be made by fishing in the troubled colonial waters. He wrote to Secretary Blathwayt that, if he and his friend Guinn would further his schemes in England, they should share equally with himself in the plunder; and there seems good ground for assuming that Blathwayt consented, and that the disgraceful administration which followed lasted as long as it did by virtue of the complicity of the bribed secretary in England.[4] Cranfield's astonishingly cool letter asking for a frigate, much as a highwayman might undertake to supply himself with a pistol, on

---

[1] *Cal. State Pap., Col., 1681–85*, pp. 49 f., 52 f., 138 f., 140 f.

[2] *N. H. Laws*, vol. I, pp. 48 ff. His instructions, in part, are on pp. 56 ff. Cf. *N. H. Prov. Papers*, vol. I, pp. 433 ff.

[3] Osgood, *American Colonies*, vol. III, p. 348.

[4] Cf. Cranfield's letters to Blathwayt in *Randolph Papers*, vol. VI, pp. 124, 138 ff., 145. From the last it would seem that Blathwayt's customary share was a third.

the ground that it would not only assist His Majesty's affairs, but would let himself and his accomplices "in to other advantages," is one of the most delightfully frank state papers on record. He estimated that the troubles in Maine might be brought to yield £3000; that, as both parties to the Narraganset dispute had money, £3000 or £4000 would "not be felt"; that selling pardons in Boston might yield £10,000; while, besides other possibilities, the £5000 "collected for the Evangelizing of Indians" might be "inspected into and regulated" — a suggestion delicately veiled, but sufficiently obvious. While these enterprises, fortunately, proved beyond his powers, no amount was too small to attract him, and he showed an amazing adroitness in turning every incident of his administration into money for himself, however remote the possibility of doing so would have seemed to the casual observer.

Besides the disreputable deal with Blathwayt, which had probably helped to procure his appointment, Cranfield had also made one with Mason, by which the latter agreed to pay him £150 a year, mortgaging the whole province to him as security.[1] It was, therefore, to the advantage of the new Governor to force the people to accede to Mason's demands. Although on his arrival, he expressed himself as friendly to the colony,[2] and had little difficulty with his first Assembly, he fell out with it in its second session, and dissolved it, determined to rule without one.[3] As a result of the feeling over this action, a disturbance, too insignificant to be called a revolt, was started by one Edward Gove, who was claimed to be of unsound mind. However, he was condemned to death by Cranfield, who confiscated his estate,— of which he promised one third to Blathwayt,— and shipped the offender to England, where, after a short stay in the Tower, he was released, in part owing to appeals by Randolph.[4]

[1] Belknap (*History*, vol. 1, p. 153) states that he found the "Mss. in the files."   I have never seen the paper, but there is a contemporary reference to it in *N. H. Prov. Papers*, vol. 1, p. 517.

[2] *Cal. State Pap., Col., 1681–85*, pp. 312 *f*.   [3] *Ibid.*, pp. 373 *f*.

[4] *Ibid.*, pp. 379, 389; *Randolph Papers*, vol. VI, p. 145, and *passim; N. H. Prov. Papers*, vol. 1, pp. 458 *ff*.

It is needless to follow Cranfield's disreputable course in detail. It was that of a petty but thoroughly unscrupulous tyrant, who had no thought for the rights of the people whom he governed, or for the interests of the Empire, and whose whole mind was concentrated on picking pockets.[1] Although the Assembly was twice convened again, the deadlock between it and the executive was complete. Finally, after an effort to collect taxes illegally, it became evident that the people would stand no more, and Cranfield, who, somewhat unnecessarily, seems to have been in fear of his life, wrote home asking for recall on the score of his health and the difficult climate.[2] Meanwhile, however, the unfortunate inhabitants of the colony had succeeded in getting their case before the Lords of Trade in England, who at once took action.[3] They wrote a sharp letter to Cranfield, demanding explanations; and upon receipt of his defense, which they did not consider satisfactory, reported to the King that he had exceeded his authority, committed illegal acts, and failed to carry out his instructions.[4] They also requested that the King allow an immediate appeal in the case of one Vaughan against Mason, in the matter of his land-title, and that all proceedings in similar cases be suspended until His Majesty's decision was known. Unfortunately, Vaughan lost the appeal, the King deciding in favor of Mason; but at least Cranfield was removed as governor, and his commission revoked, at the end of 1684.[5] In order to get rid of the troublesome private claims of Mason, a plan seems also to have been proposed by the English government, the following year, by which he was to surrender all his rights to the Crown in exchange for an annuity and the governorship of Bermuda, as it was thought the people might more willingly recognize the claims of the Crown than those of an individual.[6] Nothing, however, came of it, and, like a

---

[1] *Cf.* Vaughan's Journal, in *N. H. Prov. Papers*, vol. I, pp. 519 *ff.*

[2] *Cal. State Pap., Col., 1681–85*, p. 649; *Randolph Papers*, vol. VI, p. 150.

[3] *N. H. Prov. Papers*, vol. I, pp. 515, 557; *Cal. State Pap., Col., 1681–85*, pp. 666 *ff.*

[4] *N. H. Prov. Papers*, vol. I, pp. 562 *f.*, 569 *ff.*, 572; *Cal. State Pap., Col., 1681–85*, pp. 670, 697 *ff.*

[5] *N. H. Prov. Papers*, vol. I, pp. 570 *f.*, 574; *Cal. State Pap., Col., 1681–85*, p. 739.

[6] *Randolph Papers*, vol. IV, pp. 59 *f.*

family curse, the Mason claims continued to plague everyone concerned, including the proprietor himself.

That at this crisis in New England affairs, when the attempt was being made to alter the relations of the colonies to the Crown, and to make sweeping administrative changes, such a man as Cranfield could be chosen to be the first representative of a royal executive, boded ill for the practical success of any plans, however statesmanlike they might be in conception. There would seem to be no room for doubt that his appointment had been due to corruption and jobbery, which were likely to be the stumbling-blocks in the way of any real improvement in imperial government under the Stuarts. The Lords of Trade, indeed, as well as Randolph, both realized and protested against the dangers of Mason's claim, legal as it might be, and of the harm to be done by such an appointee as Cranfield.[1] Back-stairs intrigues and sordid schemings, however, were too strong to be overcome in the court of Charles, nor had there yet developed that powerful tradition of integrity and honor, which has been so marked a quality in the civil service of later England, although the foundations of such a tradition were being laid at this very time by the excellent work being done by a number of royal officials in other colonies.

Nor must it be forgotten that there was little or nothing to attract a man of first-rate ability, of high integrity, or of statesmanlike quality, in the post of royal governor in the seventeenth century. Owing to the remoteness of the colonies, their small populations, their lack of culture and social life, the pettiness of their problems, and the proneness of their inhabitants to quarrel with any royal official simply as such, the office of governor could mean only exile, without prestige or adequate pay, for any man to whom, from ability or position, a public career was open in England. As for the hungry schools of smaller fish who swam in their wake, eager to pick up a living in minor officialdom, it may be said that they were wont to apply all too thoroughly our later American maxim,

[1] *Randolph Papers*, vol. IV, p. 17.

"to the victor belong the spoils." They were of the universal type, transcending time or party, place or race.

In respect to the higher officials, the new policy of the Stuarts, which, by the time Cranfield was removed, had become clearly marked, might indeed, have brought an advantage. None of the New England colonies — which ranged in population from the four thousand of Rhode Island or New Hampshire, to perhaps ten times that number in Massachusetts — could offer a problem, or a legitimate recompense, sufficient to attract an able man as governor; but a dominion extending from Virginia to New France, impossible as it was for other reasons, might have done so. Nor were there less apparent advantages to be gained from the administrative point of view, in a dominion which should embrace all New England, such as was now being planned. After the fall of the Massachusetts charter, and the dismissal of Cranfield, there were seven jurisdictions in New England, some with settled governments and some without: Connecticut, the King's Province, Rhode Island, Plymouth, Massachusetts, New Hampshire, and Maine. To provide seven complete sets of administrative machinery for the seventy thousand persons included in these seven districts naturally seemed to the government in England to be not only a waste of money and energy, but likely to interfere with the best interests of the colonists themselves. The tariff wars, the constant bickering over boundaries, and the lack of unity in military affairs, which latter might easily prove fatal when opposed by a unified, centralized power like France, all seemed to point to a consolidation of the colonies as being a distinct step forward. New England, at least, formed a geographical unit, with a population fairly homogeneous in character; and a general government might be expected to work with not more friction than had been developed from the absorption of New Hampshire and Maine by Massachusetts.

Nor was the scheme confined solely to the minds of English statesmen, or to Randolph, who had urged it as early as 1681.[1]

[1] *Randolph Papers*, vol. VI, p. 90.

Not to mention others, so staunch an upholder of the old order as Samuel Sewall could write to Increase Mather, then engaged in trying to obtain a new charter, after the downfall of Andros, that, on account of the lack of voluntary cohesion on the part of the colonies in the face of the French danger, "it seems necessary that in the most convenient way as can be procured, these lesser Governments be firmly compacted into one." [1] The difficulties in the way of the plan, however, were great. The local feeling of loyalty, on the part of the colonists, to their particular colony, and distrust of the others, was amazingly strong in these little commonwealths, the total population of any one of which was not greater than that of a town or village of to-day. Although the inhabitants were all Englishmen, of much the same faith, and engaged in the same pursuits, the corporate and community life of the various colonies had, in the short space of two generations, become differentiated to a degree which is truly astonishing, and which the contemporary English government may well be forgiven for not having been able to realize. Moreover, the extent of territory and inadequacy of communication made a centralized government peculiarly difficult for those governing, and inconvenient for the governed. Lastly, the want of the right sort of men for officials, and their probable lack of tact, and of sympathy with the New Englanders at any time, and, particularly, in this one of transition, would seem to have doomed the dominion to failure from the start.

Fortunately, however, New England was saved, largely by Randolph, from the presence of a governor who would have been far worse than Cranfield, in the person of the subsequently notorious Colonel Percy Kirke, who had been appointed by Charles.[2] The death of the King made the commission void; and Randolph's wise and persistent opposition carried the day, so that James II found other work for the brutal colonel.[3]

[1] Sewall, *Letter Book*, vol. I, p. 115.

[2] *Cal. State Pap., Col., 1681–85*, pp. 718, 731 *f.*

[3] Randolph wrote that nothing could be done if the people "be condemned to that misery to have Coll. Kerk to be their Govr."; and that he himself would "rather have 100 lb. a yeare in New Engd. under a quiet prudent Govr. then 500 lb." under Kirke. *Randolph Papers*, vol. IV, pp. 29, 3, 6, 18, 40, 88.

Randolph, indeed, had not hesitated to write that "whoever goes over Governor with expectation to make his fortunes, will dis-serve his Majesty, disappoint himself and utterly ruine that Country"; and that there was "more need of a prudent man to reconcile then of a hot heady, passionate Souldier to force." [1]

In August, 1685, he suggested, in view of the inevitable delay in settling New England matters, resulting from the death of the King, that a temporary government be installed; and, a week later, the Lords of Trade recommended the plan to James.[2] It had been Randolph's wish, as well as that of those citizens in the colony who saw that a change was inevitable, that the governor and other officials, during the transition period, should, as far as possible, be local men; and to this the English government agreed, appointing Joseph Dudley as Governor.[3] It was well for Massachusetts in this critical time that some, at least, of her leading men were not fanatically irreconcilable, and that, in spite of the opposition of the clergy, so able an administrator as Dudley was willing to take the hated office, and serve at once both his colony and England.[4] If the colonists preferred, as they undoubtedly did, an administration formed from their own citizens rather than from strangers, then the question before them was similar to that put by General Lee to those irreconcilables in Virginia, in 1867, who refused to vote for the Constitutional Convention. "The question is," wrote the general, "shall the members of the convention be selected from the best available men in the State or from the worst? Shall the machinery of the State government be arranged and set in motion by the former or by the latter?" [5] The colonists, indeed, were given no choice as to the fundamental frame of their government; but the

---

[1] *Randolph Papers*, vol. IV, pp. 16, 18.

[2] *Cal. State Pap., Col., 1687–88*, pp. 77, 80.

[3] *Randolph Papers*, vols. III, pp. 317, 325, and IV, p. 13.

[4] Sewall, *Diary*, vol. I, p. 139. The old view of Dudley as a traitor, which was held by the strong defenders of Puritanism and theocracy, is largely passing. *Cf.* Osgood, *American Colonies*, vol. III, pp. 385 *f.*

[5] J. F. Rhodes, *History of the United States*, vol. VI, p. 86.

powers given to the governor and council made the character of those who held those offices, particularly the former, of vital importance.

Dudley's commission, which appointed him Governor of New Hampshire and the King's Province, as well as of Massachusetts, and was thus the first constructive step taken toward consolidation, also named the members of his Council.[1] With two exceptions, they were all New Englanders, representative of the several districts, and included such men as the Bradstreets, father and son, the two Winthrops (Wait and Fitz-John), Stoughton, Bulkley, Pynchon, and Tyng, although the Bradstreets and Saltonstall refused to serve.[2] The exceptions were Mason and Randolph; and when the latter heard that Mason had been named, he hurriedly wrote to Sir Robert Southwell, begging that the New Hampshire proprietor be advised "to moderation" or that he would "putt all in a ferment."[3]

Although the Dudley government was avowedly temporary, its organization foreshadowed the more permanent one soon to be provided, with Andros as head. All executive and judicial power was placed in the hands of the Governor and Council, except that appeals to England were provided for in cases involving not less than £300. There was no provision for the laying of new taxes or for passing laws, and the refusal to allow a popular assembly was a serious administrative blunder. In spite of the restricted franchise and the great influence of the clergy and a few families in the public life of Massachusetts, the representative assembly was the foundation of her political liberties, actual or potential; and after being accustomed to it for fifty years, the people could be counted upon not to submit willingly to a form of administration in which they were deprived of all voice. Randolph, Andros, and the Lords of Trade all seem to have been in favor of such an assembly for purposes of legislation and taxation; and the new government

---

[1] The commission is in *Colonial Society of Massachusetts Publications*, vol. II, pp. 37 ff.

[2] *Randolph Papers*, vols. VI, p. 171, and IV, p. 86. [3] *Ibid.*, vol. IV, p. 48.

under Dudley recommended that it be granted.[1]   In spite of
this, however, and of the opinion of the Attorney-General
that, even after the forfeiture of the charter, the inhabitants of
Massachusetts still had the right to be directly represented in
the making of their local laws and levying of taxes, the King
refused his consent.[2]   While the refusal was a stupid error,
which was certain to provoke the people without any material
advantage to the imperial organization, it may be doubted
whether, in truth, it was illegal.   The whole matter of the
legal position of the residents in the dominions, as compared
with the dwellers in the realm, was an anomalous one.   The
situation resulting from the expansion of England was un-
provided for in the theory of the constitution, much as the
acquisition of dependencies by the United States was unforeseen; and it is difficult to prove what legal rights an Englishman may or may not have carried with him in emigrating
beyond seas in the seventeenth century.   Although, largely
as a result of the so-called tyranny of Andros, New Englanders
from this time onward began to praise, and claim rights under,
the common law of England, the force of that law had previously been denied by themselves in statement and practice.[3]
In similar case, it may be noted, our own Congress has laid
down the principle that constitutional rights do not of themselves apply to the citizens of dependent territories, but only
when expressly extended by statute.[4]

Randolph arrived with Dudley's commission in May, 1686,
and on the 17th the new government assumed office at a
meeting of the General Court.   The members of that body
unanimously protested against the legality of Dudley's commission, but there was no forcible opposition, though, as
Sewall records, there were "many tears shed in prayer and at

[1] *Cal. State Pap., Col., 1685–88*, pp. 81, 87 *f.*; *Randolph Papers*, vol. v, p. 3; "Records of Council Meetings under Dudley," in *Mass. Hist. Soc. Proceedings*, Series II,
vol. xiii, p. 244 (hereafter cited as *Dudley Records*).

[2] *Cal. State Pap., Col., 1685–88*, pp. 9, 81, 89.

[3] P. S. Reinsch, *English Common Law in the Early American Colonies* (Bulletin of
the University of Wisconsin, No. 31, 1899), pp. 8, 23.

[4] Willoughby, *Territories and Dependencies*, p. 51.

parting." [1] The actions of the new government showed so much moderation that Randolph soon began to chafe under restraint, and complained that "twas still but the Govr & Company," and that the Navigation Acts were no more enforced than formerly. [2] Sewall, indeed, in his diary, dwells only on such minor imperial events as the reintroduction of the cross in the ensign (which led him to resign his commission), the drinking of healths, the desecration of Saturday evening (considered in New England as part of the Sabbath), the increase of periwigs, and the holding of services by an Anglican clergyman, in accordance with the religious toleration insisted upon by the King. [3] Randolph, however, who perhaps understood the colonies better than any other Englishman of the day, probably represented the feeling more truly when he wrote that the people were dissatisfied for want of an assembly, and that otherwise their main desires were for a general pardon, for the confirmation of their land-titles, and for the legal establishment of Congregationalism. [4] We also get a glimpse of the fire smouldering beneath the surface, in the refusal of the Council to permit Captain St. Loe, Commander of H. M. frigate Dartmouth, to have a celebration and bonfire ashore, not only, as the Council declared, because the town was built of wood, but because "the spirits of some people are so royled and disturbed that inconveniency beyond your expectation may happen." [5]

With the appointment of Sir Edmund Andros, who arrived in December, after Dudley had been in office about seven months, the Stuart policy was advanced another step, and the Dominion of New England was soon to receive a larger extension. The appointment also marked a distinct advance in the quality of royal official; for Andros was of a type far superior to the burglarizing Cranfield or the bureaucratic Randolph.

---

[1] *Massachusetts Records*, vol. v, p. 516; Sewall, *Diary*, vol. i, p. 140; *Dudley Records*, p. 237.

[2] *Randolph Papers*, vol. iv, pp. 92, 114 f., 120 ff.; *Dudley Records*, pp. 227 f.

[3] Sewall, *Diary*, vol. i, pp. 147 f., 156, 151, 142.

[4] *Randolph Papers*, vol. iv, p. 118. He was presumably speaking of the voters.

[5] *Dudley Records*, pp. 270 f.

He had already served with honesty and ability as Governor of New York; and, as the plans for colonial consolidation called for the eventual union of that province with New England, his previous service in the former naturally recommended him for the higher post. It is probable that he had already been considered, even before the appointment of Dudley.[1]

Although his commission of 1686 added only the small, now unimportant, colony of Plymouth to the three already combined under Dudley, the plan for uniting all those north of the Delaware had been definitely formulated, and, as part of the process of reorganization, steps had been taken to cancel the charters of Rhode Island and Connecticut.[2] After some consideration by the Lords of Trade in the previous year, it had been determined not to await the organization of a permanent government before proceeding against the two charter colonies, and Randolph had brought writs of *Quo Warranto* against each when he came over with Dudley's commission.[3] Before they could be served, the time for the return of each had expired; but, nevertheless, Randolph presented both of the "superannuated summons," as he termed them, and Rhode Island made an immediate surrender, precluding the necessity of forcing the matter to a legal issue.[4] That colony was thereupon placed under the jurisdiction of Andros.[5]

Connecticut presented greater difficulties, and, owing to delays, a second writ of *Quo Warranto*, served by Randolph, also became legally void before service. Governor Dongan, of New York, who had hopes that his province, and not Massachusetts, might be made the nucleus around which the larger administrative unit would be built, was also making efforts to

---

[1] *Randolph Papers*, vol. IV, p. 13.

[2] The commission of 1686 is printed in *R. I. Records*, vol. III, pp. 212 *ff.*; *Colonial Society Massachusetts Publications*, vol. II, pp. 44 *ff.*; and *New Hampshire Laws*, vol. I, pp. 146 *ff.* The instructions of that year are in the latter only, pp. 155 *ff.*

[3] *Cal. State Pap., Col., 1685–88*, pp. 65, 67, 77, 87, 173, 182; *Conn. Col. Records*, vol. III, pp. 347 *ff.*, 356 *ff.*

[4] *Cal. State Pap., Col., 1685–88*, p. 211; *Randolph Papers*, vols. IV, pp. 97, 100, and VI, pp. 173, 178; *R. I. Records*, vol. III, pp. 193 *ff.*

[5] *Cal. State Pap., Col., 1685–88*, p. 242; *New Hampshire Laws*, vol. I, p. 168; *Randolph Papers*, vol. IV, p. 134.

annex Connecticut, either in whole or in part.   Although twice saved by delay, that colony realized that the tendency of the time toward consolidation would probably prove too strong for her to remain permanently isolated.[1]   Not only were her social and religious affinities far closer with New England than with New York, but so, also, were her economic ties.   After some triangular fencing, therefore, with Dongan, Randolph, and the home authorities, and the service of a third writ, the General Court wrote to the English Secretary of State, that, though the colony would prefer to remain independent, yet, if the King's pleasure were otherwise, she would rather be placed under the administration of Andros than joined with any other province.[2]   This was taken to mean acceptance of the royal wishes, the *Quo Warranto* proceedings were dropped, and Andros was ordered to add Connecticut to the Dominion, which, six months later, was extended to embrace New York and the two Jerseys.[3]

The difficulties involved in attempting to administer so vast a territory, possessed of wholly inadequate means of communication, and embracing such a variety of social, religious, and economic communities, were virtually insuperable in the seventeenth century.   Difficult as the task would have been in any case, it was rendered hopeless from the outset by the opposition of all the colonies involved, and by the lack of properly qualified men to administer the government, as well as by those faults of the Stuarts which, it was now evident, could be counted upon to wreck any administrative policy.

The choice of Andros, however, as the man to be entrusted with bringing about the enormous changes incident to the new policy, while not altogether happy, was probably as good a one as the circumstances of the case allowed.   The task of making the new government successful from the standpoint

---

[1] *N. Y. Col. Docts.*, vol. III, pp. 385 *ff.*; *Conn. Col. Records*, vol. III, pp. 366 *f*; *Randolph Papers*, vol. IV, p. 78.

[2] *Conn. Col. Records*, vol. III, pp. 377 *f*.

[3] *Ibid.*, pp. 379 *ff.*; *New Hampshire Laws*, vol. I, pp. 171 *ff.*; *Cal. State Pap., Col., 1681–85*, pp. 382, 387, 463, 472.

of the King, and acceptable to the inhabitants, was beyond the power of any man; and under James few were available for foreign administrative posts who would be likely to be sympathetically inclined toward the peculiarities of New Englanders. In an exceedingly difficult position, with his choice of subordinates mainly limited to greedy place-seekers from home and honestly disaffected colonials, Andros seems to have carried out his orders with loyalty and probity, though not always with tact or discretion.[1]

The powers given to him in his commission and instructions were very broad, and, under the conditions existing in the colonies, had he, in truth, been the "tyrannical Bajazet" which he was proclaimed by the Reverend Mr. Mather, the story of his brief rule would have been very different from what it was in reality. As had been the case in the temporary government of Dudley, there was no provision made for a popular assembly, although Andros himself had no objection to such a body, and had even tried to secure one for the inhabitants of New York when Governor of that colony.[2] The King, however, had steadily opposed it in both provinces; and instead, the Governor, "by and with the advice and consent of" the Council, or the majority of them, was empowered to make all laws — which, it may be noted, was the exact wording of the Act passed by Congress in 1804 for the government of Louisiana after its purchase from France.[3] The judicial and taxing functions of the government were bestowed under the same conditions, though the laws passed were to be approved in England, and appeals were allowed in cases involving over £300. Although, apparently, the consent of the Council was required in the above matters, the further

[1] Of the modern scientific historians, Professor Channing is, perhaps, the one who takes the most unfavorable view of Andros. *History*, vol. II, pp. 180 *ff*. *Cf.*, however, Osgood, *American Colonies*, vol. III, pp. 394 *ff*., and Kimball, *Dudley*, pp. 43 *f*. The change in attitude toward Andros, which dates from the publication of the *Andros Tracts* in 1868, does not seem to me to be as much invalidated by the later publication of the *Andros Records* as Professor Channing considers.

[2] *N. Y. Col. Docts.*, vol. III, p. 235.

[3] *Colonial Society Massachusetts Publications*, vol. II, p. 46; *Organic Acts for the Territories of the United States* (Senate Doct. No. 148, 56th Congress, 1st Sess.), p. 18.

power granted the Governor, to suspend summarily any member of it "from sitting voteing and Assisting therein," if he should find "just cause," gave him virtually sole authority in the event of disagreement between them and himself, in any case which he considered just.

Such clauses in his instructions as those which required that, except in cases of extraordinary necessity, he was to act with not less than seven members of his Council, although his commission placed the limit at five, and that, further, he was to permit the members to "enjoy freedom of Debate and Votes in all things," would seem to indicate that the English authorities intended the Council to occupy a position of importance in the scheme of government. But the scheme was one which could hardly be workable. If the Council were, in reality, a body of representatives of various sections and parties, it would necessarily contain a large number of irreconcilables, who would constantly be outvoted, as the Crown could not be expected to appoint a majority from the opposition. Had the Governor, as was the case in many of the royal colonies, possessed the executive power, and an elected assembly the legislative, then the struggle between them would have taken the course with which the student of colonial history is so familiar. In the scheme of government which Andros was supposed to carry out, however, as in that temporarily provided for Louisiana, the usual rôles of governor and legislature were reversed, and Andros could quite legitimately consider himself the sole legislative power, his acts being merely subject to approval by a body the members of which were, in the first instance, at least, removable by him. For a half-century, the one policy of the leaders of Massachusetts, in their effort to balk England's efforts at control, had been to "avoid or protract," and it is not likely that that policy would be suddenly laid aside. The complaints made in general terms by five of the later accusers of Andros, that in legislation he did not give sufficient opportunity for debate, that laws were passed with only a bare quorum, and that, sometimes, the votes were not counted, cannot, even if true, be taken as very serious charges, considering his actual powers, and the practical difficulties which beset him.[1]

An attempt was, indeed, made to have the Council, which at first comprised twenty-seven members, roughly representative of the various parts of the Dominion; and, as other provinces were added, the membership was enlarged to permit the seating of members from them. Nor were prominent names wanting in the list, which included Dudley, the two Winthrops, Stoughton, Hinckley, William Bradford, Arnold, Tyng, Pynchon, Treat, and Allyn.[2] Under the circumstances, however, such an attempt was bound to break down, for important men from other parts of the Dominion could not be expected to remain permanently in Boston, or to make frequent and long journeys thither, in order to attend meetings of a body whose only powers were those of advice and veto, and even those of none too strong a character. It was entirely natural, therefore, that, during the brief rule of Andros, the actual conduct of affairs should tend, more and more, to be guided by his own will and that of a clique among the councillors, and that attendance at the meetings should have steadily dwindled.

As in the case of New Hampshire, the question of the establishment of a new administrative machinery was complicated by the distinct one of titles to the land. In the former case the unhappy complication had been forced upon the English government, as the question in that province had not been as to the rights of the Crown against those of its subjects, but as to the legal claims of one subject against those of others. In Massachusetts, the case was entirely different; and although the colonists were technically at fault in not having taken out valid titles when they might readily have done so, nevertheless, the course of the English government was both stupid and unjust.

Throughout all the colonies in the early period, there was a general and rather likeable prejudice against professional

---

[1] *Andros Tracts*, vol. 1, pp. 140 *ff.*

[2] *Andros Records*, in *American Antiquarian Society Proceedings*, N. S., vol. XIII, pp. 239, 483.

lawyers. But, unfortunately, that prejudice, if indulged in too rashly in civilized society, is apt to entail some *mauvais quarts d'heures* on occasion. In New England, not only was there an almost total absence of professional lawyers, but there seems to have been very little legal knowledge among any class in the community. The most marked difference between the libraries of that section and those of Virginia, in the seventeenth and eighteenth centuries, is the rapidly increasing number of law-books to be found on the shelves as we journey southward. In New England, not only was the whole administration of justice in the hands of laymen who had little or no knowledge of law, but the most important legal questions with reference to the charter were, in virtually every case, referred to the clergy, who seem to have been delightfully ignorant of legal theory and practice, as evidenced both by their decisions and by the fairly complete absence of any books on the subject in their studies. They had proved but blind leaders of the blind, and the insistence upon popular, but erroneous, interpretations of charter rights, which had necessitated the voiding of that instrument, now threatened an overwhelming disaster, which might easily have been averted had the leaders been possessed of better legal training.

As we saw in an earlier chapter, virtually all the land granted in Massachusetts, as well as in those other New England colonies which possessed charters, had been bestowed upon towns in their corporate capacity, and by them granted to individuals. But as the original company had had no power to create other corporations, the towns, as such, had no legal existence, and could not, therefore, give valid title to land. Moreover, a company could not act except under its seal; which the Massachusetts Company had rarely used in giving title. It may well be that Randolph was far nearer the truth than usual in his figures, when he wrote to Blathwayt that he did not believe that "10 men hold of better Title then Town Grants or Indian Purchase and not Three have a Grant legally executed."[1] Just as the substitution of Exodus, Deuteronomy,

[1] *Randolph Papers*, vol. VI, p. 218.

and the discretion of the magistrate for the common law of England could continue workable only so long as too many alien elements, which would naturally find such a system "uncongenial and oppressive," were not added to the population, so a land-title, as derived by the Reverend Mr. Higginson from "the Grand Charter in Genesis 1st. and 9th. Chapters," from Adam through Noah, could remain satisfactory only until questioned by purchasers more used to modern forms.[1] One of the last acts of Connecticut under her charter, before submitting, had been to validate land-titles by confirming under seal, to individuals, all lands previously granted through towns; thus there was no land question in Connecticut.[2]

But, aside from land in individual possession, there were, in most of the colonies, very large amounts as yet ungranted at all, or still possessed and used by towns in the then essential form of "commons" for wood and pasture. Andros, in his instructions, had been directed to dispose of all lands "yet undisposed of," and others "for which Our Royall Confirmation may be wanting," for a moderate quit-rent, not under two shillings and sixpence for every hundred acres. He was also instructed that no man's "Freehold or Goods" were to "be taken away or harmed," but by laws agreeable to those of England.[3] How far it may have been the considered policy of the home government to take advantage of the technical invalidity of title to allotted land, and how far such attempts as were made may have been due to Andros's own reading, correct though it was, of his orders, it is impossible to say. That the Crown came into possession of the unallotted lands could be disputed by no one. In regard to those that had been improved, the only statesmanlike action would have been to confirm existing titles without rent. They were, to a great extent, in the hands of innocent holders, who had naturally believed that the colony's leaders, lay and clerical, who for two generations had constituted the government, would have

[1] Reinsch, *English Common Law*, p. 11; *Andros Tracts*, vol. 1, p. 88.

[2] *Conn. Col. Records*, vol. iii, pp. 177 *f*. *Cf.* C. J. Hoadly, *Hiding of the Charter* (Acorn Club, 1900), pp. 14 *f*.

[3] *New Hampshire Laws*, vol. i, pp. 159 *f*., 162.

known enough to give a valid title when they granted land.

Not only had the people for a long period enjoyed undisturbed possession, but, to a considerable extent, as we have already pointed out, New England had been settled by emigrants to whom such possession of land in fee simple had been the main attraction. In fact, in respect to land, the New England migration had accomplished what the English Revolution had failed to do, and had virtually redistributed property. It has often been said — not quite truly, perhaps — that the English movement did not succeed because it left the injustices and inequalities of the English property system untouched. To have done otherwise would have meant the expropriation of a large and powerful class. In the wilderness of America, the unlimited fund of free land could be drawn upon for the purpose, and an economic leveling be accomplished with no disturbance of existing rights. It was another of the results of the influence of the frontier, to which, in the story of America, we have to come back over and over again; for it was in this free and abundant land that were sown the seeds of democracy and revolution. In New England, owing in part to social and in part to geographic factors, the equalizing of economic status had proceeded further, perhaps, than anywhere else at that time; and the resultant wide distribution of small holdings would there cause the maximum, both of dissatisfaction with any policy attacking titles, and of difficulty in enforcing it.

It is, perhaps, only fair to say that the English government may not have realized the full extent of the popular feeling, and that they probably thought that the sum asked, which was less than a third of a penny per acre, would be willingly paid as a means of permanently validating the imperfect titles. All those residents of Boston interested in the Narragansett country had voluntarily offered, a year previously, to pay such a quit-rent as the amount asked later, and the government of Massachusetts itself had collected quit-rents from its own citizens in Maine.[1] The policy of questioning all titles consti-

---

[1] *Cal. State Pap., Col., 1681–85,* pp. 22, 386, 527; *supra,* chap. xv; *Dudley Records,* p. 276.

tuted a typical example of Stuart injustice and ineptitude; and the few test cases which Andros brought were handled in a way to afford the greatest degree of apprehension and irritation. The needy and ill-paid minor officials, upon whom he had to depend in large part for the details of his administration, immediately scented plunder, and sought recklessly to profit by it. Although the actual number of cases in which titles were attacked individually was very small, the theory on which the cases were based threatened virtually every individual outside of Connecticut; and it is hard to conceive of any other blunder that the government could have made which would, so instantly, have arrayed an entire population in opposition. It is unnecessary to go into the details of the cases, for there is but one answer to the question, "What people that had the spirits of Englishmen could endure this?" [1]

Cranfield, who had had hopes of getting the governorship of Massachusetts for himself, had predicted that all might go well there, "provided that Religion and Tertenancy doe not hinder"; and, at least, had thus shown himself capable of picking out two of the probable rocks on which the Dominion policy might founder.[2] The fact that the new government was pledged to allow liberty of conscience to all persons would, in itself, have been sufficiently obnoxious to the clergy and old church party, even had not the clause been added that the Church of England was to be especially encouraged.[3] Andros had been preceded in his arrival by the Reverend Mr. Ratcliffe, a minister of that church, and "extraordinary good preacher," [4] and Randolph and Mason had petitioned for the use of one of the three Boston meeting-houses in which to hold services. This, quite naturally, had been refused, and the services were being held in the Town-house when the new Governor reached Boston. Andros repeated the request, and was again refused,

---

[1] *Andros Tracts*, vol. I, p. 87. The cases are given on pp. 88 *ff*. *Cf.* Palmer's defence, *Ibid.*, pp. 49 *ff.*; Also, Sewall, *Letter Book*, vol. I, p. 68 *n.*; Bond, *Quit-rent System*, pp. 42 *ff.*

[2] *Randolph Papers*, vol. VI, p. 123.

[3] *Colonial Society Massachusetts Publications*, vol. II, p. 54; *New Hampshire Laws*, vol. I, p. 161.

[4] *John Dunton's Letters*, p. 138.

the Town-house continuing to be used until the following March, when the Governor once more reopened the question. Having no better success than before, he obtained the key of the South Meeting-house from the sexton, and forced the issue.[1] From that time forward, the two congregations held services there on Sunday mornings, the one following the other. The sermons of the Puritan divines were of such inordinate length that even the late Dudley government, though firm in the faith and New England bred, had to pass a resolution that "the minister that preaches on Thursday next be prayed from this Court to hasten his Sermon because of the short days";[2] and one Sabbath morning was scarcely long enough for two clergymen. Moreover, the wholly warranted sense of injustice felt by the Congregationalists would not tend toward easing a situation which, in the best of cases, would have been likely to breed constant ill-feeling. Ecclesiastical quarrels are never lacking in venom, and the intensity of the friction developed in the present case was naturally intense. Within the year, however, the Episcopalians made an effort to build a church of their own, though not without difficulty, for Sewall, who was one of those who complained of their using the Meeting-house, refused to sell them land upon which "to set up that which the People of N. E. came over to avoid."[3]   But a new church was at last built, although Andros never worshiped in the King's Chapel, as it was called, the Revolution occurring before its completion. His religious sincerity is witnessed by the fact that, when he sailed for England, virtually a prisoner, he left £30 as a gift toward the building.[4]

Arbitrary and unnecessarily irritating as was the Governor's course in the matter, it must be confessed to have been a very mild form of religious tyranny, as compared with that customarily indulged in by the Puritans themselves. But in various minor ways he gave additional offense to the clergy and more bigoted laymen, whose Puritanism had at this time

[1] Sewall, *Diary*, vol. 1, pp. 141, 162, 171 *f.*   [2] *Dudley Records*, p. 277.
[3] Sewall, *Diary*, vol. 1, p. 207. Sewall's remark was evidently made to work off his spleen, for he adds, laconically, "besides 'twas Entail'd."
[4] H. W. Foote, *Annals of King's Chapel* (Boston, 1882), vol. 1, p. 90.

reached its narrowest point.   On Christmas Day, the observance of which was punishable by fine under the colony's
laws, Sewall sadly observes that the "governor goes to the
Town-House to Service Forenoon and Afternoon"; though
he takes some heart by noting that "shops open today generally
and persons about their occasions." [1]   A little later, Increase
Mather writes in his diary, that "this Sabbath [Saturday]
night was greatly profaned by bonfires &c. under pretence of
honor to the King's Coronation." A sort of secondary Sabbath
had been developed by the clergy about the mid-week "lecture," and on one of these days, Mather notes that "Sword
playing was this day openly practised on a Stage in Boston
& that immediately after the Lecture, so the Devil has begun
a Lecture in Boston on a Lecture day which was set up for
Christ." [2]   Happily, the old order was changing, and the community was gradually loosening the shackles of what, for most,
had become merely a dreary formalism.

In an earlier chapter, we attempted to show what a change
was wrought in the attitude of the Puritans when they passed
from opposition to the government in England to the control
of that in the colony.   Under Andros, they now once more
found themselves in opposition; and it is instructive to note
in how many particulars they again proclaimed as tyranny
what they had themselves been practising.   We have seen
how laws had been passed prohibiting anyone from settling
in the colony, or leaving it without the consent of the rulers.
These laws had never been repealed by the colonial authorities,
but it was now complained that "whereas by constant usage
any person might remove out of the countrey at his pleasure,
a Law was made that no man should do so without the Governours leave." In view of the continuous refusal of the Puritan
government, when in power, to permit any dissatisfied citizen
to go to England to lodge complaint against their arbitrary
acts, of which refusal many examples have been cited, the
complaints against Andros in the matter are an amusing in-

stance of immediate change of feeling upon discovering whose ox was being gored.   There is nothing to indicate that Andros had any intention of preventing anyone from carrying an appeal; but the same writer who complained of the above act goes on to say, with an entire lack of humor, considering the past history of the colony, "how should any dissatisfied persons ever obtain liberty to go to England to complain of their being oppressed by Arbitrary Governours?"[1]   As a matter of fact, dissatisfied persons now possessed that liberty for the first time in the history of Massachusetts.

Under the former régime, the right to organize churches, the regulation of the schools, and the licensing of printing, had all been kept rigidly under the control of the government, which meant the representatives of the minority of the population constituting the Congregational church.   But a loud cry of tyranny was raised when the new government passed an act that no schools should be kept except "such as shall be allowed," and established Dudley as censor of the press, which Hutchinson admits merely changed its keeper.[2]

The order that all records of the former governments should be lodged at Boston undoubtedly entailed hardship for anyone who wished to examine them; and the requirement that final action in the probating of wills or granting letters of administration, in estates of the value of over £50, must take place in Boston was also an unpractical attempt at bureaucratic centralization.[3]   Moreover, West, to whom Randolph had farmed out the office of Secretary, was a peculating subordinate, of whom Randolph later wrote that he "extorts what fees he pleases, to the great oppression of the people, and renders the present government grievous."[4]   The legal fees, as enacted in 1687, were fair and moderate,— that for the

[1] *Andros Tracts*, vol. I, pp. 80, 142.   The act is given in vol. III, pp. 92 *f.*

[2] *Andros Records*, pp. 467, 249; Hutchinson, *History*, vol. I, p. 318.   Andros was required by his instructions not to allow unlicensed printing.   *New Hampshire Laws*, vol. I, p. 166.

[3] *Andros Records*, p. 467; *Cal. State Pap., Col., 1689–92*, p. 202; *Randolph Papers*, vol. VI, p. 271; *Conn. Col. Records*, vol. III, pp. 423 *f.*

[4] *Randolph Papers*, vols. VI, p. 223, and IV, p. 108.

probate of a will, for example, being ten shillings,— and there is only questionable evidence for Hutchinson's statement, inaccurate in another respect, that the usual charge was fifty shillings.[1]   But there is some evidence that West and some of the minor officials attempted extortion even after the establishment of an official scale; and Randolph complained that two of them, West being one, were insubordinate in Maine, where they "were as arbitrary as the great Turke," and were upsetting matters already settled by Andros.[2]   How far Andros might have been able to organize the enormous and administratively unwieldy dominion, and rid himself of unreliable subordinates, had he been given time, cannot be known, as he was to have only a few months in which to do so after the addition of the southern provinces.

Aside from these and other difficulties, his administration would undoubtedly have been wrecked on the question of taxation, whether the Revolution had occurred in England or not.   He himself, and every one else apparently, except the King, realized the necessity for an elected assembly; but it had been denied, and there was, therefore, nothing to do but to levy the taxes without the direct consent of the people. Under his commission, Andros, "by and with the advice and consent" of a majority of his Council, had been given power to levy such taxes as might be necessary for the support of the government;[3]   and at the session of March 1, 1687, a general bill, embodying some former ones, was presented for consideration.   It aroused warm discussion over details, and both the records, and the long subsequent complaint of Stoughton and others that Andros had "held the Council together unreasonably a very long time about it," would indicate that on that day, at least, there had been no suppression of freedom of debate.[4]   After a second reading, and a lapse of two days, it

---

[1] Hutchinson, *History*, vol. I, pp. 320 *f*.   For the legal fees under the Dudley and Andros administrations *vide Dudley Records*, pp. 242, 245, 283; *Andros Records*, pp. 266, 467; *Randolph Papers*, vol. IV, pp. 147 *ff*.

[2] *Ibid*., pp. 226, 228.

[3] *Colonial Society Massachusetts Publications*, vol. II, pp. 46 *f*.

[4] *Andros Records*, pp. 256: *Andros Tracts*, vol. I, pp. 139 *f*.

was passed on the third day, *nemine contradicente*, according to the records, though the complainants, several years later, claimed that the vote had not been counted, and that many of the councilors had remained silent, under "great discouragement and discountenance." [1]

The attempt to levy the tax met with immediate resistance in Essex County, and particularly in the town of Ipswich, where the men assembled in town-meeting refused to elect an assessor. Under the leadership of John Wise, certain of the inhabitants drew up a protest, stating that their liberties as Englishmen had been infringed, and refusing to pay any taxes not levied by an elected assembly.[2] Twenty-eight were at once arrested, of whom a number, "appearing more ingenuous and less culpable," were promptly released.[3] Six, however, supposed to be the ringleaders, were thrown into prison at Boston, a writ of *habeas corpus* having been denied.[4] When they were later brought to trial, Dudley was the presiding judge, and Wise claimed that the jury was packed for the occasion. The six were fined, in all, £185, and forced to pay heavy charges in court fees, while Wise was suspended from his ministerial functions. The fines were large, but the offense naturally was serious in the eyes of Andros, who had, perforce, to carry out a policy not of his own making; and it may not be unfair to recall that, in the days when the "saddle was upon the Bay mare," the Puritans had levied fines of £750 upon Dr. Child and his fewer associates.

Although the towns, as has been stated, had never had legal standing as corporations, and, with the overthrow of the charter, had ceased to have a political one, the new government had, nevertheless, allowed them to continue functioning much

[1] *Andros Records*, p. 258; *Andros Tracts*, vol. I, p. 140. Part of the complaint is disproved by the written record.

[2] *Ibid.*, pp. 83 *ff.*; *Randolph Papers*, vol. IV, pp. 171 *ff.*

[3] *Andros Records*, pp. 477 *f.*

[4] The right of *habeas corpus* under the Statute of Charles II, 1679, did not apply to the colonies. It is questionable whether our rights to it depend upon that statute or the common law. *Cf.* A. H. Carpenter, "Habeas Corpus in the Colonies," *American Historical Review*, vol. VIII, pp. 19 *f.* In spite of the charges against Andros, the leaders apparently took the ground, before his arrival, that the right did not extend to the colony. *Cf.* Mather Papers, *Mass. Hist. Soc. Coll.*, Series IV, vol. VIII, p. 390.

as usual. As a result of the attitude of those in Essex on the tax-matter, however, the Council passed a law limiting town-meetings to one a year for the purpose of electing local officers, and thus struck at the very root of popular government in the colony.[1]

The addition of one colony after another, in rapid succession, to the province for which Andros was responsible, raised administrative problems of the gravest sort, and had necessitated journeys from Boston to Rhode Island, Connecticut, and New York. When the last-named had been placed under his rule, in 1688, he had also been given the main control over Indian affairs for nearly all English North America, and had also had to journey to Albany for a conference with the Mohawks. With wholly inadequate assistance from the greedy office-seekers, who in large part formed his staff, his position was certainly an unenviable one. It was not long before the Indian question on the eastern frontier, with the larger danger of the French lurking in the background, also arose, to add to the difficulties of the harassed Governor. It was, unquestionably, a wise policy to unite the Indian affairs of all the colonies under one head; for the French in the valleys of the St. Lawrence and the Mississippi now threatened the entire rear of the English empire on the continent, and in the impending struggle between the two, the allegiance of the Indian tribes dwelling between them would become a factor of supreme importance. The disunited English colonies, quarreling among themselves, and wholly selfish in the various policies pursued by them in relation to the natives, offered a contrast, palpable enough to the savages, to the unified control of the French.

Andros had already made one trip to the eastward, in the spring of 1688, for the purpose of restoring the fort at Pemaquid; and while there, had despoiled the home of St. Castine, an intruding French trader, who was living a half-savage life with an assorted selection of Indian wives, more notable for number than for virtue.[2] The Governor called together the

---

[1] *Andros Records*, p. 494; *Conn. Col. Records*, vol. III, pp. 427 ff.
[2] *Randolph Papers*, vol. IV, pp. 224 ff.

sachems of the local tribes, endeavored to bind them to the English cause, and then had to proceed to New York. While he was detained there, several minor Indian attacks occurred at New Haven, up the Connecticut River, and in Maine, resulting in the killing, in all, of some twenty-six whites.[1] After a proclamation ordering the Indians to restore their prisoners and surrender the murderers had proved unavailing, Andros organized an expedition of several hundred men, and himself marched with them into Maine, destroying many of the Indian settlements, and capturing much of their ammunition and supplies.[2] Randolph claims, however, what is confirmed by other documents, that Boston merchants sent the enemy a vessel of forty-two tons loaded with powder, shot, and food, and so undid much of Andros's work.[3]

The Indian troubles were made the basis for the spreading of alarming rumors that Andros was intending to turn the colonies over to France, and introduce popery, and even that the Mohawks were to be called in to destroy Boston. All sorts of trumpery evidence was adduced to lend color to these unfounded libels, to which even Increase Mather did not hesitate to lend his influence.[4] While they were utterly without foundation so far as Andros was concerned, who treated them with deserved contempt, they fitted in with both the religious and political fears of Protestant Englishmen in the closing years of the Stuarts. Moreover, recently published letters of Randolph now show that he, at least, had begun to trim his sails to meet a possible breeze from Rome, should James make England a Catholic country; and his suggestion as to the superior usefulness of Jesuits, as instruments among the Indians, and even of the possibility of establishing a monastery, may have been noised abroad.[5] As we have already noted, the mentality of the Massachusetts of this period was

[1] *Hutchinson Papers*, vol. II, p. 309; *Randolph Papers*, vol. IV, p. 276; *Andros Tracts*, vol. II, p. 207.

[2] *Cal. State Pap., Col., 1685-88*, p. 615; *Andros Tracts*, vol. III, pp. 21 f.

[3] *Randolph Papers*, vols., IV, p. 277, and VI, p. 294. This is confirmed in *Cal. State Pap., Col., 1689-92*, pp. 212, 564, 585. *Cf.*, also, *Andros Tracts*, vol. III, p. 24.

[4] *Ibid.* vols. I, pp. 30, 101 ff., and II, pp. 50 f.

[5] *Randolph Papers*, vol. VI, pp. 242 f., 246, 251.

peculiarly liable to panic and fantastic fears; and whether or not the leaders believed the fables they spread, they undoubtedly realized that the readiest way to organize a revolution against Andros would be by religious prejudice.

It is probable that the fundamental weakness of the King's policy would have borne its natural fruit, even had there been no Revolution in England; but that event was to offer the most favorable opportunity for the minor movement in the colony. Andros was still at Pemaquid when he received what was probably his first intimation of the coming attempt to overthrow the government in England, in the form of a proclamation, which the King ordered to be published, calling upon all subjects to show their loyalty in view of a threatened invasion from Holland.[1] By the end of March, 1689, the Governor was back in Boston, and, ten days later, young John Winslow arrived from the island of Nevis, with news of Prince William's landing in England and a copy of his declaration.[2] Rumors had also reached Andros, who requested Winslow to show him the declaration as confirmation. On Winslow's refusal, Andros told him he was "a saucy fellow," and had him committed to jail for overnight, releasing him in the morning, when he showed the paper to the magistrate.[3]

Andros's position was a difficult one. Although not in sympathy with much both in the religious position and in the absolutist tendencies of his Stuart masters, he had to the full the soldierly qualities of obedience and loyalty, and on the 16th of April, he wrote to Brockholls in New York that there was "a general buzzing among the people," and warned the magistrates and officers to be on their guard against probable trouble.[4]

Two days after, on the 18th, the storm broke in Boston. There is evidence to indicate that the leaders had laid their plans some time in advance, and that the staging of the events

[1] *Andros Tracts*, vol. i, p. 75 n.
[2] *Ibid.*, pp. 77 f.; *Randolph Papers*, vol. iv, p. 277; *N. Y. Col. Docts.*, vol. iii, p. 581.
[3] *Andros Tracts*, vols. i, p. 78, and ii, p. 209; *Randolph Papers*, vol. v, p. 57.
[4] Cited by Hutchinson, *History*, vol. i, pp. 332 f.

followed a preconcerted arrangement, in spite of their feigned ignorance.[1] Early in the morning, armed crowds of men and boys proceeded to the centre of the town from either end, captured Randolph, several of the justices, the sheriff, a number of the captains, and others of the government, and locked them in the jail. Andros had already taken refuge in the fort, while Dudley was absent on Long Island. Bradstreet, Danforth, and others of the popular leaders were escorted to the Town-house, and at noon a lengthy, and certainly not hastily prepared, declaration was read to the assembled people from a balcony.[2] It was an able, but exceedingly biased, indictment of the Andros government, while the art of the demagogue was evident in the weaving in of old slanders as to the Governor's pretended treachery with the French and Indians, the raking up of the Popish Plot in England, and a passing tribute to the "Scarlet Whore." It ended with flattering references to the Prince of Orange, and the statement that the persons of "those few Ill men," who had been the authors of the colony's misery, had been seized lest they should have given the province "away to a Forreign Power," before orders might be received from the new Parliament. The wording would indicate that it had been expected that Andros, and perhaps Dudley, who, with Randolph, were certainly the chief of the "ill men" in popular estimation, would already have been in custody by the time it was read. Andros's having taken refuge in the fort probably upset the plans in that respect. The paper contains every internal evidence, indeed, of having been prepared some time before, and certainly not after, the mob had begun its work on that eventful morning. Nevertheless, Winthrop, Bradstreet, Stoughton, Danforth, and others of the leaders immediately drew up another, stating that the action of the people was a surprise, of "the first motion whereof" they had been entirely ignorant, and calling upon Andros to surrender the government, and

[1] For the events of the revolution, *vide*, *Andros Tracts*, vols. I, pp. 3 *ff*., II, pp. 191 *ff*., and III, pp. 22 *ff*., 145 *ff*.; Hutchinson, *History*, vol. I, pp. 334 *f*.; *Randolph Papers*, vol. IV, pp. 264 *ff*.; *Cal. State Pap., Col., 1689–92*, pp. 33, 66 *ff*., 92 *ff*.

[2] Given in *Andros Tracts*, vol. I, pp. 11 *ff*.

deliver up the fort, which otherwise would be carried by storm.[1]

To have held the little fort, or the defenses on Castle Island, for any length of time, in the face of overwhelming odds, would have been impossible. To have defended the fort temporarily against attack would merely have caused useless bloodshed; and, fortunately for the colonists, Andros, throughout his whole career, had never shown the bloodthirsty vindictiveness of an Endicott or a Norton. That he was no coward is shown by the fact that he abandoned the shelter of the fort, and made his way through the tumultuous streets to a personal conference with the revolutionary leaders gathered in the council chamber. The meeting, however, effected no compromise; Andros was made prisoner, and, through one of his subordinates, but apparently on his orders, the fort was surrendered. The following day, the Castle also was yielded, and possession taken of the frigate, though the latter, in order to save the men's pay, was not required to be formally surrendered. Some days later, Dudley was located in the Narragansett country, brought to Boston, and placed in the common jail. In Europe, James II had dropped the Great Seal of England in the Thames, and fled to France. In America, his Dominion of New England lay shattered.

[1] *Andros Tracts*, vols. I, p. 20, and III, p. 145 *n.*; Osgood, *American Colonies*, vol. III, p. 419.

CHAPTER XVII

THE NEW ORDER

JUST a year before the events of that 18th of April, described at the close of the last chapter, the Reverend Increase Mather had sailed for England as representative of "many congregations" in the colony, in an effort to secure from King James the restoration of an assembly, confirmation of land-titles, and as many of the old charter privileges as possible. Although he was more than once received in audience by the King, before the Revolution brought the negotiations to an abrupt end, it had been evident for some time that the churches' agent was likely to gain little more than fair words and memories of royal interviews.[1] He had, however, succeeded in making useful friends, one among whom, Sir Henry Ashurst, became associated with him as agent, and another, Lord Wharton, introduced him to the Prince of Orange a month before the coronation, enabling him thus early to present a petition for the restoration of the charter.[2]

Three days after that interview, a circular letter was prepared, to be sent to all the English colonies, ordering officials then in office to continue to administer affairs temporarily until the new government could send different instructions.[3] Word of this was given to Mather by Jephson, a cousin of Wharton and an under-secretary to the King. Mather's alarm, when he heard of it, would seem to indicate that he either had definite information of the uprising planned in Boston, or very strong suspicions of what might occur. Prince William had already been two months in England, and it is

[1] Mather sailed April 7, 1688. *Andros Tracts*, vols. III, pp. 130 *ff*., and II, pp. 274 *ff*. As the addresses which he carried with him were unsigned, and as they were merely issued "in the name of many Congregations," it is impossible to say whom he really represented when he sailed.

[2] *Andros Tracts*, vol. III, pp. 146 *f*.   [3] *Cal. State Pap., Col., 1689–92*, pp. 4, 7.

incredible that Mather should not have sent home some word
of an event of such overwhelming importance to the colony
as the overthrow of the Stuart monarchy. His later censure
of the colonists for not having promptly resumed the charter
government, instead of temporizing, and his laying the blame
for his partial failure in England upon their not having done
so, may also suggest the nature of the advice sent by him.[1]
He could hardly have expected the new King to determine
offhand the form of government for the Dominion of New
England, then constituting over one half of the empire in
America. An order for a few months' longer continuance of
the Andros government, under the circumstances, would not
have been a serious matter, unless that government had already
been overthrown, or was about to be, by the colonists' acts.
However that may be, Mather and Sir William Phips, now
also temporarily in London, petitioned against the dispatch of
the letter to New England, and succeeded in having orders
issued instead for a new governor in place of Andros, and a
temporary form of government, to include a popular assembly.[2]

News of the revolution at Boston reached London the last
week in June, and soon letters from Randolph and others
supplied the English government with the details of what had
occurred.[3] Toward the end of July, orders were issued to the
provisional government in Boston to send Andros and the
other prisoners to England "forthwith," on the first ship bound
thither, and that they be treated civilly.[4] The order was not
received in Massachusetts until November 24, and then was
not complied with.[5] Although two ships were ready to sail
in December, an embargo was laid upon the vessels, and it
was not until the middle of the next February that the prisoners,
after treatment which they considered unnecessarily harsh,

---

[1] *Andros Tracts*, vol. II, p. 291. *Cf.*, however, Cotton Mather, *Diary*, vol. I, p. 138 *n*.

[2] *Andros Tracts*, vols. II, p. 274, and III, p. 148; Palfrey, *History*, vol. III, p. 591 *n*.; *Cal. State Pap., Col., 1689–92*, pp. 6, 8, 11.

[3] Sewall, *Diary*, vol. I, pp. 261 *f*.

[4] *Randolph Papers*, vol. IV, pp. 290 *f*.; *Andros Tracts*, vol. III, p. 111. The list of prisoners is in *Cal. State Pap., Col., 1689–92*, p. 109.

[5] *Randolph Papers*, vol. V, p. 23.

were allowed to start.[1] It had probably been felt that their presence in London might interfere with the success of the colony's agents.

The leaders who had planned the Boston revolution had undoubtedly desired the eventual restoration of the old charter, and the return of the Church and themselves into control of the government. It is probable also that the majority of the inhabitants wished for the reëstablishment of charter government, which they looked upon as ensuring themselves against arbitrary acts by England or English officials. The desires of the people as a whole, however, were by no means identical with those of the leaders who formed the temporary government in Boston, or were acting as agents in England, virtually all of whom were of the narrowest clerical party. When the fall of the Andros government necessitated the formation of another, those who had taken the lead on the day of its overthrow associated twenty-two others with themselves, and formed a "Council for the safety of the people and conservation of the peace," with Bradstreet and Wait Winthrop in the chief offices.[2] The decision of a convention, held May 8, as to a new government was not considered sufficiently decisive, and another was convened, which included representatives from fifty-four towns. Hutchinson says that "two days were spent in disputes," and that "the people without doors were also much divided in sentiments." Apparently the representatives of forty towns voted in favor of resuming the charter, and those of fourteen against it.[3] A compromise, not only between those for and against the charter, but also between those for and against the expediency of immediate resumption, resulted in the formation of a government composed of those officials who had been chosen in the last election under the old charter. Within a few weeks, Plymouth, which had never had a charter, and Connecticut and Rhode Island, the legal

---

[1] *Randolph Papers*, vols. II, pp. 110, 116, 118, 121, V, pp. 20, 26 ff., and VI, pp. 325, 331, 334; *Andros Tracts*, vol. I, p. 174; *Cal. State Pap., Col., 1689-92*, p. 263.

[2] Hutchinson, *History*, vol. I, p. 340.

[3] *Ibid.*, p. 344; *Mather Papers*, pp. 708 f.

proceedings against which had never been consummated, also quietly resumed their former governments.[1]

Of the points to be considered in granting a new charter for Massachusetts, or the resumption of the old one, those most likely to be discussed by the people — outside of the question of land-titles, as to which the colonists were naturally unanimous — would be the assembly, the governorship, and the franchise. As to the justice and necessity of a representative body for legislation and taxation, there was probably no difference of opinion in the colony. For that matter, as we saw in the last chapter, there was virtually none in the English government at home, or among its officials in Massachusetts, with the all-important exception of the late, but unlamented, monarch. As to the governor, it was natural that the majority of the people should prefer a chief magistrate elected by themselves rather than one appointed by England, though it is not at all certain that they were right. The old oligarchical government had grossly misused its power, and those who had a keen recollection of what toleration had meant in the days before Andros, and who realized the military danger in the old system of small, disunited, and contentious colonies, can certainly be accused of no lack of "patriotism" in their preference for a royal governor, to serve as a check upon the intolerance and military incapacity of the old régime.

Probably the most disputed point, and the one on which the leaders in control were opposed to the best opinion among the people at large, was that of the franchise. The question was, whether Massachusetts was to remain the private preserve of a persecuting religious sect, or was to be the home of a free people. For half a century, the leaders and the old church party had resisted, by every means in their power, — by fraud, trickery, and bloodshed, as well as by legitimate influence, — the granting of a voice in the government to any individual who could not be counted upon to uphold the power and authority

---

[1] *Plymouth Colonial Records*, vol. VI, pp. 206 *ff*.; *R. I. Records*, vol. III, p. 266; *Cal. State Pap., Col., 1689–92*, pp. 34, 62; *Conn. Col. Records*, vol. III, pp. 250 *ff*., 463 *ff*.

of the priesthood and the Church. Little by little, that power and authority had been declining as, on the one hand, the people had grown in intellectual independence, and, on the other, the leaders had shown themselves less and less worthy of their exalted position. But, in England, Mather was exerting every means to fasten the shackles permanently on the colony by insisting upon the old Congregational test for the suffrage. In acting thus, he claimed to be the representative, not of one element, but of the whole people, a majority of whom would have been disfranchised by his success. What the people themselves were thinking was shown by the vote at the town-meeting of Watertown on May 20, 1689, to choose representatives for the convention. After it had been agreed that they should be instructed to vote for the resumption of the charter, until further orders were received from England, it was added, as the only but significant restriction, that the number of freemen "be inlarged further then have been the Custom of this Colony formerly."[1] In this crisis, therefore, as has been the case all through our narrative, it is necessary to distinguish clearly the two separate struggles for freedom — that between the colony as a whole and England, and that between the liberal element among the people and the narrow oligarchical leaders, lay and clerical, of the theocratical party in control.

The weakness of the provisional government, due both to the character of the men composing it, and to the lack of a clear mandate from the people, was evident from the start. When, for example, Dudley was released from prison on account of illness, on a bond for £1000, and confined to his own house, a mob broke into it and carried him back to jail. The keeper refused to retain him without a warrant, and he was again confined, in another house. The mob having discovered this, the excitement became so great, and the control of the government was so slight, that Bradstreet, the Governor, had to write to Dudley, and abjectly beg him to reincarcerate himself voluntarily, as otherwise the authorities could not protect his

[1] *Watertown Records*, vol. ii, p. 37.

family.[1] A fortnight later, a writer from Boston stated that there was much division among the people, and that "every man is a Governor." Another wrote, July 31, 1689, that "all is confusion"; and, in October, Elizabeth Usher sent word to her husband that "there is little trade and the ferment is as great as ever." A few days later, Governor Bradstreet himself was complaining to the Lords of Trade of the people who "are busy to weaken the hands of the Government," and lamenting the Indian depredations and the empty treasury.[2]

Almost the first act of the provisional government had been to draw off and disperse many of the troops left by Andros to guard the eastern province, while the discipline of all was ruined by the dismissing of a number of officers on religious and political grounds.[3] The Indians realized the situation, and, with the arms and ammunition previously supplied to them by the Boston merchants, descended upon the unhappy settlers. The fort at Pemaquid, the great importance of which had always been denied by the colonists because it was urged by Andros, was captured, owing to the carelessness of the small garrison left there, and about twenty houses were destroyed by the savages. At Saco, Oyster River, and other places, houses were burned, and the inhabitants murdered, and all the horrors of Indian warfare once more came thick upon the border. The sudden disintegration of the Dominion, the inability of the separate colonies to act together quickly and harmoniously, and the lack of authority and military ability, left the frontier defenseless. In April, 1689, war had been declared between France and England, and the colonies seemed helpless before the menace of the French and Indians from the north.

A few weeks after Massachusetts had disbanded the forces that Andros had collected, the government attempted to raise more by a draft. The people questioned both its authority

---

[1] *Cal. State Pap., Col., 1689–92*, pp. 111, 120. Bradstreet's letter is cited from Board of Trade Mss., by Kimball, *Joseph Dudley*, pp. 52 f. The *Cal. State Pap.* reference gives the bail as £10,000. I have followed Kimball in stating it at £1000.

[2] *Cal. State Pap., Col., 1689–92*, pp. 82, 111, 120, 158, 167.

[3] *Andros Tracts*, vol. III, pp. 24 ff. The colony's defense against Andros's charges in this connection is weak and far from truthful. *Ibid.*, pp. 34 ff.

to press men, and its ability to pay them, and, for the most part, flatly refused either to volunteer or to be drafted.[1] A large part of Maine and the country eastward was overrun, and in October the inhabitants were reported to be flocking into Boston.[2] In that month, Bradstreet wrote to the Lords of Trade that there had been great depredations in Maine, New Hampshire, and even in Massachusetts, and that the government's efforts to check them had been of no avail, although a joint force had finally been raised by Plymouth, Connecticut, and Massachusetts.[3] Part of this force, wretchedly clothed and poorly supplied, had been sent eastward under Colonel Church, the veteran of Philip's War, but had accomplished little. Indeed, so carelessly was it outfitted and officered, that it was only when unexpectedly forced into action that the unhappy soldiers discovered that the ammunition did not fit their guns.

In January, 1690, the people of Maine sent a petition to England, complaining of lack of protection by Massachusetts, begging for help, and placing their losses at three hundred lives and £40,000 in goods.[4] The people of Great Island, New Hampshire, likewise wrote to the mother-country, complaining of Massachusetts and of the danger from the French and Indians.[5] In midwinter, came the frightful massacres at Schenectady and Salmon Falls; and even Bradstreet and the Council, on behalf of Massachusetts herself, wrote to the Lords of Trade, begging for arms and ammunition. The request was granted, and stores, including two hundred barrels of powder, were ordered shipped to Boston by the English government, although too late for the purpose that the colonists had had in mind but had not stated.[6] In addition, the English navy was active in providing convoys for all the colonial shipping, including that of New England.[7] Such items in the English records as "the convoys for Virginia, Maryland, Newfoundland and New England will sail on the 31st. October,

[1] Cal. State Pap., Col., 1689–92, pp. 111, 120. [2] Ibid., p. 158.
[3] Ibid., p. 167. [4] Ibid., p. 212.
[5] Ibid., pp. 262 f. [6] Ibid., pp. 240, 273, 282 f.
[7] Ibid., pp. 322, 575, 577 f., 675.

and that for Africa on the 20th.," or a list of ninety merchant ships, forming only one of the convoyed fleets from America, or the request by Massachusetts for a royal ship-of-war to guard her coastwise commerce, were the best answers to such premature "patriots" as the Reverend Joshua Moody, who was telling the men of Boston that they had no dependence on the Crown, and that the power of England was of no authority over them.[1]

The plan which had been conceived, and for which additional resources were needed, was that of attacking the French, who were the driving force behind the Indian raids, at their headquarters in Canada, instead of carrying on an almost impossible system of defensive tactics along a frontier several hundred miles long. The theory was good; but to put it in practice would require leaders with military ability, and a whole-hearted willingness on the part of the separate colonies to sink their petty jealousies and act together. Unfortunately, both the ability and the spirit of coöperation were lacking.

Massachusetts, indeed, carried out an easy and successful raid upon Acadia, whither Sir William Phips sailed from Nantasket, on April 28, 1690, with five ships and several hundred soldiers.[2] Phips, who is said to have been one of twenty-six children of a Maine backwoodsman, and who in his youth was unable to read or write, had acquired wealth and social position, first, by the not very original method of marrying a rich widow, and, secondly, by the more unusual one of locating a sunken treasure-ship with £300,000 sterling, of which his share was a considerable one. He had already married the widow. When he arrived at Port Royal, in command of the Massachusetts fleet, he had no difficulty in securing the surrender of the fort, as his force outnumbered the garrison ten to one. A succinct diary tells, in admirable style, the important events of his short sojourn, it being pertinent to note that the Reverend Joshua Moody was his chaplain.

---

[1] *Randolph Papers*, vol. vi, p. 295.

[2] The number of men and vessels varies in different accounts. *Cf. Cal. State Pap., Col., 1689–92*, pp. 275 *f.*, 376; Parkman, *Frontenac*, p. 247.

"May, 11. The fort surrendered. May, 12. Went ashore to search for hidden goods. We cut down the cross, rifled the church, pulled down the high altar, and broke their images. May, 13. Kept gathering plunder all day. May, 14. The inhabitants swore allegiance to King William and Queen Mary."[1] All very satisfying, doubtless, to the Reverend Mr. Moody. But, unfortunately, the plunder, about the distribution of which some unpleasant things were later said in Boston, was found to amount to £3000 less than the cost of the expedition.[2]

The easy conquest, however, inspired larger hopes, while the common danger to all the colonies might have been counted upon to induce them to lay aside their particularism, and join in a common effort, if anything could. A meeting of commissioners from Massachusetts, Plymouth, Connecticut, and New York was held at the latter city, and a combined attack on Canada was planned.[3] A land force, made up of troops from Maryland and the four colonies just mentioned, was to march from Albany to capture Montreal, while, simultaneously, a fleet from Boston was to attack Quebec. There seems to have been no realization of the difficulties of carrying out such a complex joint operation, although, to the very letter notifying the English government of the grandiose scheme, had to be added a postscript, to the effect that there were already "great distractions amongst the Forces." Everything went wrong. New York provided only one hundred and fifty of the four hundred men promised. The hundred and sixty sent from Massachusetts were recalled on news of the sacking of Casco. Plymouth sent none, and Connecticut less than her quota; the Indian allies, always uncertain, declined to move, and there were desertions among the whites. The colonies fell out over the appointment of a commander, agreement, but not harmony, finally being attained with the selection of Winthrop.[4] Although the unfortunate force, ill-equipped and

---

[1] *Cal. State Pap., Col., 1689–92*, pp. 275 f.   [2] *Ibid.*, p. 376.
[3] *N. Y. Col. Docts.*, vol. iii, p. 732.
[4] *Ibid.*, vols. iv, p. 194, and iii, pp. 727, 752; *Documentary History of New York*, vol. ii, p. 266.

badly organized, reached Wood Creek, near the southern end of Lake Champlain, they were unable to advance farther, and, save for a little skirmishing, the whole expedition was a costly failure, demonstrating conclusively that, even in the face of overwhelming danger, the colonies, if left to themselves, were as yet unable to unite in effective action.

Although the naval expedition against Quebec reached its objective, it also was unsuccessful, and was a mixture of farce and tragedy. Phips, who was quite incompetent as the leader of such an undertaking, was put in chief command, and on August 9 sailed from Boston with a force of about twenty-two hundred men, in thirty-two vessels of all sorts, mostly small. For some reason, which does not appear, nine weeks were consumed in reaching Quebec, of which the last three were spent within a few days of the city, owing to the lack of a pilot.[1] The failure of the land expedition against Montreal, and Phips's delay in ascending the river, had allowed Frontenac to reach Quebec with reinforcements before the hostile fleet dropped anchor a little below the town. The conqueror of Port Royal first tried the effect of a demand for surrender, and sent a summons "as severe as our four clergymen (who were joined to the Council of War) could make it."[2] Frontenac treated it with contempt, and refused to send more than a verbal reply, except by his cannon.

Phips then called another council of war, and delayed action while seven hundred more reinforcements arrived at the city. The plan finally decided upon was a simultaneous attack by land and water. About twelve hundred men were to be landed, and after crossing a small river, were to ascend to the rear of the city, which they were to attempt to carry by assault, while the fleet bombarded it from the front. The land forces, under Major Walley, were set on shore, where they remained

---

[1] Walley's Journal, in Hutchinson, *History*, vol. 1, p. 477; *Cal. State Pap., Col., 1689–92*, p. 384. Most of the contemporary accounts, French and English, are conveniently brought together by E. Myrand, in *Sir Wm. Phips devant Québec;* Quebec, 1893.

[2] *Cal. State Pap., Col., 1689–92*, p. 384. The summons is in Mather, *Magnalia*, vol. 1, p. 186. *Cf.* Parkman, *Frontenac*, p. 279 *n.*

for some days, unable to advance, and suffering greatly from disease, hunger, and exposure. The necessary and expected support which the fleet was to provide them was almost wholly lacking, and neither boats, ammunition, nor food was supplied in proper quantities. On the other hand, Phips, with a total disregard of the land expedition with which he was supposed to be coöperating, fired away all the fleet's scanty store of powder and shot, expending a considerable portion of it in an unsuccessful effort to hit a picture of the Holy Family, which had been hung on the cathedral spire. Nothing having been accomplished by the futile cannonading, except to provide the Quebec gunners with shot for their guns, and the English ammunition being exhausted, the incompetent commander had nothing to do but to order a retreat and return to Boston. The land forces under Walley had behaved well, but in reëmbarking lost all semblance of discipline, took to the boats much like a base-ball crowd to the street cars, and abandoned their cannon.[1] The self-flattering belief of democracy that training of any sort is a waste of time, and that, in military affairs, competent commanders and disciplined troops can be found at any moment in a crisis, had again proved a costly fallacy.

In November, Phips reached Boston with the first of his armada; and other vessels continued to straggle in at intervals until February. Some of them were never heard of at all. As the colony gradually came to a realization of the magnitude of the disaster, it was in despair, as it well might be. Few men had fallen in fighting, but, owing to the incompetence and thoughtlessness of the leaders, both civil and military, the mortality had been great. The lack of clothes and food, the cold, smallpox, fever, and exposure had killed men by scores. The loss was estimated as high as a thousand, and certainly ran into many hundreds.[2] Moreover, the government, with an empty treasury, had recklessly financed the expedition by

---

[1] Parkman, *Frontenac*, p. 287; Walley's Journal, pp. 470 *ff.*; Phips's own account is in *Cal. State Pap., Col., 1689–92*, p. 45.

[2] *Ibid.*, pp. 376 *f.*, 385, 369, 387.

promises to pay, expecting to be reimbursed from the anticipated plunder. There was no plunder, and the colossal failure
had cost £50,000.[1] A Boston merchant wrote to a correspondent in London that, since assuming office, the new government
had involved the colony to the extent of, possibly, £200,000,
and that it was almost "run aground."[2]

Virtually bankrupt, and with the discharged soldiers and
other creditors clamoring for their pay, the government took
the first step on the road to paper money, which was later to
cost it dear. The debts were ordered paid with certificates
receivable for taxes, ranging in denomination from two shillings
to ten pounds.[3] An original issue of £7000 was increased in
a few months to £40,000; and owing to the government's
lack of credit and stability, the notes fell quickly in value, and
were soon at a discount of thirty to fifty per cent.[4] Taxes rose
to formerly unheard-of amounts, and the depression both of
business and of sentiment became extreme.[5] Cotton Mather
was said to be satisfied to attribute all the colony's troubles
to the presence of the Episcopalian congregation worshiping
in the King's Chapel; and the Governor and Council wrote
to England, pointing out that the whole disaster must have
been due to God, who had "spit in our faces" — a phrase for
a state paper which darts a vivid light, in several directions,
among the colony's elect.[6] There were many, however, who
were inclined to lay the blame for the growing ruin of all their
affairs in less exalted quarters. The government did its best
to suppress or refute all criticism, and the press, whose lack of
freedom had been so bitterly complained of only a few months
before under Andros, was quickly taken in hand again, and a
stricter censorship than ever established.[7] Although nothing

[1] *Cal. State Pap., Col., 1689–92*, pp. 377, 369; Parkman, *Frontenac*, p. 297; *Andros Tracts*, vol. II, p. 238.
[2] *Cal. State Pap., Col., 1689–92*, p. 377.
[3] A. McF. Davis, *Currency and Banking in the Province of Massachusetts Bay* (New York, 1900), vol. I, pp. 10 ff.
[4] Davis, *Currency*, vol. I, pp. 16 f.; *Cal. State Pap., Col., 1689–92*, p. 377.
[5] *Ibid.*, pp. 385, 387, 399.
[6] *Ibid.*, p. 369; *Andros Tracts*, vol. III, p. 53.
[7] Duniway, *Freedom of the Press*, pp. 67 ff.

could be printed except propaganda in favor of the provisional government, the increasing discontent of many in all classes made itself heard, both in the colony and in England.

Despite all that has been written of the town-meeting, and the general impression that the average New Englander was almost solely a political and religious animal, there is little evidence to prove that the ordinary man in that section cared any more about government than the ordinary man in Virginia or Maryland. In fact, at a little later period, the more accurate election returns would seem to indicate that he then cared even less.[1] The small minority that ran the government and the churches was naturally active and vocal. But the fact that four fifths of the people were reasonably content to join no church, and to have no voice in the government, certainly does not argue, in that time and place, any very high degree of political, religious, or intellectual interest as compared with the rest of America. In the blue haze of that incense in honor of the colonial New Englanders, lighted by themselves and tended by their descendants, we are apt, a little absurdly sometimes, to lose sight of coarse fundamentals. The average man or boy in the New England of this period probably looked upon the theory that the main end of the colony's existence was to make the world safe for the Congregational church, in very much the same way in which those of us who happened to be in France lately found that the average "doughboy" regarded his main end there to be making the world safe for democracy.

Such very truthful remarks as that already quoted, made by the residents of Cape Ann, when they replied to an early whiff of the incense by saying that their main end had been fish, cannot be too much emphasized. They are as precious as they are rare. Impersonal love of liberty is about as common as uncombined oxygen; and so long as the average man could catch cod, sell whiskey to the Indians, raise crops on land he felt was his own, or stand at his little shop-counter, he did

[1] McKinley, *Suffrage Franchise*, pp. 47, 357. *Cf.*, also, L. G. Tyler, in *William and Mary Quarterly*, vol. xxvi, p. 278.

not much care — much as, by way of conversation, he might talk — about the governor in Boston or the king in England. But let him believe that either was threatening his God-given right to accumulate pine-tree shillings, and there would be trouble.

This, the Governor and Council, by their evident inability to handle the situation, were rapidly bringing about. There is nothing unexpected in the cry now beginning to ascend to England, that "we mightily want a government," [1] or unpatriotic in the attitude of those who did not desire the complete restoration of the former conditions. In England, however, that was exactly what the agents, with Mather at their head, were striving for. Their charges against Andros had entirely broken down, as had their hopes of a restoration of the old charter.[2] Attempts to have it restored by Parliamentary action or by a Writ of Error had both failed, and the agents' efforts were thereafter directed to obtaining from the King a new charter, with as favorable terms as possible.[3] It may be pointed out that the agents were not representatives of the colony as a whole, but only of the old church party, and that the terms which would be considered favorable by them would be such as would ensure continued control by the theocratic element.

The echoes of the events in the colony that we have been describing had been sounding in England with increasing loudness and frequency, in the shape of private letters and formal addresses.[4] Mather, indeed, attempted to minimize all complaints from the colony, from whatever source, and was somewhat reckless in his imputations and disregard of facts. Thirty-four petitioners of Charlestown, including many substantial men, he characterized as "a few bankrupt Publicans and Vagabonds," "persons brought up and educated in all

---

[1] *Cal. State Pap., Col., 1689–92*, p. 300.

[2] No one would sign even the brief charges submitted, and they were dismissed. *Andros Tracts*, vols. II, pp. 173 ff., I, pp. 150 ff., and III, pp. 19 ff.

[3] *Andros Tracts*, vols. II, pp. 15 ff., 75 ff., and III, pp. 149 ff.

[4] *Cf.*, besides the authorities already cited, *Cal. State Pap., Col., 1689–92*, pp. 212, 213 (2), 343, 366, 368, 409.

manner of Debauchery and Depravation," "greedy as Hell." [1]
In his effort to prove the great prosperity and importance of
New England under the old theocratic government, he gro-
tesquely claimed that, whereas New England had turned a
wilderness into a fruitful field, most of the other colonies had
"turned a fruitful field into a barren wilderness." The facts
were probably far better known to the Lords of Trade than
they were to Mather, and these showed that the population
of the other colonies outnumbered that of New England more
than two to one, while of England's colonial trade seven
eighths was with the "barren wildernesses" of the sugar and
tobacco colonies, and only one ninth with New England's
"fruitful field." [2] In that very year, of the two hundred and
twenty-six ships sailing from England to colonial ports, but
seven were bound for New England.[3]

Mather's anonymous but scarcely veiled threats that the
colony would revolt, if the old theocracy and its charter privileges were not restored,[4] failed to impress the government,
which, however, had been seriously endeavoring to meet all
the legitimate aspirations of the colonists. Mather, who had
had several interviews with King William, and had enlisted
the sympathy of the Queen,[5] had little difficulty in getting a
number of proposals altered, when the reasons were pointed
out; but the King and government were both firm in favor
of a governor appointed by England, and a property, not a
religious, qualification for the franchise. Mather bitterly
opposed both these suggestions, particularly that relating to

[1] *Andros Tracts*, vol. II, pp. 230, 240 *ff*. A report to the Board of Trade, in regard
to these "vagabond" signers, probably exaggerated on the other side, puts down two
as worth £12,000 each, two at £10,000, three at £6000, two at £5000, two at £4000,
five at £3000, etc. *Cal. State Pap., Col., 1689–92*, p. 422.

[2] *Andros Tracts*, vol. II, pp. 254 *f.*; *A Century of Population*, p. 9, gives 82,000 in New
England and 124,000 in the south, in 1690. To the latter figure must be added those
for the island colonies; Beer, *Old Colonial System*, vol. I, pp. 41 *ff*. The trade figures
are for 1697.

[3] Beer, *Old Colonial System*. Of the remainder, 103 went to Virginia and Maryland, 71 to Barbadoes, 23 to the Leeward Islands, 20 to Jamaica, one to Bermuda, and
one to Pennsylvania.

[4] *Andros Tracts*, vol. II, pp. 245, 248, 269.

[5] *Ibid.*, vols. II, pp. 277 *ff*., and III, pp. 156 *ff*.

the suffrage, saying he would sooner part with his life than consent. The ministers of state, however, were growing somewhat tired of the clergyman's representations and misrepresentations, and curtly told him that his consent was neither "expected nor desired"; that he was not a plenipotentiary from a sovereign state; and that, if it was true, as he claimed, that Massachusetts would not accept the new charter, then she could "take what would follow," for "his Majesty was resolved to settle the Countrey." [1]

The obvious fact that the colonists were not by any means unanimous in their desire for the old charter, the genuine wish of the English government to provide toleration, the long record of delays and bickerings in the colony's relations with England, and the necessity for a different organization if the Navigation Acts were to be enforced, probably all had their influence in shaping the government's policy. Of still greater immediate import, perhaps, was the military situation. With the prospect of a life-and-death struggle with France, the Franco-British frontier in America became a sphere of the highest military interest and importance; and, aside from previous records or any preconceived ideas on the part of English statesmen, the colonists had, within the past year, shown that, if left to themselves, they were unable properly to safeguard either their own homes or the interests of the Empire.

As a matter of fact, the new charter, as finally granted, was a far better document than the one desired by Mather. What he had tried to get was a constitution for a virtually independent theocratic state, the fundamental law of which should provide for the perpetual retention of political power in the hands of a religious sect. What the English government granted was a charter by which the colony took her natural place, indeed, in an empire without whose protection she was defenseless, but which, at the same time, gave to her citizens a degree of self-government and political freedom which the theocratic group would never have been willing to concede.

[1] *Andros Tracts*, vols. II, p. 281, and III, p. 165.

The substitution of a moderate property qualification for the franchise, in place of any other whatsoever, at once placed the colony abreast of the most liberal political thought of the day; while local self-government was restored in the form of a popular assembly. Regardless of the whims or religious prejudices of any clique in power, and irrespective of his class or creed, any resident of the colony who had been sufficiently industrious or fortunate to acquire a freehold estate worth forty shillings per annum, or real or personal property to the value of forty pounds, could now claim, as a right, a voice in the government of his commonwealth.[1] Thanks to England, the final deathblow had legally been dealt to the theocracy, and the foundation laid for genuine self-government and religious toleration in the colony. Those elements in its future development which we are apt to consider as typically American had, in fact, in the case of Massachusetts, been forced upon her leaders, fighting against them to the last ditch, by an English King who could hardly speak the language of his subjects.

One important aspect of this change in the franchise must not be overlooked. Under the old religious test, there had been, within the body of enfranchised voters, no social question. All had possessed the vote, without distinction between rich and poor. The struggle for the franchise, therefore, would always have remained a purely religious one between those within and those without the pale of a particular church. With the abandonment of the religious test, and the substitution of a property qualification, the question became a social one, and the way was opened for that struggle for the democratization of the state and society which became the dominant motive in the Revolution of a century later. The colonies could never have united on a question of religion, or even of trade. The basis had to be so wide as to appeal to the most numerous class in every colony; and that appeal could only be social, and was found to lie in the demand for the abolition of privilege and the extension of democracy.

[1] The charter is printed in *Colonial Society Massachusetts Publications*, vol. II, pp. 7 *ff*.

The new charter of 1691 must be regarded as an honest effort to devise such a governmental system as should allow to the colonists the greatest degree of local liberty consistent with the welfare and administrative necessities of the Empire as a whole, in the light of existing political theory. It cannot too often be pointed out that the colonial period *was* a colonial period, and that the relations subsisting between England and the colonies were necessarily those subsisting between a sovereign state and its dependencies. There was no more reason for the colonist of Massachusetts or Barbadoes to consider himself entirely independent of English control, than there is for the settler in Alaska to consider himself wholly independent of the United States to-day. It is inconsistent to claim that the authority of Congress, in the twentieth century, should reach to Guam or Nome, but that the authority of Parliament, in the seventeenth, should have stopped at Land's End. To find fault with administrative arrangements proper under the above conditions, merely because they would have been unsuitable had the subsequently revolting colonies then been the independent states they later developed into, is to look through the wrong end of the historian's telescope. If we are to judge the governments provided for the colonies in comparison with models in later American history, they should not be compared with the constitutions of our sovereign states, but with those provided for our own dependent colonies and territories; and in their broader features, the constitutions granted by Congress to organized territories reproduce very closely the old royal governments of the earlier period.

In the first place, we may note that the governor of a territory is not elected by the people, but is appointed by the president, and is removable by him, as the Massachusetts charter of 1691 provided that her governor should be removable by the king. In territories, as in the colonies, laws passed by the bicameral legislature are subject, not only to veto by the governor, but also to disallowance by the higher sovereign power. The review of colonial legislation, to which our forefathers objected so strongly when colonists, we adopted ourselves when we, in turn became a "mother-country"; and in some cases, at least, the laws passed by territorial legislatures were specifically made subject to review by Congress. It is needless to remind the reader that the citizens of our territories are no more directly represented in that body than the colonists were in Parliament, and that taxation without direct representation is as much a factor in our present state as it was in the British Empire. In one respect, the Massachusetts charter of 1691, indeed, was more liberal than our territorial governments; for in Massachusetts the judges were appointed by the governor with the consent of the council, or upper house of the legislature, while in American territories they are appointed by the president without the consent of the inhabitants.[1]

To many in the colony, however, the change from the old charter form to the new seemed a loss of independence. The former governing element felt that their control had been vastly weakened. The church party anticipated that the end of all things might be due when the Congregational church no longer legally controlled the elections. The presence of a governor and other officials appointed by the Crown, the review of legislation, the right of appeal, and other evidences of the colony having become part of a great organization instead of a practically independent, even if insignificant, little collection of towns, was unwelcome to those who had had a false idea of the rôle which, in that time and place, it was possible for them and the colony to play in the world.

On the other hand, there were very substantial advantages under the new régime. Although, owing to an obscure and probably not very reputable intrigue, New Hampshire was given a separate government, the bounds of the new Massachusetts were extended to include Plymouth, Maine, and the

---

[1] Willoughby, *Territories and Dependencies*, pp. 54 *ff.*; Bryce, *American Commonwealth*, vol. 1. pp. 553 *ff.* The constitutions of the territories may be found in *Organic Acts*, Senate Document No. 148, 56th Congress, 1st Session. As an example of legislative review, *cf.* p. 96 (New Mexico): "All the laws passed by the legislative assembly and governor shall be submitted to the Congress of the United States, and, if disapproved, shall be null and of no effect." Under the act organizing a government in Alaska, in 1884, it was specifically provided that there should be no legislative assembly. *Ibid.*, p. 206.

eastern country as far as Nova Scotia.[1]   Moreover, the colonists had never really possessed anything like the rights
which they had claimed and exercised under the old charter.
The whole system of town government, for example, had been
extra-legal.   The infliction of the death-penalty was illegal,
and there was no question that the colonists had exceeded
their rights in taxing the non-freemen.   Now all the false
reasoning and sophistries that the settlers had indulged in,
in their efforts to prove the old charter adequate as the basis
of a government, were no longer necessary.   Massachusetts
at last had, what she had never possessed before, a written
constitution, which clearly set forth her form of government,
and validated, to a very great extent, those institutions which
she had cherished.[2]   The royal officials, disliked as their presence might be by the irreconcilables, actually and symbol-
ically brought the colony into relations with the larger life
of the empire.   In her thought, her commerce, and her political
relations, New England's largest colony was at last forced out
of that position of defiant isolation which her former leaders
had chosen for her, and made to participate, so far as her
provincial position allowed, in the main currents of the world's
activities.   The new charter definitely marked the end of
one era and the beginning of another.

This change was more than political and economic.   It has
been evident from the foregoing narrative that the power of
the clergy had been felt in every sphere of the colony's life.
In the pulpits, in the schools, in the colleges, in the censorship
of the press, in the legislature, even in the councils of war and
the courts of justice, their influence had been incalculable.
The story of the struggle against it, and of its gradual yielding
to defeat, as the people more and more made good their right
to believe as they would and live their lives as they chose,
has occupied many of our pages.   The course of development,

[1] For the form of government established in New Hampshire, which became a
royal province, vide Fry, New Hampshire, pp. 71 ff.
[2] Cf. Greene, The Provincial Governor, pp. 92, 179.   For a discussion of the charter,
vide Osgood, American Colonies, vol. III, pp. 439 ff.

however, which was to make Massachusetts the leader of liberal thought among the states, was a long one, and, in part, it was but a reaction and a protest against the theological repression of this earlier period.

Although the charter of 1691 had definitely ended the legalized control of the Congregational church, which was still to maintain a privileged position until 1812, the organization desperately struggled to retain its power. The members of the new government, thanks to the efforts of Mather in England, were nearly all of the clerical party. He had, indeed, succeeded in having the more important offices filled with the most fanatical, or the most subservient, of the men in the colony's public life. His son, the Reverend Cotton Mather, when he heard of the list of officials, wrote ecstatically in his diary: "The time for Favour was now come; the sett Time was come! . . . all the Councellors of the Province are of my own Father's Nomination; and my Father-in-law, with several related unto me, and several Brethren of my own church, are among them. The Governour of the Province is not my Enemy but one whom I baptized, namely Sir William Phips, and one of my own Flock, and one of my dearest Friends." [1] He might have added that the savagely bigoted Stoughton was made Deputy Governor.

At the very time when this effort was being made still to control the government, in spite of its altered form, events occurred that gave a staggering blow to that unofficial power which the clergy had been accustomed to exert as the acknowledged intellectual leaders of the community. For, in the generation of 1690, the witchcraft frenzy, in which the clergy took a leading part, brought about the same sort of anti-clerical reaction that had been a result of the Quaker persecutions by them in the generation of 1660.

We shall not concern ourselves with the details of the horrible delusion, which, for the last time in New England, caused the blood of innocent victims to be shed as a result of

[1] Cotton Mather, *Diary*, in *Mass. Hist. Soc. Coll.*, Series VII, vol. VII, p. 148.

theological beliefs.   They may be found amply set forth elsewhere, and concern rather the antiquarian and the psychologist
than the historian.[1]   For us, the interest lies in their influence
upon the intellectual development of the colony, and the growth
of its people.

It is quite true that communities in all ages and places have
been occasionally subject to being thrown off their mental
balance, and during the period of frenzy or panic have committed acts of folly or crime, for which they have subsequently
been heartily repentant.   But to state a fact is not to explain
it; and to find the underlying cause of the psychologic disturbance in northeastern Massachusetts in 1692 — during
which two hundred persons were accused of being in league
with the devil, one hundred and fifty were imprisoned, and
twenty-nine put to death,— in such influences as the loss of the
charter, or the "harsh aspects of the scenery," seems to me
wholly inadequate, to say the least.[2]   The scenery of the native
American wild "invited to stern and melancholy musing,"
as New England's best-known historian phrases it, for about a
thousand miles north and south of Mr. Mather's study in
Boston, or the Reverend Mr. Parris's cottage in Salem Village,
and would seem to be rather dispersed as the cause of a very
localized phenomenon.

It is needless to point out that the belief in witchcraft had
been widespread throughout the world; but since the days of
King James I, there had been, among English people, only
isolated cases, save during the years of the Puritan political
supremacy in England and the closing days of that same
supremacy in Massachusetts.[3]   Of the more than seventy cases
in England since the Restoration, the great majority had resulted in acquittals, and in two cases only had the unfortunate
victims been executed.

---

[1] *Cf.* C. W. Upham, *History of Witchcraft and Salem Village*, Boston, 1867, 2 vols;
Palfrey, *History*, vol. IV, pp. 96 *ff.*; the works of Cotton Mather and Robert Calef,
edited by S. G. Drake and published as *The Witchcraft Delusion in New England*,
3 vols., Roxbury, 1866; I. Mather, *Remarkable Providences*, London, 1890.

[2] Palfrey, *History*, vol. IV, pp. 128 *f.*

[3] W. Notestein, *History of Witchcraft in England* (American Historical Association,
1911), pp. 400 *ff.*

We have seen, in an earlier chapter, the extraordinarily large sphere accorded to the devil in Puritan theology, and that theology's virtual repudiation of science by its considering every event in the universe, from the sun's course in heaven to a spider's falling into the porridge, as a direct interposition of the divine will. While Boyle, Newton, and other founders of the new scientific age in England, were tracing the reign of law, the intellectual leaders of New England were engaged in gathering together collections of "remarkable providences," ranging in interest from the sudden death of a Sabbath-breaker to the evident marking for destruction, out of a whole library, of a copy of the book of Common Prayer, by a mouse evidently brought up in the "New England way." Of the moral earnestness of such men there is no question, nor of the abiding stamp which they have left upon the New England consciousness. Happily, much of the good they did has survived, while much of the political and intellectual damage they likewise did, and would have continued to do, had they had their way, has passed.

In 1681, a group of the most eminent of the clergy around Boston determined upon a large coöperative work, to involve the research of many authors, and the labor of some years. It was to be a collection of remarkable providences, of divine judgments, of "thunders as are unusual, strange apparitions, or whatever else shall happen that is prodigious, witchcrafts, diabolical possessions, judgments upon noted sinners," and the like.[1] Each clergyman was to make diligent search among his congregation, and it is obvious what a stimulant such a wholesale inquiry among the people, by the intellectual leaders of the community, would be toward arousing interest, and intensifying the belief, in such matters. A few years later, Increase Mather published his book on the subject, in which he gave numerous cases of witchcraft and possession, and recited the signs by which it might be known. It became the study of the young Cotton Mather, whom in 1686, at the age of twenty-three, we find wrestling in prayer to cast the devils out

---

[1] I. Mather, *Remarkable Providences*, Preface.

of New England, and undertaking to track down those leagued with them.[1]

Interest in the subject continued to be stirred up, and in 1688, the criminal nonsense of some children of Boston, and their accusations against a washerwoman, resulted in her being denounced as a witch. Cotton Mather, who had now found the case for which he had been longing, and in which he might do ghostly battle, took the eldest girl home with him. She played upon the clergyman's colossal vanity, and, on evidence which ought not to have shut up a dog, the unfortunate washerwoman was hanged. Mather now proceeded, by another book and by frenzied sermons, to arouse the fears and superstitions of the crowd. With one of the most noted clergymen in Boston doing all he could to foster it, the belief deepened and spread, and the minds of many, who would not otherwise have given thought to it, were prepared to believe in that " plot of the Devil against New England " which Mather preached.

Early in 1692, some children of Salem feigned the symptoms of which they had heard their elders speak. Two of them belonged to the family of the local clergyman, Mr. Parris, who now entered on the devil-hunt, with a fanaticism which knew no bounds, and an honesty which seems to have been questionable.[2] To his efforts were added those of the Reverend Mr. Noyes. Charge after charge was launched against innocent people, and by the time Phips arrived in the colony as governor, in May, over a hundred persons were already in prison awaiting trial. Vain of his undeserved authority, the appointee and pliant tool of Mather, he immediately appointed an illegal court to try the witchcraft cases, with Stoughton as presiding judge. In the frenzy of superstitious fanticism which followed, justice, legal evidence, even a verdict of the jury, were set aside, and victim after victim hurried to the gallows, while one, with horrible tortures lasting several days, was

---

[1] C. Mather, *Diary*, vol. I, p. 114.
[2] *Vide* the remonstrance against him, in Upham, *Witchcraft*, vol. II, pp. 497 *f.*, and Drake, *Witchcraft Delusion*, vol. II, p. 142.

pressed to death under heavy weights.[1] The clergy, formally referred to by the Governor and court for advice, while carefully hedging as to certain particulars, urged the court on to "speedy and vigorous prosecution"; and Mather wrote to one of them, extolling "the noble service" of "Encountering the Wicked Spiritts in the high places of our Air, & of detecting & of confounding of their confederates."[2] The Reverend Mr. Burroughs, of Wells, who avowed that "there neither are, nor ever were witches," was condemned; and although the spectators at his hanging were so moved as almost to prevent the sentence from being carried out, Mather, who was witnessing the spectacle from horseback, told the people that the victim was not an ordained clergyman, and that, in any case, the devil often appeared as an Angel of Light.[3]

Finally, the reaction set in, and the sober sense of the community set itself against the ravings and goadings of the more fanatical clergy and church members. The commission of the special court expired with the assembling of the General Court, and was not renewed. Phips, evidently fearing criticism from England, wrote to the Earl of Nottingham, disingenuously laying all the blame for the judicial proceedings on Stoughton, and quoted Increase Mather and the other divines.[4] Courageous laymen, like Thomas Brattle and Robert Calef, both merchants, exerted their influence against the delusion; and when Mather tried to start another alarm in Boston, less than a year after the last execution at Salem, public opinion was arrayed solidly against him. In 1700, Calef's book in answer to Mather's "Wonders of the Invisible World" was printed in London and quickly imported into the colony. Though the rage of the Mathers, father and son, was unbounded, their cause had been thoroughly discredited, and their day was past. They belonged, in reality, to the sixteenth century, while Calef, the merchant, defending the cause of intellectual freedom with

[1] Sewall, *Diary*, vol. I, p. 364.
[2] Hutchinson, *History*, vol. II, pp. 52 f.; *Mass. Hist. Soc. Coll.*, Series IV, vol. VIII, p. 391.
[3] Sewall, *Diary*, vol. I, p. 363; Drake, *Witchcraft Delusion*, vol. III, pp. 38 f.
[4] *Cal. State Pap., Col., 1693-96*, p. 30.

no weapon but that of common sense, belonged to the eighteenth, the dawn of which was now at hand.

It was the voice of that century to which the people were now to hearken. Thenceforth, happily for itself as well as for America, the church was to be unable to rely either upon political power or upon blind fanaticism to uphold its leadership — a leadership which now, perforce, took on a nobler form. The work of the founders was over. In the extension of their influence throughout the country, wherever we find groups of settlers from the New England states, we find, indeed the church, the common-school, and the town-meeting; but it is a liberalized church, a non-sectarian school, and a town-meeting in which the citizen's vote is not dependent upon the possession of any peculiar theological belief.

It was usual, in an earlier and less critical day, to trace all of New England's greatness, and of her noble contributions to our common American life, to the same little group of leaders, who were supposed to have done all because they did much. Life is not so simple as that, and in the founding of New England, and the development of her liberties, we must find place for English kings and statesmen, for colonial liberals and martyrs, as well as for Pilgrim Father and Puritan Priest.

INDEX

INDEX

The abbreviated form "Mass.," refers to the Governor and Company of Massachusetts Bay — the "Bay Colony."